# The Office

## Procedures and Technology

**Dr. Mary Ellen Oliverio**
Graduate School of Business
Pace University
New York, New York

**Dr. William R. Pasewark**
Office Management Consultants
Lubbock, Texas

Contributing Authors

Dr. Anthony A. Olinzock
College of Education
The Ohio State University
Columbus, Ohio

Dr. Bonnie Roe White, CPS
College of Education
Auburn University
Auburn, Alabama

Published by

K35 **SOUTH-WESTERN PUBLISHING CO.**

CINCINNATI    WEST CHICAGO, IL    CARROLLTON, TX    LIVERMORE, CA

# Contents

## THE OFFICE IN MODERN BUSINESS LIFE

CHAPTER 1  THE OFFICE AND ITS PLACE IN THE
ORGANIZATION                                         2

Topic 1:  What the Office Is                          3
Topic 2:  The Setting in Which Offices Function      18

CHAPTER 2  EMPLOYEES AT WORK IN OFFICES             36

Topic 1:  Specialization in the Office Workforce     37
Topic 2:  Introduction to a New Job                  54

## THE SKILLS OF WORKING TOGETHER

CHAPTER 3  COMMUNICATION SKILLS IN
THE OFFICE                                           70

Topic 1:  Reading                                    71
Topic 2:  Writing                                    86
Topic 3:  Speaking and Listening                    104

CHAPTER 4  INTERACTING WITH OTHERS                 120

Topic 1:  Human Relations on the Job                121
Topic 2:  Improving Interpersonal Skills            132

AT WORK AT DYNAMICS:   SIMULATION 1                 153

# INFORMATION PROCESSING

CHAPTER 5   INFORMATION PROCESSING:
AN OVERVIEW   156

Topic 1:  Information Systems in Modern Organizations   157
Topic 2:  Organization and Technology for Information
Processing   176

CHAPTER 6   WORD/TEXT PROCESSING: COMMON
BUSINESS DOCUMENTS   204

Topic 1:  Letters   205
Topic 2:  Memorandums, Reports, and Tables   228

CHAPTER 7   WORD/TEXT PROCESSING: HOW
DOCUMENTS ARE PROCESSED   250

Topic 1:  The Setting in Which Documents Are Processed   251
Topic 2:  Equipment for Entering Words/Text for
Processing   269
Topic 3:  From Formatting to Storing   285

CHAPTER 8   DATA PROCESSING:
SOME COMMON APPLICATIONS   304

Topic 1:  Customer Services: Processing Orders   305
Topic 2:  Purchasing and Inventory Maintenance   325

CHAPTER 9   DATA PROCESSING:
FINANCIAL APPLICATIONS   344

Topic 1:  Cash and Accounts Receivable   345
Topic 2:  Payments Due from the Company   369

*AT WORK AT DYNAMICS:   SIMULATION 2*   *387*

# TIME AND TASK MANAGEMENT

CHAPTER 10   ACTIVITIES MANAGEMENT                         390

Topic 1:   Workstation and Time Management                391
Topic 2:   Using Reprographic Services                    410
Topic 3:   Office Safety and Security                      429

CHAPTER 11   MANAGEMENT SUPPORT ACTIVITIES               448

Topic 1:   Calendars, Business Meetings, and Travel       449
Topic 2:   Business Reports                                475

# RECORDS ADMINISTRATION AND TECHNOLOGY

CHAPTER 12   RECORDS MANAGEMENT                           500

Topic 1:   Maintaining Office Records                      501
Topic 2:   Paper Filing Systems                            519

CHAPTER 13   MANAGING RECORDS                             544

Topic 1:   Managing Paper Files                            545
Topic 2:   Managing Magnetic and Micrographic Media        563

AT WORK AT DYNAMICS:   SIMULATION 3                       587

*Contents continues onto next page*

# MAIL AND TELECOMMUNICATION SYSTEMS

CHAPTER 14    PROCESSING MAIL                                      590

Topic 1:    Incoming Mail Procedures                               591
Topic 2:    Outgoing Mail Procedures                               604

CHAPTER 15    TELECOMMUNICATIONS                                   628

Topic 1:    Incoming Telephone Communications                     629
Topic 2:    Outgoing Telephone Communications                     643
Topic 3:    Telecommunications Technology                          655

# PERSONAL AND CAREER DEVELOPMENT

CHAPTER 16    ADVANCING YOUR CAREER                                678

Topic 1:    Focus on You                                          679
Topic 2:    Focus on Your Career                                  693

*AT WORK AT DYNAMICS:    SIMULATION 4*                            *719*

## REFERENCE SECTION

Section A:    Standard Proofreader's Marks                        720
Section B:    Punctuation                                         722
Section C:    Capitalization                                      729
Section D:    Math                                                732
Section E:    Two-Letter State Abbreviations                      737
Section F:    Alphabetic Indexing Rules                           738
Section G:    Legal Rights of the Employee                        748
Photo Acknowledgments                                             749
Index                                                             750

# AN INTRODUCTION

*THE OFFICE: Procedures and Technology* is a completely new textbook. The content is comprehensive, up-to-date, and organized in a manner designed to ensure effective and realistic learning. Students will find this textbook invaluable as they prepare for rewarding careers in present-day offices, as well as in offices of the future.

## The Challenge Business Teachers Face

Business teachers face a critical challenge: to prepare students for a dramatically changing workplace. In the next ten years, experts predict that offices will adopt markedly different information processing technologies and procedures than they have used in the past. Students who plan to enter full-time positions when they complete their high school education must be ready to function in an environment at any stage of its transformation to the so called "office of the future." At the same time, students must be prepared to adapt to changes that are likely to be introduced in relation to their responsibilities. In the face of this challenge, business teachers must continue to bear in mind the importance of certain basic skills such as organizing work, communicating effectively, and interacting successfully with others. *THE OFFICE: Procedures and Technology* has been developed to help business teachers meet the challenge with a high level of success. The text and supplementary materials will help students to:

- understand both the role of the modern office in today's business world and the role of the office worker in the office environment
- develop marketable skills using the most current procedures and technologies
- develop an understanding of emerging technologies
- recognize the importance of organization, accuracy, and efficiency as they relate to productivity
- communicate and interact effectively with co-workers, employers, and the general public
- identify opportunities for employment and for professional growth in office occupations.

## A Text Organized for Student Comprehension

The content of *THE OFFICE: Procedures and Technology* is divided into seven general subject areas and sixteen chapters. The seven areas are The Office in Modern Business Life, The Skills of Working Together, Information Processing, Time and Task Management, Records Administration and Technology, Mail and Telecommunication Systems, and Personal and Career Development. Each chapter is subdivided into two or three smaller sections called Topics.

## Features that Facilitate Learning

*THE OFFICE: Procedures and Technology* contains many features designed to help students successfully develop the knowledges and skills presented.

*Chapter and Topic Objectives.* Chapter and topic goals focus on key concepts which serve as valuable guides to students as they become familiar with the content of each topic.

*Vocabulary Reinforcement.* General vocabulary terms that may be unfamiliar to students are defined in the margin of the page on which the term is first introduced.

*Key Business Terms.* Contemporary business terms appear in color and are defined within the text. Key terms defined in each chapter are listed at the end of the chapter for easy review.

*End-of-Topic and End-of-Chapter Activities.* Activities to reinforce important concepts and procedures and to give students practical experience are included in each topic and at the end of each chapter. End-of-topic activities include Review Questions, Making Decisions, Interacting with Others, Extending Your English Skills, Extending Your Math Skills, and Application Activities. End-of-chapter materials include a summary of the chapter's content, a list of key terms presented in the chapter, and one or more integrated activities. The purpose of these activities is to provide students with further application tasks that relate to the entire chapter.

*Productivity Corners.* The final part of each chapter is a Productivity Corner. This unique feature presents an advice-column approach to problems typically of concern to beginning office workers, such as a new job anxiety or uncertainty about handling work assignments.

*Reference Section.* Commonly needed information is provided here for students' ready access. Reference Section topics are Standard Proofreader's Marks, Punctuation, Capitalization, Math, Two-Letter State Abbreviations, Alphabetic Indexing Rules, and Legal Rights of the Employee.

*Office Simulations.* Four office simulations entitled AT WORK AT DYNAMICS are closely related to the content and skills introduced in the textbook. As in a regular business office, the tasks to be performed in the simulations are integrated and interrelated. Each simulation involves decision making, activities management, attention to detail, and the ability to deal with interruptions.

## Availability of Supplementary Materials

In addition to the textbook, support materials designed to assist in lesson preparation, instruction, and testing are also available.

*Information Processing Activities.* This student workbook contains the letterheads, memorandums, and other forms required for the completion of chapter activities. Also included are the instructions and supplies for the four office simulations and an Activities Log for students' use in maintaining a record of jobs completed.

*Teacher's Activity Guide.* This publication, available to all teachers who adopt the textbook for class use, is an invaluable aid in planning and guiding instruction. You will find information about the overall office procedures course; teaching suggestions for each chapter; solutions to all activities, simulations, and tests; and transparency masters. This information is organized in a loose-leaf binder for easy access.

*Test Package.* Available for use with *THE OFFICE: Procedures and Technology* is a set of printed tests that you will find useful in evaluating students. Included in the test package are individual chapter tests, a midterm exam, a final exam, and a performance test.

*MicroEXAM Diskette.* This computerized test bank contains all the questions from the chapter tests, midterm exam, and final exam in the printed test package. There is also space provided on the diskette for you to add your own questions to the test bank. Diskettes are available for Apple® IIe, Apple® IIc, IBM PCjr®, Tandy® 1000, TRS-80® Model III, and TRS-80® Model 4 microcomputers.

## A Commitment by the Authors

An office procedures course is an important offering in a secondary school curriculum. Students will apply what they learn in this course to a wide variety of job responsibilities. *THE OFFICE: Procedures and Technology* has been written with careful, persistent attention to the responsibilities accepted by the authors: to present relevant content within a framework that assures high-level learning; to provide activities that reinforce student understanding and help students develop a wide range of office skills; to present both contemporary and emerging office environments; and, finally, to encourage the attitude that learning can be challenging, worthwhile, and enjoyable.

Mary Ellen Oliverio
William R. Pasewark

# THE OFFICE
# IN MODERN BUSINESS LIFE

# Chapter 1

# The Office and Its Place in the Organization

Offices are universal. As you know, banks, department stores, manufacturing companies, supermarkets, medical clinics, schools, municipal agencies, and other organizations have offices. Offices are places of work for millions of Americans. Of course, many workers who consider the office their place of work are not office workers. Attorneys, bankers, buyers, and many others in the labor force work in offices. Some of them may perform tasks from time to time that are the same as those performed by office workers. However, their major responsibilities do not relate to office tasks. For example, attorneys may make telephone calls and may answer the telephone, which are tasks office workers perform. Attorneys are not office workers, though.

In this book, the spotlight is on offices in which personnel spend full time on tasks classified as office tasks. The focus of your study is on offices that create, process, store, and distribute information. You will have an opportunity to develop an understanding of these offices and of the skills and knowledge needed to handle critical office functions.

Office workers are valuable assistants to executives and managers in all types of organizations. In many instances, competent office workers are delegated a great number of tasks that they perform with no direct supervision.

In Chapter 1, you will gain an overview of the office environment. You will learn how office workers make valuable contributions to all types of organizations. The objectives of the chapter are to

- acquaint you with the unique function of the office

- help you understand the overall structure of modern organizations

2

## Topic 1

# WHAT THE OFFICE IS

When you have completed your study of this topic, you will be able to

- describe the office that creates, processes, stores, and distributes information
- identify changes taking place in the office
- explain the importance of ergonomics
- describe the general nature of productivity

Business activity would come to a standstill if there were no offices with personnel to do the many tasks related to processing information. The total office staff provides a network of human skills and understanding that supports an effective, efficient, smooth functioning of the whole organization.

*Effective:* accomplishing what is promised or planned

*Efficient:* handling a task with minimum use of time and effort

*Smooth:* achieving results without disrupting the organized way of working

The F. T. Roome Company manufactures small calculators that are sold to retail stores throughout the world. The company guarantees customers and prospective customers that orders are shipped within 24 hours of their receipt. Office workers throughout the company must cooperate in order to meet the company's promise.

3

*The office worker who carefully records the exact quantity and model of calculator ordered is processing information effectively.*

*The office worker who prepares the shipping forms promptly and properly on the first attempt is processing information efficiently.*

*The office worker who has the form to accompany the goods completed by the scheduled pick-up time is assuring smooth processing of information.*

## OFFICES ARE PLACES OF ACTION

You will have many opportunities for employment as a full-time office worker if you develop your skills and understanding of the key office functions presented in this textbook. (See Illus. 1–1.) There are also other positions not considered office jobs where you will find your skills extremely useful. Almost all employees at work today perform some tasks that are actually office functions. Here are just two illustrations:

*Bob is a member of the repair staff of the local utilities company. When he reports for work each morning, he is given a list of customers who have requested service. He must record on his list how much*

**Illus. 1–1.** Office workers contribute to the overall efficiency of an organization by performing vital office functions.

### KEY OFFICE FUNCTIONS IN MODERN OFFICES

keyboarding documents, including letters, memorandums, reports
photocopying documents
searching for information
composing letters and memorandums
editing and proofreading documents

greeting visitors
answering telephone calls
placing telephone calls
accommodating customers
arranging meetings
opening and sorting mail
preparing outgoing mail

inputting data at computer terminal
maintaining files and databases
preparing forms, including checks, orders, invoices
maintaining financial records

maintaining a calendar
establishing priorities for tasks
managing work of assistants

time he spends at each place and what repairs he makes. Also, at the end of the day, he calls the home office to report the status of the jobs assigned to him. Bob is expected to do the office-related tasks properly.

Sharon is the manager of public information for a relatively small company. A recent problem with one of the company's new products kept her at work long after the rest of the office staff had gone home. She needed to prepare a bulletin for release early the next morning. Sharon, who had studied office procedures in high school, found that her *facility* in handling the tasks required to prepare the bulletin was beneficial at times such as this. Her knowledge of filing and retrieval systems permitted her to refer easily to records in her assistant's office.

*facility:* ability to do something with ease and skill

**Illus. 1–2.** Offices are exciting places in which to work! The skills you are developing now will be useful as you investigate a variety of career opportunities.

**OFFICES
PROVIDE
VARYING
SERVICES**

*variations:* differences

All offices processing information are not alike. In fact, there are many *variations*. Even the offices of a particular organization will vary in size, structure, and nature of activity. Some offices are specialized, which means that their employees carry out a particular activity only. Other offices, where employees complete many tasks, are considered general offices.

*The Brown Lumber Company has three offices. One office is responsible for ordering and receiving products sold by the company; another handles the records required for paying for the goods and for receiving payments from customers; the third office performs a wide range of tasks, including scheduling appointments for the manager, listening to complaints and problems of customers, and processing requests for special orders.*

*Asbery Ceramics is a very small company that is operated by two ceramists who make the artistic objects in their own studio. The demand for their vases, pitchers, plates, and mugs has grown so much that they cannot manage office tasks as they did formerly. They recently hired a full-time office employee and reorganized their studio to provide an "office" for the new employee. The employee handles all office tasks including talking with customers, receiving orders by telephone and by letter, ordering raw materials, paying bills, and receiving payments from customers.*

**Illus. 1–3.** You may accept a position in either a general or a specialized office.

Brown Lumber Company has both specialized and general offices. Because of the large number of orders being placed and received, a specialized office devoted to just those activities was organized. Likewise, the number of transactions related to making and receiving payments resulted in setting up an office to direct only those financial matters. On the other hand, because the manager has a diversity of responsibilities, the staff in the general office performs a variety of tasks.

At Asbery Ceramics, the small size of the company means that there is seldom a repetition of the same task during a single workday or workweek. For example, unlike the Brown Lumber Company where goods are ordered daily, the orders at Asbery Ceramics are placed once a month. Therefore, the single employee takes care of many different office tasks. In this small company, the owners are able to spend their time producing ceramics because they have a competent office employee.

These are two of many variations in organizations. Each organization plans its office services in such a way that the goals of the organization will be achieved.

## OFFICES ARE CHANGING

Currently, much discussion at business conferences and in business periodicals centers on what is happening in offices. New types of electronic equipment are leading to changes in how office work is performed. For example, word/text processing systems have eliminated the rekeyboarding of complete letters and reports when changes must be made. Now, only the changes must be keyboarded since the original letter or report is stored electronically in the machine's memory.

*speculation:* guessing

There is much *speculation* among experts in office systems about what the future office will be. Some of those predicting the nature of the future office believe that it will be absolutely paperless. A paperless office will require that all information be created, transmitted, and stored electronically. For example, a memorandum would be prepared at a computer terminal and transmitted electronically to the recipient's computer terminal. In the meantime, the memorandum would also be stored electronically in the sender's computer system's memory. The recipient would read the memorandum at the terminal and then "file" it for future reference by striking the proper keys at the terminal keyboard. While the equipment for a paperless office is now available, the question of when this type of office will be *commonplace* is still unanswered.

*commonplace:* found everywhere

The most common descriptions of the future office include a **totally integrated workstation**. At a totally integrated workstation, an employee would have access to the electronic tools required to create, process, store, retrieve, and distribute information. This kind of workstation will permit verbal communication by telephone with other people or with machines at any location in the world. The office employee will be able to **access** hundreds of sources of information. Any collection of related items maintained in computer memory is known as a **database**. You are likely to find that businesses maintain several databases. For example, the personnel department may have an employee records database, and the sales department may have a customer database.

*access:* to enter and to use

> *An office assistant in product development has been asked by the director to find out how many men and women between the ages of 18 and 24 bought miniature television units during the past year. The office assistant, acquainted with the available databases, is able to access immediately a database that provides results of market research conducted during the past year.*

The office of the future, which is often called the *totally electronic office,* is likely to bring changes in the places where jobs are done. Many are suggesting that large numbers of office workers will be able to work at home. In fact, there are some employees already working in their own homes. **Telecommuting**, communicating at a distance, is the term for how those who work at home communicate via computer with their employers.

> *A young worker wanted to work for a large company in a nearby metropolitan area, but wanted to continue to live in a rural community about 45 miles from the city. The worker accepted a job as a word processor and was able to do the tasks at home. The company provided the equipment needed for the job, including that required for electronic transfer of the worker's output to the company office. Now this young worker handles tasks in a home office overlooking a valley where cattle graze peacefully. The letters and reports prepared in this isolated country place will ultimately be received by persons around the world.*

*elusive:* difficult to describe or understand

The future office is often referred to as the **elusive** office. The future office will be unlike offices of today, but its exact nature is not yet clear. It is not evident, for instance, what new office jobs

**Illus. 1–4.** Telecommuting gives employees the option of "going to work" without leaving their homes.

will develop as the future becomes reality. For example, many more office workers will probably be needed to design and update information maintained electronically.

You will want to be alert to what is happening in offices that you know. You must feel certain that with a sound, basic understanding of office procedures, you will be prepared to accept change and to modify your ways of working.

**TODAY'S OFFICES**

From this discussion of the office of the future, you have learned that there is much change underway and that there is no simple way to describe *all* present-day offices. However, it is possible to identify offices at three stages in the progress toward the future. These are (1) the traditional office, (2) the office in transition, and (3) the state-of-the-art office.

### The Traditional Office

The traditional office is one that is functioning with the structure and basic equipment that was available a decade or more ago. The typewriters may be manual or electric; there may be a simple copying machine. The records system may be completely manual with documents maintained on paper and stored in file drawers. The telephone system may require an operator to direct incoming calls as well as *internal* calls.

*internal:* among the departments within an organization

Generally, in the traditional office little consideration is given to more up-to-date equipment because what is already available is judged to be adequate. Neither the volume of work nor the

*perceived:* seen; judged; considered

nature of the work is *perceived* to justify changes in the manner of carrying out office tasks.

> *Withers and Layman, Caterers prides itself on the personal service provided its clients. The two women who are partners in this organization have been in business for ten years, but they have limited the number of jobs accepted, so the business has remained at the same volume for the past six years. The office staff of three works in a small office with equipment purchased secondhand a decade ago. The office staff is efficient and is able to handle tasks with ease using just the present equipment.*

> *A small manufacturing company that makes parts for computers uses the most advanced machinery in the factory, yet its office has equipment purchased 15 years ago. This company supplies components to two major computer companies and ships in large quantities only. The two office employees write few letters, and they seldom place long distance calls. The traditional office is considered adequate in every area.*

There are some offices at present that may be classified as traditional offices, but you must remember that they are likely to change in the future. As the appeal of new equipment and new systems becomes widespread, traditional offices will begin to enter into the next stage of office development.

## The Office in Transition

*transitional:* in the process of changing from one stage to another

Offices in many organizations are at some point between the traditional office and the state-of-the-art office. These *transitional* offices have long-range plans for the introduction of modern equipment. Such plans are fulfilled in phases. A company may have, for example, a highly automated payroll system and inventory system, yet still use a traditional way of handling other office functions. In some businesses, electronic equipment is used for word processing but not for the transfer of information from one location to another. One executive described a company's plans in these words:

> *Our company's office automation began about five years ago. It has proceeded in the typical manner: concentrating on installing word processing equipment first, since that is where large and immediate savings could be realized. Gradually, we are adding other office sup-*

**Illus. 1–5.** Note the differences among a traditional office, a transitional office, and a state-of-the-art office, shown here from left to right.

*port capabilities. Within another three years we should have a completely integrated office system.*

## The State-of-the-Art Office

A state-of-the-art office is one that is functioning with the most advanced equipment and systems available. This type is also referred to as a *technologically advanced office*. The technologically advanced office makes use of workstations where many different office functions can be performed. For example, at such a workstation, it is possible to produce a *hard copy* (paper copy) of a document. At the same time, the document can be transmitted to an executive's desk terminal in another part of the country or another part of the world. Every office function is part of what is known as an integrated information network. Basically, an integrated information network is one that permits interaction among the units connected for creating, processing, storing, retrieving, and transmitting information.

*The offices of a major computer manufacturing company support the company's belief that its equipment streamlines office functions. This company produces the most **innovative** equipment in the industry. As soon as the new equipment is produced, it is installed in the company's own offices. The offices serve as showplaces for customers who are interested in the state-of-the-art office.*

*innovative:* newest; representing the most recent changes

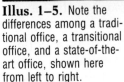

**OFFICE DESIGN**

Managers are giving increasing attention to the general design of offices and workstations. You will want to note the physical layout of the offices you visit.

To provide a comfortable, pleasant environment, managers use attractive colors for walls and floor coverings; they provide textured, flexible partitions that permit employees to work in a

*congenial:* agreeable; friendly

*congenial* setting. Artwork and living plants are frequently added to heighten the cheerfulness of the environment. Measures are taken to minimize accidents and ensure safety: carpeting is installed tightly, equipment is secured to workstations, and electrical cords are concealed.

Many companies have planned offices with consideration given to physically handicapped employees. Ramps and workstations specially designed to accommodate wheelchairs, for example, illustrate a company's goal of making the movement of the handicapped easier.

The concern for the physical environment of workers is part of a field of specialization called ergonomics. Ergonomics is the study of the effects of the work environment on the health and well-being of employees. Relationships between biological and technological factors are of interest to specialists in this field. For example, one study determined the relationship between the lighting at computer terminals and eye fatigue. The purpose of the study was to establish the nature and intensity of light that assure a low level of eye fatigue for workers at the terminals.

Workstations increasingly reflect the knowledge gained from ergonomics. Study carefully the details shown in Illus. 1–6. Notice that many of the workstation components can be adjusted by height and angle in order to meet the worker's individual needs. Also, note the comments about color of walls, noise level, and lighting. Proper attention to these kinds of factors contributes to a comfortable working environment for each employee.

## THE CONCERN WITH PRODUCTIVITY

*paperwork:* handling all documents required for business activity

Productivity, which means level of accomplishment, is important to employers of office workers. Modern businesses operate in a complex environment. They buy and sell goods in a world market; they borrow money from banks and other financial institutions throughout the world; they manufacture different products in a number of countries; they seek innovations everywhere. Such complexity has resulted in an overwhelming amount of *paperwork*. For example, a company of a hundred years ago may have had a single factory producing a single product or several related products; the company bought and sold goods in the town where it was located. A company of today may have factories in a hundred locations producing many different products; this company buys and sells goods throughout the world. Can you imagine the paperwork required for the headquarters office to

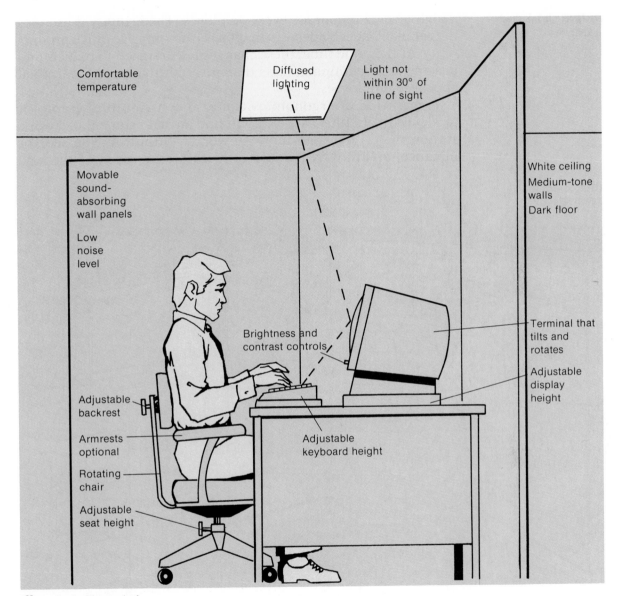

Comfortable temperature

Diffused lighting

Light not within 30° of line of sight

Movable sound-absorbing wall panels

Low noise level

White ceiling
Medium-tone walls
Dark floor

Brightness and contrast controls

Terminal that tilts and rotates

Adjustable display height

Adjustable backrest

Armrests optional

Rotating chair

Adjustable seat height

Adjustable keyboard height

**Illus. 1–6.** The goal of ergonomics specialists is to make workers more comfortable and more productive.

have complete information about everything the factories have produced and shipped out during one month only!

The pressure of increasing amounts of paperwork has led companies to try to organize office functions in a manner that allows

*output:* tasks completed

a high level of *output* for every employee. The primary reason for the rapid changes underway in offices is to improve office productivity. At the same time, these changes are designed to reduce, and in some cases eliminate, tasks that are repetitive and have limited appeal to employees.

Recognition of ergonomics can also contribute to employee productivity. In Illus. 1–7, you will find an arrangement of a workstation that is likely to increase worker output. As you see, for instance, an employee would be within easy reach of the key-

**Illus. 1–7.** Workstation layout.

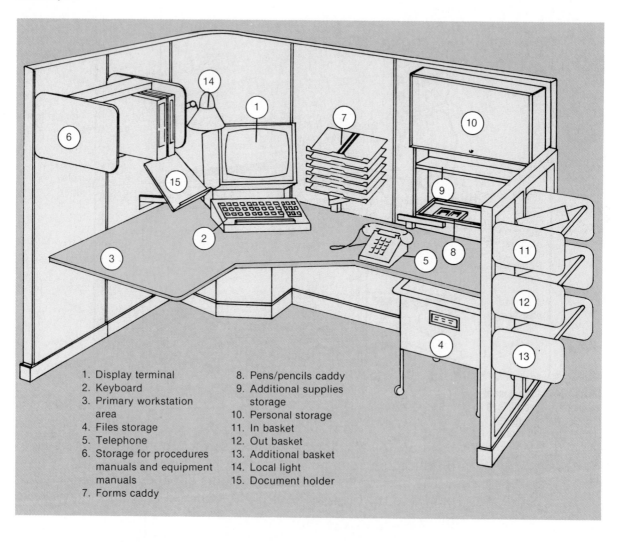

1. Display terminal
2. Keyboard
3. Primary workstation area
4. Files storage
5. Telephone
6. Storage for procedures manuals and equipment manuals
7. Forms caddy
8. Pens/pencils caddy
9. Additional supplies storage
10. Personal storage
11. In basket
12. Out basket
13. Additional basket
14. Local light
15. Document holder

board, the telephone, and storage areas. This means that the worker would not have to take time to walk to another area in order to have access to these important items. Also note the flexibility of the modular components that make up the work-station. *Modular components* are parts that can be quickly assembled, taken apart, and rearranged to meet employee needs. Storage areas and shelves hung from movable panels are examples of modular components. Adjustable work surfaces and seating also are said to be modular.

Managers are finding much success with new and more efficient ways of carrying out tasks. Comments from two managers are:

> *The word processing center in our company (a medium-size insurance company) processes 75 to 80 percent of the daily correspondence in our main office. Prior to the use of word processors, memorandums, letters, and reports were prepared at electric typewriters. We had almost twice as many people at work on the tasks. Now, needless repetition in keying has been eliminated.*

> *We (a cable TV service company) are managing customer calls far more efficiently and satisfactorily now than we were formerly. We have eight operators at computer terminals answering customer calls. Operators instantly retrieve for viewing on their screens the four-month customer service records or any other information required for a complete response. At a glance at the screen, an operator can tell an unhappy customer that the service technician knocked at the customer's door 45 minutes earlier but had no response. Then, the operator can schedule another appointment.*

> *In earlier days, we had twice as many employees taking customer calls. The person who answered had to walk to the file cabinet to retrieve the appropriate file folder. If the file was out, there was much time spent in trying to locate it. Often, the information was not up to date. For example, there was no way of knowing what happened when the technician went to a customer's home to provide service until the end of the day when the technician returned to the office. Customer inquiries seldom could be taken care of quickly; generally, operators had to promise to call back when they had located the information.*

You see, the office is a very interesting and challenging place to work. The content of this book provides a thorough understanding of what productivity is and will teach you how you can assess your own level of accomplishment as you complete the assignments.

## REVIEW QUESTIONS

1. What is the general role of the office in today's organizations?
2. Why is efficiency considered important in an office?
3. Identify five key office functions.
4. Explain in what ways offices are not all alike.
5. In what ways does new electronic equipment change offices?
6. Briefly describe an integrated workstation.
7. How is telecommuting changing where people work?
8. How does the traditional office differ from the state-of-the-art office?
9. Why are business managers interested in the findings of ergonomics?
10. What is office productivity?

## MAKING DECISIONS

Assume that you are a relatively new employee in a traditional office. You have become accustomed to the electric typewriter at your workstation. You like the typewriter; it is functioning well.

One day the supervisor stops by to talk with you about plans to buy a few new electronic typewriters. The supervisor says to you:

*"Would you be interested in participating in our experimental use of this new typewriter? If the three who experiment with the machine like it, we will then replace all our electric typewriters. The new machine positions paper automatically and has a correcting key. It also has a memory and a display panel, which allows for editing before a line is typed. There are other automatic features, too."*

What would you say to the supervisor? What would be the basis for your decision to participate or not to participate?

**What You Are To Do:**  Prepare a brief response to each of the questions raised.

## EXTENDING YOUR ENGLISH SKILLS

Read the following paragraph. You will notice that there are complete sentences as well as words that do not form a sentence.

*Many new office employees attended the workshop. The program was planned to give. While employees will be in specific departments, they still have responsibilities to the total company. The company thinks its employees. If they understand what the overall goals are. Supervisors who participated in the opening discussion. The employees listened closely.*

**What You Are To Do:**    Keyboard (type) each group of words ending with a period. At the end of each unit, keyboard an "S" if the words form a complete sentence or an "N" if the words do not form a complete sentence.

When you have completed the entire paragraph as instructed, keyboard a complete sentence for all units that were incomplete. Add any words that you believe are needed to convey a complete, realistic thought.

## APPLICATION ACTIVITIES

Word/text processing equipment can be used to complete this activity.

### Activity 1

**What You Are To Do:**    Talk with an office employee about the office in which she/he works. Get answers to the following questions:

A. What are the major tasks performed in the office where the employee works?

B. What are the major types of equipment, if any, that the employee uses?

C. What types of equipment are in the office in addition to that used by the worker with whom you are talking?

D. What does the employee think are the major goals of the total organization?

Review the answers you received in your interview with the employee. Prepare a brief report of the answers to your questions.

Word/text processing equipment can be used to complete this activity.

### Activity 2

**What You Are To Do:**    The office in your school provides a number of services required to keep your school operating properly. Prepare a list of the tasks that you believe must be performed by the office staff each week.

# Topic 2

## THE SETTING IN WHICH OFFICES FUNCTION

When you have completed your study of this topic, you will be able to

- identify general goals for the three types of organizations
- describe the contributions of employees in organizations
- describe the unique role of office employees

As you have learned, information processing tasks are the focus of this book. Such tasks are not ends in themselves. The tasks are important to the goals of the organization. Many activites are required for any organization to achieve the goals established for the day or week or year. Few, if any, of the activities in organizations can be completed without some related office tasks.

From your own observations in local businesses, you understand that information is vital to the proper functioning of a business. The management of a business must know what is happening throughout all departments. Office workers provide valuable assistance by processing and maintaining the information that relates to what is happening. Management must communicate with a variety of outsiders, including suppliers and customers. Office workers assist by preparing documents, processing financial data, and transmitting messages required for such communications. All management within a business must understand the policies and procedures that are to guide the business's activities. Office workers help in this area by preparing documents and transmitting these through interdepartmental messenger or mail service.

*Wonderland Toys, Inc., has an active department of product development. It is here that new toys are created and ideas that are sent in from outsiders are reviewed. An office employee processes the correspondence and contracts with these outsiders. The director is grateful for the excellent assistance of this office worker. It is important to the company that ideas are acknowledged quickly and that the originators get prompt, courteous responses. The follow-up for those whose ideas are accepted must be done carefully so that payment arrangements are clearly understood.*

*Teenagers Camping Council is a not-for-profit organization in a large southern state. The Council is supported by contributions from individuals and corporations. The director of the camp program has a staff of office employees who aid in preparing brochures, in sending out letters, in maintaining records of applicants, and in answering telephone inquiries. The director believes it would not be possible to serve the teenagers of the state without an efficient office staff.*

Any office task you perform will be more interesting if you understand the total organization and its goals. Also, this interest will aid you as you *assess* your own performance.

*assess:* evaluate

Organizations, in much the same manner as individuals, establish goals to guide their actions. It is possible to think of general, overall goals if organizations are viewed in three groups:

## OVERALL ORGANIZA-TION GOALS

*entities:* units with separate identities

- businesses
- not-for-profit *entities*
- governmental units

The specific goals of an organization within any of these groups can vary considerably from the specific goals of another organization within the group. However, the overall goals of the organizations within the group will be the same.

### Businesses

*subsidiaries:* units of a larger organization

Businesses range from the so-called giant corporations with *subsidiaries* throughout the world to very small businesses with a single owner/employee. The primary goal of all businesses is to provide particular goods or services that will result in a profit.

When a company earns a profit, it has *revenues* (receipts from sales) that are greater than the costs of providing the goods or services. With profit earned, a company is able to continue to operate the business and also invest in more equipment and buildings for additional production. For example, a profitable small computer company was able to buy more equipment and produce more computers. Their profits increased at a rapid rate.

Businesses use their resources in the most economical manner possible so that they can realize profits. Profit is considered very important to the well-being of the country at large. When businesses are profitable they are likely to increase the number of people they employ. This means that the country will have a lower unemployment rate than would otherwise be the case. Workers will have money to spend and to save. Furthermore,

**Illus. 1–8.** A grand opening is one way in which a company communicates with potential customers.

*segment:* part

businesses pay income taxes on their profits directly to federal and state governments. Businesses are the profit-earning *segment* of the American economy.

Businesses in the United States are organized as single proprietorships, partnerships, or corporations. Single proprietorships and partnerships are organized without approval by any governmental agencies. Corporations, on the other hand, must meet governmental requirements before they are recognized as business units. Of course, there are laws and regulations that govern business activity, regardless of the type of organization chosen.

A single proprietorship is a business owned by one individual who may or may not also be the manager of the enterprise. A single proprietorship may be of any size, but many are small.

### Jason Computer Supplies Store

*A single retail store owned by one person, who also manages the store. Two full-time general clerks and a part-time stockroom employee assist the owner/manager.*

### Aunt Annie's Pizza

*A single restaurant owned and operated by the person who actually makes the pizza. Two persons assist the owner/cook in the kitchen; two persons take orders and serve customers; one person serves as cashier; a part-time bookkeeper handles financial records.*

A **partnership** is a business that has two or more owners. There may be different types of partners in this kind of business. Some partners provide funds only, but others may be active in managing the business. Partnerships, too, may be of any size; many are small, however.

### Galman and Elwood

*An accounting firm owned by two partners who are aided by three staff accountants and two office workers.*

### The Westwood Dental Clinic

*A dental office owned by three partners, all of whom are dentists. The dentists work full-time and are assisted by a total staff of ten persons.*

**Illus. 1–9.** Organizations vary in size from a small single proprietorship (Sue's Pies) to a large corporation (Cincom Systems).

A **corporation** is a business organized under the laws of a state or the federal government. A corporation is a separate legal unit and may be privately or publicly owned. Owners have shares of stock and are called *stockholders* or *shareholders*. Most of the largest businesses in the United States are publicly owned corporations.

> *Privately owned: Reader's Digest Association, Inc.*
>
> *Publicly owned: General Motors*
>
> *Large corporations employ hundreds of executives, managers, specialists, and office workers, as well as production workers, to meet the goals of their organizations.*

*expenditures:*
amounts of money
spent

Your understanding of a business's interest in earning a profit will help you interpret what you are to do and why you are to do it. For example, an employee in the budget office will appreciate comparing actual *expenditures* for each department in the company with budgeted expenditures (the budgeted expenditures are those necessary for the proper functioning of the departments). The budget office checks figures monthly. If any department is spending more than it is allowed, immediate steps are taken to determine what changes are needed in the way funds are being used.

## Not-for-Profit Entities

A highly developed economy, such as that in the United States, has many organizations providing essential services to the people of the country. Among these organizations are associations that sponsor developmental programs for young people (4-H Clubs, Girl Scouts, Campfire Girls, and Boy Scouts). Other common not-for-profit groups include centers for performing arts, museums, libraries, hospitals, and private colleges and universities.

*Not-for-profit organizations* raise funds from individual and group contributions and from fees and dues paid by participants; in some instances, limited funds are provided by governmental agencies at the local, state, or federal level. These groups strive to keep their expenses at a level that is no higher than their contributed funds.

As you realize from the name of this group, organizations of this type do not seek to make profits. The chief goal of not-for-profit organizations is to provide a valuable service to anyone who can benefit from it. Museums strive to make their exhibi-

**Illus. 1–10.** If you work in a not-for-profit organization, your tasks may include typing display labels and dealing with the public. This young woman is conducting a tour of a museum.

tions of art appealing to increasing numbers of visitors; centers for performing arts encourage more persons to participate in theatrical productions; hospitals strive to offer high-quality health care to all patients who seek services.

If you choose to work in a not-for-profit organization, you will want to be aware of its overall goals. Then you will better understand how the tasks you perform contribute to total efforts of the organization.

## Governmental Units

*extensive:* having a wide range; including many services

In the United States, the role of government is *extensive*. There are governmental units at the local, state, regional, and federal levels. These units are called by different names, including *agency, commission, bureau, department,* and *board.* Each unit has specific responsibilities for services necessary in the life of the community, state, or country.

Local: *Office of the Mayor, Board of Education*

State: *Department of Motor Vehicles, Department of Commerce*

Federal: *Environmental Protection Agency, Federal Communications Commission*

Governmental units do not strive to make a profit. These units are supported with the money received from taxes. The units strive to provide high-quality service without wasting the tax-payers' money.

Office workers who work for governmental units participate in providing services that add to the quality of life throughout the community. Understanding the long-term goals of the particular department or agency or board contributes to the office workers' effectiveness in performing their jobs.

## TYPES OF EMPLOYEES REQUIRED

*competent:* skilled; capable

Organizations require many different types of talented, **competent** workers, including large numbers of office workers. In your job as an office employee, you will often interact with workers whose responsibilities are unlike yours. Understanding what their jobs require will help you as you cooperate with them in getting specific tasks completed properly and promptly.

The general types of workers, in addition to office workers, required in a typical large, publicly owned corporation are briefly described in the following paragraphs.

### Top Management

Persons who have overall responsibility for directing company operations are referred to as top management. Top management generally includes the chief executive officer, the president, and a small number of executive vice presidents. This group, some-

**Illus. 1–11.** The board of directors is responsible for setting policies of the company.

times identified as the *executive committee,* maintains a total view of the organization through direct visits and meetings with the operating managers of various divisions. They also have frequent meetings among themselves. In a publicly owned company there is a board of directors which sets the policies related to products to be produced, investments to be made, salaries and wages to be paid to employees, and similar matters.

The chief executive officer and the president are members of the board of directors in most companies. Other members of the board are persons who are not employed by the company. The outside board members, though, have a broad understanding of how businesses function and can contribute to the decision-making function of the company.

## Division Management

Companies are subdivided into units by lines of work or by functions to be performed. Each unit typically is called a *division* or *department* and is run by a vice president. Persons who direct division or department operations are called division management. The persons at this level **implement** the policies of the executive group described earlier. You will find a wide variety of vice presidents at this level, including vice president of manufacturing, vice president for retail sales, vice president for product development, and vice president for public information.

*implement:* put into effect

## Middle Management

Companies may have several levels of managers and supervisors. These employees are commonly referred to as middle management. Such persons oversee the carrying out of specific tasks. For example, there may be a manager for personnel. Reporting to the manager are three assistant managers: one handles hiring; another, employee training programs; a third, counseling and performance appraisals. Each assistant manager has a staff of several persons who assist in the activities provided.

One especially important group is that of managers and supervisors for administrative support services. Administrative support services refers to the activities of the total office staff, plus the managers and supervisors of the office staff. For example, if you choose to work as a word processing operator in a center, the supervisor to whom you report is an employee in administrative support services. You, too, will be an employee in this category.

Middle management employees are required in all types of companies to provide the management and supervisory skills important to a smoothly operating company.

## Persons with Technical Specializations

Many different types of specialized personnel are required in organizations. The nature of a company's activities determines what specialists are required. If you were to review the specialists in a number of companies, you would likely find accountants, financial planners, systems analysts, programmers, and economists, as well as machinists, salespersons, maintenance workers, carpenters, and engineers.

*An automobile manufacturer hires engineers who design motors and other parts for new automobiles.*

*A large bank has a staff of economists who study what is happening in business.*

*A company that manufactures custom-designed tables and chairs hires furniture makers who produce the pieces.*

**STRUCTURE OF ORGANI- ZATIONS**

*hierarchical:* placed in rank from highest to lowest

*primary:* first; chief

*structuring:* subdividing responsibility

The types of workers to whom you have been briefly introduced are assigned responsibilities that, added together, are expected to meet the goals of the organization. The structure of an organization is formally presented in an organization chart. An organization chart shows positions in *hierarchical* order. In actual practice, the organization chart for several thousand employees will require a number of pages to show all the levels of employees.

Illus. 1–12 is a partial organization chart for a publicly owned furniture manufacturing company. Note that only the *primary* divisions of responsibility are shown. Note also the positions of the executive vice presidents in relation to the president and to the vice presidents. In Illus. 1–13 on page 28, you have the staff for one department only: customer services.

These two illustrations merely introduce the concept of an organization chart. As you proceed with your study of this book, you will become familiar with more aspects of the *structuring* of organizations. Knowing how an organization is structured will help you understand more thoroughly the duties of your own job.

*A new office assistant in the frozen foods department of a large food producing company was asked by the manager to get preliminary*

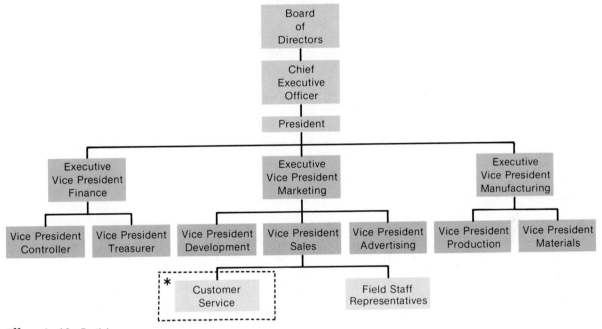

**MANSON FURNITURE MANUFACTURING COMPANY**
**PARTIAL ORGANIZATION CHART**

**Illus. 1–12.** Partial organization chart showing the primary divisions of responsibility.

*copies of forthcoming advertisements. The assistant had carefully studied the organization chart in the company manual and knew that the advertising director would be the person to call with this request.*

## UNIQUE ROLE FOR OFFICE WORKERS

As you learned from the preceding paragraphs, many employees at different levels of responsibility are required to operate a successful organization. And, at all levels of any organization there are office workers providing important information processing services. Here are just two examples:

*The executive must meet with the division heads to discuss new developments for the next year. The office worker talks with each division head to determine whether the suggested date and time are convenient. When the date and time have been established, the office worker prepares an agenda and accompanying materials to be forwarded to each division head prior to the meeting.*

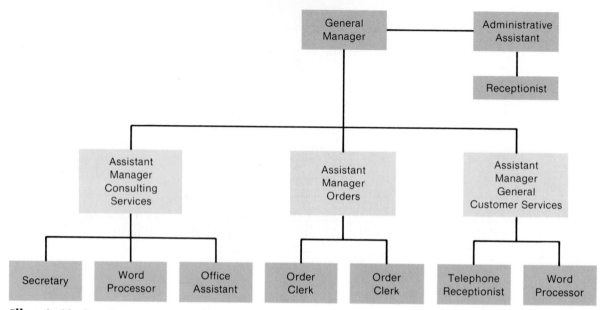

**MANSON FURNITURE MANUFACTURING COMPANY**
**ORGANIZATION CHART**
**CUSTOMER SERVICE DEPARTMENT**

**Illus. 1–13.** Organization chart for a single department within a company.

*The sales representative secures an order from a customer and then calls the order department and reports the order. Several office workers will become involved in preparing and processing the information required to deliver the merchandise to the customer, to bill the customer, and to record payment.*

*facilitate:* help ac-complish; make easier

Office workers can be compared with assistants who *facilitate* the activities of specialists. Research associates and assistants aid scientists in carrying out experiments in the laboratory; dental assistants work with dentists in providing care to patients; legal assistants help lawyers in developing background for particular cases. Office workers assist management, as well as specialists, in performing those tasks that initiate, process, and maintain the information required for the business activities of a particular department. The term *information processing* is used to describe, in general fashion, what office workers have as primary responsibility.

In Chapter 2, you will be introduced to types of office positions commonly found in present-day organizations. Skills and understandings required for each type of office job are discussed. This information will help you understand the way in which office tasks are organized by types of jobs. You will then have the basis for developing your own career goal as you consider your interests in relation to the types of office jobs in modern organizations.

## REVIEW QUESTIONS

1. On the basis of overall goals, how are organizations commonly classified in the United States?

2. What is the primary difference between a business and a not-for-profit entity?

3. How does a corporation differ from a single proprietorship?

4. Why should you be interested in the overall goals of the organization in which you have accepted an office position?

5. Identify two positions that are considered top management.

6. Identify a position that requires accepting broad operational responsibility.

7. What kinds of technical specialists might an organization require?

8. What information is provided in an organization chart?

9. What is the unique role of office workers in modern organizations?

10. In what way is an office worker like a dental or legal assistant?

## INTERACTING WITH OTHERS

Assume that you have accepted a position in a large company that provides each new employee with a copy of the company's annual report and policy manual. You go to lunch the second day with another new employee. As you are sitting in a local coffee shop, your co-worker says to you: "Look, I don't understand what is going on. I am a good office worker. I like keyboarding, answering telephones, and doing other office tasks. Why do I have to be bothered with all this other information? I don't care what the company's business is; I don't care about its policies. Why don't they just leave me alone to do my keyboarding and other tasks? Isn't that what they hired me to do?" What would you say to your co-worker?

**What You Are To Do:** Prepare a brief response to the questions raised.

## EXTENDING YOUR MATH SKILLS

You work as an office assistant in the personnel department. You have been given the following table.

**What You Are To Do:** Compute all ten missing totals. Write your answers on a sheet of plain paper.

### PERSONNEL IN REGIONAL OFFICES

| Position | Miami Office | New Orleans Office | St. Louis Office | Total |
|---|---|---|---|---|
| Regional Vice President | 12 | 14 | 16 | ? |
| Regional Manager | 16 | 12 | 14 | ? |
| Sales Representative | 20 | 18 | 17 | ? |
| Secretary | 6 | 5 | 4 | ? |
| Word Processor | 8 | 6 | 7 | ? |
| General Clerk | 7 | 6 | 8 | ? |
| Totals | ? | ? | ? | ? |

## APPLICATION ACTIVITY

You are an assistant to the executive secretary in the office of the president of a major telecommunications company. The secretary asks you to key a draft of a speech the president wrote out on the commuter train while en-route to the office this morning. The president is going to speak to the new office employees within a few days.

Word/text processing equipment can be used to complete this activity.

**What You Are To Do:** Keyboard (type) a copy of the excerpt which follows. Use double spacing and allow a one-inch margin at the left and right sides. Refer to Reference Section A for information about standard proofreader's marks.

Welcome! I know you've had several welcomes already, but I want to add mine. We are happy you have chosen Nationwide Telecommunications. We like it here. We want you to like it too.

You have a program that will give you many specifics about your jobs at Nationwide. I'll use the *short time* few minutes allocated to me to say a few words about our overall goals and interests.

Our business is developing and manufacturing telecommunications systems and equipment as well as servicing business customers throughout the country. Our goal is to be the best company in the industry! This means that we are looking ahead to the next century in our research laboratories where products that set the standard for our industry have been developed. We expect breakthroughs in electronic components that will revolutionize information *lc* Management throughout the country. And then, we expect to make our systems available in the most efficient *and appealing* ways possible.

We employ people with a wide range of skills and training. One very important group is the one you have joined — our office staff. Your contribution to our overall goal is invaluable. You will find that you are using state-of-the-art technology in your work. But, you must re-

CONTINUED ON NEXT PAGE

member that it is going to be what you do as a human worker that is the most significant part of your job. We know you have the skills for your job; we know your attitude is positive; and we know you understand the critical need for team work. We respect good workers; we care about your interest in earning your salary. We want you to succeed here. We are here to assist you. Welcome! Best wishes!

## CHAPTER SUMMARY

Offices are found in every type of organization. The office that is highlighted in this book is the place where the tasks performed are related to the processing of information.

Technological developments influence the way offices are organized and the way office work is performed. Because of the current rapid rate of change, offices are at different stages in being transformed into the so-called office of the future. Although the exact nature of the office of the future is not clearly identifiable at this time, it most certainly will involve integrated electronic equipment.

Increasing attention is being given to ergonomics. This is the field of study that considers relationships between physical facilities and the health and well-being of employees.

Productivity, which refers to the level of accomplishment of workers, is a key concern in the modern office. Many factors contribute to productivity improvement.

# Topic 1

## SPECIALIZATION IN THE OFFICE WORKFORCE

When you have completed your study of this topic, you will be able to

- identify major differences in skills required for employees in major office job clusters

- describe in general how office employees are studied by the Bureau of Labor Statistics of the U.S. Department of Labor

- describe general qualifications for all office workers

Every office worker participates in some aspects of information processing. For purposes of highlighting key types of office positions, four office position clusters will be discussed. The four clusters are:

- word/text processing

- data processing

- information management and distribution/transmission

- general assistance and customer service

You must remember, however, that the combination of tasks for a particular position may include tasks from several of the four clusters. Increasingly, technological developments in electronic equipment are allowing jobs to be classified in new ways.

Office employees are a significant segment of the total workforce in the United States. The U.S. Department of Labor, therefore, studies office workers and develops trends about employment prospects. You will find this information useful as you think ahead to job opportunities.

## WORD/TEXT PROCESSING

Word/text processing has a critical role in the total information processing environment. Word/text processing is the term used to describe the system for preparing documents (such as letters, memorandums, and reports) that are composed primarily of words. Present-day positions in which you might be interested which are *predominantly* word/text processing jobs include word/text processing specialists, word processing operators, word processors, typists, and secretaries.

*predominantly:* chiefly; mainly

### Basic Skills Required

Word/text processing positions require the employee to spend the major part of each working day preparing letters, memorandums, reports, and other documents using typewriters, word processors, or microcomputers. Proper preparation of documents requires a number of important skills and abilities. Among these are:

- rapid keyboarding skill
- skill in using text-editing equipment and software packages
- command of grammar, punctuation, and spelling
- ability to follow instructions
- ability to learn specialized vocabularies
- skill in *formatting* documents appropriately
- skill in proofreading accurately
- ability to organize tasks so that deadlines are met

*formatting:* setting up on the page

### Where Workers Are Employed

Employees who spend most of their time at word/text processing tasks are found in different settings in all types of companies. Some persons in this cluster work in word/text processing centers which service different departments within the organization. Documents may be prepared from rough drafts, from dictated notes, or from disks and tapes. Executives may have access to the center by telephone and may be able to record their dictation at any time — often from locations outside their offices.

In some instances, word/text processing employees are in decentralized clusters working on particular tasks for a single executive or for several executives whose responsibilities require many written communications. The workers in decentralized clusters become thoroughly familiar with the nature of the work of the executives. They learn any specialized vocabulary required, and they often suggest improvements in the letters, memorandums, and reports they prepare.

## Opportunities for Promotion

Along with the rising demand for employees who can perform word/text processing tasks, there is the demand for persons who can supervise the work of word/text processors. There are excellent supervisory opportunities for those persons who understand the word/text processing system in depth and who are willing to assume responsibility. Furthermore, word/text processors who

**Illus. 2–1.** Work in word/text processing requires a variety of skills and offers a number of career opportunities.

become acquainted with the content of what they are preparing
learn much about the department and the company. Their suggestions for improving what was written often reveal talent in communications. Numerous positions in general management are
considered appropriate for such employees.

If you begin your business career in a word/text processing job
and find that you enjoy the careful attention to well-written
communications, you may want to study further in a community
college or four-year college. Additional study in English, including writing, as well as study of administrative management,
may be of interest to you. Many company executives would find
further study a positive factor as they consider you for jobs of
more responsibility.

## DATA PROCESSING

Data processing refers to the collecting, manipulating, and distributing of details that are usually in the form of figures. The
final result of a data processing operation is called *output*, which
usually takes the form of a printed form or document. Output
may be tables of figures, financial reports, invoices, checks, and
other documents that present numbers of significance to the
organization. Jobs in this cluster that may interest you are payroll assistants; accounts payable and accounts receivable clerks;
order, purchasing, and receiving clerks; inventory assistants; and
junior accountants.

### Basic Skills Required

Employees who hold data processing positions spend the
greater portion of each workday handling a specific type of
information. An employee in the purchasing department may
determine the price of each item to be purchased, compute the
cost of the quantity desired, and prepare purchase orders. An
employee in an accounts receivable department records sales to
customers and payments received.

The basic skills necessary for jobs in data processing include:

- skill in entering information at a computer terminal
- skill in using electronic equipment and software
- aptitude with numbers and math processes
- ability to handle details carefully
- understanding of basic recordkeeping and accounting principles
- skill in writing legibly
- ability and willingness to check the accuracy of computations

## Where Workers Are Employed

Departments in modern organizations often require employees who can work with numbers confidently. Many employees are required in ordering, purchasing, accounts receivable, accounts payable, inventory, sales, and research and development. In some departments, there will be several workers who do the same type of activity; in other departments, there may be a few or only one carrying out the activity. For example, employees in the stockroom who keep records of items in stock and items released deal with numbers most of the workday. On the other hand, one office assistant in the advertising department keeps track of the expenditures related to trade shows which are held three times a year. Only a few hours a week are devoted to working with numbers.

## Opportunities for Promotion

Workers in data processing who grasp the significance of their tasks in relation to other tasks become valuable to the organization. They, therefore, are promising candidates for higher level positions. Frequently, successful employees are encouraged to seek additional training within the company or outside. If you

**Illus. 2–2.** Data processing skills can be applied to many areas of business.

begin your career in a data entry job, you may want to learn programming, software management, systems analysis, management information systems, or accounting. Opportunities to become data processing schedulers or supervisors of data processing centers are also frequently available to employees.

## INFORMATION MANAGEMENT AND DISTRIBUTION/TRANSMISSION

Modern organizations require personnel who devote full time to managing information properly and to distributing/transmitting information to persons within and outside the company. Positions in central records departments, mailrooms, reprographics centers, company libraries, and telephone information offices require competent workers.

### Basic Skills Required

Oganizations expect to train new employees in certain aspects of information management and distribution/transmission because each company's system is likely to have some *unique* aspects. The most common skills for beginning employees are:

*unique:* the only one

- good keyboarding skills
- excellent oral communications skills, especially for those who use the telephone frequently
- command of basic filing rules and principles
- ability to follow instructions
- ability to carry through specific tasks without close supervision
- ability to handle details accurately
- ability to work in an organized, systematic manner

### Where Workers Are Employed

Many workers are required to manage a company's business records. The records must be readily accessible to executives as they carry through their responsibilities. In some companies, records are maintained in a central computer memory for easy retrieval at an executive's computer terminal. But up-to-date records require careful employees inputting data promptly and accurately. **Inputting** is the task of entering data at a computer terminal.

Workers are needed in maintaining programs used in computer operations centers and in libraries within the organization. Mailrooms require workers who can keep up to date on costs and types of services available through the United States Postal

Service, as well as through private companies. Central reprographics departments require workers who can use assorted reproducing equipment — including equipment that will produce *graphics* (charts, diagrams, and graphs).

There are companies with departments providing telephone information to customers and potential customers. Also, customers are able to place orders by dialing 800 numbers which allow calls to be made without cost to the customer. Employees answer telephones and respond to questions, or they accept orders on a full-time basis. Such employees must be able to refer quickly to available information in order to be helpful to callers.

## Opportunities for Promotion

Company executives often look to beginning workers to find persons who can assume more responsible positions. General supervisors are frequently selected from among employees who have handled their tasks with intelligence, care, and attention to detail. Furthermore, employees who have taken the opportunity to learn more about the organization are valuable in higher level positions.

**Illus. 2–3.** One aspect of information management is the distribution/ transmission of information to persons inside and outside the company. That information often takes the form of charts and graphs or computer printouts.

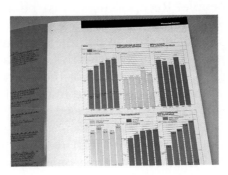

## GENERAL ASSISTANCE AND CUSTOMER SERVICE

*diversified:* varied; of different kinds

There are positions in general assistance and customer service where employees are not limited to only a few tasks, as is the case in the positions just described. You may find jobs in this cluster appealing if your interests overlap two or more clusters.

In small organizations, for example, there may be only one worker performing all the office tasks required to meet the goals of the organization. Common positions with *diversified* tasks include receptionist, general clerk, office assistant, and secretary.

### Basic Skills Required

The basic skills you need for positions that are diversified will vary somewhat. In general, the following are commonly listed requirements:

- good keyboarding skills
- skill in writing legibly
- ability to process information via a computer terminal
- skill in using office equipment such as calculators and copiers
- ability to manage telephone calls

*simultaneously:* at the same time

- ability to conduct several tasks *simultaneously*
- ability to deal with people in a friendly, cooperative manner
- skill in establishing a schedule for tasks to be completed
- ability to communicate orally and in writing

*specialized:* fitting for one particular purpose

Some of the positions in this cluster require *specialized* skills. The position of secretary is likely to require word/text processing and transcription skill. Additionally, secretaries are expected to have good judgment, organizational ability, and initiative. Secretaries for specialized offices, such as law, engineering, and medical, must understand the technical vocabulary and the types of documents basic to information processing in these offices.

For the position of receptionist, a candidate should enjoy interacting with people. Receptionists must be able to meet and talk with visitors of different backgrounds, take telephone calls, transmit messages, and be able to complete a variety of keyboarding tasks. Receptionists must know the company's personnel and schedule of activities since much of their day involves answering inquiries with accurate, up-to-date information.

Office assistants in many offices are required to learn about the technical details of the business so they can aid customers. For example, office assistants in travel agencies are expected to answer questions about advance payments required for tours,

## Job Outlook

| CLUSTER<br><br>Subgroup<br><br>Occupation | Percent change in employment 1984-95[1] | Numerical change in employment 1984-95[1] | Employment prospects |
|---|---|---|---|
| **ADMINISTRATIVE SUPPORT OCCUPATIONS** | | | |
| Tellers | 5 | 24,000 | Full-time and part-time job openings should be plentiful. |
| Bookkeepers and accounting clerks | 6 | 118,000 | Employment expected to grow more slowly than average due to technological change such as the increased use of computers. Nevertheless, because the occupation is so large, job openings will be numerous. |
| Computer operating personnel | 46 | 143,000 | Employment of computer and peripheral equipment operators expected to rise much faster than average as the use of computers expands. Employment of data-entry operators is expected to decline, however, due to the use of more efficient direct data entry techniques. |
| Receptionists and information clerks | 18 | 83,000 | Employment expected to grow faster than average as business, personal, and professional services expand. Job prospects should be most favorable for those with typing and other office skills. |
| Reservation agents and transportation ticket agents | 6 | 7,000 | Only slight change expected in employment as automation and other changes improve productivity. Competition is anticipated for jobs. |
| Secretaries | 10 | 268,000 | One of the occupations adding the largest number of jobs, reflecting information processing needs of rapidly growing industries including business services, finance, and health care. Numerous job opportunities are expected because the occupation is so large. Prospects for part-time and temporary work are likely to be excellent. |
| Traffic, shipping, and receiving clerks | 9 | 61,000 | Employment expected to increase more slowly than average due to automation and the concentration of these clerks in slow-growing industries, principally manufacturing and wholesale trade. Many job opportunities are nonetheless expected because the occupation is large. |
| Telephone operators | 19 | 89,000 | Employment expected to grow faster than average. |
| Typists | 1 | 11,000 | Employment expected to increase more slowly than the average, due to office automation. Numerous job openings are anticipated because of the large size of the occupation. Demand is likely to be particularly strong for typists who can handle a variety of office duties and operate word-processing equipment. |

[1]George T. Silvestri and John M. Lukasiewicz, "Occupational Employment Projections: The 1984-95 Outlook," *Monthly Labor Review*, 108, No. 11 (1985), 46-47.

**Illus. 2–7.** Projected employment changes.

the office jobs listed. As you see, an 18 percent increase is expected for receptionists and a 10 percent increase for secretaries. However, since there are far more secretaries than receptionists, the actual number of secretaries to be added to payrolls will increase considerably more than the actual number of receptionists.

*transformation:* involving major changes in form

*recurring:* done again and again

The projection for office employment is that it will increase by about 1,783,000 jobs by 1995.[3] Even though the office is expected to undergo considerable *transformation* in the next decade, the demand for workers is expected to continue. As you learned in Chapter 1, office employees are needed for the effective functioning of every type of organization. New technologies will aid in performing *recurring* tasks; however, employees will continue to be needed to perform those nonrecurring tasks requiring understanding and good judgment.

---

[3]George T. Silvestri and John M. Lukasiewicz, "Occupational Employment Projections: The 1984–95 Outlook," *Monthly Labor Review*, 108, No. 11 (1985), p. 46.

## REVIEW QUESTIONS

1. Identify two positions that are classified as word/text processing positions.

2. What are important skills for those who have jobs in word/text processing?

3. Identify two positions classified as data processing positions.

4. What basic skills are important for workers in information management and distribution/transmission?

5. What are two positions classified as "general assistance and customer service"?

6. To be considered for a promotion in a job with diversified tasks, what are two abilities you need?

7. What are three critical qualities all office employees are expected to possess?

8. How does the U.S. Department of Labor describe the general category of Administrative Support Occupations?

9. What skills does the U.S. Department of Labor identify as important for workers in office occupations?

10. In general, what are the future job prospects in office occupations?

## MAKING DECISIONS

Assume that one of your classmates says to you:

*"I have just read the first part of Chapter 2. I think the office jobs described are interesting. I have always enjoyed math; I liked the accounting course I took last year. At this point, I think I will take a full-time job when I graduate next June. I am wondering if I should plan now to get a job in the data processing area. Should I concentrate all my attention in this office procedures course on the tasks I would do in such a job? Is it better to concentrate on one type of work or to prepare for several?"*

What response would you make to your classmate's questions?

**What You Are To Do:**   Prepare a brief response to the question raised.

## EXTENDING YOUR ENGLISH SKILLS

Read the copy below. Note that there are several spelling errors in the copy.

*When executives are asked to choose the key attributes of office employees, they frequently indentify the following:*

- *strong knowledge of grammer, spelling, and punctuation*
- *accuracey*
- *capible of working under pressere*
- *ability to deal with people in a diplometic fashion*
- *punctuality and regular attendence*

**What You Are To Do:**   Prepare a copy of the above excerpt, correcting all spelling errors. Underscore the words which you corrected.

## APPLICATION ACTIVITY

You have been given the following handwritten draft with corrections. If necessary, refer to Reference Section A for information about standard proofreader's marks.

Mr. Leonard Medina
Placement Office
North Central High School
2156 Wilson Road
Rochester, N Y 14618-2786

Dear Mr. Medina

Our need for office workers is especially intense for the coming year. We are interested in talking with any of your seniors who are now planning careers in offices when they graduate.

The available
~~Our~~ jobs are in many departments. We think we can offer the kind of experience any student desires. Students should know how to keyboard and how to handle basic office tasks.

interested                                    (565-7300)
Please ask students to call my office any time from 9 to 5 to arrange an interview.
          a.m.    p.m.

Thank you for your help in this matter.

Sincerely

Ernest Wolffe, Personnel Dept. Manager

Word/text processing equipment can be used to complete this activity.

**What You Are To Do:** Key (type) a copy of the letter for mailing. Use letterhead for Creative Kitchenware in *Information Processing Activities* or plain paper. Use your own judgment with regard to line length and use the current date.

# Topic 2

## INTRODUCTION TO A NEW JOB

When you have completed your study of this topic, you will be able to

- describe the types of orientation provided new employees
- explain the type of learning expected on the job
- describe how performance of employees is evaluated

When you begin a new job, it is quite natural to have concerns about the company, your specific responsibilities, relationships with co-workers, and your work environment. For example, you might wonder:

- Where should I hang my coat?
- Which workstation will be mine?
- Do I get an afternoon break?
- How should I address my supervisor?
- Will I have a trial period?
- I've never used that model of word processor; how will I learn to operate it?
- Does the company have a no-smoking policy?
- How will I ever remember the names of all those people?
- Am I expected to memorize all those stock numbers?
- How will I ever learn my way around this large building?

- How will I be evaluated?

Employers expect new employees to have questions. In order to answer such questions, as well as to provide new employees with important job-related information, employers provide orientation programs. An orientation program will help you learn about the company, its products and/or services, your role within the organization, and how to carry out your assigned tasks.

This topic presents various types of orientation programs provided for new employees. Learning on the job and employee evaluation are also discussed. Regardless of the company for which you work, you will want to learn all you can about the company's goals, its policies and procedures, and the corporate structure. You also will want to learn the specific guidelines under which you will be expected to perform your specified duties.

## ORIENTATION

Initial introduction to a new company and job is called orientation. Programs of orientation may be formal or informal. A *formal orientation program* is organized for a particular time and includes a specific series of events. *Formal orientation programs* are common in large organizations where a number of new employees are beginning their jobs at the same time.

*A large insurance company planned an orientation program for the 20 new employees who recently completed their high school education. The program was arranged for the first day of work and consisted of introductions of key executives and presentations of information valuable to new employees. At lunch each employee was introduced to his or her supervisor. The afternoon sessions were held in the departments where the new employees would be working.*

**Illus. 2–8.** Formal orientation programs often are used in large organizations. It is not uncommon for such programs to include training sessions on specialized equipment to be used on the job.

*Informal orientation programs* are common in smaller organizations where fewer employees are hired. An informal program is directed by the immediate supervisor of the new employee. The supervisor explains to the employee the nature of the organization as well as the specific requirements of the job.

Regardless of the manner in which the orientation is planned, the following topics are generally included:

- goals and policies of the organization
- company structure and key personnel
- employee benefits
- policies related to office safety and security
- personnel policies
- policies and procedures for office tasks
- specific procedures and schedules related to specific positions

New employees are introduced to co-workers by supervisors in most companies. Co-workers who are meeting new employees often express a willingness to be helpful if there are any questions about the work to be done or about the work environment.

Orientation does not always end with the initial program offered when employees first arrive at the organization. Sometimes additional orientation sessions are scheduled after workers have had two to three weeks of experience on their jobs. These

**Illus. 2–9.** In a small company, orientation is likely to be given on an individual basis.

sessions give the employees a chance to ask questions about the company and their jobs that have arisen since they began. Companies want new employees to "feel at home" as quickly as possible.

## LEARNING ON YOUR FIRST JOB

Your new supervisor will not assume that you know everything your job may require. Learning on the job is expected and is considered a normal part of your introduction to your responsibilities. You should feel as comfortable about learning in the work environment as you do about learning in the classroom.

New workers can expect some introduction to the specific tasks they perform. A clearly stated job description may be provided you so that you know the extent of your responsibilities. Note the partial job description in Illus. 2–10 on page 58. As you see, there is a general statement of, and then a listing of, detailed duties.

### Equipment Instruction

*capabilities:* functions that can be performed

If you must use equipment that is unfamiliar to you, a demonstration may be planned for you. You may also be given time to become acquainted with the equipment so that you can use it properly. There is usually a manual with detailed instructions which will better familiarize you with the equipment's *capabilities*. You should refer to the manual whenever you feel unsure about particular functions of the equipment.

### Reference Sources

In addition to manuals for equipment, you may find that there are manuals on company policies and procedures. You are also likely to have available organization charts, calendars of events, directories, and other specialized reference books that will be useful in completing tasks. You will want to know about all the references that are at hand for your use. You may find it helpful

*scanning:* looking through quickly

to spend any free minutes you have *scanning* the references so that you know what each contains. Later, when you need specific information, you will know which reference will be most helpful.

Generally, new employees are encouraged to consult references and to ask questions whenever there are doubts about how to proceed with a specific phase of a task. You should check any references you have first. If you cannot find an answer to your question in a reference, then you should seek help from your supervisor or a co-worker.

## JOB DESCRIPTION

**Position Title:** Junior Secretary

**Division:** Advertising and Promotion

### Primary Functions

To help the administrative assistant to the vice president of advertising and promotion through preparation of various types of communications, handling details for travel to fashion shows out of the country, and maintaining departmental files.

### Detailed Duties

1. Uses a word processor to prepare fashion show scripts, press releases, and correspondence.

2. Makes inquiries of hotel and travel services for forthcoming travel and follows up with reservations.

3. Helps the administrative assistant in special projects and other tasks.

4. Keyboards correspondence and other documents.

5. Retrieves documents needed from files and returns documents to proper place in files.

**Illus. 2–10.** Partial job description.

**INTRODUCING CHANGES**

There are often several ways of completing a particular task. It is not uncommon to find that the current procedure may not be the most efficient one. Sometimes, you might be able to determine a better way of doing it. If this is a task that you do independently of others, you will undoubtedly be free to make the change.

New employees discover that soon after they understand their tasks well, they begin to see related tasks that are not being done by anyone. It is good to take the initiative in assuming responsibilities for these additional tasks.

*A new employee in the office of sales promotion found that frequently there was no stock of brochures for the letters that were to be mailed out on a particular day. Letters would have to be set aside until the next day when someone would go to the stockroom to get additional brochures. The new employee thought there should be some way of alerting the staff that additional brochures should be requested. So, the new employee cut a sheet of heavy paper to the size of the brochures. She wrote in large letters: Brochure 456 TIME TO REORDER STOCK. She believed that a similar card should be made for all 45 brochures that were constantly being mailed to prospective customers. After the new stock was put in place, the reorder card was to be placed above the tenth copy, counting from the bottom of the stack. Her supervisor liked her idea very much. It was soon in effect.*

*propose:* suggest

As a new employee you must understand well the task that you believe should be modified. If you do not understand, you may *propose* something that does not improve the situation.

*A new office assistant noted that the executives for whom she worked gave her jobs to do all during the day. She suggested to one of them that she would like to know by 9:30 each morning what jobs she was to do during that day. She said to the executive: "There is no way I can be efficient if I don't have all jobs by 9:30. I must be organized for the day before I can get much done."*

*Unfortunately, this assistant had not given attention to the jobs she was asked to do during the day. If she had, she would have realized that most of them could not have been anticipated early in the morning. Her failure to understand the nature of the work of the office led her to make a useless suggestion.*

Remember, it is wise to take time to understand the task that you believe requires some changes. Then, think of the consequences of the change and whether or not improvements will be realized as a result of your idea.

As you do the assignments in this textbook, think of ways of working that can improve your efficiency. This means that you will complete the task in less time than if you had not made changes in the procedures.

## EVALUATION OF PERFOR- MANCE

Companies require competent workers. Therefore, new employees are evaluated from time to time to determine if they are performing their tasks in satisfactory fashion.

New workers are given a period of time for learning their jobs. The so-called trial period may extend over three, six, or twelve months. The length of the trial period is determined by the complexity of the job and the level of skills possessed by the employee. Companies use varying methods of evaluation.

### Evaluation by the Supervisor

*appraisal:* a judgment of how well someone is performing

In many companies, the supervisor or executive for whom the office employee works prepares a job performance *appraisal* at least once a year. In the case of new workers, the evaluation may be at the end of the trial period. Sometimes the supervisor writes an evaluation, noting strengths as well as weaknesses. Comments about the potential for improvement are also added. Other times the evaluation prepared by the supervisor or executive is discussed with the employee before it is submitted to the next higher level of administration. See the following list for common matters included in the evaluation of an office employee:

- job knowledge
- quantity of work
- quality of work
- initiative
- cooperation
- adaptability
- judgment
- attendance and punctuality

Read carefully the appraisal form shown in Illus. 2–11. Note the description of behavior at the several levels for each of the factors important in doing a satisfactory job.

A supervisor's evaluation is based on observations and experiences with the employee. The supervisor's general impressions, plus specific observations, influence how the employee is judged.

*The supervisor did not keep a record of how many questions the employee asked that could have been answered by checking the procedures manual. However, the supervisor's impression was that the employee had asked too many questions. Therefore, the employee was scored at the low end of the range on the factor, "job knowledge."*

## EMPLOYEE PERFORMANCE EVALUATION

**INSTRUCTIONS:**
Evaluate the employee's performance on the job now being performed by marking an X in the box above each of the following suggested statements which best expresses your judgment about the individual's capabilities. If a pre-printed statement is not an accurate description, a more applicable statement may be entered in the comments section. In order to conduct a more meaningful appraisal you should refer to the employee's job description while evaluating and discussing the employee's job performance.

Employee's Name  Blair Cooper        Supervisor's Name  Margaret Bridges        DEPARTMENT  Marketing

| | | | | | | COMMENTS |
|---|---|---|---|---|---|---|
| **A. JOB KNOWLEDGE** Possession of information and understanding of the work to be performed. (how well employee knows the job) | ☐ Thoroughly familiar with all phases of work. | ☐ Well rounded knowledge. Requires minimum assistance. | ☒ Adequate job knowledge. Requires some guidance and assistance. | ☐ Limited job knowledge. Requires considerable assistance. | ☐ Inadequate knowledge. Requires improvement to retain job. | Has been in complex situation for past three months. Making good progress. |
| **B. QUANTITY OF WORK** Volume of acceptable work turned out and use of working time. | ☐ Rapid worker. Unusually high output. | ☒ Better than average work flow. | ☐ Average amount of work turned out, but seldom more. | ☐ Output of work is frequently less than expected. | ☐ Very slow worker. Must improve to retain job. | COMMENTS |
| **C. QUALITY OF WORK** Accuracy, neatness and dependability of results. | ☐ Consistently excellent quality. | ☒ Highly accurate with few errors. | ☐ Acceptable degree of accuracy. Occasional errors. | ☐ Careless. Frequently does unacceptable work. | ☐ Too many errors. Must improve to retain job. | COMMENTS Is a very good proofreader. |
| **D. INITIATIVE** Ability to originate, develop and/or carry out new ideas or methods. (amount of supervision required) | ☐ Continually innovative and resourceful. | ☐ Considerably resourceful. Needs little follow-up. | ☒ Shows occasional initiative. Performs some assignments without much direction. | ☐ Rarely shows initiative and requires frequent follow-up. | ☐ Needs follow-up on all phases of work. | COMMENTS Has more potential than is now realized; must encourage him more. |
| **E. COOPERATION** Ability and willingness to work with others. | ☒ Exceptionally good team worker. Always coop-erative. | ☐ Cooperative. Customarily goes over halfway. | ☐ Usually cooperative. May clash occasionally with others. | ☐ Cooperative only when has to be. Frequent conflicts. | ☐ Very poor relationships. Must improve to retain job. | COMMENTS Always willing to help co-workers meet a deadline. |

**CONTINUED ON NEXT PAGE**

**Illus. 2–11.** Appraisal form (partial).

*The supervisor gave a high score to a new employee on the factor, "quality of work," because the employee seldom submitted work that required corrections.*

## Evaluation Based on Work Measurement

*standards:* expected output

Some companies have developed *standards* for specific tasks. For example, there may be standards for how many pages of key-boarded copy should be completed in a working day. Some companies count number of lines or number of keystrokes produced per working day. With the introduction of electronic office equipment, it is possible in some cases to keep records of how much work each employee does during the course of the day. Then, at evaluation time, the record of production is reviewed in relation to the standards. A worker who meets or exceeds the standard is given a good evaluation. Beginning workers are not expected to meet the standards of an experienced worker. Allowances are made for a period of learning and development of adequate skills.

*assessment:* review to determine how well something was done

Evaluations provide a basis for determining what must be done to improve performance. As a new employee, you must interpret an evaluation carefully. You should not be discouraged by weaknesses noted. Understand that improvement is something that you can achieve. You must be willing to improve; you must have confidence that you can improve. Carefully considering the *assessment* of your work can help you identify what you must do to be more successful. Supervisors generally want to assist employees in improving their performance. Supervisors also encourage employees who perform at a high level to maintain the quality and quantity of their work.

## REVIEW QUESTIONS

1. What is the purpose of an orientation when entering a new company?

2. How does a formal orientation program differ from an informal program?

3. What are three topics commonly discussed during orientation periods?

4. Do supervisors expect new employees to learn on the job? Explain your response.

5. What can new employees learn from job descriptions for their positions?

6. What are some common types of references new employees find useful on the job?

7. Why should a new employee understand a task well before making a suggestion to change it?

8. Why is a new employee given a trial period?

9. What are three factors considered in an evaluation of an office employee?

10. Explain the value of an evaluation for an office employee.

## INTERACTING WITH OTHERS

Assume that you accepted a job as a word processor. You were introduced to your tasks by the supervisor. You did not take notes while the supervisor demonstrated the use of the equipment. You thought that what was being explained would be available in an operations manual. However, at the end of the demonstration, the supervisor said nothing about a manual. The only comment of the supervisor was: "Here are some sheets of practice exercises that you may find useful in getting acquainted with the equipment. Spend the next hour getting used to this equipment."

As soon as the supervisor walked away from your workstation, you wrote some notes from memory. However, you realized that there were some initial steps in the operation of the equipment that you did not remember.

What would you do at this moment?

**What You Are To Do:**   Prepare a brief response to the question raised.

## EXTENDING YOUR MATH SKILLS

A survey was completed that provided information about where computer graphics were being used. You have been given the information shown in the following tabulation.

**What You Are To Do:**   Refer to the table shown on page 64. Make the computations necessary to fill in the following seven blanks. Write your answers on a sheet of plain paper.

1. Total number of questionnaires mailed out _____

2. Total number of responses _____

3. Total number of responses indicating usage of graphics _____

4. Total number of questionnaires not returned
_____

5. Number of questionnaires by department that were not returned _____

6. Total number of respondents who indicated no use of graphics _____

7. Number of respondents by department who indicated no usage of graphics _____

## USE OF COMPUTER GRAPHICS

| Department | Number of Questionnaires Mailed Out | Number of Responses | Number of Responses Indicating Usage of Graphics |
|---|---|---|---|
| Accounting . . . . . . . . . . . . . | 750 | 390 | 128 |
| Finance . . . . . . . . . . . . . | 800 | 386 | 223 |
| Management Information Systems . . | 900 | 432 | 328 |
| Marketing . . . . . . . . . . . . | 900 | 475 | 228 |
| Personnel . . . . . . . . . . . . | 650 | 285 | 63 |
| Planning . . . . . . . . . . . . | 600 | 298 | 120 |
| Production . . . . . . . . . . . | 900 | 478 | 134 |
| Research and Development . . . . . | 650 | 318 | 124 |
| Totals | ? | ? | ? |

## APPLICATION ACTIVITY

You have just learned that office employees are often evaluated on the following factors:

- job knowledge
- quantity of work
- quality of work
- initiative
- cooperation
- adaptability
- judgment
- attendance and punctuality

Word/text processing
equipment can be used to
complete this activity.

**What You Are To Do:** For each of the factors listed, describe what you might do in your course assignments that will help you develop the level of skill or attitude valued on the job. (Example: I will begin all class assignments promptly so that the quantity of my work is greater than it would otherwise be.) Keyboard (type) your responses.

**CHAPTER
SUMMARY**

There are many different office jobs. Some are specialized while others are diversified. You learned about jobs in four primary clusters: word/text processing, data processing, information management and distribution/transmission, and general assistance and customer service.

For all office jobs, certain general qualifications are considered critical. These include: being a team worker; having a sincere interest in your organization's goals as well as having a positive attitude toward your work; working in systematic fashion; learning from observation and from written instructions; being flexible; being punctual; and having skill to evaluate your own work.

The U.S. Department of Labor collects information about occupations in the American economy, including office occupations. Demand for employees in office occupations is projected to continue at a high level for the next decade.

New employees can expect an orientation to their jobs. They also will be given an opportunity to learn on the job. Employers do not expect new employees to know everything at first. Employees will be evaluated from time to time. Careful interpretation of an evaluation can lead to changes in how you perform your tasks. Thus, your future performance will be considered more satisfactory than your past performance might have been.

### KEY TERMS

| | |
|---|---|
| word/text processing | inputting |
| data processing | orientation |

**INTEGRATED
CHAPTER
ACTIVITY**

You are now aware of the skills required for each of four major office position clusters: word/text processing; data processing; information management and distribution/transmission; and general assistance and customer service. Undoubtedly, as you became acquainted with these four clusters, you realized that one was more appealing to you at this point than the others were. (Remember, after your study of the complete textbook, you may find your interest has shifted to another type of office job.) It is likely that you already have some skills considered important in the job cluster of your choice.

**What You Are To Do:**
- Choose the cluster that is most appealing to you now.
- Prepare a copy of the following form or use the one in *Information Processing Activities*. Fill in the name of your chosen job cluster in the blank after "for" at the top of the form.
- List on the form the skills given in the chapter for the cluster you select (word/text processing, page 38; data processing, page 40; information management and distribution/transmission, page 42; general assistance and customer service, page 44).
- Complete the form by assessing each skill according to the three factors given.

### SELF ASSESSMENT FOR _____

| Skills required | Present skill level | | | Will develop in class | | Some learning required on the job | |
|---|---|---|---|---|---|---|---|
| | No skill | Limited | Good | Yes | No | Yes | No |
| | | | | | | | |
| | | | | | | | |
| | | | | | | | |
| | | | | | | | |
| | | | | | | | |

# PRODUCTIVITY CORNER

**Blake Williams**
*OFFICE SUPERVISOR*

## I'M LOST, BUT I LIKE MY JOB

DEAR MR. WILLIAMS:

I took a job with a brand new video production company exactly a week ago. I work for a manager who has never had an office assistant. He is a very busy man and he keeps me busy. However, I must tell you I don't know what I am doing most of the time. I get assignments at any time and all the time. I'm going around in circles. My workstation is a mess.

I think I should try to get organized. I do like the place; the people are friendly and there is never a dull moment. Do you have any ideas for me?—CRAIG FROM DALLAS

DEAR CRAIG:

I am happy to hear that you do like the company where you work. You aren't frightened by the circumstances, which is good. Keep up your confidence. You are right in thinking that getting organized will help. Here are some suggestions that will reduce your sense of being unorganized:

- Keep a log of all tasks assigned to you; check off each task as you complete it.
- Determine the order in which all tasks you have at the beginning of the day should be done; as a new task is given to you, immediately determine where it is to be fitted into your list of tasks to be done.
- Begin a personal directory of names, addresses, and telephone numbers of all persons to whom you place calls and to whom you write letters.
- Set up your workstation with supplies that you use regularly.
- Arrange references at or very near your workstation.
- Check the arrangement of your workstation to be sure it is as efficient as it can be. (For example, is your telephone placed so that you can answer it without getting up or moving your chair?)
- Remember the questions asked you that you cannot answer; you might want to write them down. When you have a free minute, determine if you do have at hand sources for answers to such questions.
- Review all incomplete jobs at the end of the day; determine which ones should be considered first the next morning.
- Begin to draw up a calendar of tasks that must be done on a regular basis, such as weekly or monthly.

Best wishes for success in getting organized.—BLAKE WILLIAMS

67

# THE SKILLS
# OF WORKING TOGETHER

# Chapter 3

# Communication Skills in the Office

Imagine bringing to an absolute stop all activity at 11:10 a.m. on Monday in any business organization. What do you think you would discover in progress at that instant? You would undoubtedly find conferences among executives, meetings between supervisors and office workers, office assistants reading manuals and incoming communications, administrative assistants keying messages at their terminals, executives and assistants composing memorandums and letters, customer service representatives listening to customers, tellers speaking via telephones to branch offices, and other similar activities. In short, much of the activity would involve communication of some kind. You can imagine, then, how important effective communication is in every organization.

You are familiar with communication skills. You have been studying them every year you have been in school. You use your communication skills in your everyday tasks. You may have also seen their value in part-time or summer jobs. These same basic communication skills are equally important for the business office.

This is a good time to improve any phases of your basic communication skills that you think are not as effective as they could be. In this chapter, you will find a general introduction to the usefulness of reading, writing, speaking, and listening in the office.

The objectives of the chapter are to

- describe the reading skill that is valuable at work

- explain what effective business writing is

- demonstrate speaking and listening techniques that assure effective oral communications

# Topic 1

## READING

When you have completed your study of this topic, you will be able to

- describe the types of reading you may do in an office job
- identify what a competent reader does
- describe techniques for improving reading skills

Your reading skills will be valuable to you at work. There will be numerous occasions when you must read information quickly in order to respond to an inquiry or to determine what you should do. Few people have reached the level of reading facility where no more improvement is possible. You, too, will find it worthwhile to improve your reading skill during your study of office procedures. Studying the barriers to effective reading and carefully analyzing how you read can lead to positive changes in your reading techniques.

Although you have been reading for many years, try to step back and think about it as if it were a new process for you. Then, the information in the following paragraphs may be more useful to you.

## THE READING PROCESS

You know how to read. You read textbooks in your courses. You read the local newspaper and your favorite magazines. You read instructions for new equipment. **Reading**, as you know, is actually quite simple when viewed in a general sense. It is the process of translating printed information or information on a screen into useful mental impressions. What you have read becomes a part of your memory and is available to you as you think and act.

> *Assume you know nothing about office employment. Then, you are given an article from which you read the following: "The employment prospects of office workers are expected to remain favorable in the future. Overall, employment in office jobs will grow 19 to 27 percent in the next five years." Remember the assumption: You knew nothing about office employment.*
>
> *What do you know now? How will your actions be influenced by what you have learned? Now you know that there will continue to be many job opportunities for persons like you who are studying office procedures. You may increase the attention you give to your study of office procedures because you know that you will have job prospects.*

An adequate reading skill is composed of several factors. As you learned in the English courses you have completed, a good reading skill means that you:

- *read naturally*
  When you read naturally, your attention is on the meaning of what you read. It is not on the process of moving your eyes from word to word.
- *read with understanding and reasonable speed*
  You need to understand what you read in order to learn something you can use—either at the time of completing the reading or later. For example, when you finish reading the instructions for formatting a report, you actually need to be able to use the ***prescribed*** format.

*prescribed:* ordered

  Reasonable speed means that you are not spending an excessive amount of time in reading. If you must complete a report quickly, yet you must read the instructions for the format, you will be grateful for your skill in reading quickly.
- *read with few pauses because of unfamiliar words*
  It is possible to understand the meaning of a passage when you do not know the exact meaning of every word. However, you are less likely to be ***perplexed*** if every word is familiar to you. Command of a somewhat extensive vocabulary is helpful.

*perplexed:* puzzled

GUIDELINES FOR SUBMITTING ARTICLES
TO THE <u>COMPUTER MONTHLY REVIEW</u>

FORMAT AND LENGTH

Manuscripts should be typed on plain 8 1/2" x 11" paper,
double-spaced, with one-inch margins all around.  Two
copies should be submitted.  Manuscript should not exceed
3,500 words.

HEADINGS

All major headings should be flush left with the margin,
with initial capital letters.  Subheadings should also
be placed flush left with the margin, and <u>underscored</u>,
with initial capital letters.  Usually only <u>two levels</u>
of headings should be used.  However, if third-level
headings are necessary, they should be indented the same
as a paragraph indention, <u>underscored</u>, with only the
initial letter of the <u>first word capitalized</u>, and followed by a period with the text immediately following.

**Illus. 3–3.** Instructions
for preparing articles submitted to a professional
journal.

## Using Equipment

From time to time office employees are given new equipment
to make their work easier. Sometimes demonstrations of the
equipment are provided. However, workers generally find that
they must read and understand the instruction manual in order
to use the equipment properly.

*The three office assistants in the advertising department attended a
demonstration on the new telephone system that was being installed
throughout the company. They heard the explanations of how to forward calls, how to have a three-way conversation, and how to hold a
call. Workers attending the demonstration were given a brochure that
described the features of the new system.*

**Illus. 3–4.** "Are you *sure* all these cords go with this equipment?" This office worker's question could easily be answered if only she would read the equipment manual!

## Using Forms

Businesses develop forms to simplify the task of getting appropriate and complete information. You will find forms that facilitate such tasks as recording telephone messages, requesting supplies and equipment, ordering goods, reporting travel expenses, and submitting overtime hours. It is very important that you read all instructions on forms and fill in all information requested. If some item of information is not needed in a particular instance or is not available, some comment should be added. Note Illus. 3–5, which shows a telephone message recorded on a form. What information did the person who recorded the message fail to add?

*An office worker is employed by a photographic studio that specializes in food photography. She was asked to return some camera equipment that was not the type ordered. To complete this task, the office worker filled out the merchandise return form that was packaged with the camera equipment. She read each section of the form carefully and provided all necessary information.*

**Illus. 3–5.** Telephone message recorded on a form. Can you identify what information is missing?

**MEMO OF CALL**

To _Steve Franklin_ _10/17_ 19_--_

M~~s~~ _Gail Talbot_ called from _Coleman & Perry_

Telephone No.: _(212) 565-7921_

**I TOLD THAT PERSON YOU WERE:**

Out _____ ☑
Not in today _____ ☐
Not in your office ____ ☐
Talking on telephone __ ☐
In conference _____ ☐
Out of town _____ ☐

**THE REPLY WAS:**

No message _____ ☐
See message below ____ ☑
Will call again _____ ☐
Answering your call ___ ☐
Please call back _____ ☐
It is urgent _____ ☐

ADDITIONAL REMARKS _Contract has been reviewed; there are a couple of questions about utilities. Please call ASAP_

Message taken by _____

Time _____

## Responding to Inquiries

Office workers must often respond to inquiries from other departments and from customers directly. The subject of the inquiries can vary considerably. Employees are not expected to know every requested detail from memory. However, they are expected to read quickly and accurately the information needed. Increasingly, office workers are reading the details which appear on their terminal screens.

*The office worker in the central reservation office for a worldwide chain of motels handles incoming calls throughout the day. She sits at a terminal where she has access to details about any location. When a prospective traveler asks: "Do you have a motel in San Diego, California?" the worker has the information on her screen only a moment after the caller has completed the question. Additional questions are answered quickly as the office worker accesses the information and reads the appropriate details from the terminal screen.*

### Using References

Several key references will probably be available for your use in the office. Some references commonly found at an office employee's workstation include a dictionary, an atlas, telephone directories, and a general office procedures manual. You will want to become acquainted with the information in the references as well as with the abbreviations and codes used to present the information in **condensed** form. You should scan the table of contents to gain an idea of the scope of the information contained in each reference.

*condensed:* reduced; shortened

## IMPROVING READING SKILLS

*impede:* block

High-level reading skill will allow you to be more productive in an office position than you would otherwise be. To improve your reading skill, you must first believe that you *can* improve. "I'm not a good reader and I never will be," reflects an attitude which will **impede** your progress. You must have a positive attitude. You must believe that you can and will improve your skill. Strive for a reading skill that is so natural you need not give detailed, deliberate attention to the skill itself. Instead, you can focus on what

**Illus. 3–6.** Office workers often need to use reference materials.

you want to achieve from your reading. The critical skills for high-level reading are comprehension, vocabulary, and speed.

## Comprehension

**Comprehension** is the ability to understand what you have read. To comprehend is "to know." It implies a transfer from the printed page or the terminal screen to your *mental storage* (your memory). A simple example is looking for a number in the telephone directory and keeping it in mind until you can dial it. A more complex example is reading about a supplier's new product and being able to determine whether it appears superior to the product your company is now using. Following are some techniques you may find helpful as you strive to increase your reading comprehension:

1. Put aside anything else on your mind when you begin to read.
2. Before you begin, ask yourself this question: "What do I want to know when I have completed this reading?"
3. Scan what you are going to read to get an overview of the topic.
4. Attempt to summarize as you move from one paragraph to the next.
5. After reading several paragraphs, try to put ideas or procedures in *sequence*.
6. As you read the words, attempt to draw mental pictures.
7. After reading the material, determine if you have learned what you have read. For example, if you have read instructions for processing a request for new equipment, see if you can outline those procedures without referring to the written version.

*sequence:* one thing following another in an orderly way

## Vocabulary

A *vocabulary* is a stock of words. Having an extensive vocabulary means that you know the definitions of a large number of words. Words that are unfamiliar to you can be a barrier to your reading. There are techniques that can expand your vocabulary and help you to be an effective reader. Consider using some of these as you study the content of this book:

*encounter:* come upon

1. When you *encounter* an unfamiliar word, try to determine its meaning from the way it is used in the sentence. After you have a meaning you think is correct, check your dictionary. If you were right, you should have increased your confidence in

*inappropriate:* not
suitable

figuring out what words mean. If your meaning was *inappropriate*, try to conclude why you were not able to establish an appropriate meaning.

2. When you encounter an unfamiliar word, see if you can determine a meaning for part of the word. You see the word "rearrange," which is unfamiliar to you. You think of "re" and "arrange." You know from earlier experience that re-do means that you must do something again. You know the meaning of arrange. You then guess that "rearrange" means to put back in a new or different order. You check your dictionary and find that your guess was right.

3. While reading, have at hand a notepad and pencil to record any word that you don't know. When you complete your reading, check the words on your list in a dictionary. As you read the definition for each word, look back to the place where the word occurred. Determine from the context which definition is the appropriate one. *Context* refers to the parts of a sentence or paragraph around a word that can throw light on its meaning.

You will possibly find that there is a specialized vocabulary required in the office where you are employed. You will want to become acquainted with the specialized dictionary or other references that will help you to master that vocabulary.

## Speed

Another reading skill is speed. Problems with comprehension and/or with vocabulary can slow the rate at which you read. Reading rapidly can improve your productivity on the job. Following are some techniques which may help you increase your rate of reading:

1. Focus your attention on a whole paragraph. Tell yourself, "I want to read this paragraph as a single thought and to know what it says." By doing so, you are forcing yourself to break the habit of *deliberately* pausing at each word or each sentence. When you have finished reading the paragraph, try to summarize it in a sentence or two. If you realize that you have not grasped the meaning, read it once again as quickly as possible. Again, attempt to summarize it. You are likely to be successful on your second attempt.

*deliberately:*
intentionally

2. Time your reading. Set a goal such as: "I will read this page, which has approximately 350 words, in 1½ minutes."

*passage:* brief portion of a written work

Check to see if you reached your goal. If you did, try the same *passage* with a reduced time allowance.

3. Deliberately force yourself ahead as you read. Do not set a specific goal. Note the extent to which you continue pushing and the extent to which you return to your slower way of reading. Try to determine why you do not continue reading quickly.

## READING AS A SINGLE PROCESS

*compensated:* offset by

The critical skills of comprehension, vocabulary, and speed were highlighted separately in this topic. However, when you are actually reading, these skills interact in a variety of ways. In some cases, a weakness in one skill may be *compensated* for by strength in another skill. For example, you may comprehend well what you read. If you encounter an unfamiliar word, you are able to figure out its meaning from your understanding of the rest of the sentence or paragraph. Or, you may read rapidly, but your comprehension is not as good as it could be. By reading rapidly, you can take time to reread the material to improve your comprehension. Ultimately, you will want to be skilled in all three areas.

You will read every day when you are working in an office. Now you have an opportunity to improve your skill so that you will have no reading barrier to being a competent office employee.

## REVIEW QUESTIONS

1. Are reading skills established by the time you complete your elementary education? Explain.

2. Describe briefly the reading process.

3. Describe how a person with good reading skills actually reads.

4. Illustrate how reading might be useful in understanding tasks to be performed on a job.

5. What kind of information is generally provided in written form when new equipment is installed in an office?

6. What kind of information are you likely to find on forms used on the job?

7. What do you generally have to read before you can use reference materials efficiently?

8. Identify one technique that you believe will help you in improving your reading comprehension.

9. How can you improve your reading vocabulary?

10. Identify a technique that you believe would be effective in improving your reading speed.

## MAKING DECISIONS

One of the students in an office procedures class has had reading problems throughout his school years. He knows that he is a poor reader and that he will have to be careful in choosing a job after graduation to be sure he does not have to do much reading. He has worked part-time in the warehouse of a local supermarket. From time to time he has had difficulty in reading, but he is generally able to figure out the words he doesn't understand. Fortunately, he can complete his work most days without needing to read.

This student has made a decision that he can learn nothing more about reading. Assume that he considers you a trusted friend who will not reveal his weakness. He confesses to you and tells you that he can learn nothing about reading. What would you say to your friend about his decision?

**What You Are To Do:**   Prepare a brief response to the question raised.

## EXTENDING YOUR ENGLISH SKILLS

Read the following lines. Note that there are four errors in subject/verb agreement.

**What You Are To Do:**   Prepare a copy of these paragraphs, making the corrections required. Underscore your corrections.

*Employee communication were listed as one of the top priorities for good management according to corporate executives. Corporate executives, recently surveyed by Ralson Management Consulting Company, was in complete agreement about the importance of employee communications.*

*Based on the survey's findings, a human resources consultant recommend that efforts be made to improve the ability of supervisors to communicate on a one-to-one basis with employees.*

*The ability to communicate with employees on a one-to-one basis are even more important than ability to communicate to employees in groups.*

## APPLICATION ACTIVITIES

### Activity 1

Assume that you are an office assistant in the personnel department. The manager of the department expects you to answer routine questions that are raised by employees in the company. Read the following information about vacations.

# VACATIONS

**Eligibility:** All full-time, permanent employees are eligible for vacation time.

**Vacation Length:** Vacation time varies depending on years of service completed. The following vacation schedule is currently in effect:

| Years of Service Completed | Vacation Length |
|:---:|:---:|
| 1–4 years | 10 days |
| 5–9 years | 15 days |
| 10–15 years | 20 days |
| 16 or more years | 25 days |

**Vacation Period:** An employee may schedule vacation time during the calendar year with the prior approval of the supervisor. All vacation time must be taken during the calendar year. Unused vacation may not be accumulated and will, therefore, be forfeited at the end of the year. Exceptions are made in regard to accumulating vacation time in those cases where a department manager requests that an employee postpone vacation time until the following calendar year.

The year in which an employee is eligible for a longer vacation is the calendar year in which the relevant anniversary occurs. For example, an employee is entitled to 15 days of vacation during the calendar year in which the fifth anniversary of service occurs, without regard to the actual anniversary date.

**Use of Vacation Time:** All employees are encouraged to take at one time the full vacation period to which they are entitled. There is evidence that taking only a day or two of vacation at a time does not maximize the benefits to the employee of time away from work. When a half day of vacation is taken, the employee is to work 3¾ hours that day.

Word/text processing
equipment can be used to
complete this activity.

**What You Are To Do:** Assume that three employees in the company have called you with the following questions. Write out exactly what you would say in response to each question.

A. "I will not complete my fifth year of service until June 12. Does this mean that I cannot take the full 15 days of vacation until after June 12?"

B. "If my supervisor approves, may I take my 10 days vacation by working only 4 days a week for 10 weeks during the summer months of June, July, and August?"

C. "I've worked here for only two years and I would like to take a long vacation next year. Would it be possible to postpone this year's vacation to next year? I would like to have 20 days for a trip to England and France."

## Activity 2

Assume that you are to determine the appropriate shipping charges for packages to be sent to customers. The company for whom you are working manufactures a variety of office supplies. You have already weighed each of the following 15 packages.

| Package Number | Destination | Weight | Charge |
|---|---|---|---|
| 1 | Connecticut | 8 lbs. | _____ |
| 2 | Oklahoma | 4 lbs. | _____ |
| 3 | West Virginia | 12 lbs. | _____ |
| 4 | Nebraska | 8¼ lbs. | _____ |
| 5 | Kansas | 11 lbs. | _____ |
| 6 | Pennsylvania | 9 lbs. | _____ |
| 7 | Maine | 5½ lbs. | _____ |
| 8 | Vermont | 14 lbs. | _____ |
| 9 | Oregon | 10½ lbs. | _____ |
| 10 | Utah | 56 lbs. | _____ |
| 11 | California | 10 lbs. | _____ |
| 12 | Kentucky | 5 lbs. | _____ |
| 13 | Arizona | 15 lbs. | _____ |
| 14 | South Carolina | 9 lbs. | _____ |
| 15 | Missouri | 11 lbs. | _____ |

**What You Are To Do:** A. Prepare a copy of the information for the 15 packages (shown on page 84) or use the form provided in *Information Processing Activities*.

B. Then determine the shipping and packing charge for each package. (The chart from which you are to read the proper charge follows.) If the actual weight of the package is not an exact number of pounds, use the charge for the next higher weight. (If, for example, the package weighs 8¼ lbs., you would use the charge for 9 lbs.)

# Insured Shipping & Packing Charges

| Find your state at right.<br><br>Shipping Weight | Maine Mass. N.H. R.I. Vermont | Conn. N.Y. | Delaware Maryland N.J. Penn. Virginia Wash. D.C. W. Va. | Illinois Indiana Ky. Michigan N.C. Ohio S. C. Tenn. | Alabama Arkansas Florida Georgia Iowa Minn. Miss. Missouri Wisc. | Colorado Kansas La. Montana Neb. N. Dak. Okla. S. Dak. Texas Wyoming | Arizona Calif. Idaho Nevada N.M. Oregon Utah Wash. |
|---|---|---|---|---|---|---|---|
| 1 lb. | $1.95 | $2.04 | $2.17 | $2.36 | $2.53 | $2.71 | $2.96 |
| 2 lb. | 2.07 | 2.31 | 2.53 | 2.78 | 3.09 | 3.40 | 3.69 |
| 3 lb. | 2.21 | 2.45 | 2.70 | 3.03 | 3.44 | 3.79 | 4.15 |
| 4 lb. | 2.33 | 2.63 | 2.91 | 3.27 | 3.77 | 4.24 | 4.64 |
| 5 lb. | 2.45 | 2.76 | 3.06 | 3.51 | 4.06 | 4.63 | 5.11 |
| 6 lb. | 2.60 | 2.93 | 3.27 | 3.76 | 4.39 | 5.04 | 5.64 |
| 7 lb. | 2.69 | 3.05 | 3.45 | 4.01 | 4.71 | 5.41 | 6.11 |
| 8 lb. | 2.79 | 3.24 | 3.63 | 4.25 | 5.07 | 5.85 | 6.59 |
| 9 lb. | 2.93 | 3.36 | 3.80 | 4.49 | 5.38 | 6.26 | 7.08 |
| 10 lb. | 3.05 | 3.50 | 4.01 | 4.71 | 5.70 | 6.67 | 7.58 |
| 11 lb. | 3.20 | 3.64 | 4.17 | 4.98 | 6.02 | 7.05 | 8.06 |
| 12 lb. | 3.31 | 3.79 | 4.38 | 5.23 | 6.35 | 7.46 | 8.60 |
| 13 lb. | 3.43 | 3.92 | 4.59 | 5.47 | 6.69 | 7.89 | 9.03 |
| 14 lb. | 3.53 | 4.06 | 4.73 | 5.68 | 7.01 | 8.30 | 9.50 |
| 15 lb. | 3.68 | 4.23 | 4.95 | 5.92 | 7.32 | 8.67 | 10.03 |
| For each add'l. lb. | .17 | .19 | .23 | .28 | .36 | .44 | .54 |

# Topic 2

## WRITING

When you have completed your study of this topic, you will be able to

- describe types of writing required in the office
- write letters and memorandums that reflect the qualities of good business communications
- describe a procedure for fulfilling writing tasks

Office workers have many occasions when they must communicate with others in writing. Business writing is different from social writing. When you write a letter to a friend describing a recent trip or your life at school, you are free to write as you like. Your sentences may not be complete or they might be quite long. You may write about one matter very briefly but dwell for many paragraphs on another matter. You are likely to convey your personality in your writing. Your friend knows you and will understand what you are thinking and saying.

In the business office, the situation is quite different. You may be corresponding with persons whom you do not know and who do not know you. They cannot interpret what you mean if your thoughts are incomplete. Your message must convey the total meaning. Business people receive many letters. They do not like to read long letters that could have been brief. Writing business communications is challenging and rewarding. The task performed successfully adds to the smooth functioning of any organization. The task performed poorly subtracts from the efficiency and effectiveness of business activity.

**COMMON WRITING TASKS**

*draft:* tentative copy for review

The levels of responsibility which workers assume depend on two things. One is the nature of the work of the office. The other is the manner in which the executive chooses to handle writing tasks. If you were to visit several offices, you would find that office employees have varying responsibility for preparing written communications. You would find employees:

- preparing *drafts* of communications for executive review
- suggesting changes in drafts prepared by executives
- composing communications, revising them, and then preparing final copy

### Preparing Drafts

Often a secretary or other office employee sees the incoming mail before it is placed on the executive's desk. In many offices, the secretary prepares a draft of a response to any letter concerning matters that the secretary knows well. The draft, together with the letter it answers, is given to the executive for review. The executive reads the incoming letter and the suggested response. If necessary, the secretary's draft can be modified quickly. Final copies are then prepared.

> Susan is secretary to the department manager for consumer loans. She prepares responses to many of the letters received in her office. Numerous letters are received from customers who have questions about their loans. Susan is knowledgeable about all aspects of consumer loans.
>
> The department manager commented: "Susan really saves me a great deal of time by preparing drafts for much of the incoming mail. We are able to have responses in the mail within a day of receipt of inquiries."

### Suggesting Changes

Office assistants are frequently asked to review executives' written communications. Some executives like for their assistants to act as editors. An **editor** is a person who reviews what has been written and suggests changes in wording, organization, and content. Office assistants with editorial responsibility read carefully the drafts prepared by the executive. They determine whether the message will communicate clearly what the executive had in mind. Drafts which are responses to incoming letters are checked against the letters to be sure the responses are complete.

**Illus. 3–7.** Office workers often assist in editing rough drafts of correspondence and reports.

*Mrs. Richards, director of human resources, discussed the role of her secretary in these words: "I must send many memorandums to our employees. These memos discuss personnel policies about vacations, schedules, pensions, and health insurance provisions. They must be written carefully so that no misunderstandings develop. The secretary reads what I write and then marks improvements on the copy. We review the suggestions before final copies are prepared."*

Note the draft prepared by a personnel manager shown in Illus. 3–8. Then read the revision suggested by an office assistant. What do you think are the improvements reflected in the assistant's revision?

*Overtime Hours*

At certain periods of the year various departments find it necessary to work overtime, and it is a condition of employment that employees work overtime if at all possible when it is requested of them. Department managers will notify those employees who are expected to perform overtime work. Employees should try to arrange personal matters so that they can work overtime when work in the department requires it. Overtime pay rules are specified in the next section.

OVERTIME HOURS

The work of most departments requires overtime hours at certain periods of the year. The willingness of employees to work overtime is appreciated. Department managers schedule overtime as far in advance as possible. However, there are times when the need to work beyond the regular hours cannot be determined in advance. Employees who can arrange personal matters so that they are able to work overtime hours will be contributing a great deal to the effective functioning of their departments. Overtime pay rates are specified in the next section.

**Illus. 3—8.** Handwritten draft and revision of policy statement regarding overtime hours.

## Composing Messages

You may one day have to write letters and memorandums on your own. In some instances, what you prepare will be signed by the executive. In other cases, you will sign memos and letters with your own name. When you are doing the entire job of composing and signing letters, you serve as your own editor. You will want to be sure to reread carefully what you have written. If you feel it is not adequate, you may need to rewrite your message. Letters which office assistants often prepare on their own include the following:

- letters requesting reservations for hotel accommodations
- letters acknowledging the receipt of reports and other materials
- letters making inquiry about a particular good or service
- letters in which goods are ordered

*The secretary to the director of training commented on her writing tasks in these words: "I often write letters on my own. The director may say, 'Please write to the publisher of this book to find out if we can get large quantities at special prices.' or, 'Would you find out if the seminar leader we used last month will be available for another seminar next month.' The director expects me to write such letters, sign them, and send them out. As soon as I receive a response, I give it to the director."*

**BUSINESS WRITING HAS A SPECIFIC PURPOSE**

Most activity in business is *purpose-driven*. This means that there is a practical reason for the activity. Therefore, each written communication has a purpose. Among the most common purposes are those discussed in the following paragraphs.

### Seeking Specific Information

There are times when someone in the organization needs specific information in order to make a decision. Information is needed from outsiders who can provide the organization with equipment, supplies, and professional services. Also, there are times when messages are exchanged within the organization for the purpose of seeking information. Illus. 3–9 is a memorandum that seeks information from sales representatives throughout the company.

### Providing Specific Information

Many written communications provide specific information. A department within an organization often provides information to other units. Customers and prospective customers make numerous inquiries that generally get prompt, courteous attention. Note the information about hotel accommodations in Illus. 3–10 on page 92.

## Laynor Pharmaceutical Corporation                    MEMORANDUM

TO: All Sales Representatives

FROM: Gary H. Jenkins, Vice President, Sales

DATE: October 5, 19--

SUBJECT: Program for Spring Regional Meetings

The planning committee here at the home office wants to organize a program for the regional meetings that is of value to you. There are several topics that must be included in the program. But there also is time to deal with matters of primary concern to you. You will see on the attached tentative program that there are about nine hours of time yet to be scheduled.

Please give me your suggestions for topics and speakers on the attached suggestion sheet. Return the sheet to me no later than November 1. Thank you.

rp

Attachments

**Illus. 3–9.** Memorandum requesting information.

### Following Up Oral Discussions

Much interaction among business people is oral. Discussions may be in person, by telephone, or by teleconferences. Sometimes a written communication is necessary as a follow-up to an oral discussion. The written communication may make sure everyone understood the topic in the same way, or it may serve as a summary of what happened. A written communication is a useful reference later.

*The advertising director asked her secretary to attend a meeting with the company's new advertising agency representatives. The secretary's task was to record the key points of the plans developed during the meeting. After the meeting, the secretary prepared a copy of the notes for the director. The director reviewed and edited the notes. She also prepared a letter to be sent with the notes to the advertising agency representatives.*

**Illus. 3–10.** This letter was written to provide specific information about hotel accommodations. Notice that an alternative hotel is being recommended.

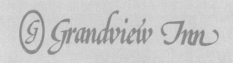

122 Cottonwood Drive
Irvington, VA  22480-8914
(703) 662-5000

August 17, 19--


Mr. and Mrs. Willard E. Rollins
4689 Heritage Hills Road
Melrose, MA  02176-4703

Dear Mr. and Mrs. Rollins

We thank you for your request for a double room for the nights of October 11 and 12.  Unfortunately, our inn is completely booked for the dates you want.  Our local tennis tournament runs from October 9 through October 16.  Our tournament attracts many visitors from out of the state each year.

A new hotel at the water's edge still has rooms available. We suggest that you write to Hotel Belmar.  This hotel is about a mile from our inn and has complete service.  You should find it a very attractive place for your visit to Irvington.  Enclosed is a Hotel Belmar brochure which gives you rates and other details.

We look forward to having you as guests in our inn in the near future.

Sincerely yours

Alan Heitzler
Alan Heitzler
Reservations Manager

tn

Enclosure

## Sending Messages to Customers and Prospective Customers

Often, written communications encourage greater demand for the products and services of businesses. Letters, brochures, fliers, and catalogs are used to announce new products, special

*delinquent:* late

sales, extended hours of service, and new methods for making payments. Letters are also needed to remind ***delinquent*** customers of amounts still due and of the actions that will be taken if payment is not forthcoming. Office workers often assist in the preparation of such communications. See Illus. 3–11 for a letter that the owner of a gourmet foods shop prepared for a monthly catalog.

**Illus. 3–11.** This letter was written to customers and potential customers of Edwards Gourmet Foods, Inc. Notice that it provides information about gift wrapping and gift certificates.

*Edwards Gourmet Foods, Inc.*
*Fall, 19––*

*Dear Customer*

*Every season has its particular pleasures, and fall is somehow a very domestic time. We start to plan for holidays, decorating the house and filling cupboards with special foods and gifts. All the specialty food items in this catalog make wonderful gifts for your friends as well as for yourself. Food is always a most welcome and appreciated gift.*

*It seems to me that just as the attractive presentation of a meal heightens our enjoyment, so the packaging of a gift adds to the pleasure of receiving it. So as a special service to our customers, we provide simple but tasteful gift wrapping. Your message will be attractively written on a card. Give us the names and addresses of those to whom you wish gifts sent and we will do the rest. You will receive confirmation of your order. (See details on order form.)*

*For food-minded or cooking friends for whom it is difficult to buy, we can send gift certificates, boxed with a copy of our catalog. They can be purchased in increments of $5.00 in any amount over $20.00.*

*Bon appetit*

*Rick Edwards*

*Rick Edwards*

**Illus. 3–12.** As an office worker, you may have an opportunity to help prepare brochures, booklets, and catalogs that are used to communicate with customers.

## CHARACTERISTICS OF EFFECTIVE WRITING

*potential:* to be realized in the future

Effective business writing reflects certain characteristics which you will want to understand well. Then you will know how to evaluate your own writing and its *potential* effectiveness in communicating your messages.

### Clearness

Stating what you wish to communicate is what clearness means. To have a clear message, you must know *why* you want to communicate, *what* you want to communicate, and *who* your recipient will be. A clear message is *logically* arranged. This means the information is in an order that is easy to understand.

A clear message eliminates the need for requests for additional information. A clear letter or memorandum allows the receiver to respond immediately. The person reading a clear message need not ask when finished: "What is the meaning of this message?"

The manager of computer services in a medium-sized firm learned of a book which would be interesting to the rest of the staff. Study the following for clarity.

NOT CLEAR:     *I noted in a recent copy of BUSINESS TODAY that you publish a handbook on WISE USE OF SOFTWARE PACKAGES. I would like a copy. What is the price of the book?*

*Questions raised:*     Does the writer of the letter want a copy of the book? Or, does he/she just want to know the price and will determine later whether the book will be purchased?

*CLEAR:*     In the September issue of BUSINESS TODAY, I noted that you publish a handbook entitled WISE USE OF SOFTWARE PACKAGES. Please send me one copy and enclose an invoice. Upon receipt of the book and invoice, I shall send you a remittance.

## Conciseness

Stating what you want to communicate in the fewest and most direct words possible is the meaning of **conciseness**. An efficient message gets right to the point. Conciseness in written communications means that the recipient will waste no time in reading words and thoughts that add nothing to understand the message.

*NOT CONCISE:*     We have your letter of October 15 in which you indicate that our letter of October 4 did not include the price list as we promised. We are not sure what happened in our office. We have enclosed the price list with this note.

*inadvertently:*
accidently

*CONCISE:*     Enclosed is the price list we **inadvertently** omitted from our earlier letter to you. We regret any inconvenience the omission may have caused you.

**Illus. 3–13.**

CATHY, by Cathy Guisewite. Copyright, 1984, Universal Press Syndicate. Reprinted with permission. All rights reserved.

## Courteousness

A written communication reflects courteousness when it conforms to the expected civil, considerate behavior of the business world. Expressions such as "Thank you," "Please," and "You are welcome" are commonly used in business correspondence. As you know, most letters include a salutation and a complimentary close which are evidence of courtesy. The "you approach" is recommended for letters and memorandums. When you write from the point of view of the recipient—the "you approach"—you are likely to prepare a courteous message. Courteous letters and memorandums encourage good relations and cooperation with the recipient. Discourteous letters and memorandums create strained relations and ill will on the part of the recipient.

DISCOURTEOUS:        *You write that you want a dozen packages of our file folders. However, you should know that we manufacture folders in two dozen sizes, five styles, and twelve colors.*
*We have no idea what you want. You must be more specific. Read the enclosed form carefully, then fill it in precisely. When we receive the form, we will send you the file folders.*

COURTEOUS:        *Thank you for your Order No. 4356. However, before we can forward the file folders to you, we need to know the quantity, size, and color you desire.*
*Enclosed is a brochure and order form. Please note that you are to record on the order form the quantity, size, and color for each type of file folder you want.*
*Your order will receive our immediate attention upon receipt of your choices.*

## Completeness

Completeness means providing all the information necessary for the message to be understood. Think of the recipient by asking yourself: "Are we answering all the questions the recipient might raise about this matter?"

NOT COMPLETE:        *We will meet on Wednesday, November 3, at 9:00 a.m. at the Astor Hotel.*

*The recipient wonders:*      *How long is the meeting?*
*In what room will the meeting be held?*
*Who will be there?*

COMPLETE:      *Our Community Service Committee meeting will be held on November 3 from 9:00 a.m. to 3:00 p.m. at the Astor Hotel. We will meet in the Franklin Room where we will also have lunch from 12 noon to 1:00 p.m.*

## Correctness

Correctness means that the information in a document is accurate and up to date. The details should be verified before the message is prepared in final form. You should not assume, for example, that a price in effect when you last wrote a letter is still in effect. Changes are common in business, and any correspondence should carry current information.

Incorrect information causes many problems in business. Further correspondence often is required; the goodwill of customers is lost; and, at times, customers discontinue their association with the organization.

*Part of Kathy's job was to answer inquiries about products and prices. A prospective customer wanted a price quotation for a large volume of an item no longer in demand but still in stock. Kathy quoted a figure from an old price list. The prospective customer compared this price with those from other competitors and found Kathy's to be far out of line. What should Kathy have done?*
*She should have questioned the price since it was not a recent one. She should have questioned the price for a large volume.*

In addition to correct content, a message should have no grammar, punctuation, or capitalization errors. Furthermore, all words should be spelled correctly. In the next section, you will have a review of the English skills that are basic to good business writing.

**ENGLISH SKILLS FOR BUSINESS WRITING**

Your business writing should reveal a good command of the English language. Sentences should be complete. Grammar should be correct. Punctuation and capitalization should follow standard rules. Words should be spelled correctly. You have studied these components many times during your school years.

You will now want to focus on enhancing your understanding of the rules and applying them as you complete assignments in this course.

## Use Proper Grammar

*cultivate:* develop

Almost everyone is likely to have some uncertainties about composing a letter or memorandum. You should *cultivate* the habit of checking a reference manual if you have even a slight doubt about what is correct.

Can you identify the grammar errors in the following sentences? Can you explain what rule or rules have been disregarded? Refer to a reference manual, if necessary.

1. *A article about our company appears in today's paper.*
2. *Miss Johnson thinks that Ruth and me are not doing this project as quickly as we should.*
3. *Sally is the best typist of the two.*
4. *Do you think this job should be divided between Patricia and I?*
5. *The range of seminars are far more than the personnel director imagined.*

## Follow Rules of Punctuation

You know the basic rules of punctuation. As you write or edit business documents, you will want to consider whether your marks of punctuation add to the clarity of your message. Reference Section *B* is a valuable source for answering many questions you may have. Can you determine where punctuation marks are needed in the following sentences? Refer to Reference Section *B*.

1. *Will Dr Hanley be able to meet with us today*
2. *Two years ago the ABC Company's decision was to make a considerable investment in computers*
3. *Documents are needed from our offices in Chicago Indianapolis and Kansas City*
4. *Customers always get fast accurate information*
5. *As you know the Roland Company has installed an automated tracking system*

*distracting:* shifting attention away from primary focus

## Spell Words Correctly

*indifference:* lack of interest

Misspelled words are *distracting* to the recipient of your message. Such words convey an impression of sloppiness and *indifference* to quality. Your message will not be persuasive or believable if there are spelling errors. You will want to have a dictionary at hand to check the correct spelling of any word about which you are uncertain.

Can you find the spelling errors in the following lines? Refer to a dictionary if necessary. Few communications will ever have so many errors among so few words! What would be your impression of the company that sent you a letter with so many errors?

*Under seperete cover we are sending you, with our complements, a copy of our latest report. We believe you will be especially interested in the questionaire used as the bases of the report. The report underscores our commitment to quality products. We will be happy to recieve your comments.*

## PERFORMING WRITING TASKS

Writing tasks must be managed wisely if they are to be completed successfully and on schedule. The following steps will prove useful to you whenever you are given a writing assignment:

1. Identify the reason for the written communication.
2. Secure all the information required for the message.
3. Compose a draft of your message.
   A. You may want to make an outline before you write out your response.
   B. You may choose to key your message directly at your typewriter or word processor.
4. Edit what you have written.
5. If required, submit the draft to the supervisor or executive for review.
   A. If you have made only a few corrections on your original draft, you may choose to submit the draft without rekeying it.

**Illus. 3–14.** Writing and editing are complex tasks. You will want to take every opportunity to improve your written communication skills.

    B. If you made many corrections, you should key another draft before submitting it to the person who asked you to prepare the message.

6. Prepare a final copy of your communication.
7. Proofread carefully.
8. Sign and prepare the communication for distribution or leave it for the person who is to sign the communication.

You will have numerous occasions during your study of office procedures to develop your writing skills. Use the preceding steps as a guide.

All written communications do not need to be of the same quality. For example, a memorandum to the manager of the stockroom, whom you know personally, might be written informally at the typewriter or word processor. But a letter to thousands of customers might be rewritten several times before it is exactly as it should be.

With practice, you will gain sufficient facility to prepare simple messages the first time you try. Also, you will gain a sense of what a good message should be and you will learn how to edit what you have written.

## REVIEW QUESTIONS

1. Do you write a business letter in the same way you write a personal letter?

2. What are some common writing tasks of office workers?

3. What is the information sought by the writer of the memorandum shown in Illus. 3–9 on page 91?

4. Why might a written communication follow an oral discussion?

5. Identify a reason a business might write to customers.

6. In what way does a clear message help communication between the writer and the recipient?

7. Why is a concise letter considered efficient?

8. What is meant by *completeness* in a message?

9. What English skills are reflected in a well-written letter?

10. What procedures should you follow in preparing a draft of a message for the executive for whom you work?

## INTERACTING WITH OTHERS

The director of personnel, during an early morning meeting with her secretary, said: "Would you find out if Ms. Sally Terman will be free at 9 a.m. on November 9? While I am in New Orleans, I'd like to have an appointment with her."

To know how to take care of this request, what questions do you think the secretary must ask?

**What You Are To Do:** Prepare a brief response to the question raised.

## EXTENDING YOUR MATH SKILLS

Assume that you are an office assistant to the general manager. From time to time, the manager places orders for office forms and supplies.

**What You Are To Do:** Prepare a copy of the form on page 102 or use the form in *Information Processing Activities*. Perform the calculations required to complete the order shown in the form. **NOTE:** The office is 500 miles from Vincent Office Supplies.

## APPLICATION ACTIVITIES

### Activity 1

You are an office assistant to Mr. Timothy Peters, who prepared the draft of the letter shown on page 103. Mr. Peters said to you: "Do whatever you want to improve this letter. I don't need to see what you do. Edit it; then prepare a copy for me to sign."

Word/text processing equipment can be used to complete this activity.

**What You Are To Do:** Follow Mr. Peters' instructions using letterhead in *Information Processing Activities* or plain paper.
(**Note:** From the incoming letter, you learn that this letter is going to Mr. Edward G. Haney, Director of Purchases, Wells Oil Refinery Corporation, Houston, TX 77081-1212. The manager for whom you are writing the letter is Manager of Production for Davisson China, 6360 Lowry Boulevard, Boston, MA 02169-8062.)

# ORDER FORM

## Vincent Office Supplies

821 Marshall Street  Jackson, Mississippi  39202-9404 (601) 841-9253

**BILL TO▶**

COMPANY Leland Corporation

ATTENTION Cindy Alphonse

STREET ADDRESS 39 Thornton Ave.

CITY Mobile  STATE AL  ZIP 36610

TELEPHONE ( 205) 545-9147

**SHIP TO▶**

IF DIFFERENT FROM BILL TO

COMPANY _____

ATTENTION _____

STREET ADDRESS _____

CITY _____ STATE ___ ZIP _____

Special Shipping Instructions _____

| QUANTITY DESIRED | | CATALOG NUMBER | SPECIFY COLOR | PAGE NO. | DESCRIPTION | UNIT PRICE | TOTAL PRICE Unit Price X How Many | |
|---|---|---|---|---|---|---|---|---|
| HOW MANY? | UNIT (Specify ea., doz., etc.) | | | | | | Dollars | Cents |
| 4 | each | 851-14 | TN | 218 | Multi-Tier Trays | 17.19 | | |
| 1 | each | 851-B-19 | | 161 | Word Dater Stamp | 4.99 | | |
| 12 | doz. | 851-72020 | | 153 | Steel Binder Clips | .93 | | |
| 3 | each | 851-C15 | BN | 155 | Desktop Tape Dispenser | 1.59 | | |
| 2 | each | 851-Tu-712 | | 49 | Collators | 26.39 | | |
| 6 | pairs | 851-END-20 | BN | 198 | Clamp-on Bookends | 3.69 | | |
| | | | | | | | | |
| | | | | | | | | |
| | | | | | | | | |
| | | | | | | | | |

Unit is shown in each ordering chart after the words "Priced Per __"

*FOR OFFICE USE ONLY*

| | | |
|---|---|---|
| Subtotal | | |
| **SMALL ORDER PROCESSING CHARGE** (Add $2.50 if subtotal is less than $20) | | |
| Mississippi residents only add 6¼% sales tax. | | |
| **TOTAL** (Shipping charges, if applicable will be added to your total. See NOTE below.) | | |

**OUR TERMS:** 1% 10 days, net 30 days.

*Thank You*

*for ordering from*
*Vincent Office Supplies*

**We pay shipping charges for the first 750 miles when your total order exceeds $45.00.**

(Refer to this form when completing the "EXTENDING YOUR MATH SKILLS" activity on page 101.)

    I have in hand your letter of October 3.  I am happy to
have the time now to respond to your request.

    We cannot, in any way, honor your order immediately.  As
you may not know, custom-designed china is not the major production of our company.  We produce such china when we can
fit a special order into our schedule.  Companies like our
high-quality china for their executive dining rooms.  They,
therefore, are willing to wait until it is convenient for us
to produce their special china.  Some of these companies place
orders that are ten times the size of yours, and they wait six
to nine months to receive their orders.

    If you are willing to wait, let us know.  We'll be happy
to put your order in our file of special orders.

Draft of letter prepared by
Timothy Peters. (Refer
to Application Activity 1
on page 101.)

## Activity 2

You are an office assistant to Mr. Louis E. Valdez, director of promotion for Ridge Office Machines, 45 Ridge Road, Mansfield, OH 44904-6332.

Word/text processing
equipment can be used to
complete this activity.

**What You Are To Do:** On a plain sheet of paper, draft a letter of inquiry to Modern Video Equipment, 3912 De La Ra Road, Palo Alto, CA 94302-4567. You are to request information about small portable video screens that are appropriate for use in relatively small exhibit booths at trade conferences and shows. Then keyboard (type) the final document on letterhead in *Information Processing Activities* or plain paper.

# Topic 3

## SPEAKING AND LISTENING

When you have completed your study of this topic, you will be able to

- describe what successful speaking is
- identify techniques that aid in active listening

The tempo of business activity would be drastically slowed if there were no oral communication. Executives know the value of oral communication in meeting the demands of business life. They provide telephones and paging equipment for employees. They expect employees to talk face-to-face about common tasks and plans for jobs to be done. Executives depend on employees who can communicate easily and successfully with each other and with outsiders.

Many problems in offices can be traced to ineffective oral communication. As you have learned, much of what happens in an office requires the cooperation of several people. You can imagine what happens when an important link in the activity is misunderstood because of incomplete or inefficient oral communication.

*An executive gave an assistant oral instructions for a job. The assistant thought she had all the information required. The executive left the office for a meeting in another town. As the assistant prepared to do the job, she realized that there were questions about the exact procedures to be used. The assistant had to put the job aside until the executive returned. However, the executive assumed the job would be completed immediately.*

*What happened in the meeting between the executive and the office assistant that resulted in inadequate instructions? Did the executive overlook some key points? Did the assistant fail to ask appropriate questions? Did the assistant fail to listen to all the details?*

## UNIQUENESS OF ORAL BUSINESS COMMUNICA- TION

*parallel:* similar; comparable

You might be asking: "Aren't speaking and listening at work exactly the same as speaking and listening at home? or with my friends? or with my teacher and classmates in school? Aren't there situations *parallel* to the one described in the preceding illustration at home and school?" A quick answer to both questions is: "Yes and no." It is true that you *are* communicating orally at home and at school. It is true that misunderstandings arise in your personal communications. However, the style and rules of speaking in business are not as important in your personal communications. Oral communication in business is expected to be efficient and effective. Your family and friends probably will not impose such demands on your oral communications with them—at least, not all the time!

Personal situation:

*A friend calls you on Wednesday evening to invite you to a party on Saturday night. You hesitate to give a firm answer because of some uncertainty about your Saturday plans. You and your friend talk about a number of common interests and you even talk about your hesitancy to respond to the invitation. Your friend tells you the party is informal and you can make a decision as late as Saturday afternoon.*

Business situation:

*You serve as a member of a company-wide employees' committee. The chairperson calls to ask you to represent the committee at a Board of Directors' meeting scheduled for the following Thursday at 3:00 p.m. The chairperson is at work and expects you to look at your calendar, quickly think about your Thursday afternoon work schedule, and respond either that you can or cannot go. The person arrranging the Board meeting needs*

**Illus. 3–15.** Your co-workers cannot use a crystal ball to determine what you are trying to say. You must make a conscious effort to communicate effectively.

**Illus. 3–16.** New employees listen attentively as a supervisor explains how to use the company's computer terminals.

*to know who will be present so a list of those expected to attend can be prepared. You cannot postpone your decision. The chairperson would not expect you to spend several minutes discussing why you are not sure what your response should be.*

*aspects:* features

Oral communication in business is powerfully important to the smooth functioning of every department. You will find the opportunities to talk with and listen to your co-workers one of the most satisfying *aspects* of your job — if you are confident of your skills. Two important communication skills are the ability to speak successfully and the ability to listen actively.

## SPEAKING SUCCESSFULLY

There are commonly accepted characteristics of successful speech in the business environment. You will want to apply these as you study and work with your teacher and classmates in your office procedures class.

### Be Interested in Communicating

Being indifferent, or not caring, destroys effective communications. Have you ever listened to a speaker who seemed to be reading a speech with no understanding of the words? The speaker seemed to have no involvement with the content. Did you enjoy what you heard? Did you learn much? Probably not. On the other hand, you may have seen a demonstration of a new office machine. The demonstrator was so involved in what she or he said that your interest was captured and held throughout the demonstration. The interest of the demonstrator in communicating with the listeners *enhanced* the effectiveness of the experience for those present.

*enhanced:* raised; improved

*When Miss Williams asked Beth, an office assistant with six months' experience, to introduce a new assistant to the staff and acquaint the new employee with the facilities, she got an immediate "Yes." Beth recalled how much she appreciated the thoughtful, careful introduction she had received. She wanted to communicate equally well with the new assistant. Would you guess that she was successful?*

### Speak Clearly

*modulated:* adjusted to the situation

You will not be able to communicate if the listener is unable to hear your words exactly. Generally, you can improve the quality of your voice by deliberately speaking in a *modulated* tone which

**CHAPTER
SUMMARY**

The basic communication skills of reading, writing, speaking, and listening are important in the business office. You have developed each of these skills to some extent during your studies in school. However, these skills need constant attention if you are to reach higher levels of effectiveness and efficiency.

Reading is a basic skill that you will use every day in the business office. You will use your reading skill to understand the tasks you must do, to use equipment skillfully, to use various office forms, to respond to inquiries, and to use references. You will find it worthwhile to improve your comprehension, your vocabulary, and your rate of reading.

Office workers, as you learned, have varying responsibilities for writing tasks. You may write drafts of letters and memorandums that are reviewed by a supervisor or executive. You may be responsible for making suggestions for change in the written communications of an executive. You may have the complete responsibility for preparing written communications. To write well, you will want to remember the importance of clearness, conciseness, courteousness, completeness, and correctness. You also must remember that proper use of your English skills is important in all your written communications.

Oral communication, requiring good speaking and listening skills, will be a common phase of your everyday interactions with your co-workers. You will want to speak clearly, express your ideas carefully, and use standard language. You also will want to be a good listener, which requires focusing your attention on what is being said and mentally summarizing and understanding every word. Taking notes and asking questions will often enhance your listening power.

Communication skills are a part of practically every office task. As you study office procedures and complete the activities for each chapter, take advantage of the opportunities to practice effective communication techniques.

## KEY TERMS

| | |
|---|---|
| reading | completeness |
| comprehension | correctness |
| editor | standard language |
| clearness | colloquialisms |
| conciseness | listening |
| courteousness | |

## INTEGRATED CHAPTER ACTIVITIES

### Activity 1

**What You Are To Do:** Prepare a copy of the following form or use the form in *Information Processing Activities*. Evaluate your own communication skills.

| | YOUR OWN APPRAISAL | | |
|---|---|---|---|
| | **Very Good** | **Good** | **Poor** |
| **Reading Skills**<br>Ability to comprehend what you read | | | |
| Ability to understand an extensive vocabulary | | | |
| Ability to read with considerable speed | | | |
| **Writing Skills**<br>Ability to use proper grammar | | | |
| Ability to use appropriate punctuation | | | |
| Ability to spell correctly | | | |
| **Speaking and Listening Skills**<br>Ability to speak clearly | | | |
| Facility in using standard language | | | |
| Ability to express ideas clearly | | | |
| Ability to keep attention on the person(s) with whom you are speaking | | | |
| Ability to focus attention on the speaker | | | |
| Ability to maintain an attitude of interest in the speaker | | | |
| Ability to follow the person speaking | | | |

Word/text processing equipment can be used to complete this activity.

### Activity 2

**What You Are To Do:** Prepare a brief statement about what you plan to do during the course in office procedures to improve each of the skills listed in Activity 1.

# PRODUCTIVITY CORNER

**Blake Williams**
*OFFICE SUPERVISOR*

## WHY DON'T I EVER DO A JOB RIGHT?

DEAR MR. WILLIAMS:

I work in a relatively large company where I am an office assistant to the general manager. He is a very, very busy person. He calls me into his office shortly after 9:00 a.m. to give me jobs to do. He talks rapidly; he moves quickly from one job to the next. Before I've heard one job, he's on to the next one! And when he's finished, he's likely to dash out of his office before I can get up to leave. I go back to my workstation and I work very hard trying to get all the jobs done. I leave them on his desk. Later, he calls me in and says: "You didn't get the information I really wanted when you called John Smith," or "You didn't set up this report as I wanted it," or "You didn't make the right number of copies of this letter."

Is something wrong with me? Is something wrong with him? What can I do?—DIANE IN HUNTSVILLE

DEAR DIANE:

Communication is a two-way activity and sometimes you must step in to do what the other person fails to do. From what you describe, I'd say the manager isn't giving you complete instructions when he talks with you at the beginning of the day. However, it is possible that you are not able to write them down or you may not be remembering similar jobs that you have done. You will need to take the initiative in getting complete instructions. Here are some pointers:

1. Take notes on everything he tells you.
2. Think ahead to what you must know to do the job while you are listening and recording the instructions. Make a mental note of anything that is missing.
3. Review complex tasks by saying to the manager: "Could I just double-check that these instructions are right? I'm to call the controller at headquarters to get the November production schedule of Product XTB by individual plant?"
4. Follow your notes as you complete each task.
5. Make the best decision you can when you find specific instructions are missing in your notes and it is not appropriate to check with the manager. Base such decisions on the past experience you have had in doing similar jobs. If you think it necessary, you might attach a note to the job explaining to the manager the basis for your decision.
6. Review any decisions you made (point 5) that the manager did not accept. Ask yourself why you didn't make a good decision. Try to learn from each wrong decision.

I hope you will find these pointers useful every day.—BLAKE WILLIAMS

# Chapter 4

# Interacting with Others

You interact with others every time you ask your supervisor a question, coordinate your schedule with a co-worker, explain a procedure to a new employee, answer a question, participate in a meeting, listen to a visitor, greet someone in the elevator, or work with others to solve a problem. The quality of this interaction affects your productivity and your level of job satisfaction.

Your attitude, actions, appearance, and voice have a bearing on your interaction with others. These factors are examined in this chapter to help you work produc-tively with those in your office as well as with the public. You will learn specific techniques to help you interact well with supervisors and co-workers on a daily basis. Suggestions for keeping positive interaction under stressful conditions are also presented.

The objectives of the chapter are to

- help you understand the importance of good human relations on the job

- improve your interpersonal skills

# Topic 1

## HUMAN RELATIONS ON THE JOB

When you have completed your study of this topic, you will be able to

- describe your role in getting along with others

- explain how attitude influences working relationships

- explain how actions, appearance, and voice affect human relations on the job

- describe your role in representing the company to the public

As a beginning office worker, you will probably already have good technical skills such as keyboarding and machine transcription. An equally important skill which you may need to develop is the ability to get along with others while on the job. The term human relations refers to the relationships between people—and *good* human relations improves productivity and makes the work environment more pleasant. Your ability to work well with others under a variety of circumstances is important as you advance in your career.

You may change jobs. You may lose some technical skills and gain others. Yet wherever you work—in a small bank or large insurance company, in a formal reception area or a word processing center—you always will have to deal with people.

## YOUR ROLE IN INFLUENCING THE OFFICE ENVIRONMENT

*tone:* mood

*compatible:* able to work well together

*influence:* affect

*self-image:* how you think of yourself

*nurture:* help something grow and mature

The interaction among co-workers affects the *tone* of an office. How well you and your co-workers get along with each other will affect communication, productivity, and office morale. When your relationships are positive, even heavy workloads or tight schedules seem less burdensome. You and your company profit when you and your co-workers are *compatible.*

You *influence* the office environment by your attitude (how you think), how you exhibit your attitude, and how you look and sound. You are not responsible for how your co-workers think, act, look, and sound, but you are responsible for yourself. You play an important part in making the office an enjoyable place in which to work.

### Your Attitude — Your Mental Self

Your attitude is your outlook on life. It includes your *self-image* and your opinions. Attitude is guided by your mind. For example, if you spend your mental energies worrying about what *might* happen next, your outlook on life (your attitude) is probably negative. If, however, you spend your mental energies taking each day as it comes and appreciating the people or events that are helping you, your attitude is probably happy and healthy.

No one can control what you think and feel, except you. Your attitude is your mental self; *nurture* it! Following are three elements of a positive attitude.

**Illus. 4–1.** You will project a positive attitude if you have a good self-image.

### Realize That You Are Important

Never think of yourself as *just* a billing clerk, *just* a secretary, or *just* a receptionist. Your role as an office worker is vital to the company for which you work and you, personally, make a valuable contribution to any job you hold. Without competent office workers, the entire business system would **collapse.**

*collapse:* fall apart

When you realize that your job is important, you can feel good about yourself—which is the first step toward achieving success in your job. When you realize that your job is important, you can go about your tasks more enthusiastically and with greater purpose. You will be happier and you will do your job better.

### Do Not Take Yourself Too Seriously

While it is very important to realize the contribution you make to the company, it is wise not to take yourself *too* seriously. Learn to laugh at yourself, and allow co-workers to laugh with you. Your sense of humor will help you **cope** with stress and get along better with others.

*cope:* handle well

### Accept Your Co-workers

To accept others, you must believe that it is not necessary for everyone to think and act as you do. Co-workers come from different backgrounds, have different responsibilities, experience different daily pressures, and have needs and feelings different from your own. Instead of demanding that they be like you, listen to and learn from them, and respect their differences.

**Illus. 4–2.** "But I *am* succeeding as fast as I can!"

## How You Exhibit Your Attitude

Your attitude is reflected by how you act toward others. Having a positive attitude enables you to act in a manner that is pleasant and encouraging. Following are a few ways in which you can exhibit a good attitude.

### Look for Favorable Qualities in Others

It is important for you to search for favorable qualities in every person with whom you must deal. When you search for good points in others, you will not have time to criticize them.

### Be Courteous

It is not necessary to consider every co-worker a personal friend, but it *is* necessary to treat all people with courtesy and respect. A good way to show courtesy is to use common-sense etiquette. For example, remember the simple courtesies of saying, "Please," and "Thank you." Smile at people! Your goal should be to treat others the way you want to be treated.

### Empathize with Others

Empathy is the ability to look at situations through the eyes of others and to try to understand their points of view. Empathizing helps you feel and understand what the other person is experiencing.

> *Jerri, Paul, and Linda are co-workers in the accounting department of Tollimar & Reese, Inc. During the morning break, Jerri and Linda were chatting:*
>
> Jerri: *Why isn't Paul friendlier? He seems nice, but he hardly talks to anyone unless he has to.*
>
> Linda: *I used to wonder the same thing. But he is still new on the job. I think he's just nervous about doing his work correctly. He will probably relax and visit with us more when he feels more confident about his work. We'll just have to be patient, and let him know he's doing a good job!*

### Look for Ways to Help Co-workers

"How may I help?" is a question that workers should ask themselves throughout the day. Of course, the best way to help is to be sure you are doing your own work completely and efficiently. Helping others while your work is left undone is not productive.

However, if you complete your work you may offer to help co-workers finish theirs if a deadline needs to be met. Or, as you are doing your work, you may offer to help a busy co-worker: "June, I'm going to the mailroom. Do you have anything you'd like me to mail while I'm there?"

### Be Dependable

An important part of being dependable is accepting responsibility for your actions. If you say you will do something, do it. If you promise to be somewhere, be there. If you schedule a meeting at a certain time, be on time. If you start a job, finish it.

## How You Look

Your appearance influences your working environment in much the same way as does your attitude. To an extent, it can determine how pleasant and productive your office will be.

### Your Dress

*appropriately:* properly

Even before you speak, others begin to form an opinion about you based on your appearance. If you are dressed *appropriately* for the office and you take pride in your appearance, others will think you take equal pride in your work. If, however, your appearance is sloppy, it will be difficult to convince others that you are an efficient, capable worker.

Dress attractively and in a businesslike manner. Extreme or faddish styles will detract from your professional image, so select a wardrobe with care. Let your appearance say to others, "I take my job seriously." More about your appearance will be presented later in this chapter.

### Facial Expressions

Are you aware of your facial expressions? Do you appear to be pleasant? hostile? neutral? From a practical standpoint, it is easier for others to deal with you if you look pleasant. A smile is a simple way to put others at ease.

### Nervous Habits

Nervous habits such as twirling your hair, drumming your fingers, humming to yourself, and frequently clearing your throat can be extremely annoying to those around you. Fortunately, these habits, which look and/or sound unprofessional, can be changed. Work hard to eliminate them.

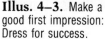

**Illus. 4–3.** Make a good first impression: Dress for success.

### *Your Voice*

Many modern offices are arranged in such a way that conversations can be easily overheard. When you are on the telephone or are discussing something with a co-worker, try to speak loudly enough so the listener can hear you without straining. But do not speak so loudly that you disrupt other conversations around you. Speak at a moderate rate of speed so others can understand you easily.

The pitch of your voice has to do with how high or low your voice sounds. When you become emotional—both happy and angry—the pitch usually goes up—and a higher pitched voice tends to carry farther than a lower pitched voice. You cannot change the natural pitch of your voice, but you can try to control raising it. Overall, a lower pitched voice is more pleasant to hear.

**YOUR ROLE IN REPRESENTING THE COMPANY TO OTHERS**

Your job may involve dealing with the public. You may be a receptionist in a doctor's office, a customer-service worker in a large department store, a reservationist for an airline, a telephone operator, or a teller at a bank. You are the person representing your company to the public. Your appearance and attitude are as important — if not more important — in representing your company to others as they are in influencing your office environment.

## Project a Businesslike Image

If you deal with the public in person, you should project a businesslike image so the public will have confidence in the company. Some companies have dress codes to ensure that employees project a proper image. Other companies allow you to determine your own manner of dress as long as it is appropriate. Either way, your businesslike image begins with good personal **hygiene.**

*hygiene:* bodily cleanliness

Be sure to shower or bathe daily, and use an effective deodorant or antiperspirant. Brush your teeth regularly. You may want to keep some breath mints in a drawer to use if necessary. If you enjoy wearing perfume or cologne, be sure the fragrance is not overpowering.

Your clothes should always be neat and clean. Choose styles and colors that flatter you. Your hair should be clean and styled in such a way that it is not distracting to you or to the public.

Remember, when you look your best you will feel good about yourself. And when you feel good about yourself, you will be more relaxed and confident. This will help you to represent your company in the best way possible.

## Have a Businesslike Handshake

Shaking hands is a common custom that is used when people greet one another or when they are introduced to one another. How you shake hands is important in the business environment. Remember to step or lean forward slightly as you extend your hand, shake hands firmly, and look the other person directly in the eye.

## Listen Attentively

The attitude of a worker who deals with the public should be, "I want to help you in any way possible." To convey that attitude to others, you must take time to listen carefully. When you listen, your voice and body language should say, "There is nothing else I would rather be doing right now than listening to you."

*impatient:* in a hurry to do something else

While you listen, look at the person. Do not check your watch, thump your pencil on the desk, think about where you will eat lunch, interrupt the speaker, or act **impatient** in any way. If you deal with the public over the phone, respond to their comments by saying, "I agree," "I understand," or whatever other response is appropriate to let the caller know you are listening with interest. Listening attentively is the only way you can learn what the caller or visitor needs.

## Be Prepared to Help

To help a caller or visitor most efficiently, you should be completely familiar with the policies and procedures of your company. This is so you can explain accurately and clearly the action you will take or the action the caller should take. It is also important to know as much as possible about the services or products provided by the company. If you access information from a computer, you must understand the capabilities of the computer software so you can retrieve information quickly.

> Marian works for Bachman Books, a large bookstore. During the day, Marian often receives calls from customers asking whether a particular book is in stock, how long it will be before an order can be filled, and what the cost will be. She quickly accesses the needed information on the computer. When she receives new books or revised price lists, she promptly keys these changes on the computer. She knows her references must be current to help customers.
>
> Sometimes customers want to know about a book, but they cannot remember the exact title or the author's name. For example, one caller asked if "the book about stress written by Reeves — or something like that" was in stock. Marian quickly searched the computer's memory for a book fitting that description. She found a book entitled Managing Stress by Benjamin Reyes. The customer was delighted: "Yes, that's it! Thank you for finding it. I didn't give you much to go on!" Marian was able to help because she was knowledgeable and prepared.

If you do not know, or cannot find, the answer to a question, tell the caller you will ask for assistance. Most callers will wait patiently if they believe you are trying to help them. If the wait will be longer than a few minutes, don't keep the caller waiting; ask for a telephone number and call back.

## Put Yourself in the Caller's Place

When you must answer the same question over and over, remember to treat the last caller as courteously as you treated the first caller. Be patient.

*Suppose you called an airline reservationist and asked when Flight 389 was scheduled to arrive. You would expect a quick and courteous reply. You would not know how many other people had asked the reservationist the same question. You called because you needed the information.*

When you deal with the public, remember that a caller's anger is probably not directed toward you personally. Use these situations as opportunities to build goodwill between your organization and the caller.

*Suppose you call Customer Service because you are upset that a filing cabinet was not delivered on time. Are you personally angry with the representative who answered the phone? Probably not, but you may express your frustration to the person anyway. If the representative can work out a satisfactory solution, you may be willing to do business with that store again.*

People who call or visit your company are individuals who have differing needs. Be flexible enough to laugh with one caller one minute and to discuss a problem seriously with another caller the next. Remember to be courteous and tactful—it's your job to help others.

## Be Loyal to the Company

Being *loyal* means you do your part to achieve company goals and to build a positive, professional image of your company. As a loyal worker, you will speak positively about the company to customers. You should not complain about your job or company policies to a customer. If you disagree with a policy, talk with the appropriate company personnel—not the customer! Even in social gatherings outside the office, what you say about the company to others will affect—either positively or negatively—their perception of your company.

Being loyal also involves keeping confidential company matters to yourself. Just as gossiping about individuals is harmful, gossiping about your company is harmful to its corporate image. Your actions should show others you believe in your company. Being loyal will cause customers to believe in the company as well. In Chapter 16, you will learn about some of the policies and practices established by businesses to encourage company loyalty.

## REVIEW QUESTIONS

1. What affects the tone of an office more than workloads or schedules?

2. What is your role in making the office a pleasant place in which to work?

3. What is one trait that will help you not take yourself too seriously and will help you get along well with others?

4. Describe several ways in which you can exhibit a good attitude.

5. What message should your appearance send to others?

6. What is a simple way to put others at ease?

7. Why do some companies have dress codes?

8. Describe a proper business handshake.

9. What should your attitude be if you deal with the public?

10. What is the only way you can learn what a caller or visitor needs?

## INTERACTING WITH OTHERS

For the last two years you have worked in the office of a department store. You and your three co-workers enjoy a friendly working relationship. Last week the store hired a new worker, Darla, to key bookkeeping entries into the computer. She is very shy, and it appears to be difficult for her to relax and feel at ease with you and the other workers.

**What You Are To Do:**  What can you and your co-workers do to help Darla feel more at ease and welcome in the workplace? Make a list of your suggestions.

## EXTENDING YOUR MATH SKILLS

Kay, your co-worker, is keying a marketing report. One of the pages, which is shown, contains four columns of figures. Kay would like you to help her by adding the figures in each column to verify her answers.

**What You Are To Do:**  On a sheet of paper, write the column heading and the total you get for each column. Circle any totals that are different from Kay's totals.

The research team, directed by Edwin Broyles, conducted a six-week study, gathering valuable data about which new snack food consumers would be most willing to buy. Following are the statistics showing how many consumers preferred each product.

| | Products | | | |
| Test Target | Crunchy Munchies | Fruit Scoops | Lite Flavors | Nuts 'n' Such |
| --- | --- | --- | --- | --- |
| Chicago | 482 | 842 | 596 | 217 |
| Denver | 267 | 991 | 322 | 431 |
| Detroit | 770 | 572 | 145 | 292 |
| Little Rock | 321 | 885 | 287 | 658 |
| Pittsburgh | 890 | 139 | 661 | 543 |
| San Diego | 367 | 372 | 350 | 220 |
| Topeka | 253 | 283 | 739 | 965 |
| Tucson | 444 | 744 | 413 | 109 |
| | 3,744 | 2,848 | 3,523 | 4,135 |

## APPLICATION ACTIVITY

Assume you are responsible for observing beginning office workers employed by Trek Tours Travel Agency. These workers are expected to interact effectively with the general public as well as with co-workers. What would you expect to observe in order to give a particular employee a high rating for each of the following areas?

- attitude
- actions
- appropriate appearance

Word/text processing equipment can be used to complete this activity.

**What You Are To Do:**  Keyboard (type) your response.

# Topic 2

## IMPROVING INTERPERSONAL SKILLS

When you have completed your study of this topic, you will be able to

- describe ways to interact successfully with those to whom you report
- identify ways of working compatibly with co-workers
- explain how to cope effectively with others under stressful conditions

Accomplishing company goals requires a team effort on the part of all workers. On every team there are different positions, and the people in those positions must work together in order to win the game. In baseball, you will find a pitcher, a catcher, and an outfielder, to mention just a few positions. In a company, the team positions include secretaries, receptionists, general clerks, mail workers, bookkeepers, and managers. Each team member must be able to interact with the other members in order to be productive and help the company reach its goals.

You will want to develop your own interpersonal skills so that you can be an effective team member. Interpersonal skills involve the attitudes and communication techniques that help you get along with others. In order to complete your assigned office tasks, you will be expected to interact with those to whom you report, as well as with co-workers. Effective interaction with other employees may be critical to doing your job to the best of your ability.

Interacting with others is not always easy. Deadlines, differences of opinion, and circumstances beyond your control will test your ability to interact with others. You must learn to expect such stressful situations and to handle them in a professional and productive manner.

This topic will explore the interpersonal skills you need to be successful on the job. Specific suggestions are given for interacting with those to whom you report, interacting with co-workers, and interacting with others in stressful situations.

**INTERACTING
WITH THOSE
TO WHOM
YOU REPORT**

*authority:* the right
to guide or direct

No matter what your position is in the company, you will have someone to whom you report—someone who is responsible for your performance. As an office worker, you may report to an office manager. The office manager may report to a vice president. The vice president will have to account to the president of the company. Even the president must act in accordance with the board of directors or laws of the state or country. Interacting with someone in authority is a reality of everyday business life. Interacting effectively could mean the difference between continued employment and being fired.

In this section, the term supervisor will be used to refer to the person who has *authority* over your position. There are many ways to enhance the interaction between you and your supervisor.

## Accept Work Assignments Pleasantly

When you are given a task to complete, how you respond will make a difference in how your supervisor feels about you and your work. Following are two situations where an office worker is given a task. Notice the responses of the workers and the supervisors.

| WRONG | Mr. Hill: | *Ken, I'd like to have this report typed for today's meeting at 3 p.m.* |
|---|---|---|
| | Ken: | *All right. (Sighing and frowning, he tosses the report into his in basket without even glancing at it.)* |
| RIGHT | Mr. Imoto: | *Jill, I'd like to have this report typed in time for my meeting this afternoon, please.* |
| | Jill: | *Yes, of course! (Smiles pleasantly and quickly scans the report.) Do I need to make copies of the report before the meeting?* |

Both Ken and Jill agreed to type the report. What made the responses so different? What did the responses contribute to the worker-supervisor relationships? Let's examine both responses.

### Ken's Response

Ken's verbal response indicated he would complete the task. But the message he sent with his nonverbal response (sigh, frown, tossing the report aside) was, "I'll do it if I have to, but I don't want to."

Mr. Hill sensed Ken's resistance to typing the report. Becoming anxious about whether the report would be ready on time, Mr. Hill began to remind Ken frequently about the assignment. Ken wondered why Mr. Hill was nagging him. Ken thought to himself, "I told him I'd do it. Why doesn't he trust me?"

When the job was completed, Mr. Hill felt as if he had had to squeeze the work out of Ken, and Ken felt unappreciated. What an unpleasant cycle to experience every day on the job!

### Jill's Response

Jill's response was pleasant. Unlike Ken's, Jill's verbal and nonverbal messages were consistent. Her words, tone of voice, smile, and actions all said, "I'll be glad to type the report." She stopped the task she was doing to briefly examine the report. She tried to identify questions she would have about completing it and to anticipate the needs of Mr. Imoto. What supervisor would not appreciate that kind of response?

*diminished:* decreased

The most important issue, of course, is to complete the assigned task. In this situation Ken and Jill both completed the report accurately and on time. But Ken's attitude *diminished* Mr. Hill's view of his work, whereas Jill's attitude enhanced Mr. Imoto's opinion of hers. As a general rule, your accepting work assignments pleasantly will help make your worker-supervisor relationship productive and enjoyable.

## Agree on Priorities

Setting priorities means ranking tasks in the order in which they should be done. Assume that you had to process an expense report, transcribe three letters, and make 25 copies of an agenda. How do you choose which task to do first? Priorities are often based on deadlines. A deadline is a specific time or date by which a project, task, or assignment must be completed. If the expense report is due this afternoon, but the letters and copies of the report are not needed until tomorrow, you should process the expense report first. That is just common sense. But since priorities are not always easy to recognize, it is important to discuss them often with your supervisor.

### *Setting Priorities with One Supervisor*

You may work in an office where you report to only one supervisor. If you do, communicating priorities could be as simple as this:

> *Peggy:*      *Mrs. Paulson, I'm planning to transcribe the first draft of the conference program now. Is there anything else that should be done first?*
>
> *Mrs. Paulson:*      *Yes! I'm glad you asked. Please copy these minutes first. I need them by noon.*

By communicating their priorities, Peggy and Mrs. Paulson work compatibly as a team.

If your work schedule is heavy or if your supervisor is frequently unavailable, it is helpful to have a written priority list. If your supervisor has time, you both can rank tasks in priority order together. If your supervisor is not available, rank the tasks in the order in which you believe they should be completed. Leave a copy of the written list with your supervisor so he or she can review it later. Whether you communicate in person or in writing, it is important that the two of you agree on the priorities so you can work toward the same goal.

**Illus. 4–4.** Work together with your supervisor when setting priorities.

### Setting Priorities with More Than One Supervisor

When you work for more than one supervisor or executive, it is essential that you establish work priorities. Unless there is an immediate deadline, a company may adopt a "first-in, first-out" policy. Then, tasks are completed in the order in which they were received.

*Work Log.* There will be times when one supervisor may submit work with an immediate deadline, even though others have submitted work first. A work log is a record that helps you keep track of when work is submitted, when it is needed, and when it is completed. Illus. 4-5 is an example of a work log.

| WORK LOG | | | | | |
| --- | --- | --- | --- | --- | --- |
| Supervisor's Name | Work to Complete | Date | | | |
| | | In | Needed a.m. | p.m. | Out |
| *Avery, J.* | *Ferguson Report* | 2/1 | | 2/4 | |
| *Stewart, M.* | *Graphics for Fuller* | 2/1 | 2/4 | | |
| *Miller, L.* | *Statistical Analysis* | 2/1 | | 2/5 | |

**Illus. 4–5.** Work Log

Notice that the work log includes a column for the supervisor's name and a column for the description of the work to be completed. You will see that J. Avery and M. Stewart both submitted work on 2/1 and that both need their work on 2/4. The a.m. and p.m. columns under "Date Needed" help you recognize priorities. M. Stewart's project should be completed first since it is due before lunch, while J. Avery's project is due in the afternoon. By frequently checking the "Date Needed" column in your work log, you can keep an accurate idea of priorities.

*Conflicting Priorities.* Sometimes several supervisors all want their work completed "right now." You need to inform the supervisors of the conflicting priorities. Perhaps a meeting among the several supervisors and yourself will help you work out priorities. One supervisor may change a deadline. Or you may have to delegate work.

By focusing on priorities, you and your supervisors can direct your energies toward finding effective ways to get the work done. You can work productively as a team and reduce the chances of becoming frustrated with one another. Setting and communicating priorities is vital to good worker-supervisor relationships.

## Don't Bring Me Problems, Bring Me Alternatives

After beginning a task, you may run into a problem trying to complete it. The problem may not be your fault; yet you must still deal with it. In the following situation, see how differently Nina and Mark handle the same problem:

| WRONG | Nina: | Ms. Foster, I can't make copies of this report in time for your meeting. The copier broke down. |
| | Ms. Foster: | Oh, Nina! You know I need that report right away. |
| RIGHT | Mark: | Mr. O'Neill, the copier is out of order. Should I go down the street to the copy and quick-print center to make copies of the report? |
| | Mr. O'Neill: | That's a good idea, Mark. Go right now and make the copies. |

The facts in the two examples above are the same: The copier is not working and the report cannot be completed without a copier. Why did the supervisors react so differently? Let's examine Nina's and Mark's approaches to the problem.

### Nina's Approach

Nina began the conversation poorly by saying, "I can't . . . ." When an obstacle (the copier not working) got in Nina's way, she gave up. Ms. Foster was impatient with Nina for giving up so easily instead of searching for other solutions. If Nina says "I can't" enough, Ms. Foster will start to believe that she probably can't do her job. Why should the company keep employees who can't do their jobs?

Ms. Foster thinks Nina does not really care about getting the job done. Nina believes Ms. Foster is blaming her for the problem. Their working relationship is strained. Nina's inability, or unwillingness, to look for alternate solutions to problems *discredits* her professionalism.

*discredits:* takes away from

### Mark's Approach

Mark's approach to the situation was both professional and helpful. First he identified the problem and then proposed an alternate method of completing the job. His approach showed Mr. O'Neill that he was dedicated to getting the job done and was willing to find another way to copy the report. Mr. O'Neill appreciated Mark's professional attitude and his *resourcefulness* in solving problems.

*resourcefulness:* ability to find solutions

Of course, some problems are more complex than a copier breaking down. In those situations it will take a little longer to think of alternative solutions. But when you think problems through and present alternatives to your supervisor, you save yourself and your supervisor valuable time. You are an *asset* to the company. People who are assets are more likely to be promoted than those who say, "I can't."

*asset:* a benefit

## Keep Your Supervisor Informed

Supervisors need to know what is happening within their areas of responsibility. When they are informed, supervisors do their jobs better and are regarded as competent by *their* supervisors. As an office worker you will naturally see and hear situations throughout the day that your supervisor will not. For example, an important client may unexpectedly drop in while your supervisor is out of the office. Be sure to tell your supervisor. Perhaps you are working on a project such as making arrangements for a national sales conference. Keep your supervisor aware of your progress. Advise your supervisor when circumstances arise that affect the project.

Keeping your supervisor informed does NOT involve reporting on co-workers about petty matters. There may be times when differences between you and a co-worker cannot be resolved without your supervisor being called in. But on a day-to-day basis, informing your supervisor means keeping the communications lines between you open so you both can do your jobs better.

thoughts. If you still believe you need to discuss the issue, go to the person when *you* feel mentally prepared to talk calmly and directly.

### Concentrate on Your Job

Concentrate on doing your job well, not on what others think of you personally. Trying to please people who are frequently angry or extremely critical will usually result in frustration. Instead, do your job to the best of your ability. When you have done your best, *you* can be pleased with your work. Of course, always look for ways to improve. Listen to criticism of your work even though it may be unpleasant. If a criticism is accurate, work to improve the weak area. Do so because you want to improve yourself— not because you want to please the critical person.

### Be Patient

Remember that co-workers who are difficult to get along with are human, too. Many of them know that they offend and upset others. They may be trying to improve, even though you may not be able to **detect** their efforts.

*detect:* notice

## Resolving Problems

From time to time a problem may arise between you and another person. You should try to resolve the problem as quickly as possible because problems that are ignored seldom disappear. Go to the person involved with the problem and discuss it with him or her *first*. Do not discuss the person and/or problem with everyone else in the office. Respect the other person's privacy and dignity.

How you approach the problem with the other person will affect how easily the problem can be resolved. Here are two approaches.

Betty:   *Stan, I can't believe you are so absent-minded. You know the mail is picked up every day at 3:30. I'm tired of your ignoring your duties and then asking me to help you get the mail ready in a hurry.*

Jack:   *The mail hasn't been ready in time for the afternoon pickup all week. Perhaps if you began getting the mail ready at 2:45, we could avoid this frantic rush every afternoon.*

Betty's approach is harsh and critical; Jack's approach is direct, yet tactful. His approach is better than Betty's because he followed three problem-solving principles:

1. Attack the problem—not the person. Betty ridiculed Stan ("I can't believe you are so absent-minded"). Jack focused instead on the problem. When people feel attacked they will spend their energies defending themselves instead of solving problems.
2. Describe the problem—do not evaluate it. Jack described the problem ("the mail hasn't been ready in time"). Betty, however, gave her opinion of the problem (you are "ignoring your duties"). Describing the problem instead of evaluating it helps both people view the problem objectively.
3. Courteously describe the action you want the other person to take. Jack suggested that Stan begin preparing the mail earlier. Betty was more concerned about *venting* her anger towards Stan than she was about correcting the problem.

*venting:* getting rid of; expressing

## Sexual Harassment

Sexual harassment is a difficult term to define. The Equal Employment Opportunity Commission (EEOC) has issued guidelines that define sexual harassment as any unwelcomed sexual advance that:

- is used as a condition of employment
- affects your chances for promotion
- creates an unpleasant, hostile, or offensive working environment

Sexual harassment is not present in every office. You may never have to deal with the problem. But if it does occur, do not ignore it. To eliminate sexual harassment, you will have to take action. Reference Section G outlines specific action you should take if the unwelcome advances persist. Sexual harassment is illegal. You will not be alone in your fight against it.

## Controlling People Interruptions

One of the benefits of working in an office is that you have the opportunity to be with and enjoy people. On the other hand, people can be a source of frustration when they interrupt you often and lessen your productivity. Some interruptions are necessary—

perhaps a co-worker has a question or must tell you something important. Interruptions unrelated to work, however, should be controlled.

It is acceptable to have brief, social conversations with co-workers throughout the day. Lunch and breaks provide opportunities for more lengthy social conversations. But you may discover one or two co-workers who *monopolize* your work time by talking about activities unrelated to the job. There may be times during the workday when you must tactfully communicate to a "talker" that you are busy.

*monopolize:* take over

**Illus. 4–9.** Use your break and lunch time to socialize with co-workers.

## REVIEW QUESTIONS

1. Define interpersonal skills.

2. Why is it important for you to be able to interact well with others as team members?

3. Why is it important for you and your supervisor(s) to agree on priorities?

4. What is the purpose of keeping your supervisor informed?

5. Give an example of being specific when expressing appreciation to a co-worker.

6. How can you act professionally when dealing with unpleasant co-workers?

7. Why should you continue to do a good job even when your supervisor is never pleased?

8. Briefly identify three problem-solving principles.

9. How does the Equal Employment Opportunity Commission define sexual harassment?

10. Why is it necessary to control "people interruptions?"

## MAKING DECISIONS

Terri asks you to help her complete a report for Mr. Sturzenberger. You agree to prepare several charts while Terri finishes keying the report. You were under considerable pressure and you did not proofread your work before giving it to Terri.

After the report and the charts are submitted, Mr. Sturzenberger discovers errors in the charts. He points out the errors to Terri and asks her to proofread more carefully. Since your workstation and Terri's are side by side, you hear Mr. Sturzenberger's remarks. What should you do or say? Why?

**What You Are To Do:**  Prepare a brief response to the questions raised.

## EXTENDING YOUR ENGLISH SKILLS

Read the typed paragraphs on page 149 which are from a rough draft copy of an employee recommendation your supervisor is composing. Note that there are several misspelled words in the paragraphs.

**What You Are To Do:**  Prepare a copy of these paragraphs, making the necessary spelling corrections. Underscore your corrections.

## APPLICATION ACTIVITY

Miss Sherman, one of your supervisors, was out of the office all day today. To keep Miss Sherman informed, you jotted down notes during the day about important events and circumstances. You plan to key the handwritten notes and place them on her desk before you leave for the day.

Word/text processing equipment can be used to complete this activity.

**What You Are To Do:**  Following are the handwritten notes. Key (type) them attractively on an 8½" × 11" sheet of paper. (Use colored paper, if available, since it will attract Miss Sherman's attention.) Use your own judgment with regard to format. Sign the page of notes at the bottom before placing it on Miss Sherman's desk.

Sara is an efficent worker with a pleasant personality. She willingly accepts responsability and is able to follow through.  She listens well to instructions and asks intelligant questions.  Sara posesses good technical skills as well as common sense.  I particularly appreciate being able to trust her completly with confadental information.

Sara also enteracts well with co-workers.  She is able to impathise with people and encourage them.  Her actions, her apropriate business attire, and her desire to maintain compateble working relationships with co-workers reflect her positive atatud towards work.  I believe Sara Barker will be an excellant employee.

---

Notes to Miss Sherman
2/18/--

1. Samuel Pebsworth came by to see you at 9:30 a.m. He said it wasn't urgent. He will call you Thursday morning.

2. Mr. Carlyle wanted the letter to Michael Vinson that you dictated transcribed and mailed right away. I signed your name with my initials in parentheses. A copy of the letter is in the files.

3. The first draft of the marketing report should be ready by tomorrow afternoon.

4. The customer mailing we discussed yesterday was prepared and sent today.

5. Mr. Crane asked about the budget proposed today. He seemed anxious to have it ready soon.

6. Tomorrow, Bob Wiggins in Purchasing will have been with the company 25 years. Just thought you'd like to know.

7. Your telephone messages are clipped together next to the telephone.

**CHAPTER SUMMARY**

Being able to interact well with others is an ability that will always benefit you, regardless of your position. Compatible business relationships improve communication, office morale, and productivity. Your role in making the working environment a pleasant and productive place is to treat others with the same respect and courtesy you would like to receive.

To enjoy good human relations on the job, you need a positive, professional attitude. You want your actions and your appearance to help you say, "I feel good about myself and I take my job seriously."

The same factors that affect human relations in your office also affect the public's opinion of your firm. Your appearance, voice, and actions should reflect a helpful, courteous attitude.

Stress is present in every office, but in varying degrees. Learning to deal successfully with co-workers under stressful conditions is important.

You are an important member of the office team. Be sensitive to the needs and viewpoints of co-workers, and keep the lines of communication open so your interaction with others will be pleasant and productive.

---

### KEY TERMS

| | |
|---|---|
| human relations | supervisor |
| attitude | setting priorities |
| empathy | deadline |
| pitch | work log |
| interpersonal skills | sexual harassment |

---

**INTEGRATED CHAPTER ACTIVITIES**

Word/text processing equipment can be used to complete this activity.

## Activity 1

Your teachers have authority over you as a student. Teachers are in the school environment what supervisors are in the work environment. How well you are able to interact with teachers will give you insight as to how well you will probably get along with a supervisor.

**What You Are To Do:** Take time to analyze how you interact with your teachers. Describe in writing how you can apply three techniques you have learned for good human relations to the relationships you have with your teachers. As you change your attitudes and actions, see if you notice an improvement in your student-teacher relationships. You can begin practicing good human relations skills now.

## Activity 2

Maxine, a receptionist at First City Bank, is attending a seminar for office workers. To help workers realize the importance of their jobs, the seminar leader asks them to answer three questions. Maxine answered the questions as follows:

A. What is your company's main product or service?
*Maxine's answer:* First City Bank provides financial services.

B. How does your company benefit the community?
*Maxine's answer:* It provides a secure place for individuals and businesses to keep their money; it lends money so businesses can expand and individuals can buy such things as cars and houses, take vacations, and make home improvements.

C. What is your personal contribution to the company?
*Maxine's answer:* I greet customers and make them glad they chose First City Bank. I direct callers to the appropriate people so their needs can be met quickly.

Maxine saw that doing her job helped the company benefit the community. Her job really was important!

**What You Are To Do:** Select a neighborhood company you would like to work for and a position you would like to hold. Then prepare answers to the same three questions that Maxine answered.

Word/text processing equipment can be used to complete this activity.

# PRODUCTIVITY CORNER

**Blake Williams**
*OFFICE SUPERVISOR*

## STRESS SIGNALS

DEAR MR. WILLIAMS:

As a receptionist for a large law firm, I am very, very busy. I open the mail, answer the telephone, and process legal documents on a word processor. But my primary responsibility is greeting the endless stream of clients who come to the firm each day. Most days are so busy that I don't take breaks or go to lunch!

Lately, however, I'm beginning to develop headaches—especially in the afternoon. And I'm so tired and weary at the end of the day.

The people I work with are great, and I especially like what I do. I don't want to quit this job—but it's wearing me down! What can I do?—JULIE FROM ATLANTA

DEAR JULIE:

Stress can drain your energy in a hurry and cause you to become discouraged. Happily, though, there *are* steps you can take both on and off the job to reduce stress:

- My first suggestion would be to take your scheduled breaks and lunch—even in the midst of a busy day. Taking a break will give you a chance to "re-energize" yourself.

- When you take your breaks, leave your workstation. Take these opportunities to relax. Close your eyes and think about happy thoughts such as your vacation plans or a lazy day by the pool.

- You also may want to slowly stretch your muscles, especially if you've been sitting for hours. Roll your head slowly from side to side. Stretch your arms above your head. Slowly bend down to touch your toes. All of this may not take five minutes, but you will benefit from it for hours!

- Take advantage of everyday opportunities to exercise—such as taking the stairs even when there is an elevator, or walking to lunch instead of driving. You will feel more energetic during the day.

- Set realistic expectations for yourself. Trying to meet unrealistic expectations is a sure-fire way to cause stress.

- Finally, do something pleasant during your non-working hours. Find a hobby you enjoy. Develop other interests by joining civic or service organizations. Do something helpful for someone else. And while you're at it, do something nice for you. After all, you've worked hard and deserve it!—BLAKE WILLIAMS

## AT WORK AT DYNAMICS: Simulation 1

DYNAMICS is a local manufacturer of health and fitness products, which are distributed nationwide. Last week your teacher announced that several local firms, including DYNAMICS, were hiring temporary office personnel to work after school, on Saturdays, and during the holidays. You and several of your classmates completed resumés and sent them to the firms. You were invited for an interview with Miss Joy Lancaster, human resources manager of DYNAMICS. You felt that the interview went very well. Yesterday, Miss Lancaster telephoned you to offer you a job. She asked that you give her an answer within a week. You liked the company, so after two days you called and accepted the job.

At your first meeting with Miss Lancaster after you were hired, you learned that you would be working at the headquarters complex. This complex has approximately 2,500 manufacturing employees and 170 management and office employees. In addition, DYNAMICS employs a select group of temporary office workers to help during peak work periods and to fill in during employee vacations. Working as a "temporary" will be an excellent opportunity for you to learn about the various functions and activities of different divisions of DYNAMICS. At the conclusion of your meeting with her, Miss Lancaster said, "I'm certain you will enjoy working here. We always look for responsible employees who are conscientious about completing their work assignments. I know you will do a fine job."

Your job assignments will be coordinated by Miss Lancaster, who will assign you to different divisions as the need arises. Turn to your *Information Processing Activities* workbook to learn of your first assignment at DYNAMICS.

# INFORMATION PROCESSING

# Chapter 5

# Information Processing: An Overview

One of the most challenging tasks facing business today is managing information. Practically all those who work in business require some type of information in order to do their jobs properly. That information must be organized for easy reference and must be up to date to be useful. Most businesses—whether single proprietorships or giant corporations—have someone responsible for reviewing new technological methods and equipment in information processing. Such new methods and equipment are viewed as potential means of improving the management information systems presently used.

You, as an office worker, may participate in answering the question "Should changes be made in the way we maintain our information system?" This question leads to careful study of how tasks, including the ones you perform, are done and whether the purchase of new computer technology would be a wise expenditure. In some companies, after existing methods have been studied, the decision is made to introduce no changes. In other cases, there may be major changes over a period of time. Few companies have failed to evaluate their information systems. Increasingly, computer technology is being added.

As an office worker, you will participate in tasks that maintain the flow of information. You will want to understand the purpose and nature both of management information systems and of information processing systems so that you can perform your tasks in a meaningful manner. Comprehending the total system will make your job more interesting. This chapter helps you focus on the overall systems rather than on specific tasks of office employees.

The objectives of the chapter are to

- acquaint you with the reasons businesses need management information systems and what a management information system is

- acquaint you with present-day and emerging information processing systems

# Topic 1

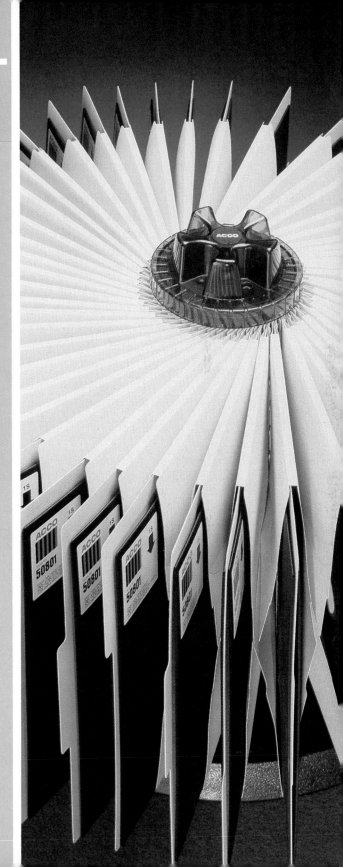

## INFORMATION SYSTEMS IN MODERN ORGANIZATIONS

When you have completed your study of this topic, you will be able to

- explain why information systems are important in today's organizations

- describe what a management information system is

- describe the relationship between a management information system and an information processing system

You have undoubtedly heard that this is the Information Age. It is a time when everyone—regardless of the activity underway—has much use for information. Modern companies require a great deal of up-to-date information.

*A company manufactures automobiles and sells them through dealers in every part of the country. The headquarters office, via computer network, gets a report of the number of sales at each dealership at the end of each day's business. Plans for production are influenced by the pattern of sales.*

*A large retail store is able to accumulate details of inventory levels as sales are recorded at the cash registers throughout the store and transmitted to the computer center. The manager of inventories has immediate access to what items are selling and what items are still on hand. Decisions about what should be purchased are influenced by this constant flow of information.*

From your own understanding of business activity, you realize that *systems, management,* and *procedures* are key words in any business that strives to be successful. Because so much information is required, the following aspects of businesses have been developed:

- *systems* for the organization of information
- methods for *management* of information systems
- *procedures* that guarantee timely and accurate flow of information

Today's business managers focus much attention, therefore, on their need for information. As an office worker, you will assume an important role in assuring users of the information you process that the information is accurate and timely.

**Illus. 5–1.** Information *must* be kept up to date and accurate.

## WHAT INFOR-MATION IS

Information is a general term for all types of organized facts, policies, procedures, and other details that modern business must have readily available for the completion of activities.

> *The manager of payroll must have information about hours worked by each employee in order to prepare paychecks.*

> *The office worker in the shipping department must have information about the date each shipment was made to answer a customer's inquiry as to when a particular shipment was made.*

> *The secretary in the sales office must have information about the sales manager's travel plans in order to prepare an itinerary.*

Information in business takes several forms. The most common forms are identified in Illus. 5-2. As you know, though, some words are used with varying meanings. For example, note that in Illus. 5-2 the term *data* refers to numbers. However, in some instances the word *data* is used to mean any type of unprocessed detail. When processed and organized, such *data* become *information*.

| COMMON TYPES OF INFORMATION | |
| --- | --- |
| **Type** | **Examples** |
| **data** | amounts, quantities, sizes, weights, capacities, ages |
| **text** | words organized to convey meaning, as in letters, memorandums, or reports |
| **image** | charts, graphs, photographs |
| **voice** | messages conveyed in person; messages conveyed by telephone |

**Illus. 5–2.** These are the most common types of information.

> *Donna, an office assistant, was asked to find out how many people each conference room in the building would accommodate. When she had obtained the information and had prepared a simple report, she said to her supervisor, "Here are the data you requested." Donna was using data to mean "bits of information" about conference room capacity.*

*Ms. Raines said to Hugh, her assistant, "Please take all this data and prepare a list of best-selling books in alphabetic order." The executive was using data to mean unorganized details — all words — of names of books, their authors, and their publishers.*

**Illus. 5–3.** Data in the form of figures can be presented attractively in graph form.

## NEED FOR INFORMATION SYSTEMS

Can you think of a recent occasion when you called or visited a business office or retail store with a question? Did the person with whom you talked have an organized way of locating information for you? Think of calling a retail store to find out why something you ordered was not delivered. You would not expect the person responding to your inquiry to *remember* what happened. You would expect the employee to locate quickly the record of what you ordered and the store's schedule for delivery. You would expect the store to have an explanation for the delay in delivery. In fact, if the store's employee told you, "I don't really know what happened — we have no record of your purchase," you might wonder whether you should shop at the store again.

There are a number of reasons for the value of information in business. You should understand these reasons because they will help you see the importance of every information-processing task you perform.

### Complexity of Business

*complex:* made up of several interrelated components

Even a small business is quite *complex* in the present-day world. In a very small business, the owner may take care of all activity. The owner might try to keep all information about the business in his/her memory and may believe that all business people with whom he/she interacts could do the same. Picture the following situation:

> *Joanne is the owner/manager of a newsstand at a busy downtown street corner. She sells one morning paper and one afternoon paper only. She keeps her cash in a box. Her papers are delivered twice a day, and she pays for them in cash out of the box. She pays the rent on the stand in cash from the box each Friday. Any other business payments are made from this cash.*
>
> *Only on Friday afternoons does she count the cash, taking out what she will not need to pay for papers on Monday morning. She takes the cash not needed for papers to the bank to deposit.*
>
> *Joanne has all her business information in her head, except for the cash deposit that is recorded each Friday at the bank. She gets no receipt for the payment of her rental fee or for her payments for the deliveries of newspapers. She has been doing business with the same people for two years, and she trusts them to remember that she has paid her obligations, just as she has remembered.*

What do you think of such an information system? Joanne does not have a good system because she is relying on her memory. She is not likely to make good decisions because she will not recall important details accurately. Joanne could develop an effective information system by doing two things.

1. By setting up records of:
   - number of papers received at each delivery and amount paid
   - number of unsold papers
   - amount received from the sale of each paper
   - amounts deposited in the bank
   - amounts taken for personal purposes
   - amounts paid for rent and other expenses
2. By maintaining the records in up-to-date fashion so that she is able to:
   - estimate how many papers she should order in the future
   - determine whether or not she is actually paid for each paper (that is, that the amount of cash received during the sale of a paper equals the number delivered less the number unsold multiplied by the price per paper)
   - determine how much she is earning each day and each week
   - know accurately how much money is being used for personal purposes

*interrelated:* having
something in common

As you now can see, there is much to be gained from organizing information—even in a small business that is owned and managed by a single person. Efficient organization of information will be *more* critical in large organizations with thousands of employees. You will find that the jobs of employees in a large organization are *interrelated* and that many workers need the same information. Key executives in a large organization must have information about the total organization in order to make decisions. It is not possible to get such information solely through first-hand observation. Key executives must rely on the information provided by others.

*controller:* the chief
accounting officer of
a business

*The **controller** in the home office of a large manufacturer of household linens is responsible for all financial information management. Every week, the controller receives a report from each of the six plants in four southern states. The weekly reports give the controller a way of knowing what is being produced and what the total production costs are.*

## Volume of Transactions

Organizations must deal with thousands of transactions each day. Consider the following examples:

- banks process millions of checks, receive millions of deposits, and issue millions of dollars in cash each day
- insurance companies receive thousands of premium payments, issue thousands of new policies, and send out notices to thousands of customers each day
- manufacturing companies complete the production of millions of products, ship thousands of orders, and receive payments from thousands of customers each day

*adequate:* satisfactory

Think of the problems that would occur if the organizations did not maintain *adequate* information. The volume of transactions would be overwhelming in a bank that kept customer accounts in no particular order. The tasks of processing and keeping track of many transactions of the same type have motivated companies to set up efficient information systems.

*As you may recall from your study of American history, the first business letters in the Colonies were carefully written in longhand, often by the owner of the business. As business increased, letter writing often was delegated to a clerk with an especially attractive handwriting style.*

*Can you imagine a large, modern corporation sending a letter to its 200,000 shareholders by having a staff of assistants write the letters by hand? How long would the task take if 20 assistants worked at it full time?*

As an office worker, you will help keep your company's information system current and accurate. You will follow procedures that allow you to process numerous transactions in the most efficient way possible.

**Illus. 5–4.** "Allan, I can't believe you don't remember where you filed that account! The Olmstead file should be right here after the Glenn file."

## Central Concern for Timely Information

Information must be available when needed. When business managers ask for information, they do not want to be told that it will be available in approximately two weeks. Customers do not expect to wait weeks for answers to their inquiries. In fact, the general public is aware of the technological developments that

**instantaneous:** occurring without delay

make possible almost ***instantaneous*** communication. People expect such communication technology to result in getting needed information quickly. Furthermore, that information is expected to be up to date.

*Modern airlines have been able to maintain an international network of service because of the availability of timely information. It is possible to call an airlines office, request a reservation for a flight between two cities anywhere in the world, and get information about the availability of seats immediately. Customers requesting reservations are not willing to receive a response such as: "We are happy to have your reservation. We can let you know in about a week whether or not we have a seat available."*

## Value of Accurate Information

Information that is not accurate is worthless. Accurate information is required so that quality decisions can be made throughout a company. Accurate information means that plans can be effectively made. Think of the value of accurate information in each of the following examples:

*A company keeps detailed information about its need for cash. It also knows exactly how much cash is on hand. Therefore, the company is able to transfer cash not needed immediately to accounts that earn interest. The company earns money because it has accurate information about cash. If this information were not available, there would be no way to determine if some of the cash on hand could be temporarily invested.*

**Illus. 5–5.** Accurate information is necessary in order for office workers and managers to make decisions.

*A publishing company sells books to bookstores with the provision that unsold books can be returned. The company maintains and updates a record of what the sales actually are in the various bookstores throughout the country. Decisions about reprinting are made not only on the basis of how many books are still in the company warehouse but also on the basis of the number of books unsold in all the bookstores throughout the country.*

## MANAGEMENT INFORMATION SYSTEMS

Large volumes of information are not likely to be of much use to modern businesses unless they are properly organized and easily accessed. In recent years, the availability of electronic equipment has caused much attention to be focused on appropriate ways of organizing information.

**Illus. 5–6.** "Organized information" is an important key to the success of a management information system.

A number of terms are used for the total information a business maintains. You will hear references to information systems, and to management information systems, or MIS. A management information system is essentially all the facts, decisions, policies, and interpretations that form the organized pool of information resources for everyone who participates in the activities of a company. A key word in this definition is "organized," which implies that there is a system. A *system* is a logical structure that is evident throughout the collection of information. Furthermore, a system means that there is clear understanding of how to collect information, how to update information, and how to delete information.

*A company treasurer needed to know if a bank in which the company maintained an account had received a particular deposit. The treasurer called the bank to inquire about the deposit. The response from a bank employee was: "Oh, goodness, we are now recording deposits of two weeks ago. I have no idea when we will get to the deposits of this week." The company treasurer was surprised at such a response. The treasurer expected the bank to have up-to-date information at all times. Do you think the treasurer might have some thoughts about changing banks if such failure to provide timely information continued?*

Timely information is critical when an organization is dealing with its customers and other outsiders. However, the demand for timely information is just as critical within organizations. Progress in getting tasks done sometimes is impeded because timely information is unavailable. Decisions about what should be done cannot be made until the results of past decisions are available.

## Organization of Management Information Systems

Management information systems differ from company to company. Often the company's information system is organized along functional lines, like the tasks in the company. Look at Illus. 5-7 to see the organization of Manson Furniture Manufacturing Company. The functions of finance, marketing, and manufacturing are the primary divisions of the total company. In such a company, there may be a separate management information system for each function. Look again at Illus. 5-7 and notice the kind of information maintained by each of the three divisions of Manson Furniture Manufacturing Company. For example, all the information required for all persons having responsibility for financial matters is maintained as a separate collection. If someone from another division of the company needs information from the financial division, for example, a telephone call or a memorandum is necessary.

In some companies, there is a single *management information system*. This means that all information for the several divisions of the company is maintained as one collection. Generally, such systems are maintained in computer memories.

Although maintained as a single collection, all the information is not available to everyone. Access to information is carefully determined since matters of confidentiality and privacy are critical. This subject will be discussed in more detail in Topic 2 of this chapter.

In the early stages of getting acquainted with a new job, you will learn how the information in the company is organized for administrative purposes. You also will be informed about the procedures you are to use to get the information required to complete tasks delegated to you.

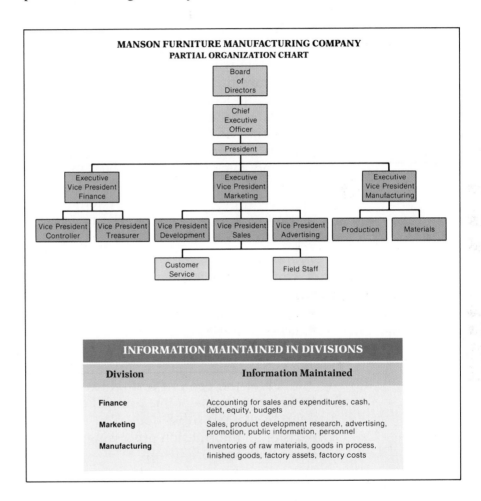

Illus. 5–7.

## Administration of a Management Information System

As companies are increasingly giving attention to the overall design of their management information systems, new positions are being created. Within a company there is likely to be one executive who has overall responsibility for the company's management information system. Under the direction of this executive are other executives responsible for specific subsystems. A subsystem is a unit of a system. There also may be employees who spend all their time reviewing parts of the subsystems and making recommendations for significant improvements in the management information system as a whole.

## INFORMATION PROCESSING SYSTEMS

There could not be an effective, efficient management information system without a companion information processing system. Sometimes the two are considered as a single system. However, because the focus of your studies is information processing, the processing system is spotlighted in this book as if it were a separate entity. An information processing system is defined as the policies and procedures for the efficient flow of data, text, images, and voice organized to meet the needs of the company.

Just as management information systems are subdivided in a manner appropriate to a particular company, so is an information processing system. The most commonly identified subsystems are:

- word/text processing
- data processing
- records management
- reprographics
- distribution/transmission

Much of the content of this textbook deals with information processing. At this point, you will be introduced to a brief identification of each subsystem. You then will understand how the parts of an information processing system are interrelated as you study each in more detail.

### Word/Text Processing

Office workers who are responsible for word/text processing transform what originators create (primarily with words) into output that is communicated to a wide variety of recipients. Note the summary of tasks performed by word/text processing employees in Illus. 5-8. You will learn about procedures for word/text processing in Chapters 6 and 7.

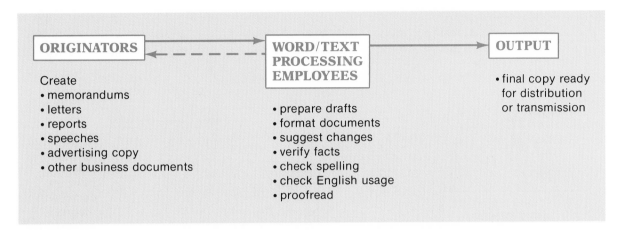

**Illus. 5–8.**

### Data Processing

Numbers are very important to most businesses. Therefore, transforming numbers into useful information is what office workers in data processing departments do. Such workers classify, sort, record, and merge numbers in the preparation of useful reports. Note the summary of tasks performed by data processing employees in Illus. 5-9 on page 170. You will learn about some common data processing tasks in Chapters 8 and 9.

### Records Management

The main concern of records managers is to ensure that information is stored according to the plan designed for the management information system and can be retrieved readily. Office workers who are responsible for records management spend their time storing and retrieving information. Note the summary of tasks performed by records management employees shown in Illus. 5-10 on page 170. You will learn about policies and procedures for records management in Chapters 12 and 13.

### Reprographics

Office workers who prepare copies through the use of copying and duplicating equipment are specialists in reprographics. Common tasks for such workers are shown in Illus. 5-11 on page 171. You will learn more about this important subsystem of information processing in Chapters 10 and 13.

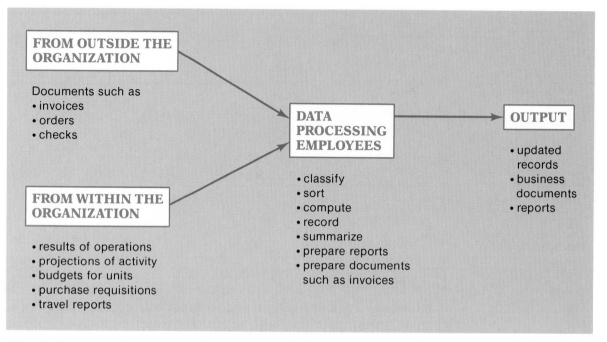

**Illus. 5–9.**

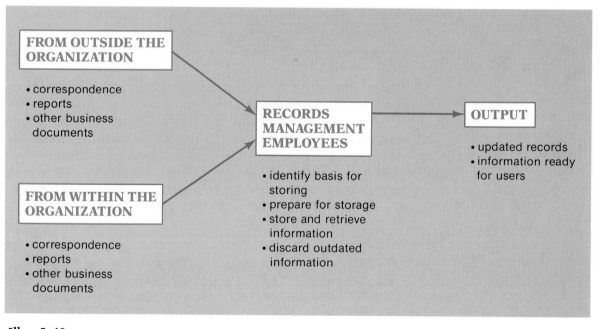

**Illus. 5–10.**

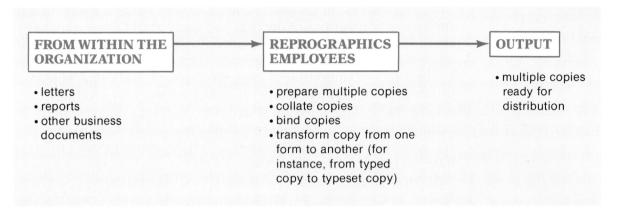

**Illus. 5–11.**

## Distribution/Transmission

Seeing that information ready for forwarding to recipients is processed promptly is the responsibility of office workers who carry out distribution/transmission tasks. More and more, such workers are using telecommunications that have markedly increased the speed of sending messages. However, postal services are still used for the distribution of much written communication. Note the summary of tasks performed by employees in Illus. 5-12. You will learn more about this important subsystem of information processing in Chapters 14 and 15.

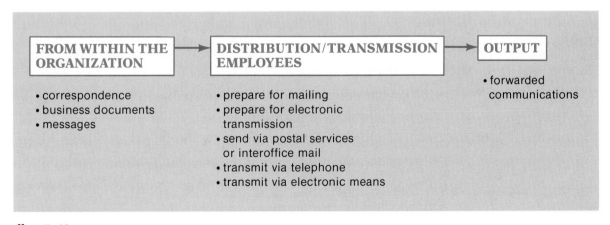

**Illus. 5–12.**

## THE ROLE OF OFFICE WORKERS

As you learned in Chapter 1, office workers play a major role in modern organizations. Now that you understand what a management information system and an information processing system are, you can understand better the importance of these systems to the efficient operation of modern business. Data that is part of a company's management information system changes constantly. New data must be added. Current data must be updated or deleted. Once a management information system is in place, its success depends on competent office workers who process data accurately and efficiently.

In this topic, you learned that an information processing system is the means for keeping a company's management information system complete and up to date. Information processing is almost a continuous activity since much of what happens each business day results in some change in a company's total collection of information. You see, therefore, that the quality of a management information system is dependent on office workers performing their information processing tasks competently.

## REVIEW QUESTIONS

1. What is information?

2. What are common forms of information?

3. What problems can a businessperson face if he or she keeps no records but simply relies on memory?

4. What would be likely to happen in a bank if the volume of transactions was high but there were no established procedures for processing the transactions?

5. How does timely information aid a company's employees in responding to customer inquiries?

6. Why would a company want accurate information?

7. What is a management information system?

8. How does an information processing system differ from a management information system?

9. What are the five most commonly identified subsystems of an information processing system?

10. Describe in a general way how the input for data processing employees differs from the input for word/text processing employees.

## INTERACTING WITH OTHERS

Vicki, an office assistant in a recently established office responsible for special promotional activities, has had to learn much of what she does from oral instructions given by the department manager. Vicki is competent; she has been able to implement all the instructions given her by the manager. The work of the office is done without any problems.

One morning, while the manager and Vicki are talking about the work for the day, the manager says: "Vicki, this memorandum has just come from our systems manager. We're being asked to prepare written procedures for what we do in this new department. Why don't we start with your recording all the procedures you have so skillfully developed thus far for all recurring activity?"

If you were Vicki, what comment would you make at this point in your meeting with the manager? What questions might you ask in order to clarify what you should do?

**What You Are To Do:**   Prepare a brief response to the questions raised.

## EXTENDING YOUR MATH SKILLS

Assume that you are an office worker in the central office of a professional organization that sponsors seminars for various occupational groups. Just recently the company completed a series of seminars in five cities throughout the United States. The standard fee for each participant at one seminar was $700. However, two of the seminars (Update on Software for Business and Assessing New Technology) had a $500 fee per participant. You were given the task of calling the manager at each seminar site and getting enrollment figures for the several courses. On page 174 are the details you recorded from your telephone calls.

**What You Are To Do:**   Using a sheet of plain paper, write the titles of each of the five seminars on a separate line. Set up columns that will aid you in the following computations:

1. the total number of participants for each seminar for all five cities considered together
2. the total revenue earned from each seminar for all five cities considered together
3. the total number of participants in each city for all five seminars considered together
4. the grand total of participants for all seminars in all cities

| TITLE OF SEMINAR | NUMBER OF PARTICIPANTS | | | | |
|---|---|---|---|---|---|
| | BOSTON | NEW YORK | WASHINGTON | CHICAGO | SAN FRANCISCO |
| Management Information Systems for Small Offices January 6-10, 19-- | 125 | 245 | 110 | 117 | 97 |
| Controlling and Managing Computerized Management Information Systems February 15-18, 19-- | 105 | 325 | 175 | 130 | 110 |
| Security for a Computer System March 1-4, 19-- | 78 | 110 | 45 | 72 | 70 |
| Update on Software for Business March 19-22, 19-- | 170 | 295 | 140 | 110 | 115 |
| Assessing New Technology April 1-5, 19-- | 210 | 410 | 175 | 102 | 117 |

## APPLICATION ACTIVITY

Assume that you are employed in the office of a weekly newspaper devoted to computers. One of the reporters gives you the rough draft which follows. The notes are from an interview with the Manager of Information Services at Seagrove Pharmaceutical Co.

**Word/text processing equipment can be used to complete this activity.**

**What You Are To Do:** Key (type) a revised copy of the interview. Key the word *INTERVIEW* on line 10. Use your own judgment with regard to line length. Make all corrections noted. If necessary, refer to Reference Section A for information about standard proofreader's marks.

INTERVIEW
*September 22, 19--*

REPORTER
QUESTION:  What is the priority of office automation in a giant
           company such as Seagrove Pharmaceutical?

LISA HOLT
RESPONSE:  It's mixed.  Obviously, when you have different operat-
           ing companies, there are different priorities.  We
           started a decade ago to look at office automation and
           personal computers.  We actually bought our first
           personal computer about nine years ago.

REPORTER
QUESTION:  What services are presently available through your
           system?

LISA HOLT
                                                    *four*
RESPONSE:  We offer a variety of services to ~~all five~~ floors of
           our building.  There's electronic mail and electronic
           messaging.  We can also transfer documents--we do a
           great deal of that.                      *electronically*

REPORTER
QUESTION:  Will you expand to more floors?

LISA HOLT
RESPONSE:  As the need arises, we will respond.  One of the reasons
           we started slowly was to give ourselves time to learn
           about local area networks and their impact upon office
           automation.  It was our belief early on that we would
    *be*    soon doing work much differently than we'd done in the
           past.  Things began to change as soon as we put in our
           first workstations with computer capabilities.  We've
           learned a lot from those early pilot studies!

REPORTER
QUESTION:  What have you learned?   *specifically*

LISA HOLT
RESPONSE:  One very important lesson is that relationships between
           people change.  Let's take the case of a secretary who
           works for two executives.  In the past, the secretary
           was directly involved in the document preparation task.
           Both executives would dictate letters and memos and
           the secretary would transcribe them at ~~the~~ typewriter.
           Now that both executives have computer terminals on  *it*
           their desks, they can ~~compose~~ documents and send ~~them~~
           electronically to the terminal at the secretary's work-
                                            *edit*
           station.  The secretary can either ~~process~~ the docu-
           ment and print a final copy or send the document
           electronically to the word processing center for pro-
           cessing.  We're also finding that some executives
           prefer to edit and print their own documents.  That
           way, the secretary may not even see the document before
           it is ready for distribution!

# Topic 2

## ORGANIZATION AND TECHNOLOGY FOR INFORMATION PROCESSING

When you have completed your study of this topic, you will be able to

- describe a manual information processing system
- describe a computer-assisted information processing system
- describe an integrated electronic information processing system

Currently, as you learned in Topic 1 of this chapter, much attention is given to the most appropriate organization and technology for information systems. A large company considers each of its offices as a separate unit when reviewing the adequacy of the information processing system. Different offices perform different functions. Therefore, it is not always possible to have the same level of efficiency and effectiveness with the same organization and technology.

You are likely to experience firsthand how offices are changing to become more productive. The technological advances reflected in equipment encourage companies to analyze their information processing systems and introduce changes. In many companies, the discussions and analyses require the services of a number of specialists. The employees whose tasks will be affected if changes are recommended and put into effect are also involved. You will enjoy your participation in reviewing what you do and how your work would be done if a different organization and different equipment were used. To help in such an analysis, you may be asked to keep a complete record of what you do. The person responsible for the overall task generally needs to know how many times you are doing the same task, how often you must make judgments about how something is done, and what you accomplish during a given time period. At times, an analysis results in the conclusion that changes should be made. At other times, the conclusion is that no changes should be made.

*Mr. Arroyo, an executive in a large company, attended a conference where an amazing new robot was exhibited. The manufacturers claimed that the robot could replace a human receptionist—even to the point of answering questions raised by visitors.*

*Mr. Arroyo thought the robot might be an effective and efficient addition to the company. To determine whether a robot could really do the job, he asked Nick, one of the receptionists, to tape record all conversation Nick had with visitors to the reception area.*

*After a week, an analysis was made of the conversations. Mr. Arroyo concluded that there were too many different types of discussions and that the receptionist needed to exercise too much independent judgment for a robot to be successful. The robot was not recommended for purchase.*

A discussion of how information processing systems can be organized and equipped follows. This discussion will help you understand why present-day organizations constantly review office operations. Only through careful review and analysis can an organization be assured that the information processing system is as good as it can be for dealing with current and *emerging* tasks.

*emerging:* in the process of being developed

## A MANUAL SYSTEM FOR INFORMATION PROCESSING

*economical:* done with the least expense

A manual system for information processing relies primarily on the skills of office personnel. There is limited help from technology. You will often find manual systems in very small offices where there are few transactions and in offices where there is much variety in what is done. It is not considered *economical* to use computers in offices where many different tasks are done but no one task is repeated often.

**Illus. 5–13.** You may work in an office where information processing tasks are completed using a manual system.

*systematically:* me-
thodically; in a regular
and predictable manner

Information processing follows essentially the same cycle, however, whether you are using manual or computer procedures. The
basic cycle is shown in Illus. 5-14. Notice that it includes *input,
processing, output, distribution/transmission,* and *storage/retrieval.*
The term "cycle" implies that data is transformed **systematically**
into usable information. Remember that the output of one information system often is the input for another system.

---

### INFORMATION PROCESSING CYCLE

| | |
|---|---|
| INPUT | Words and figures accepted by an employee or computer. |
| PROCESSING | Transforming input into a prescribed form; for instance, keying a handwritten letter or preparing a sales order from a computer's purchase order. |
| OUTPUT | Producing what was processed in a form that can be transmitted to others or in a form that updates computer-maintained records. |
| DISTRIBUTION/ TRANSMISSION | Forwarding the output to designated recipients. |
| STORAGE/ RETRIEVAL | Saving and accessing output according to the records management system. |

**Illus. 5–14.** Information
Processing Cycle

Actually, a **manual information processing system** can be defined as a system where office employees do the processing with
the aid of basic office equipment.

*Leah works in the office of an importer of high-quality antique rugs.
The company specializes in one-of-a-kind rugs for a limited number of
customers. A general office manager and six additional workers are in
the small office. Leah's workstation includes an electric typewriter, a
small calculator, and a telephone. She was surprised to learn that the
inventory for the rugs was maintained on cards on which she was to
write in longhand!*

## Organization

In a manual information processing system, there must be clearly specified tasks for each office employee. Additionally, the office employee must have complete instructions about each processing detail to provide the quality of performance expected. Consider a small office for a company that manufactures sweaters for children.

*An office staff of five is responsible for the information processing tasks required by the work of the executives, sales representatives, and factory foremen. From the design of sweaters to the payments for sales, the office workers perform vital tasks. They make telephone calls, prepare letters and purchase orders, process incoming orders, and record and deposit checks. To aid the office workers, the executives purchased electric typewriters, telephones, files, and workstations, as well as supplies.*

*In Illus. 5-15, you will note some major tasks for each of the five employees in the office. Each office employee is held responsible for specific tasks. Yet, in such a small office, you are likely to find much cooperation among employees, since each understands the job of the others. From the tasks listed for secretary and office assistant, how would you describe the differences between their assigned tasks?*

### HEIDI'S CHILDREN'S SWEATERS, INC.
### PROCESSING TASKS OF OFFICE PERSONNEL

| Mail/Messenger Clerk | Secretary | Receptionist/ Typist | Office Assistant | Bookkeeper |
|---|---|---|---|---|
| • opens mail | • reads incoming mail and distributes to executives | • answers telephone calls | • keeps records of inventory | • records sales |
| • delivers mail | | • greets callers | • determines when items must be purchased | • records payments |
| • takes orders to wholesalers | • composes letters and memos | • makes appointments | | • keeps all employee payroll records |
| • takes mail to post office | • types letters from machine dictation | • keeps travel schedules for executives | • files all correspondence and forms | • writes checks |
| • delivers packages in the city | • retypes and proofreads letters and memos | • prepares purchase orders | • makes bank deposits | |
| | • places telephone calls | • types form letters | | |
| | • answers telephone calls | | | |

**Illus. 5–15.**

## Equipment

Office workers functioning within a manual processing system usually have some equipment to help them in performing their tasks. It is important for you to understand these basic types of equipment.

### Typewriters

The most common typewriter in an office with a manual system is the electric typewriter. There are, of course, a few manual typewriters, especially in offices where little time is required to do the few typing tasks that occur. The electric typewriter you will have available may or may not have a correcting device. As you know, you will have to make all formatting decisions as you undertake each keyboarding task.

One of the first steps in changing from a manual system to a computer-assisted system is the introduction of electronic typewriters to replace electric ones. You will learn more about electronic typewriters in Chapter 7. Regardless of the kind of typewriter you use, you should find available a detailed instruction manual supplied by the manufacturer.

### Calculators

Machines that perform calculations for you reduce the time you will need to process numbers. Such machines help you in the basic arithmetic processes of adding, subtracting, multiplying, and dividing. But your particular machine may also have features that simplify many business computations. For example, there may be an automatic constant for multiplication and division and for chain calculations. See Illus. 5-16 for an example of the use of an *automatic constant*. There may also be *non-add keys* that print numbers which do not become part of your calculations. In Illus. 5-16 you will see an example of the use of a non-add key. Indeed, newer types of electronic calculators have capabilities which simplify many computations.

### Photocopiers

There is some type of photocopying machine in most offices today. The features vary considerably on photocopiers. You may encounter a basic machine that requires hand feeding of each sheet and does not permit copying on both sides of a sheet of paper. Or you may have available a machine that automatically feeds the sheets you want to copy, allows copying on both sides

***accommodates:*** permits; makes room for

of each sheet, ***accommodates*** varying sizes of sheets, and permits reduction or enlargement of the size of the text you are photocopying. Instructions for use of the features often are maintained at the machine itself. You will learn more about these machines in Chapter 11.

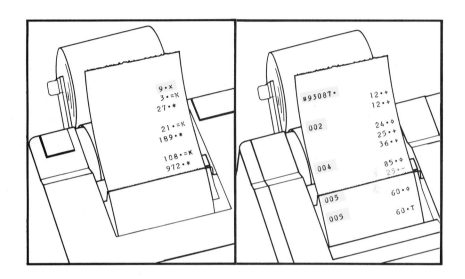

**Illus. 5–16.** Automatic constant and non-add keys are two features of some calculators.

### *Telephones and Postal Equipment*

Telephones are standard equipment in all offices. You may have a telephone with several lines. You also may have a telephone with special features, such as call forwarding. The telephone company provides detailed instructions so that you know how to use your telephone properly. More information about telephone services and equipment will be presented in Chapter 15.

Offices generally prepare their own outgoing mail and provide scales and postage meters for employees to use when preparing mail. Such equipment is relatively easy to use, and instructions are generally available if any questions arise. Chapter 14 provides more information on this topic.

## The Critical Role of Office Workers

The critical component in information processing is the skill and understanding that the workers themselves possess. There are often detailed procedures for each processing task you are asked to do. Furthermore, your general processing skills which you have been developing in your business courses (such as key-boarding, business communications, and business math) are of much value in such manual processing systems. For example, your ability to format letters and memos properly and to proof-read carefully are essential skills in an effective manual word/text processing system. Knowing how to check your calculations when you are preparing a weekly payroll means that no employee's pay will be inaccurately determined.

**Illus. 5–17.** Businesses need many employees who possess a variety of different skills.

While you have been introduced to the manual system as though it applied to every aspect of an office's activities, you must remember that many offices have what might be called a *mixed system of processing*. For example, this means that an office may use electronic typewriters for word/text processing but use simple calculators for all data processing. Since offices are under-going changes, there is no way of predicting what kind of office you will work in when you accept your first job. Increasingly, though, you will be using equipment that simplifies more and more processing tasks.

**COMPUTER-
ASSISTED
SYSTEMS**

*transform:* change
the form of

Since the introduction of the computer in business organizations in the mid-1950s, there has been a steady shift from manual to computer-assisted systems in many types of organizations. A computer-assisted information processing system is a logical series of procedures that enables a computer to *transform* data into meaningful information. There are few modern offices which have not introduced some aspects of computer operations into their information processing tasks.

Basically, what the computer provides is a transfer of processing tasks from human employees to an electronic processing method. Think for a moment of the way in which you prepare a letter at an electric typewriter. You must insert the paper, determine what your margins will be, determine where you should begin the date line and the letter address, and follow through on a number of decisions before you are at the end of the task. With a word processor, many of the decisions—and processing—would be taken care of merely by depressing an appropriate key or keys at your terminal.

You will encounter a variety of computer-assisted systems in offices. It is possible to identify three structures for computer systems. Additionally, there are common features of computer systems regardless of the specific equipment in use. The remainder of this topic is devoted primarily to helping you gain an understanding of the general nature of computers in an information processing system. With such an understanding, you will be able to adapt easily to the particular equipment you are expected to use in your office job. Note the information processing cycle when computer capability is available, shown in Illus. 5-18 on page 184.

## Organization

Information processing tasks often are restructured when a computer-assisted system is installed. The organization of the system is determined by the *particular* needs of the company.

*particular:* specific;
individual

### Centralized Structure

When all processing tasks or all processing tasks related to one phase of the company's activities are performed in a single location, the system is *centralized*. When all computer facilities are in one place, there is likely to be a single processing unit that handles all types of processing. However, the centralization may be by type of task. For example, all word/text processing may be performed in a word processing center. All data processing may be performed in a data processing center. With a centralized system, office employees throughout the company must provide the processing centers with the information in the format that is required for prompt processing.

*Sandra collects the time cards for workers in the factory. She organizes the information (regular and overtime hours worked) in the proper form for the data processing center. The payroll is actually prepared in the center and the checks are printed there.*

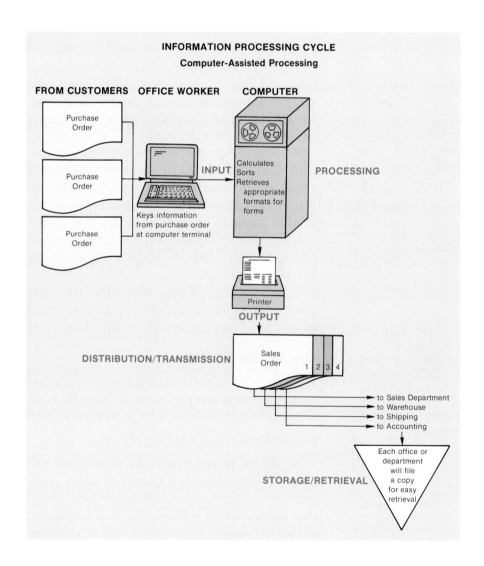

**Illus. 5–18.** A computer-assisted information processing system follows essentially the same cycle as does a manual information processing system. The cycle includes input, output, processing, distribution/transmission, and storage/retrieval.

### *Decentralized Structure.*

In the company where you choose to work you may find that computer facilities are located throughout the company. In a decentralized structure, there will be office employees in practically every department who work at computer terminals to carry out the processing tasks of their departments.

> *Kara and Brian work at word processing tasks in the consumer services department of a large manufacturer of kitchen appliances. They and two other employees handle all the word processing tasks for the entire department. There are similar clusters of word processors in departments throughout the company.*

### *Distributed Structure*

Many organizations have a distributed structure that combines features of centralized and decentralized structures. At one and the same time, a local office can carry out processing tasks and also interact with the computer *facilities* in another center where there is a central processing unit.

*facilities:* equipment or space established to serve a particular purpose

> *An organization of motels has a microcomputer at each motel as well as a mainframe computer at the headquarters office. Each motel is able to process information locally and to interact with the mainframe. A database of room availability is maintained at headquarters. Each location is able to get information about room availability at any of the motels through the connection with the mainframe. Office employees at the motels input the data for local use as well as for transmission to the mainframe computer.*

## Equipment

While references are often made to "the computer," there are actually many variations among computers now available. There are three types of computers commonly used in business. These are:

- mainframe computers
- minicomputers
- microcomputers

*Mainframe computers* are large, multipurpose machines that have traditionally done tasks such as payroll, accounting, and personnel recordkeeping for large organizations. *Minicomputers* are essentially smaller versions of mainframe computers. They can perform a wide variety of processing tasks. *Microcomputers* are the smallest of the three types of computers. A microcomputer system typically is made up of several interacting components. Microcomputers (also called micros or personal computers) are being used more and more by workers at all levels within organizations. Illus. 5-19 shows the three types of computers.

**Illus. 5–19.** Shown here are the three types of computers: mainframe computer (top left), mini-computer (top right), and microcomputer (bottom).

*distinctions:* differences

As new technological devices are introduced, the ***distinctions*** among types of computers become somewhat difficult to identify. Increasingly, companies are able to find computers that exactly match their own processing needs. Further, when you are at work in business you will find that many companies own several different types of computers to meet their varying needs.

As you have learned, a computer is essentially a processing machine. To accomplish processing tasks, every computer system includes:

- devices for inputting data and making data available for processing
- a central processing unit
- storage (memory) where data and information are retained for later use
- devices for outputting information to the people who need it

### Media for Inputting Data

Data that represent business transactions normally consist of handwritten, typewritten, or printed facts that can be understood by people. Before data can be processed by a computer, however, that data must be changed into a machine-readable form that the computer will understand.

Input media are the recording forms on which data are encoded in machine-readable formats. Some of the most common types of input media are:

- magnetic tapes
- magnetic cassettes
- magnetic disks
- magnetic diskettes

Some input forms are shown in Illus. 5-20 on page 188. Data captured on these media can be read automatically by computer-controlled devices.

Many office workers are employed to prepare data that can be read by a computer. These office workers typically use keyboards very similar to a typewriter keyboard to prepare magnetic tapes, cassettes, and diskettes. In effect, what the office worker is doing is storing the data on the appropriate medium for immediate or later processing. Computer systems where information is first stored on one of the media and later processed are known as *batch systems*. A system where the data inputted is immediately accepted by the computer for processing is called an *on-line system*. This means that you can use the keyboard of your terminal to enter data directly to the computer, since your terminal is connected to the computer.

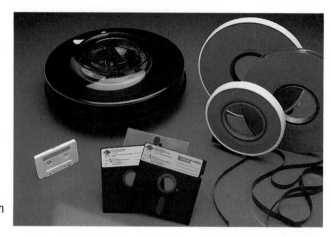

**Illus. 5–20.** Magnetic disks, tapes, cassettes, and diskettes are common types of input media.

### Central Processing Unit

*essence:* core; most important part

The computer's action (the processing of inputted data or words) takes place in the **central processing unit.** Here is the *essence* of a substitute for your human (or manual) processing of office tasks. Naturally, the central processing unit (CPU) must have a storage area to accept the inputted data. The CPU also is the location of the instructions that guide the processing to be completed. Some of the instructions are considered part of the hardware, while others which are specific to particular tasks to be performed are considered software.

### Storage

*sufficient:* adequate; providing what is needed

While *primary storage* is in the central processing unit, it is often not *sufficient* for all information retained by a computer system. Primary storage temporarily holds the data needed for the forthcoming processing task. To accommodate all of the data that computers process again and again, there is so-called *peripheral* or *secondary storage*. This is on line to the central processing units but is separate from the memory which is a component of the central processing unit. This type of storage is, in effect, memory of the computer system maintained outside of the central processing unit but *readily* available to the computer when needed.

*readily:* easily; quickly

**Illus. 5–21.** Magnetic tapes are a common secondary storage medium.

### Devices for Outputting Information

A computer must have at least one output device. An output device prints, displays, or records information in usable form. The most common output devices are terminals and printers. However, the output of a computer also may be in the form of magnetic tape, magnetic disks, diskettes, or microfilm. Illus. 5-22 shows output displayed on a terminal screen, and Illus. 5-23 shows output from a high-speed printer.

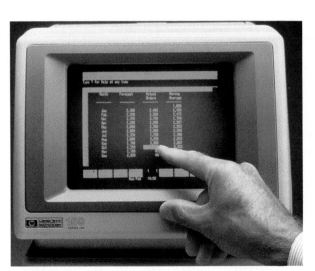

**Illus. 5–22 and 5–23.** Output could be displayed on a terminal screen or it could be in the form of a printout from a printer.

## Software

Computers are **versatile** because of software availability. Software is the general term for instructions that direct a computer in performing specific jobs. Software can be classified in a number of ways. For the purposes of this brief overview, two major classifications are noted: operating (or system) software and application software.

**Illus. 5–24.** Because of the wide variety of software available, computers can be used to perform many different tasks.

### Operating Software

A variety of programs is needed to set up the central processing unit to function properly and to handle common tasks. A program is a detailed set of instructions that guides the action of the central processing unit. The most common programs (software) in the category of *operating software* include:

- systems:      software which provides the instructions for guiding the input, processing, storage and output of a computer. Be aware that in some computers these instructions are a part of the hardware, while other computers (for example, a microcomputer with two floppy disk drives) require operating instruction software.
- compilers:    software which has the capability to translate symbolic language into machine language, which the central processing unit will "understand." The program translates a program written in COBOL or BASIC, which are called high-level languages, into a form acceptable to the central processing unit.

- utility:  software that handles common tasks of processing such as sorting, finding errors, and similar tasks.

### Application Software

*Application software* programs direct a wide range of specific tasks. Word processing programs will help you format, edit, store, and retrieve letters and reports. Data processing programs, such as spreadsheets, will permit a variety of calculations, statistical analyses, and *forecasts.* Other programs aid in the maintenance of files, inventories, and financial transactions, including accounts receivable and accounts payable.

*forecasts:* predictions based on information presently available

**OFFICE WORKERS' TASKS**

*tutorial:* an instructional guide to aid individual learning

While computers will assist you in handling tasks, you will find that there are still responsibilities which you must assume. You undoubtedly will find that you must learn to handle new equipment from time to time. Procedures manuals, demonstrations, training seminars, and *tutorial* disks all will aid you in gaining familiarity with the equipment you use.

**Illus. 5–25.**

THE WALL STREET JOURNAL

"Just act casual and try to remember which buttons you pushed."

From THE WALL STREET JOURNAL—permission Cartoon Features Syndicate.

You must remember that the power of the machines is simply an aid to you in completing your tasks. Machines are not able to do anything that you and other workers could not do. These machines have been introduced because they are able to process far more rapidly and more accurately than human employees. However, the value of having computer assistance is reduced if employees are not careful and thoughtful about the tasks they perform in relation to the computer-assisted processing activity.

## INTEGRATED ELECTRONIC SYSTEMS

The development of the totally integrated electronic information processing system is underway in American businesses. Companies are at varying stages of the transformation from computer-assisted systems to fully integrated systems. An integrated electronic system refers to the capability of computer units to transfer and accept data from each other. Integration of a total system is considered a worthwhile goal in many organizations.

When office systems are fully integrated, most, if not all, office employees will work at computer terminals. They will have instantaneous access to up-to-date information throughout the computer system.

*Cheryl is an administrative assistant in a large company. From time to time, she must get information from the sales department for use in a draft of a report she is keying for an executive. At such times, she must call the sales office where an employee can access a terminal to get the requested information.*

*If Cheryl were working at a desktop computer that was integrated with the mainframe or other microcomputers, she would be able to access her computer for the information. She would save considerable time by using her computer rather than making a telephone call and waiting for someone in another office to get the information for her.*

### Organization

Since totally integrated information processing systems are not yet widespread, it is not clear what the most appropriate plan of organization will be. It does seem clear that location is not critical, since information can be transmitted in seconds from one location to another. This means that companies may transfer some office functions from a central city location, for example, to a suburban or rural area some distance from the home offices.

In the process of integration, local area networks are developing. *Local area networks* (LANS) interconnect equipment within a

Helen considered keeping such a record a nuisance and something that would interfere with her getting her work done. She decided that she would just take the sheets home with her on Thursday evening and fill them in from memory. She would fill in the form for Friday then, too, because she would have a good idea of what she would be doing on Friday. The sheets were to be given to the supervisor at the end of the day on Friday.

**What You Are To Do:**  Evaluate Helen's decision. Would you have made the same decision in the same situation? Why? Why not? What might the supervisor have said to Helen that might have changed Helen's attitude toward keeping a record of her activities? Prepare an answer to each of the questions.

## EXTENDING YOUR ENGLISH SKILLS

The excerpt from a report to be sent to shareholders (on page 198) contains a number of punctuation and capitalization errors.

**What You Are To Do:**  Prepare a copy of the excerpt, making all corrections required in punctuation and in capitalization. If necessary, refer to Reference Section B for punctuation guidelines and to Reference Section C for capitalization guidelines. Underscore your corrections.

## APPLICATION ACTIVITY

Assume that you are an office assistant to Natalie B. McCardle, Manager of Information Systems at Pacific-First Bank. The bank has several branches throughout the metropolitan area. Mrs. McCardle has prepared a draft of a memo, which is on page 199. Mrs. McCardle says to you: "Please key this memo. Reprographics will make the needed copies. Also, compose a brief memo to Kenneth C. Withers, Vice President of Operations. Invite him to attend the demonstration and enclose a copy of the memo for his information. Please give me the completed memo to initial."

Word/text processing equipment can be used to complete this activity.

**What You Are To Do:**  Follow Mrs. McCardle's instructions, using two sheets of memo stationery from *Information Processing Activities* or plain paper.

In june of last year, the board of directors approved future expenditures from the reserve fund for two purposes

- for the acquisition of land the construction of a building in bergen county new jersey and for such moving and related costs as may be required in an amount not to exceed $2000000. As of june 30 of this year $1311000 had been transferred. The additional funds to complete the project were obtained through the issuance of $4000000 of industrial development bonds by the new jersey economic development authority.
- for the implementation of a comprehensive marketing and promotional effort in the amount of $300000. As of June 30 of this year $204500 had been expended.

The cash is held by a broker and earns interest at a rate which approximates the weekly 90-day u. s. treasury bill rate.

(Refer to this form when completing "EXTENDING YOUR ENGLISH SKILLS" activity on page 197.)

To:            All Branch Managers
From:          Natalie B. McCardle, Information Systems
Date:          October 20, 19--
Subject:       Voice Mail Demonstration

We think our experimental use of voice mail here in headquarters and at one office *branch* supports its introduction throughout the organization.

*of all branch managers* A meeting is planned for November 14 15 at 9:00 30 a.m. in the conference room here at the Embarcadero Center. We hope you can plan to attend. There will be a discussion of our experience s, a demonstration, and a tour of several offices so you can talk with personnel who use this means of communicating. The meeting will end no later than 11:00 30 a.m.

If you have any questions, just call my office.

(Refer to this form when completing "APPLICATION ACTIVITY" on page 197.)

## CHAPTER SUMMARY

Information is valuable in every organization, regardless of its size or purpose. As you have learned, the most common forms of information that you will find in business offices are data, text, image, and voice.

There are several reasons for the present-day need for information. Among the major reasons are complexity of business, volume of transactions, concern with timely information, and value of accurate information.

Companies currently are giving a great deal of attention to their management information systems because of the technology that has become available to them. A management information system is the organized collection of knowledge resources needed for the proper functioning of the business. Such a system may be organized according to the functions of the company, with each function maintaining its own system. Or the system may be one where all the information needs of the total organization are combined in an integrated system.

The effectiveness of a management information system is dependent on a good information processing system. An information processing system consists of all the policies and procedures for the flow of data and for the preparation of data in appropriate form. Common subsystems of an information processing system are:

- word/text processing
- data processing
- records management
- reprographics
- distribution/transmission

Information processing systems may be manual, computer-assisted, or integrated electronic. The tasks office workers perform will differ from one system to another. Office workers may perform tasks related to maintaining the security of the system. They also have responsibility for maintenance of diskettes.

### KEY TERMS

information

management information system

subsystem

information processing system

manual information processing system

computer-assisted information processing system

# Topic 1

## LETTERS

When you have completed your study of this topic, you will be able to

- describe how a letter conveys a positive initial impression
- describe the basic parts of a business letter
- prepare letters that are formatted according to commonly used standards

Each day millions of letters are processed by office workers in American businesses. These letters are extremely valuable in the total communications of companies.

Even though many companies are providing new equipment to assist their word/text processing employees, the need to understand the formats of letters persists. One of the most important contributions to your productivity as you prepare letters is your knowledge of the various parts of the business letter. You will want to use this opportunity to learn the letter parts thoroughly. This will reduce the occasions when you must check references to learn how you should format a particular part.

A standard format for a business letter increases efficiency. Both the person who prepares the letter and the recipient of the letter gain from a standardized format. You, as an office worker processing letters, will not need time to decide how to set up the letter. You will use a standard format that your company has established. And, when the recipient receives the letter, the task of reading and comprehending is simplified because the format is basically familiar.

*Walter works as a word/text processing operator for a large insurance company. During a typical day, he processes many business letters. Walter discovered very quickly that his knowledge of basic letter parts and their correct placement increased his efficiency in processing the documents.*

## A LETTER'S INITIAL IMPACT

The primary purpose of a business letter is to convey a message. However, even before the message is read, the recipient is likely to make a judgment about the letter and its sender. An attractively formatted letter on quality paper will encourage the recipient to read the message with care. On the other hand, a carelessly formatted letter on smudged paper may result in a negative attitude toward the sender and may fail to get close attention.

A letter gives a good first impression if it has the following characteristics:

- The margins, indentions, and spacing are pleasing to the eye.
- Each letter part is correctly placed within the letter.
- Appropriate stationery is used.
- There are no obvious erasures or strikeovers.
- The typed or printed letter is neat and clear.
- There are no smudges or fingerprints.

Make your letters as attractive as possible. If the appearance of the letter is pleasing to the eye, the receiver will want to read the letter.

## PARTS OF A BUSINESS LETTER

In Illus. 6-1 you will find all the parts that could be included in a business letter. Of course, few letters will include all these parts. There are some parts that generally are included in most letters, and there are parts that are included only when needed.

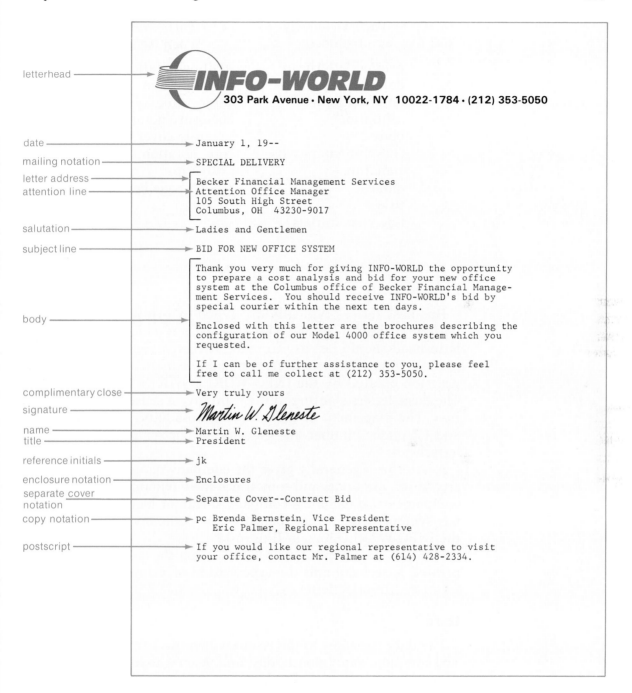

letterhead

**INFO-WORLD**
303 Park Avenue · New York, NY 10022-1784 · (212) 353-5050

date — January 1, 19--

mailing notation — SPECIAL DELIVERY

letter address —
attention line —
Becker Financial Management Services
Attention Office Manager
105 South High Street
Columbus, OH 43230-9017

salutation — Ladies and Gentlemen

subject line — BID FOR NEW OFFICE SYSTEM

body —
Thank you very much for giving INFO-WORLD the opportunity
to prepare a cost analysis and bid for your new office
system at the Columbus office of Becker Financial Management Services. You should receive INFO-WORLD's bid by
special courier within the next ten days.

Enclosed with this letter are the brochures describing the
configuration of our Model 4000 office system which you
requested.

If I can be of further assistance to you, please feel
free to call me collect at (212) 353-5050.

complimentary close — Very truly yours

signature — *Martin W. Gleneste*

name — Martin W. Gleneste
title — President

reference initials — jk

enclosure notation — Enclosures

separate cover — Separate Cover--Contract Bid
notation

copy notation —
pc Brenda Bernstein, Vice President
   Eric Palmer, Regional Representative

postscript —
If you would like our regional representative to visit
your office, contact Mr. Palmer at (614) 428-2334.

**Illus. 6-1.** Business letter shown in block format with open punctuation.

| Parts Generally<br>Included | Parts Added<br>When Needed |
|---|---|
| printed letterhead | mailing notation |
| date | attention line |
| letter address | subject line |
| salutation | enclosure notation |
| body | separate cover notation |
| complimentary close | copy notation |
| signature | postscript |
| name | second-page heading |
| title | |
| reference initials | |

## Printed Letterhead

Business letters typically are typed or printed on stationery with preprinted headings. This stationery is called *letterhead.* The letterhead should be easy to read, attractive, and representative of the company that sends it. For example, notice the positive impression created by the INFO-WORLD letterhead on page 207. The large letters slanting to the right give a sense of forward motion. The placement of the street address, city, state, ZIP Code, and telephone number gives a sense of horizontal balance to the letterhead.

A letterhead generally gives the company name, street address, city, state, ZIP Code, and sometimes the telephone number. Some companies also include a company slogan or logo. A logo is a letter, symbol, or sign that identifies the company. Can you locate the INFO-WORLD logo in Illus. 6-1?

Plan the placement of your letter so that the combination of the printed letterhead and the typewritten or printed message will form an attractive letter.

## Date

The date indicates to the reader when the letter was prepared. The complete date (month, day, and year) is used as the dateline. Abbreviated forms of the date are not acceptable in business writing, and *st, nd, rd,* or *th* is never used in the dateline of a business letter.

|                          |                            |
|--------------------------|----------------------------|
| Proper                   | Not Proper                 |
| January 2, 19--          | 1/2/--                     |
|                          | 2nd of January, 19--       |

Military offices (and offices where military style is used) key the date as follows: *28 February 19--.* Notice that the order is day, month, and year. Notice also that there is no punctuation.

*blueprint:* a detailed
outline or plan

Many companies have adopted standard formats for letters and other business documents. A standard format is a *blueprint* for arranging the document on the page. Standard letter format often specifies that the date should be entered or typed on a specific line (line 15 is a common placement) for all letters. Formatting documents and common letter and punctuation styles will be discussed later in this topic.

## Mailing Notations

Mailing notations are used when the letter requires some type of special postal service. Common services are *certified mail, registered mail, special delivery, insured mail,* and *air mail* (for overseas mail). When a special mailing service is used, you should identify that service by keying the appropriate notation a double space below the dateline. Be sure to use all capital letters for the mailing notation.

Mailing notations on the letter provide a record of the specific mail service used. Other notations, such as *PERSONAL* or *CONFIDENTIAL,* remind the reader of the nature of the letter's content. These other notations can be shown between the date and the letter address. Such notations also appear on the envelope to inform the mailroom staff that the envelope is to be delivered to the addressee without being opened.

## Letter Address

Complete information about the addressee is given in the letter address. The addressee is the organization or the person to whom the letter is directed. The letter address matches the information on the envelope, which includes:

- name
- title (when appropriate)
- department or division
- complete mailing address

By including the complete address on all letters, you will have a file copy that serves as a good reference for the organization's or person's address.

A common practice is to begin the letter address on the fourth line space below the date. If a mailing notation is used, the letter address is keyed a double space below it.

### Name and Title

The name of the addressee is keyed on the first line of the letter address. If the letter is addressed to more than one individual, each name should be keyed on a separate line. When more than one name is included in the address, the names are placed either in alphabetic order or in order of *prominence* (for example, Vice President before Office Manager).

*prominence:*
importance

```
Mrs. Janet L. Gollmar        Mr. Samuel F. Kusnerak
Mr. Kenneth G. Stewart       Vice President
                             Mrs. Martha A. Rutkowski
                             Office Manager
```

A courtesy or personal title should precede each name. Commonly used courtesy titles are *Mr., Ms., Mrs., Miss, Dr., Professor, The Honorable, Sister,* and *The Reverend.* When known, use the courtesy title the addressee prefers. If a woman's title *preference* is not known, use *Ms.* This is an acceptable title for either a single woman or a married woman and is being used more and more frequently. Also be careful to spell the addressee's name correctly. A misspelled name creates a negative impression for the reader. If you are unsure of the appropriate courtesy title or the correct spelling of a name, check previous correspondence received from that individual. As a last resort, call the individual's company and inquire about the courtesy title or the correct spelling of the name. There are a few companies where courtesy titles have been eliminated from all correspondence. This means that the addressee would be identified simply as *Patrick L. Plizga* or *Betsy J. Wells.*

*preference:*
one that is
liked better

Business titles (Marketing Manager, Personnel Director, Vice President) may be keyed either on the same line as the person's name or on the next line. The length of the business title will determine on which line it will be keyed. You want to achieve a balanced look within the lines of the letter address:

```
Ms. Maryann C. Appelt, Treasurer        Mr. Alfred L. Vinci
Amalgamated Plastics & Supply Co.       Advertising Manager
921 California Avenue                    Leisure Sports
Pittsburgh, PA  15202-9481               5110 Transit Boulevard
                                         Buffalo, NY  14221-3741
```

### Company Name

The name of the company should be keyed exactly as the company name appears on the letterhead. For example, if the letterhead shows Reynolds, Frazier, & Crum, you would not use Reynolds, Frazier, *and* Crum. The company name follows the individual's name, unless a department or division is included in the address. If a department or division is used, the company name follows it.

```
Mrs. Kiki Komura, Manager        Mrs. Kiki Komura, Manager
Reynolds, Frazier, & Crum        Internal Audit Department
                                 Reynolds, Frazier, & Crum
```

### Delivery Address

When the name of the street is a number from one through ten, the street name is spelled out (2819 Tenth Avenue). Use figures for street names that are numbers above ten (127 East 15th Street). When house or building numbers consist of the digit 1 (one), spell out "One." Use figures for other single digits (3 Waycross Road).

Some companies use a post office box number as well as a street address. The post office box is added for correspondence. The street address only is used for shipments of products or supplies made to a specific location. Other information, such as an apartment number or suite number, generally is keyed after the delivery address and on the same line.

```
For Correspondence              For Shipments


Craftmaster Lumber Company      Western Wildlife Publications
31 Duck Creek Road              One Park Circle, Suite 119
P.O. Box 779                    San Marcos, CA  92069-9703
Berwick, ME  03901-9142
```

### City, State, and ZIP Code

The last line of the letter address contains the city, state, and ZIP Code. The United States Postal Service has designated two-letter abbreviations for states to be used with the ZIP (Zoning Improvement Plan) Code. A list of two-letter state abbreviations is provided in Reference Section E. The ZIP Code appears on the same line as the city and state. Use of the ZIP Code reduces mailing costs and speeds mail deliveries because it allows the Postal Service to use automated equipment to sort the mail. The last four *digits* of the nine-digit code allow faster and more accurate sorting of mail to small geographic segments, such as city blocks or single buildings.

*digits:* figures

### Attention Line

Frequently, when a letter is addressed to a company, an attention line is used to direct the letter to a particular person or department within the company. The attention line indicates that, while the letter concerns company business, the writer prefers to direct the letter to a particular individual or department named in the attention line. If the individual is no longer employed by the company, someone else will take care of the matter of the correspondence. The attention line is keyed immediately below the company name in the letter address. The word *Attention* should not be abbreviated. It may be keyed in all capital letters or it may be keyed with a capital "A" and the rest of the word in lower-case letters. A colon may be used to separate the word *Attention* from the name, but the current trend is to omit the colon.

```
Kamarski Office Supplies        Kamarski Office Supplies
Attention Mrs. Ellen Reynolds   ATTENTION ACCOUNTING DEPARTMENT
1010 Anderson Pike              1010 Anderson Pike
Uniontown, PA  15401-9127       Uniontown, PA  15401-9127
```

```
          Kamarski Office Supplies
          Attention:  Mrs. Ellen Reynolds
          1010 Anderson Pike
          Uniontown, PA  15401-9127
```

Remember the addressee is the company—not the person or department in the attention line. The salutation always agrees with the first line of the letter address, not with the attention line.

## Salutation

*greeting:* expression of good wishes

The salutation is a ***greeting*** to the addressee. The first line of the letter address influences the salutation that is appropriate. If the addressee is a company, you use *Ladies and Gentlemen* as the salutation. If the addressee is an individual, the salutation may be as informal as *Dear Jack* or as formal as *My dear Mr. Sharp.* Often the salutation the letter originator chooses is determined by the relationship with the recipient. The following are acceptable salutations:

FOR MEN

Commonly Used:

```
Dear Brian
Dear Mr. Bennington
```

Less
Commonly Used:

```
My dear Brian
My dear Mr. Bennington
```

FOR WOMEN

Commonly Used:

```
Dear Margaret
Dear (Ms., Mrs., Miss) Fagerstrom
```

Less
Commonly Used:

```
My dear Margaret
My dear (Ms., Mrs., Miss) Fagerstrom
```

Sometimes the name of the addressee is not known. For example, the addressee may be *Advertising Manager.* The acceptable salutation, therefore, would be *Dear Sir or Madam.* The salutation is keyed a double space below the letter address.

## Subject Line

The writer of a letter sometimes will include a subject line to highlight the key topic of the letter. If a subject is included, it is keyed a double space below the salutation (See page 207). The trend today is to key the line in all capital letters and omit the word *Subject.* However, all of the following are acceptable:

```
BID FOR NEW OFFICE SYSTEM
SUBJECT:  BID FOR NEW OFFICE SYSTEM
SUBJECT:  Annual Automation Conference
Subject:  Annual Automation Conference
```

## Body

The message is called the body of the letter. It begins a double space below the subject line, if one is included. If there is no subject line, the body begins a double space below the salutation. Paragraphs of the body are usually single-spaced with a double space between paragraphs. If appropriate, strive to have at least two paragraphs in the body. Avoid paragraphs that are too long or too short. If a letter is very short, you may double-space the entire body. You always should take special care to keep the right margin as even as possible.

## Complimentary Close

*farewell:* a wish of well-being made at parting

The complimentary close is the *farewell* of the letter. Like the salutation, the complimentary close can be informal or formal. It is important to remember that the complimentary close and the salutation should convey the same degree of informality or formality. Use an informal complimentary close with an informal or friendly salutation. Use a formal complimentary close with a formal salutation. The following complimentary closings are listed in order from informal to formal:

Commonly Used:

```
Cordially
Sincerely
Yours truly
```

Less Commonly Used:

```
Cordially yours
Yours cordially
Sincerely yours
Yours sincerely
Yours very truly
Very truly yours
Yours respectfully
Respectfully
```

The complimentary close is keyed a double space below the last line of the body. Capitalize only the first letter of the first word of the complimentary close.

## Signature, Name of Originator, and Title

The handwritten name of the originator is called the signature. Because handwritings vary, the signature may not be easily read. Therefore, the typed name below the signature is there to overcome problems caused by poor handwriting. The typed name is keyed on the fourth line space below the complimentary close. It may be followed on the same line or on the next line by a business or professional title such as *Manager, Vice President,* or *CPA.*

Yours truly

*Renaldo E. Lopez*

Renaldo E. Lopaz
Claims Adjuster

Very sincerely yours

*John R. Ruel*

John R. Ruel, CPA

Personal titles, such as Mr., Ms., Mrs., or Miss, are not generally used before the signature or typewritten name. If a name could be that of a man or woman, (Robin or Leslie, for example), then it is appropriate to add a personal title so that the receiver knows how to address the sender if a response is needed. The use of parentheses around such titles is optional.

*Robin M. LaFabre*

(Mr.) Robin M. LaFabre

*Leslie W. Webster*

Ms. Leslie W. Webster

Some women prefer to be addressed by a certain personal title. This preference can be indicated as part of the typewritten name or the signature. Some examples of how a woman's name might appear follow:

*Claudine A. Reynolds*

(Mrs.) Claudine A. Reynolds

*Miss Ruth P. Bezdek*

Ruth P. Bezdek

*Joanna Manjerovic*

Mrs. Joanna S. Manjerovic

*Ms. Donna C. Antonacceo*

Donna C. Antonacceo

If your employer is not available, you may be asked to sign his or her name to letters. To do this, sign your employer's name in your own handwriting and place your initials after the signature.

*Michael B. Gillespie*

Michael B. Gillespie

Sometimes the name of the company is keyed as part of the closing lines. This practice is unnecessary if the company name appears on the letterhead. If used, the company name is keyed in all capital letters a double space below the complimentary close. The originator's name and title then are keyed four lines below the company name.

Sincerely yours                            Yours respectfully

DATA SYSTEMS SPECIALISTS                    GLOBAL TRAVEL INCORPORATED

*Alan F. Conrad*                           *Judi R. Bronstein*

Alan F. Conrad                             Miss Judi R. Bronstein
Regional Vice President                    International Consultant

### Reference Initials

Reference initials identify the person who keyed the document. These initials are placed at the left margin, a double space below the sender's name and title. It is not necessary to include the sender's initials if the name is typed. If you are the originator as well as the person who keys the document, no reference initials are needed.

*Marybeth is a staff assistant to the public information director of a large communications company. The director has delegated to Marybeth the task of getting up-to-date reports in a wide range of fields. Marybeth writes many letters requesting reports. She writes such letters, keys them, and signs her own signature. No reference initials are added to her letters.*

### Enclosure Notation

Items included in the same envelope with a letter are called enclosures. Enclosures should be noted at the end of the letter. Such a notation will remind you to check to be sure the items are in the envelope.

The enclosure notation is keyed a double space below the reference initials (See page 207). One enclosure is indicated by the word *Enclosure*. More than one enclosure may be indicated by any of the following. However, the preferred notation indicates what is actually enclosed.

```
Enclosures
Enclosures 2
Enc. 2
2 Enc.
Enclosures:   Sales Catalog
              Order Form
```

### Separate Cover Notation

If a letter refers to items sent in another envelope or package and not included with the letter, you should include a separate cover notation. This notation is keyed a double space below the last enclosure line, if one is included. One item is indicated by the words *Separate Cover*. More than one item may be indicated in either of the following ways:

```
Separate Cover 2

Separate Cover:   "Strategy for the Year 2000"
                  "Forecasting Computer Capability"
```

### Copy Notation

A copy notation indicates that copies of the letter have been sent to individuals other than the addressee named in the letter address. This notation is keyed a double space below the separate cover notation, if included. When you prepare a photocopy, use *pc* for photocopy. Use *cc* when you prepare a carbon copy. It also is acceptable to use the words *Copy to* or *Copies to*. Refer to the examples which follow:

```
pc Lee Ann Cloonan        Copy to Leonard Kincaid

pc Kimberly Lewis         Copies to Carolee Fender
   Jerry Steiner                    Howard Ewald
```

When copies are sent to several individuals, a check mark often is placed beside the name of the individual to receive each copy. This procedure aids you in preparing envelopes for all who are to receive copies.

pc✓Alan Oldfield
    Wesley Schmidt
    JoAnne Winiarski
    Jessica Ziobro

The notation *bpc* or *bcc* is used to indicate a blind copy. A blind copy notation refers to the practice of omitting the copy notation on the original copy. It is used when the sender does not want the addressee to know to whom a copy of the letter is being sent. Refer to the following examples.

bpc Howard Miller          bcc Geraldine O'Conner

The blind copy notation should appear only on the copies of the letter. When using carbon paper, the copy notation may be keyed before the letter is removed from the machine. Simply place a small sheet of paper over the notation position on the original before keying the notation. On photocopies, the blind copy notation must be keyed on one photocopy which then is photocopied to produce as many copies as are required.

## Postscript

Some writers include a postscript. A postscript is a short message at the very end of the letter. It usually is used to add information omitted from the letter or to add special emphasis to an important point. Although the letters *PS* may precede the postscript, the trend today is to omit these letters and to treat the postscript as a separate paragraph. It is keyed a double space below all other notations. (Refer to page 207.)

## Second-Page Heading

Occasionally, a letter will require more than one page. In such instances, each page except the first page is numbered. The second-page heading should include the name of the addressee, the page number, and the date. The second-page heading may be blocked at the left margin or placed horizontally across the page as shown in Illus. 6–2.

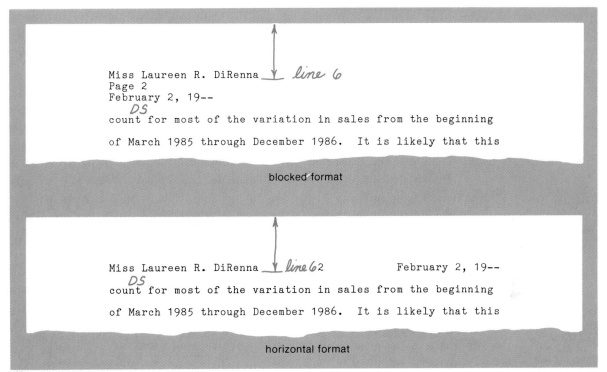

**Illus. 6-2.** Second-page headings

## LETTER FORMATS

Letters are formatted in several different ways in offices today. The most commonly used formats are *block, modified block,* and *AMS simplified.* As you read about each format, locate the appropriate sample letter on page 221.

### Block

All lines in the block format begin flush with the left margin. The popularity of this format is due to the ease of keying all the special lines. Block format is highly efficient because it saves time in moving from one part of the letter to another.

### Modified Block

There are two variations of this format. In the first variation all letter parts except for two are keyed exactly as they are in block style. As you will note, the dateline and the closing lines begin at the horizontal center of the page rather than flush with the left margin. In the second variation, paragraphs are also indented.

## AMS Simplified

The Administrative Management Society is the sponsor and promoter of this letter format. The following are characteristics of this format:

- Block placement is used throughout.
- The address begins on the fourth line space below the date.
- There is no salutation.
- The subject line is keyed in all capital letters three line spaces below the address.
- The body of the letter begins three line spaces below the subject line.
- Enumerated items begin at the left margin; unnumbered items are indented five spaces.
- There is no complimentary close.
- The writer's name and title are keyed in all capital letters on the fourth line space below the body of the letter.
- The operator's (typist's) reference initials are keyed in lower-case letters a double space below the writer's name.
- All notations after the reference initials are double-spaced.

*vocal:* inclined to talk about freely

Supporters of this simplified letter format believe it is more appropriate for modern communications than the other formats. Supporters are especially *vocal* about the use of salutations and complimentary closes, which they believe are now outdated.

**PUNCTUATION STYLES**

Currently there are two commonly used styles for punctuating the special lines of business letters. These are open punctuation and mixed punctuation. As you read about each style, locate the appropriate sample letter shown in Illus. 6–3.

## Open Punctuation

Open punctuation actually means no punctuation marks are used after the salutation and the complimentary close. Open punctuation is considered a time-saving style, and it often is used with a block format letter. See Illus. 6–3 for an example of a block letter with open punctuation.

## Mixed Punctuation

When the mixed punctuation style is used, the salutation and complimentary close are followed by punctuation marks. The

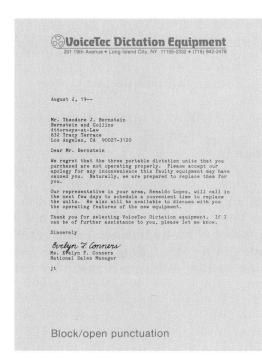

Block/open punctuation

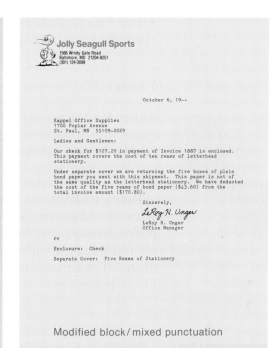

Modified block/mixed punctuation

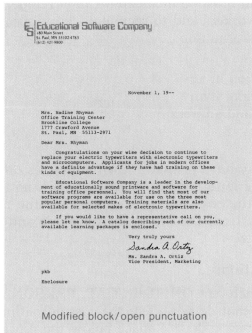

Modified block/open punctuation

AMS simplified

**Illus. 6-3.** Letter formats

proper punctuation with this style is a colon or a comma after the salutation and a comma after the complimentary close.

| Formal | Informal |
|--------|----------|
| `Dear Mr. Nassar:` | `Dear Mark,` |
| `Ladies and Gentlemen:` | |

Refer to Illus. 6–3 for an example of a modified block letter with mixed punctuation. The persistence of the use of this style of punctuation reflects the belief of many businesspeople that there should be some punctuation after salutations and complimentary closes. Traditions in letter writing in business last a long time in many instances!

## ENVELOPE FORMAT

There is a parallel between several parts of a business letter and the information that must be included on an envelope. To be informative to postal workers and to recipients, envelopes must include the following information:

- the return address
- special address notation, if any
- special mailing notation, if any
- the recipient's name and address

### The Return Address

Most companies today have printed return addresses on their envelopes similar to the letterhead of the company. If no return address is printed on the envelope, you should key the return address a double space from the top of the envelope and three spaces from the left edge.

### Special Address Notations

Special notations, such as CONFIDENTIAL, PERSONAL, or HOLD FOR ARRIVAL, that do not affect the cost of mailing are keyed in all capital letters a double space below the return address and three spaces from the left edge of the envelope.

## Special Mailing Notations

Special notations, such as REGISTERED MAIL or SPECIAL DELIVERY, that affect the cost of mailing are keyed in all capital letters below the area where the stamp will be placed.

## Recipient's Address

If mail is to be handled efficiently by postal workers, it is important that the address on the envelope be accurate, complete, and easy to read. The address on the envelope should include the same information given on the letter enclosed. When an address contains an attention line, it should be keyed as the second line of the address.

If you are using a No. 10 envelope (9½″ by 4⅛″), begin the address on line 14 and five spaces to the left of center. If you are using a No. 6¾ envelope (6½″ by 3⅝″), begin the address on line 12 and ten spaces to the left of center. Addresses should be single-spaced and in block format, as shown in Illus. 6–4.

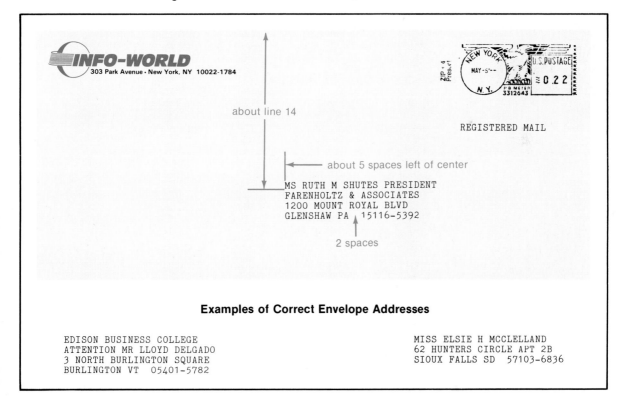

**Illus. 6–4.** Recommended envelope format

The United States Postal Service has a recommended style for addresses on envelopes. Note in Illus. 6–4 that all words are shown in capital letters and no punctuation marks are used. The only exception is the hyphen used within the nine-digit ZIP Code. Keying the address in this manner facilitates the handling of envelopes by automated postal equipment such as *OCR*'s (optical character readers). You will learn more about the use of such equipment in Chapter 14.

In some companies today where modern word/text processing equipment with storage capabilities is used, the letter address is keyed in the same form as that recommended for the envelope. The address is then recalled from storage and printed automatically on the envelope.

## REVIEW QUESTIONS

1. Why is a standard format used for business letters?

2. What parts of a letter always will be included in any letter?

3. What information generally is included in a company's letterhead?

4. How is the date of a letter keyed?

5. Where should a mailing notation appear on a letter?

6. Describe what generally is included in a letter address.

7. Why do you include the ZIP Code in a letter address?

8. In what ways does the block letter format differ from the AMS simplified format?

9. Where are punctuation marks required when you are using mixed punctuation?

10. What information shown on a letter must also be shown on the envelope?

## INTERACTING WITH OTHERS

Brenda is a new office worker at Capital Wholesale Distributors. Three other employees work in the same office. The first day Brenda reports to work, her supervisor, Ms. DeAngelo, tells her to take some time to become acquainted with the office equipment and the company procedures manual.

While she is studying the procedures manual to see how various company documents are prepared, Ms. DeAngelo interrupts her and says, "I have drafted several letters which I would like you to prepare for my signature. I will be out of the office for about three hours. I'll sign the letters when I return."

Brenda took the letters from Ms. DeAngelo and placed them in her in basket until she finished studying the procedures manual. Later, when Brenda began to process the documents, she found that Ms. DeAngelo did not include the recipient's full name and address on any of the letters. Since each salutation identified the recipient by last name only, Brenda felt that she had no way of locating the missing information. Therefore, she went back to the procedures manual to review some sections and did not key the letters. When Ms. DeAngelo returned, she approached Brenda and said, "I'll sign those letters now."

If you were Brenda and you were not able to complete the letters before Ms. DeAngelo returned, what would you say to her when she asked for the letters? What might Brenda have done when she discovered that complete names were missing?

**What You Are To Do:** Prepare a brief response to the questions asked.

# EXTENDING YOUR MATH SKILLS

Assume that you are an office worker in the Accounting Department of The Computer Depot, a small retail computer store. Your supervisor, Mrs. Lowell, asks you to compute manually the figures needed for departmental reports. Mrs. Lowell hands you the report shown on page 226 and asks you to determine the total sales, the cost of units sold, and the gross profit on the sales of each product.

**What You Are To Do:** Write the headings *Product No., Total Sales, Cost of Units Sold,* and *Gross Profit* across the top of a sheet of plain paper. Then list each product by its product number. Compute the total sales for each product. (Multiply units sold by the selling price.) Compute the cost of units sold for each product. (Multiply units sold by the wholesale price.) Compute the gross profit for each product. (The gross profit is the difference between the total sales and the cost of units sold.) Finally, add the gross profit column to determine the total gross profit figure.

```
                          THE COMPUTER DEPOT

                        PRODUCT EARNINGS REPORT
```

| Product Description | Product Number | Units Sold | Wholesale Price | Selling Price | Total Sales | Cost of Units Sold | Gross Profit |
|---|---|---|---|---|---|---|---|
| Monitor | M2021 | 15 | $173.90 | $ 248.50 | $___?___ | $___?___ | $___?___ |
| Keyboard | K001 | 5 | 126.18 | 180.25 | ___?___ | ___?___ | ___?___ |
| CPU | C3011 | 82 | 995.60 | 1,422.32 | ___?___ | ___?___ | ___?___ |
| Disk Drive | D8929 | 111 | 145.55 | 207.93 | ___?___ | ___?___ | ___?___ |
| Computer Desk | K3723 | 15 | 134.40 | 192.00 | ___?___ | ___?___ | ___?___ |
| Diskettes (box) | T5221 | 722 | 20.65 | 29.50 | ___?___ | ___?___ | ___?___ |
| Computer Paper (box) | P0010 | 57 | 13.30 | 18.98 | ___?___ | ___?___ | ___?___ |

```
     TOTAL GROSS PROFIT.................................................$___?___
```

## APPLICATION ACTIVITY

Word/text processing equipment can be used to complete this activity.

Assume that you are an office worker for Pfeifer Office Furniture. Your supervisor, Louis Nicolas, asks you to key a corrected copy of the letter to Wolff Pharmacies. The letter, which follows, originally was prepared by a temporary office employee and is not mailable. Mr. Nicolas indicates that some of the required letter parts are missing and that other letter parts are keyed incorrectly. The letter was to be keyed in block style with open punctuation.

**What You Are To Do:** Key a corrected copy of the letter. Use letterhead in *Information Processing Activities* or plain paper. If necessary, refer to Illustration 6–1 on page 207.

PFEIFER OFFICE FURNITURE
2700 West Haddon Avenue  Chicago, Illinois  60622-9022


April 21st, 19--

Special Delivery

Wolff Pharmacies
1192 Goshen Street
Attention Accounting Department
Hartford, Ct.  06106-9202

Sir

     Enclosed are the price list and catalog you requested in
your letter of April 5.  As you will notice, we stock over fifty
different workstations, each designed to accommodate different
configurations of computer equipment.

If your company decides to stock five or more of our computer
workstations, we can offer you an additional 5 percent discount
off the list price.

Thank you very much for your interest in Pfeifer Office Furniture.
If you need additional information, please feel free to call me
collect at 312-286-2987.

Yours Truly


Louis W. Nicolas, Sales Manager

ly

# Topic 2

## MEMORANDUMS, REPORTS, AND TABLES

When you have completed your study of this topic, you will be able to

- identify the basic parts of formal and informal memorandums
- explain how memorandums differ from letters
- identify the basic parts of informal (unbound) reports
- identify the basic parts of a table
- describe the ways in which documents are originated
- describe the usefulness of form letters and paragraphs

Letters are used for communicating with people outside the company; memorandums are used for communicating with people within the company. As you can imagine, there are numerous occasions when persons within a company must write to each other. Personnel directors send memorandums to all employees informing them of vacation and holiday schedules. Payroll department managers send memorandums to employees informing them of new social security rates or income taxes. Credit managers send memorandums to sales representatives describing new terms for extending credit to established customers.

Company managers, with the aid of office workers, produce many reports and tables for both external and internal purposes.

Regardless of the department you choose as your place of employment, you undoubtedly will aid in the preparation of many memorandums, reports, and tables. For example, it is not uncommon for managers of departments to report on a regular basis to their superiors. Such reporting is done in written form. Additionally, managers are responsible for suggesting changes in company procedure. Often such suggestions must be reviewed by superiors, who expect to read a report as a part of the review process.

Often internal communications must be developed and prepared under considerable pressure because of the need for prompt decisions. In such an environment, you can imagine how your skills as a word processing worker become critical. An alert, competent office worker is an important partner in getting memorandums and reports done promptly and properly. Many office workers find the preparation of communications under pressure one of the most challenging jobs they face. You, too, may enjoy such a challenge.

*Jill is a word processing worker in the office of the director of product development. A new product that was being sold on an experimental basis in only seven cities across the country was received by the public with far more enthusiasm than anticipated. Sales were beyond projections; stock was insufficient to meet demand. It became clear that new production facilities were required. The entire department moved into high gear as plans were developed for increasing production. Jill was invaluable in preparing drafts of reports as they were being developed. Several workdays extended well into the night. However, Jill worked the additional hours willingly because everyone was so cooperative and all were contributing to doing an exceptionally good job. She liked being a member of such a hardworking team.*

## MEMORAN-DUMS

*streamlined:* containing only the essentials

A memorandum is a *streamlined* business document used to communicate with an individual or a group of individuals within an organization. Memorandums (also called *interoffice memos* or *memos*) do not contain all the parts used in letters. For example, the salutation, complimentary close, and formal signature are omitted. Many offices use preprinted memorandum forms in either full or half sheets. Memorandums typed or printed on these forms are called *formal memorandums.* In some cases, memorandums are typed or printed on a sheet of plain paper or a sheet of letterhead. These are called *simplified memorandums.*

As more and more electronic equipment enters the office, more companies are using computer-generated forms. These basic forms are stored electronically in computer memory and recalled when needed. The computer user calls up the form on the screen and keys the appropriate information. (Refer to page 230.) The document (exactly as it is seen on the screen) then is printed on plain paper or sent electronically to another computer terminal.

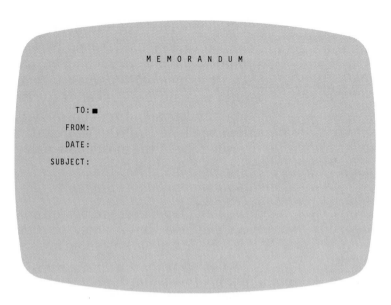

```
                    M E M O R A N D U M



            TO: ■
          FROM:
          DATE:
       SUBJECT:
```

**Illus. 6–5.** Computer generated form

Illus. 6–6 shows the various parts of a memorandum on a preprinted form. Refer to this illustration as you read about the purpose and proper placement of each part.

### Heading

The guide words TO, FROM, DATE, and SUBJECT constitute the heading. The guide words should be printed to allow for double spacing between the lines of the heading. Note that in Illus. 6–6 the guide words are placed in such a way that the same margins may be used throughout the keying process. It is quite common for a memo to be sent to more than one individual. The situation can be handled in either of the following ways:

```
   TO:  Adam Brown, Carole Matthews, and Kim Ling

 FROM:  Tracey Flannagen
```

                        or

```
   TO:  All Regional Vice Presidents
        (See distribution list below.)

 FROM:  George Hayduk, Executive Vice President
```

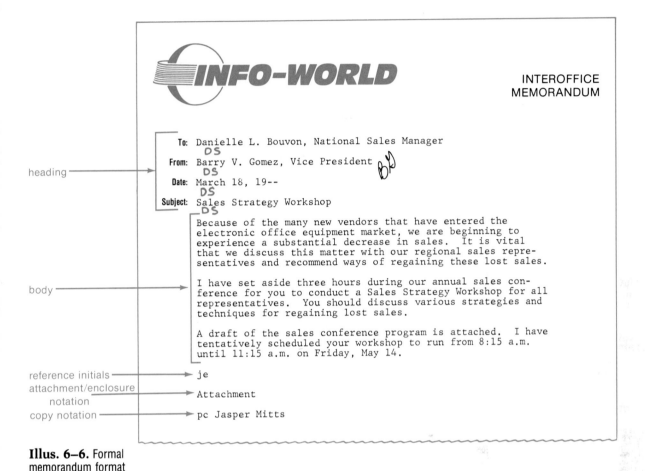

heading

body

reference initials

attachment/enclosure notation

copy notation

**Illus. 6–6.** Formal memorandum format

The distribution list mentioned in the heading in the second example would be keyed a double space below the reference initials at the end of the memo. This procedure aids you in making sure that all intended recipients receive a copy of the memo.

Personal preference will determine whether or not handwritten initials are included after the sender's name in the heading.

```
                    cd

          Distribution List:
          Alson, T. F.
          Balsas, Richard W.
          Cantwell, Mary Sue
          Dodwell, Winter
          Flanders, Ross
```

## Body

The body begins either a double space or a triple space below the last line of the heading. The traditional triple space is being replaced by a double space in order to make efficient use of today's automated equipment. Paragraphs may be blocked at the left margin or indented five spaces.

## Reference Initials

Reference initials identify the person who keyed the document. These initials are keyed at the left margin, a double space below the last line of the body.

## Attachment/Enclosure Notation

Sometimes an item or items are attached to a memorandum with a paper clip or a staple. In such cases, an *attachment notation* is used. When the item or items are placed in an envelope with the memorandum, an *enclosure notation* is used. More than one attachment or enclosure may be indicated in any of the following ways:

```
Attachments
Attachments 2
Attachments:   Flextime Policy
               Vacation Schedule


Enclosures
Enc. 2
2 Enc.
Enclosures 2
Enclosures:   Software Price List
              Order Form
```

## Copy Notation

The copy notation is keyed in the same manner for memorandums as for letters. Use *pc* for photocopy and *cc* for carbon copy.

## The Envelope

If the person to whom the memo is going is located nearby, the memo may be placed in the receiver's in basket. In this case, an envelope may not be needed. However, if the receiver is in a different part of the building or in a different building altogether, the memo typically is sent in an interoffice or intra-company envelope or in a plain color envelope used only for intra-company mail. A confidential document always is placed in an envelope and the envelope is marked <u>CONFIDENTIAL</u>.

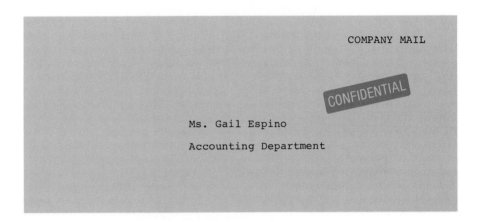

## THE SIMPLIFIED MEMORANDUM

In recent years, a simplified memorandum has been developed. This type of memo is easy to keyboard and does not require a preprinted form. As you learned earlier, simplified memos can be prepared on either letterhead or plain paper.

Standard format for a simplified memo often specifies that the date be entered on a specific line (line 10, for example) or a double space below the letterhead, if letterhead is used.

As you look at Illus. 6–7 on page 234, note the following characteristics of this format:

- One-inch margins are used.
- Block placement is used throughout.
- Only single, double, or quadruple spacing is used, which takes advantage of special features of electronic word/text processing equipment.
- The name of the addressee is keyed on the fourth line space below the date.
- The subject line is keyed in all capital letters.
- The writer's name and title are keyed on the fourth line space below the body of the memo.
- All notations after the reference initials are double-spaced.

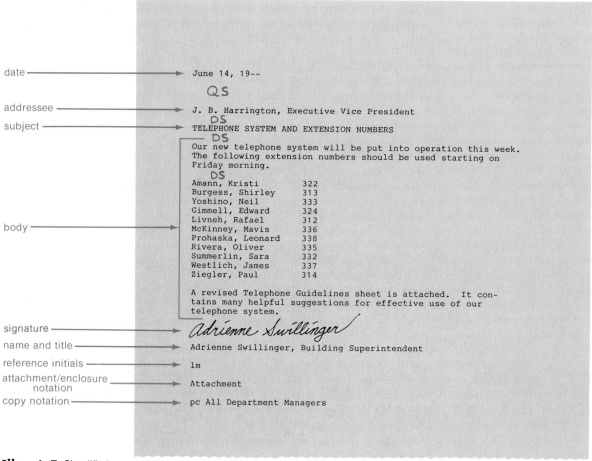

date

addressee

subject

body

signature

name and title

reference initials

attachment/enclosure
notation

copy notation

**Illus. 6–7.** Simplified memorandum format

## INFORMAL, BRIEF REPORTS

A business report, whether formal or informal, is written to convey information in a clear, concise manner. You probably know something about reports in general if you have written such documents as assignments in various classes at school.

All reports include both a main heading (or title) and text, called the body of the report. Informal, brief reports also may include the following additional parts:

- secondary heading
- side headings
- reference citations
- reference list (or bibliography)
- title page
- abstract

The number of additional parts included will depend upon the nature of the report and the subject matter covered. Essentially, reports are organized to communicate the intended message or information quickly and clearly.

Informal, unbound reports of no more than five to six pages will be discussed here. You will learn about long reports in Chapter 11.

**PARTS OF INFORMAL REPORTS**

Illus. 6–8 on page 236 shows an informal, unbound report. This type of report may fit on one sheet of plain paper or it may require several sheets of paper. If the report requires several sheets, it is stapled in the top left-hand corner. Unlike bound reports, unbound reports do not have extra space left in the margin for fastening the pages together.

Because these documents are informal, they do not require all the parts of more formal reports. In this topic, you will learn about the main heading, the secondary heading, the body, and side headings. Other report parts will be discussed in Chapter 11.

### Main Heading

Standard format for an informal, unbound report often specifies that the main heading or title be entered on a specific line (line 12 is a common placement). The main heading is centered and keyed in all capital letters. If two lines are required for the heading, the lines may be either double-spaced or single-spaced. In order to take advantage of the automatic features of word/text processing equipment, standard format often calls for the main heading to be double-spaced.

### Secondary Heading

Some reports require a secondary heading such as the one shown on page 236. The secondary heading is centered a double space below the main heading, and only the first letters of key words are capitalized. The body of the text begins either a triple space or a quadruple space below the secondary heading, if there is one. Because alternating between single and double spacing is often difficult when using some of today's automated equipment, standard format may call for a quadruple space between the last line of the heading and the body of the report. (Refer to page 236.)

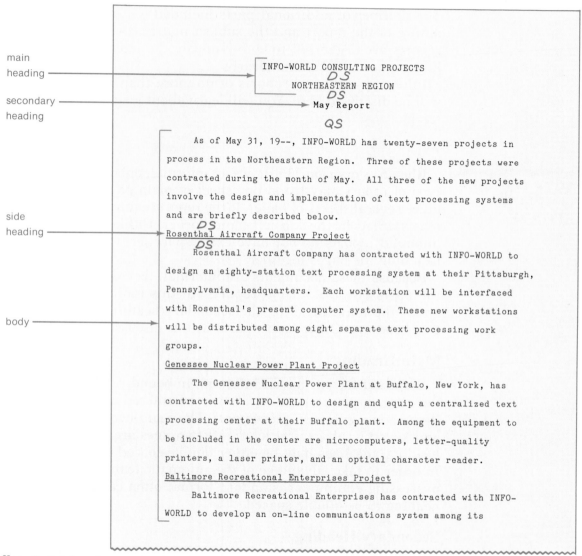

main heading

secondary heading

side heading

body

INFO-WORLD CONSULTING PROJECTS
*DS*
NORTHEASTERN REGION
*DS*
May Report
*QS*

    As of May 31, 19--, INFO-WORLD has twenty-seven projects in process in the Northeastern Region.  Three of these projects were contracted during the month of May.  All three of the new projects involve the design and implementation of text processing systems and are briefly described below.
*DS*
Rosenthal Aircraft Company Project
*DS*
    Rosenthal Aircraft Company has contracted with INFO-WORLD to design an eighty-station text processing system at their Pittsburgh, Pennsylvania, headquarters.  Each workstation will be interfaced with Rosenthal's present computer system.  These new workstations will be distributed among eight separate text processing work groups.

Genessee Nuclear Power Plant Project
    The Genessee Nuclear Power Plant at Buffalo, New York, has contracted with INFO-WORLD to design and equip a centralized text processing center at their Buffalo plant.  Among the equipment to be included in the center are microcomputers, letter-quality printers, a laser printer, and an optical character reader.

Baltimore Recreational Enterprises Project
    Baltimore Recreational Enterprises has contracted with INFO-WORLD to develop an on-line communications system among its

**Illus. 6–8.** Informal, unbound report format

## Body

    The body of the report presents the information that the sender wants the reader to have regarding the subject of the report. The body may be double-spaced or single-spaced. Double spacing is used between paragraphs whether the paragraphs are single-spaced or double-spaced.

## Side Headings

A side heading is used to divide a main topic into subdivisions. Side headings are keyed in capital and lowercase letters at the left margin and are underscored for *emphasis*. In order to take advantage of the automatic features of word/text processing equipment, standard format may call for a double space before and after all side headings.

*emphasis:* special stress; insistence on something

## Page Numbers

A report frequently takes more than one page. In such instances, each page except the first is numbered. The page number is placed at the right margin on line 6. If a heading is used on succeeding pages, the page number is part of that heading. The heading may be blocked at the left margin or placed horizontally across the page, as shown in Illus. 6–9. The text continues a double space below the heading and/or page number.

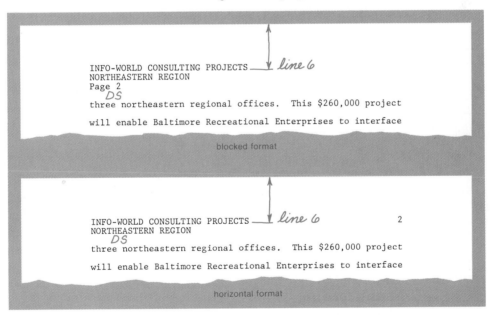

**Illus. 6–9.** Formats for second and succeeding page headings

## TABLES

A **table** is an organized arrangement of facts, figures, and other information. A table should be self-explanatory and not require referring to any text that might *accompany* the table. For example, tables often are used to make comparisons. Look at the

*accompany:* go with

table in Illus. 6–10. Which employee received the highest commission? How much were his or her total sales for the first quarter? Which employee received the lowest commission? How much were his or her total sales for the first quarter?

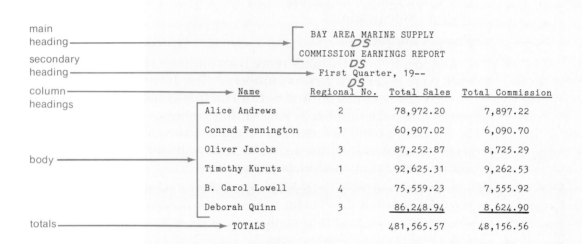

main
heading

secondary
heading

column
headings

body

totals

BAY AREA MARINE SUPPLY
DS
COMMISSION EARNINGS REPORT
DS
First Quarter, 19--
DS

| Name | Regional No. | Total Sales | Total Commission |
|------|--------------|-------------|------------------|
| Alice Andrews | 2 | 78,972.20 | 7,897.22 |
| Conrad Fennington | 1 | 60,907.02 | 6,090.70 |
| Oliver Jacobs | 3 | 87,252.87 | 8,725.29 |
| Timothy Kurutz | 1 | 92,625.31 | 9,262.53 |
| B. Carol Lowell | 4 | 75,559.23 | 7,555.92 |
| Deborah Quinn | 3 | 86,248.94 | 8,624.90 |
| TOTALS | | 481,565.57 | 48,156.56 |

**Illus. 6–10.** Table format

## PARTS OF A TABLE

Illus. 6–10 shows the standard parts of a table. Some simplified tables will not include all these parts. More complex tables will include other parts such as a source note, ruled lines, and leader dots. Refer to the illustration as you read about standard table parts.

### Main Heading

The main heading is the title of the table and describes its overall content. The main heading of a table is treated in the same manner as the main heading of an informal report.

### Secondary Heading

Some tables require a secondary heading such as the one shown in Illus. 6–10. The secondary heading is centered a double space below the main heading, and only the first letters of key words are capitalized. The column headings begin either a double or a triple space below the secondary heading. In order to take advantage of the automatic features of word/text processing equipment, standard format may call for the column headings to begin a double space below the secondary heading, if there is one.

### Column Headings

Column headings are used to tell the reader what information is provided in particular columns. A column heading is centered above the longest line in that column and is keyed in capital and lowercase letters. Column heads may be underscored in order to set them off from the body of the table. A double space precedes and follows the column head.

### Body

The body of the table contains the information indicated by all the column headings. You may either double-space or single-space the body. Unless a table is very long, it usually will be double-spaced. When the table is part of the text of a letter, memorandum, or report, the spacing of the table will be determined by the amount of space available on the page. Notice in Illus. 6–10 that word columns (such as Name) are *aligned* at the left and figure columns (such as Total Sales) are aligned at the decimal point.

*aligned:* lined up

### Totals

The last entry in a column is underscored in order to indicate that figures in that column have been added to get a total. The word *Totals* is indented and keyed a double space below the last entry in the body of the table.

## ORIGINATING DOCUMENTS

A common responsibility of managers is to originate letters, memorandums, and reports. As an office worker, at times you will assist managers in doing this task. Managers differ in the way in which they originate their written communications. Also, you will find variations in what office workers do to assist managers.

Equipment availability and personal preference generally will influence how a manager prepares written communications.

However, even one manager may use several methods, choosing the one best suited to the particular writing task at hand.

> *Marian Yanlow is responsible for writing many letters, memorandums, and reports in her position as vice president for systems engineering for a large manufacturing company. If she has a letter to write which she thinks is difficult to compose, she begins by making notes in pencil on a yellow pad. However, for the many relatively straightforward letters she writes, she dictates on-line to machines in the word processing center.*

Some managers have substituted a microcomputer keyboard for pad and pencil in the origination of memordandums, letters, and reports. Managers who choose this method for preparing documents are enthusiastic about how much time they can save.

## Manual Methods

Some managers think best with a sheet of paper and a pencil when they must compose a letter or report. So they prepare drafts of all, or at least some, correspondence in longhand. Other managers like to think without having to worry about writing down their thoughts, so they choose to dictate to an office worker with shorthand skills. These are both examples of manual methods of composing documents.

As you might guess, manual methods are not likely to be as economical as machine methods, if you consider only the time involved. However, since companies care about the quality of written communications, managers are often free to use a method that helps them do the best job possible.

**Illus. 6–11.** This manager is using a microcomputer to originate documents.

You'll be pleased to learn that a new,
more comprehensive benefit package
was approved ^at by the Board of ~~(May)~~
directors at its last May meeting.
A 12-page pamphlet describing the
new package is attached.

This package will take effect on July 1.
If you have any questions concerning
the specifications of this package,
feel free to ~~call~~ contact Jody Hall
at Extension 1258.

## Activity 2

Word/text processing
equipment can be used to
complete this activity.

Assume that you are an office assistant at Brown-Corwin International. Harold Owens, your supervisor, has made some minor revisions to a one-page informal report he needs for a meeting tomorrow. He asks you to key a revised copy of the report shown on page 246.

**What You Are To Do:**  Use plain paper and key a corrected copy of the report. Be sure to follow all handwritten directions. If necessary, refer to Illus. 6–8 on page 236.

*Begin the main
heading on line 12.
Use a 6-inch line.*   H. O.

## Document Storage

The diskettes used with our system are the 5¾/inch,
double/density, single/sided, soft-sector type.  With this
type of diskette, as many as 100 documents can be stored on a
single diskette.  The diskettes used to store our processed
documents represent the paper less files of our company.

☐ The storage medium used with our Word/Text Processing System is the diskette.  It is very important that each
processed document be copied onto a diskette and deleted from
the internal memory of the text-editing system.

## Formatting *Diskettes*

Before a new diskette *can* be used to store documents, it must
be formatted.  Formatting gets the diskette ready to recieve
and store documents.  When you format a diskette, the text-
editing system will check the diskette for bad spots, it will *set up*
make a directory for the document identification you assign to
each document stored, and it will delete (erase or wipe off)
documents already stored on the diskette.

It is only necessary to format a diskette once.  The
format procedure should only be used when you are using a new
diskette or when you wish to erase all of the documents stored
on the diskette.  If you format a diskette on which documents
are already stored, those documents will be deleted.

**CHAPTER
SUMMARY**

Office workers who are responsible for word/text processing must have a thorough understanding of how to format commonly prepared written communications. In this chapter, you have learned all the parts that might be included in business letters, as well as the standard placement for each part. While you were introduced to accepted formatting and styling, you also learned that you can expect to find variations in the way companies format letters and other documents. In some cases, these variations make more efficient use of modern word/text processing equipment.

You also were introduced to formatting for memorandums, reports, and tables. You learned that memorandums are used for internal communications. Reports, which are prepared for both internal and external purposes, generally follow a standard format. Short reports, however, often have fewer parts than long reports. Tables also are prepared frequently in business offices. Each table should be self-explanatory, which means that the reader should not have to refer to the body of a report to determine the meaning of a table.

You had an opportunity to become acquainted with the variety of means used by managers to originate written communications. You learned that managers can write out their communications, dictate them to an office worker, or dictate them to a machine (either at their desks or at a centralized location). You learned about the types of equipment used for machine dictation. These include portable units, desk-top units, and centralized dictation systems.

You also have learned about the origination and use of form letters and form paragraphs. These letters and paragraphs take advantage of the automatic features of word/text processing equipment.

---

### KEY TERMS

| | |
|---|---|
| logo | report |
| standard format | table |
| addressee | centralized dictation system |
| memorandum | |

---

**INTEGRATED
CHAPTER
ACTIVITY**

You work for the general manager of Dibert Real Estate Company. The manager likes the way you compose responses to incoming letters. He gives you the letter which follows, and says: "Please draft a response to this letter from Professional Office Equipment. I've made some notes in the margin that should be of help to you."

**Word/text processing equipment can be used to complete this activity.**

**What You Are To Do:** Compose a letter to Professional Office Equipment, to be signed by the general manager of Dibert, Kenneth L. Breman. Use modified block format with mixed punctuation. If necessary, refer to Illus. 6–3 on page 221. Use plain paper.

---

**Professional Office Equipment**

974 Hudson Avenue    Pontiac, Michigan   45058-8409

June 27, 19--

Dibert Real Estate Company
700 South Washington Avenue
Lansing, MI  48933-9012

Ladies and Gentlemen

It has been nearly three months since we delivered and installed your new copy machine, Model No. 1022. Payment for this machine was due within 30 days after delivery.

We have sent you three statements, but you have not forwarded your payment.  Please send us your payment today so that it is not necessary for us to take legal action.

Yours truly

*Christine M. Latkovic*

Christine M. Latkovic
Credit Manager

lp

*The copy machine has not worked properly since it was installed.*

*We sent Professional a letter on April 2 indicating that we would not submit a payment until the machine was repaired or replaced.*

*Called Professional on May 22 and explained the problem to a Mrs. Thomas.*

# PRODUCTIVITY CORNER

**Blake Williams**
*OFFICE
SUPERVISOR*

## WHY CAN'T THERE BE ONE SET OF RULES?

DEAR MR. WILLIAMS:

My first full-time job is that of an office assistant in the accounting department of our local college. I like my work, but I do have a major problem: I key documents for eight different professors who don't seem to want their letters prepared in the same way! Just last week, I did some letters for the first time for one professor. He returned them to me, asking me to add "Ph.D., CPA" after his name. He was very nice about it, and it was easy enough to add these letters. Then yesterday I did some letters for another professor. I checked her credentials in the college catalogue, and I saw that she was also listed as Ph.D., CPA. So I typed these initials after her name. She, too, was nice; but she said, "Under no circumstances are you ever to type those initials after my name. Simply type 'Department of Accounting' after my name." I've also learned that some professors want block format for their letters, while other professors prefer modified block with five space paragraph indentations.

What am I supposed to do to keep track of *what* to do?— TRACY IN TRENTON

DEAR TRACY:

Unfortunately, there isn't one set of rules anywhere. Individuals have different opinions about identifying their credentials. There is nothing wrong with listing such credentials as Ph.D. and CPA. However, many individuals are more comfortable when they do not include such information in their correspondence.

Some organizations have established format guidelines, yet you may still find individual variations within these guidelines. Therefore, it's wise to ask about format preferences before preparing any correspondence so that rekeying is not necessary.

You might find it helpful to set up your own reference manual—possibly a loose-leaf notebook. You could have a section for each of the eight professors for whom you are likely to prepare written correspondence. When you prepare the first letter properly, make an extra copy (unless the subject matter is confidential) and put it in your notebook for future reference.

Good luck in your new job!—BLAKE WILLIAMS

# Chapter 7

# Word/Text Processing: How Documents Are Processed

The preparation of written communications is a critical task in today's offices. Conveying accurate and appropriately worded messages is the concern of executives as they compose letters, memorandums, and reports. Processing letters, memorandums, and reports in proper form with no errors in spelling, grammar, or punctuation is the concern of office workers. Your command of English will be invaluable as you complete word/text processing tasks.

The preparation of business communications is a high-volume task in many modern offices. Between 20 and 30 million letters and memorandums are composed, processed, and mailed each business day. Additionally, over 70 billion document pages (other than letters and memorandums) are prepared, processed, and distributed yearly by busi-

nesses. Many competent office employees are required to process this volume of written communications.

As discussed in Chapter 5, the word/text processing system is a sub-unit of an organization's information processing system. You have learned that organizations strive to maintain high-quality written communications.

The objectives of the chapter are to

- introduce you to the ways in which word/text processing is organized

- acquaint you with the types of equipment office workers use to enter words and text for processing into documents

- develop your understanding of formatting, editing, printing, distributing/transmitting, and storing/retrieving documents

250

# Topic 1

## THE SETTING IN WHICH DOCUMENTS ARE PROCESSED

When you have completed your study of this topic, you will be able to

- explain the phases of the word/text processing cycle

- describe how word/text processing tasks are organized in multipurpose offices

- describe how word/text processing tasks are organized in satellite clusters and centralized units

- explain the purpose and types of performance evaluation used in word processing centers

Certain basic tasks require essentially the same steps regardless of how the office is structured. Word/text processing is such a task. You will be introduced to the basic word/text processing cycle in this topic. With a thorough knowledge of this cycle, you will be able to understand any variations you may find in the office where you choose to work.

The volume of work to be completed and the type of equipment available largely determine how the steps of word/text processing tasks are organized. For example, in offices where there are few written communications to be processed, any office assistant who is free is delegated the task of preparing the occasional letter or memo. The office assistant may be given some instructions orally or may be expected to determine

251

on his/her own what to do. Because word/text processing tasks are limited in these offices, you are not likely to find the most advanced equipment used. However, you may find that a micro-computer—used primarily for other tasks—is available for the limited amount of word/text processing required.

In companies with a great deal of word/text processing, care-fully established procedures are developed for each step of pro-cessing. Such companies may use the most advanced equipment so that office workers perform word/text processing tasks with high-level productivity. Furthermore, word/text processing may be done in centers devoted exclusively to this task.

Major changes are taking place in today's offices as businesses make the transition from the traditional office to the electronic office. Therefore, while on the job you may be faced with changes in how word/text processing tasks are done. You will be expected to be adaptable and flexible as new equipment is purchased, as procedures are revised, and as word/text processing is restruc-tured. If you understand the common organizational structures for word/text processing, you will be well prepared to respond to changes that are made in your work assignments. Also, you will be able to understand how procedures for completing your tasks are influenced by a new structure.

## WORD/TEXT PROCESSING CYCLE

*recipient:* one
who receives

The same word/text processing cycle must be completed for each document processed, regardless of how the tasks are orga-nized. In general, each document must be composed, keyed, mailed or transmitted electronically, and filed. The final result is a document on its way to the **recipient** and a file copy stored for easy retrieval whenever it is needed.

A typical workflow for a letter requiring revisions by the origi-nator is shown in Illus. 7–1. Note that the word/text processing cycle includes *input, processing, output, distribution/transmission,* and *storage/retrieval.* Your responsibilities within that cycle will depend on how the overall word/text processing task is orga-nized. In many offices, the cycle requires the cooperation of sev-eral persons within the company.

*Tama works as an office assistant to the manager of operations in a large textile manufacturing company. The manager composes many letters, memorandums, and reports. He dictates some on a machine; he writes some in longhand; and, at times, he prepares rough drafts at his microcomputer at home.*

**Illus. 7–6.** A WP center manager and a center employee discuss the performance appraisal form used for evaluation.

## EVALUATING YOUR OWN PERFORMANCE

You learned in Chapter 2 that independent review of your own work is expected. To grow in your job, you will find it a valuable practice to ask yourself from time to time: "How well am I doing my job? " To answer that question, follow these steps:

1. *Determine the factors that are used in evaluations made by your supervisor or manager.*
   You may have a copy of the evaluation appraisal form used, or you may have to determine from what the manager says to you what the factors are.
2. *List the factors in a notebook.*
3. *Review the list, thinking about your performance in relation to each factor.*
4. *Keep notes of all problems you encounter on the job.*
   For example, a job may be returned to you because it was not formatted properly.
5. *Review each problem noted to determine what, if anything, you failed to do.*
   For example, in the problem identified in 4, you might determine that the instructions clearly included formatting details. You had failed to read the instructions clearly.
6. *Analyze why you did not perform successfully.*
   You must be honest with yourself at this point. Again, in the problem identified in 4, if you had clear instructions, think about the reason you did not follow them.

7. *Introduce changes in your way of work.*
   For example, if you feel you were careless in reading instructions, make a point of carefully reading every word of instruction.

8. *From time to time, review your total performance.*
   Note if the changes in your way of work have reduced the number of problems.

9. *If possible, compare your own evaluation with the one given by the supervisor at the time of the yearly appraisal.*

Evaluating your own performance does not need to take much time. It simply involves being alert to what you do and being willing to make changes in what you do to improve your overall performance. *Wanting* to do a good job is likely to be transformed into *doing* a good job when you evaluate what you do and act on your evaluation.

**THE SETTING IS SUBJECT TO CHANGE**

Because companies constantly review how tasks are done, you will find that word/text processing may be reorganized from time to time. The availability of new, more efficient equipment also leads to changes in the way in which tasks are completed. An increase or decrease in the volume of work also leads to changes in organization and procedures.

**Illus. 7–7.** "Let's try it one more time. It says here to insert cord A into plug B."

Change is an accepted part of today's modern office scene. Word/text processing is becoming integrated with other subsystems of information processing, including data processing, records management, and reprographics. Workers will need to adapt to new structures and new procedures. When you find yourself faced with changes, remember that you have the basic understanding of word/text processing tasks. With this background, you will be able to develop new skills and understandings. If you are able to be flexible and to learn, you will have no difficulty working in a new environment.

## REVIEW QUESTIONS

1. Describe the word/text processing cycle.

2. Describe how word/text processing is likely to be organized in a multi-purpose office.

3. Why might you keep a notebook for your use in completing word processing tasks?

4. What is an appropriate basis for determining who gets to use a workstation that is shared by several employees?

5. Describe a situation in which an office worker would have responsibility for the entire word/text processing cycle.

6. Where are satellite word processing clusters likely to be located?

7. How does a centralized unit differ from a satellite cluster?

8. Identify four common responsibilities of managers and supervisors in WP centers.

9. Identify three types of evaluation commonly used in word processing centers.

10. Describe the key steps in evaluating your own performance.

## MAKING DECISIONS

Andrea works in a word processing center. She has excellent keyboarding skills and enjoys her work very much. She has been on the job for less than three months and has received a number of compliments from her supervisor. Andrea feels that she would be able to do a much better job if two problems were resolved. She finds the lighting at her workstation inadequate. She also finds that the music that is constantly provided in the center is distracting.

One day at lunch Andrea mentioned these two problems to a co-worker. Her co-worker quickly responded: "I think the lighting is fine, and the music is very relaxing. If you complain, there will be changes that the rest of us won't like."

Later that same day, Andrea's supervisor stopped at her workstation and asked, "How are things going?"

**What You Are To Do:**  Prepare a brief response to the question Andrea's supervisor raised.

## EXTENDING YOUR ENGLISH SKILLS

You are an office assistant to B. J. Jeffreys, sales manager of Hollingsworth Book Distributors, Inc. Ms. Jeffreys has drafted the memorandum on page 268. As she hands it to you, she says: "I barely had time to draft this memo! Please read it and be sure that it isn't confusing. If necessary, change the wording to make it more understandable. If you have questions, ask me. I'll be working on another project, but I don't mind being interrupted."

**What You Are To Do:**  • Read the memo and make a list of questions you would ask Ms. Jeffreys to be sure you know exactly what she wants to communicate in the memo.

• Assume that Ms. Jeffreys answers all your questions. (**NOTE:** For the purposes of this activity, use your imagination and provide the answers yourself.) Rewrite the memo, incorporating the responses you imagined Ms. Jeffreys gave you.

• On a sheet of plain paper, key the memo in final form. Use the simplified format shown on page 234.

## APPLICATION ACTIVITY

Word/text processing equipment can be used to complete this activity.

You are a word processing operator in a relatively new center. The manager is in the process of developing a manual to be sent to all user departments. The manager has given you a rough copy of a page of the manual entitled "Responsibilities of Originators." The rough copy appears on the next page.

**What You Are To Do:** Key the copy attractively on a single sheet of plain paper. Use your own judgment with regard to line length and spacing.

Responsibilities of Originators

1.  Clarity--the originator of ~~an assignment~~ [a job] must examine the copy, ~~in advance,~~ [before submission] for clarity. ~~An assignment~~ [The copy] may be typed, handwritten, or a combination ~~of both. Most importantly, assignments~~ [jobs] must be in legible form to be acceptable for processing in the ~~WPC~~ [Word Processing Center].

2.  Completeness--~~assignments~~ [jobs] must be presented in complete form for processing. Jobs submitted in a "piece-meal" fashion are excessively time-consuming and ~~delay the completion of assignments~~ [cannot be completed efficiently].

3.  Correctness--~~when an originator receives a completed assignment from the WPC, it becomes the responsibility of the originator for the accuracy and format of the assignment.~~ The WPC is not responsible for input control problems resulting from a failure to correctly interpret illegible handwriting or scribbling, inaccurate data, etc. Although all completed ~~assignments~~ [jobs] are scanned in-house for grammar, spelling, and punctuation discrepancies, the final approval of ~~an assignment~~ [a job] remains the sole responsibility of the originator.

4.  Revision--if ~~an assignment~~ [a job] requires editing, it is recommended that standard proofreading symbols be used to specify all revisions. As a convenience, a chart of standard proofreading symbols ~~has been~~ [is] included in this manual. Insertions of additional text must be clearly stated and legible.

5.  Priority Processing--~~assignments~~ [jobs] requiring special handling must be approved by the ~~Director~~ [Manager] of Word Processing. Logical and valid reasons must substantiate such requests. Originators are urged to keep special requests for priority processing of ~~assignments~~ [jobs] to a minimum.

6.  Advance Notice of Large Projects--if an originator is aware of an impending project that will require an unusual amount of processing assistance from the WPC, it is imperative that the Center be notified as soon as possible. Wherever possible, all originators are requested to

From: B. J. Jeffreys, ^Sales Manager

Date: March 22, 19-- ^12

Subject: New Meeting Date

The meeting of sales representatives scheduled

~~on~~ for 9:00 A.M. ^on Tuesday, March 26, 19--, in

Conference Room B has been changed. The

meeting will be held on March 27.

If you are unable to attend this resched-

uled ^meeting, please call Kenneth Derby.

# Topic 2

## EQUIPMENT FOR ENTERING WORDS/TEXT FOR PROCESSING

When you have completed your study of this topic, you will be able to

- identify the types of equipment used for keyboarding

- explain differences among the types of equipment used for keyboarding

- describe useful features of word processing systems

- identify nonkeyboarding equipment for entering text for processing

This topic focuses on the types of equipment used for entering text for processing. Such equipment is undergoing a great deal of change. The equipment currently in use varies considerably from office to office. Office employees work at keyboards on electric typewriters, electronic typewriters, dedicated word processors, multi-station text-editing systems, and microcomputers. Dedicated word processors, multi-station text-editing systems, and microcomputers are all in the class of equipment referred to as *text-editing systems*. References to text-editing systems may mean one or more of these machines. Nonkeyboarding devices also are used in some offices to capture words and text for processing.

As you study this topic, note the features that are common for each type of equipment. For example, all electronic typewriters have some common features, but they also have many different features. Some features are unique to a particular model. If you understand the common features, you can readily learn the features that are specific to the model you are expected to use.

Technological developments in equipment for word processing continue to increase the productivity of office workers. You undoubtedly have become proficient on one or more types of equipment in keyboarding courses. The basic skills you have developed are readily transferable to other types of equipment. Your basic skill, plus your command of all the capabilities of the equipment you use, will enable you to meet the productivity standards of the company in which you work.

Primary emphasis in this topic will be on the newest types of equipment found in today's office. Once you have an overall understanding of the nature of the equipment available, you can readily adapt to the particular type of equipment you will be expected to use in entering text for processing. As you know, newer forms of equipment tend to perform tasks automatically that must be done manually on less sophisticated equipment.

Remember, too, that your general knowledge of keyboarding will make it easy for you to adapt to new equipment. Manuals and/or tutorial disks accompany new models. Such references are especially useful in acquainting you with the capabilities of the equipment you are expected to use. Not utilizing all features that

*undermine:* weaken        aid you in completing tasks will ***undermine*** your efficiency.

## ELECTRIC TYPEWRITERS

Electric typewriters continue to be used in offices for word processing tasks. This type of equipment is most appropriate in offices where there is not a high volume of word processing to be completed. Also, electric typewriters are considered adequate in offices where there is limited need to key documents more than once.

Some electric typewriters have a correcting feature. A special *cover-up* or *lift-off* tape installed in the machine makes it easy to correct letters that are incorrectly keyed. To eliminate an incorrect letter or letters, the typist uses the special backspace key and then strikes the incorrect letter or letters. The special tape either covers up the error or lifts it off the paper. Then the correct letter or letters are keyed.

## ELECTRONIC TYPEWRITERS

Electronic typewriters provide capabilities beyond those provided by electric typewriters. *Microprocessors* (small electronic chips) in electronic typewriters make possible many automatic functions such as centering, carriage return, and decimal alignment.

### Common Features

Electronic typewriters are not all alike. Some have a limited number of features beyond those found on electric typewriters, while others have many features similar to those found on word processing systems, such as internal text-storage capacity and auxiliary (secondary) storage media.

In Illus. 7–8, which shows an electronic typewriter keyboard, you will see far more keys than are found on an electric typewriter. The keys to the left and the right of the character keys allow you to take advantage of the additional capabilities of an electronic typewriter.

**Illus. 7–8.**  An electronic typewriter keyboard.

Note the highlighted key of one model shown on page 272. By depressing the mode select key, the typist has access to several choices. For instance, the *JUST* mode enables you to have each line of copy justified at the right margin. This means that the last characters of all lines are aligned at the right-hand position. In effect, your electronic typewriter automatically determines where additional blank spaces are to be allowed within the lines in order to have all lines end at the same point.

There are a number of common features on electronic typewriters. Read carefully the listing given in Illus. 7–10 on page 272 to become acquainted with these time-saving features.

**Illus. 7–9.** Mode key choices available on one model of electronic typewriter. Note that the JUST mode has been selected.

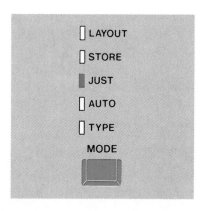

**Illus. 7–10.** Special features enhance the capabilities of electronic typewriters.

| COMMON FEATURES ON STANDARD ELECTRONIC TYPEWRITERS | |
|---|---|
| Automatic carriage return | Ability of the machine to return to the beginning of the next line automatically, based on the line length selected by operator. |
| Automatic word wrap | Ability of the machine to automatically determine if the next word will fit on the line. If it will not, the word is placed on the next line. This feature is used in conjunction with automatic carriage return. |
| Automatic decimal tab, center, and underline | Ability of the machine to automatically align columns of numbers at the decimal point, to automatically center a word or text between margins, and to automatically underline a specified segment of text as it is being entered at the keyboard. |
| Automatic relocate | Ability of the machine to return to the point where keying was interrupted to allow the operator to correct the copy. |
| Index/Reverse index | Ability of the machine to be spaced down (indexing) or up (reversing) without the need to return to left margin. |

## Optional Features

Features that further increase the capability of electronic typewriters are available. Three of the most popular features are described briefly in the following paragraphs.

### *Display*

Some electronic typewriters have what is called a *thin-window* or *one-line* display, which allows you to view a limited number of characters as they are being keyed. Other electronic typewriters include a *partial-page* display which typically allows 8 to 24 lines to be displayed. Some manufacturers of electronic typewriters provide a screen that displays a full page (56-66 lines) of copy. Such devices enable the office worker to see what is being keyed, proofread it, and make any corrections required before the lines or the document are printed. Corrections are far easier to make before a document is printed; therefore, this feature increases worker productivity.

**Illus. 7–11.** Electronic typewriter with partial-page display.

### Auxiliary Storage

Storage outside the internal memory of the electronic typewriter is called *auxiliary storage.* When the electronic typewriter is connected to a disk drive, the office worker can initiate a command to have a document stored on an auxiliary storage medium. Storing documents on auxiliary storage media expands the storage capabilities of the electronic typewriter. For example, a disk will hold approximately 100 pages of text.

### Communicating Capabilities

Electronic typewriters can become a part of a *communications network* by being connected with other electronic typewriters, word processors, or microcomputers. An electronic typewriter then is used as a means of receiving and transmitting information with other pieces of equipment. For example, if you are working at an electronic typewriter with the capability to receive data from a microcomputer, you can use the electronic type-writer as a printer for the data.

Equipment designed solely for word processing commonly is referred to as a *dedicated word processor*. Such a system often is made up of a single, self-contained station consisting of a key-board, a screen (monitor), a logic/intelligence unit, a storage unit, and a printer (page 277). In some models, several of these parts are combined in one unit; in others, each part is a separate unit.

## The Keyboard

The keyboard of a dedicated word processor to some extent will look very much like that of an electric typewriter. However, you will find that there are additional keys which permit you to perform common word/text processing functions. Because such equipment is made by many different manufacturers, you will not find identical arrangements of keys on all keyboards. How-ever, once you learn to identify the keys that will allow you to perform basic functions, you should be able to adapt your skill to other brands and models of word processors.

### Character Keys

These keys are those you know from your courses in keyboard-ing. These are the keys for letters, numbers, and basic symbols.

### Locate Keys

As the name implies, locate keys are used to move throughout a document or bring a specific portion of the document to the screen. The flashing rectangle or small hyphen which you see on the screen is called a cursor. The purpose of the cursor is to iden-tify the point on the screen where the *action* (keying, moving, inserting, or deleting text) is taking place. Locate keys include those with the directional arrows that are used to move the cur-sor up, down, to the left, and to the right. These keys are referred to as *cursor positioning keys*. You choose the arrow that will direct the movement of the cursor to a specific position within the text. Can you locate the cursor positioning keys on the right-hand side of the keyboard shown in Illus. 7–12?

Other locate keys include SEARCH, RECALL, PREVIOUS SCREEN, NEXT SCREEN, ROLL UP/ROLL DOWN, and SCROLL.

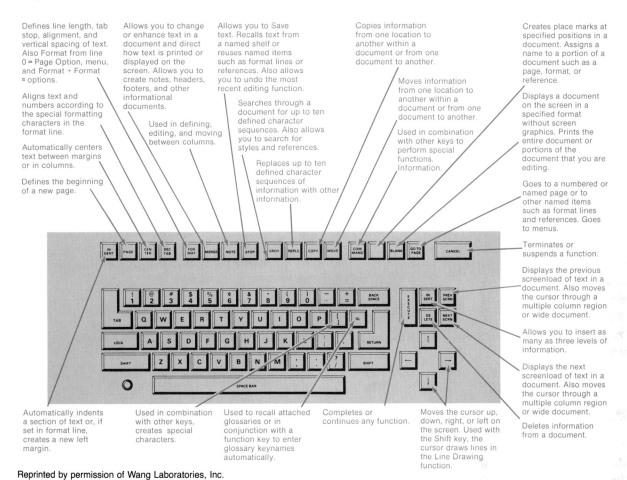

Defines line length, tab stop, alignment, and vertical spacing of text. Also Format from line 0 = Page Option, menu, and Format + Format = options.

Allows you to change or enhance text in a document and direct how text is printed or displayed on the screen. Allows you to create notes, headers, footers, and other informational documents.

Allows you to Save text. Recalls text from a named shelf or reuses named items such as format lines or references. Also allows you to undo the most recent editing function.

Copies information from one location to another within a document or from one document to another.

Creates place marks at specified positions in a document. Assigns a name to a portion of a document such as a page, format, or reference.

Aligns text and numbers according to the special formatting characters in the format line.

Used in defining, editing, and moving between columns.

Searches through a document for up to ten defined character sequences. Also allows you to search for styles and references.

Moves information from one location to another within a document or from one document to another.

Displays a document on the screen in a specified format without screen graphics. Prints the entire document or portions of the document that you are editing.

Automatically centers text between margins or in columns.

Used in combination with other keys to perform special functions. Information.

Defines the beginning of a new page.

Replaces up to ten defined character sequences of information with other information.

Goes to a numbered or named page or to other named items such as format lines and references. Goes to menus.

Terminates or suspends a function.

Displays the previous screenload of text in a document. Also moves the cursor through a multiple column region or wide document.

Allows you to insert as many as three levels of information.

Displays the next screenload of text in a document. Also moves the cursor through a multiple column region or wide document.

Deletes information from a document.

Automatically indents a section of text or, if set in format line, creates a new left margin.

Used in combination with other keys, creates special characters.

Used to recall attached glossaries or in conjunction with a function key to enter glossary keynames automatically.

Completes or continues any function.

Moves the cursor up, down, right, or left on the screen. Used with the Shift key, the cursor draws lines in the Line Drawing function.

Reprinted by permission of Wang Laboratories, Inc.

**Illus. 7–12.** The keyboard of a dedicated word processor.

### Format Keys

Format keys are used to arrange text. Typical format keys include INDENT, PAGE, CENTER, DECIMAL TAB, and FORMAT. Can you find these keys in the upper left portion of the keyboard shown in Illus. 7–12?

### Edit Keys

These keys are used to make revisions or changes to the text or to move text from one place to another. Basic edit keys include DELETE, INSERT, REPLACE, COPY, and MOVE. Can you find these keys on the keyboard shown in Illus. 7–12?

**Illus. 7–13.** Common format keys and their functions.

| KEY | ALLOWS YOU TO |
| --- | --- |
| INDENT | Indent all lines at the tab location |
| PAGE | Define the end of a page of text |
| CENTER | Center text automatically |
| DEC TAB | Align columns of numeric data at the decimal point |
| FORMAT | Design the appearance of the text |

**Illus. 7–14.** Common edit keys and their functions.

| KEY | ALLOWS YOU TO |
| --- | --- |
| DELETE | Remove text |
| INSERT | Add text |
| REPLC | Replace a character, word, or phrase with something else |
| COPY | Copy text from one part of a document to another |
| MOVE | Move text from one location to another |

### Transaction Keys

To carry through the function you wish or to reject a function, you must depress a transaction key. The two most common transaction keys you will find on a word processor keyboard are EXECUTE and CANCEL. Can you find these keys on the right-hand side of the keyboard in Illus. 7–12 on page 275?

**Illus. 7–15.** Common transaction keys and their functions.

| KEY | ALLOWS YOU TO |
| --- | --- |
| EXECUTE | Complete the operation |
| CANCEL | Stop the operation |

### The Monitor

A monitor, which is a video display screen, is a standard feature of most dedicated word processors. The monitor (also referred to as a *terminal*) allows you to see what you are keying. When an error is made, you simply backspace and strike the correct key. Because the copy is displayed on the screen, you can see the corrections and changes as you make them. Also, any text you access from memory will be shown on the monitor. The text displayed on the screen is called soft copy.

The amount of copy displayed on the screen varies from one model of word processor to another. Some models have full-page displays, while others have only partial-page displays. Most monitors have adjustments to control the brightness and intensity of the characters on the screen. Also, you can position the monitor for comfortable viewing. A special large-print video terminal (LPVT) has been developed for the ***visually impaired***.

***visually im-
paired:*** those who
experience difficulty
in seeing

Printer

CPU

Monitor

Keyboard

**Illus. 7–16.** The components of a dedicated word processor.

### Logic/Intelligence Unit

The logic/intelligence unit of a dedicated word processor, like that of an electronic typewriter, contains microprocessors. The microprocessors of a dedicated word processor, however, are much more powerful than those in electronic typewriters.

### Internal Storage (Memory)

*Standalone* (dedicated) word processors have internal storage. This storage is used for temporary storage of documents while they are being processed. The internal storage is larger in word processors than it is in electronic typewriters. In some models of word processors, hundreds of pages can be stored.

Documents to be saved generally are transferred from internal storage to an auxiliary medium, such as a diskette. Storage media are referred to as *off-line* when they can be removed and stored when not in use. Diskettes are the most popular type of off-line storage media.

**MULTI-STATION TEXT-EDITING SYSTEMS**

Multi-station text-editing systems have two or more workstations (keyboard and monitor) that share other parts of the system. Some shared systems consist of several terminals with one or two shared printers. In some instances, several terminals share a single logic/intelligence unit.

**THE MICRO-COMPUTER AS A WORD PROCESSOR**

*predates:* comes from an earlier time

The microcomputer is a highly versatile machine in today's business offices. The dedicated word processor **predates** the microcomputer as an invaluable machine for completing word processing tasks. However, with the use of software packages, the microcomputer is able to match the capabilities of some dedicated word processors.

Software packages are available at varying levels of sophistication to fit the processing needs of a particular office. There are basic packages which are relatively inexpensive that enable users to insert, delete, move, and copy blocks of text, as well as search for and replace words and justify the right-hand margin. More sophisticated word processing packages offer features such as boldface, italics, subscript, superscript, automatic footnoting and indexing, text merge, and electronic dictionaries.

There are software packages that combine word processing with other applications such as database management, spreadsheets, graphics, and communications capabilities. Such packages are called *integrated packages*. In many cases, these several applications can be accessed **interchangeably**. For example, spreadsheet and graphics applications could be integrated with a word processing application, enabling you to include details from a spreadsheet (in chart or graph form) within the body of a report.

*interchangeably:* permitting mutual substitution

The keyboard of a microcomputer looks very much like the keyboard of an electronic typewriter, except that there are additional keys. You will find variations from one manufacturer's models to those of other manufacturers.

**Illus. 7–17.** The versatility of the microcomputer makes it easy to combine word processing with other applications such as database management and graphics.

## ENTRY VIA NONKEY-BOARDING EQUIPMENT

It is time-consuming for an office worker to key every letter of every word that is to be processed. Therefore, designers of electronic office equipment are developing alternative ways of entering text for processing. Progress is being made and breakthroughs are anticipated. Presently, optical character readers and electronic shorthand machines are in use for some types of input. Also, voicewriters/talkwriters are in the experimental stage in the laboratories of some equipment manufacturing companies. These alternative ways of entering text for processing are discussed in the following paragraphs.

## Optical Character Readers

In some offices, optical character readers are being used as an alternative means of input for word/text processing. The *optical character reader* (OCR) scans a typewritten or printed page and converts the characters on it into electronic signals that are recorded on a magnetic medium, usually a floppy diskette. With the use of an OCR, the draft prepared at an electric typewriter or electronic typewriter can be entered electronically into the word processor's memory. No rekeying of the document is necessary. Then the word processing operator can recall the document, make all necessary formatting and editing changes, and print the final document.

As you might guess, there are specifications for the preparation of copy to be read by an OCR. If you are working in an office where you prepare copy that is to be entered by an OCR, you will need to read the equipment instructions carefully. Some models of OCR require that the original document be prepared on a typewriter with specific type styles; other models can read almost any standard type style.

**Illus. 7–18.** The red "glow" indicates that this OCR is scanning a document. The use of such equipment saves time because it automatically records the document on a magnetic form. No rekeying of the document is necessary!

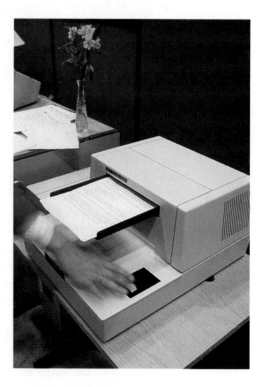

### Electronic Shorthand

A special model of the standard shorthand machine once used primarily by court reporters now is being used as a means of entering information into word processing systems. Keystrokes made on this equipment are transferred to magnetic tape and transcribed with the aid of a computer. The transcript can be displayed on a screen, printed, or recorded electronically for recall later. This process is called *computer assisted transcription.*

### Voicewriters/Talkwriters

Machines that can transcribe speech are already in experimental laboratories. There is some uncertainty as to when these machines will be commonplace in business offices. Since voices vary considerably in pronunciation, pitch, and speed, the technology required for speech recognition is difficult to perfect. However, progress is being made. Also, building the capability of equipment to "know" the range of vocabulary encountered in business communication poses problems.

The changes such machines will introduce to business offices are not clear. At this point, many forecasters believe office workers still will need to edit and format documents appropriately. Keyboarding skill is likely to be needed in many jobs for many, many more years!

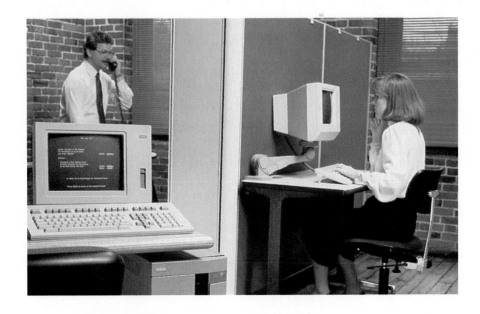

**Illus. 7–19.** This manager is using voice recognition equipment as an input form into a word processing system. As he speaks, the computer matches the spoken words to the words stored in computer memory and displays the message on the office assistant's terminal.

# REVIEW QUESTIONS

1. For what kinds of keyboarding tasks is the electric typewriter likely to be adequate?

2. What are some features of an electronic typewriter that are not available on electric typewriters?

3. How does the memory of an electronic typewriter increase the productivity of a typist?

4. In what way does auxiliary storage enhance the capability of an electronic typewriter?

5. What are the basic components of a dedicated word processor?

6. How does the keyboard of a dedicated word processor differ from that of an electric typewriter?

7. What is the usefulness of the locate keys on a dedicated word processor?

8. What is the function of internal storage in a word processor?

9. What components might be shared in a multistation text-editing system?

10. Why is an optical character reader (OCR) considered a timesaver in a WP center?

# INTERACTING WITH OTHERS

Ted is one of three office assistants in the small legal firm of Breece and O'Malley. Each office assistant has a workstation with a correcting electric typewriter. All three assistants share one workstation equipped with a dedicated word processor. Ted feels that his co-workers monopolize the use of the word processor because they use the system to keyboard nearly all the documents they process. Every time Ted tries to use the equipment, his co-workers say that they are working on a "rush job" that must be completed immediately.

Ted frequently has no choice but to use an electric typewriter to key multi-page reports in rough-draft form. After the originator reads and edits the draft, Ted often must rekey the entire report before it can be considered final copy. He feels that these long reports, which are typical of his workload, should be done on the word processing system.

If you were Ted, what would you say to your co-workers? What would you hope to achieve through your discussion with your co-workers?

**What You Are To Do:**  Prepare a response to the questions raised.

## EXTENDING YOUR MATH SKILLS

You work as an office assistant to the sales manager of Tidewater Computer Stores. You are helping with the preparation of a report comparing income earned through the first six months of this year with income earned during the first six months of last year. You are asked to complete the computations required on the report (on page 284) before you send it to the WP center to be keyboarded.

**What You Are To Do:**    Use the form in *Information Processing Activities* or use plain paper and compute the missing totals. Then determine the percentage change from the prior year to the current year. If necessary, refer to Reference Section D for information about percentages.

## APPLICATION ACTIVITY

Tanya Castillo is the supervisor in a general office with 12 employees. Each employee has an individual workstation. Some workstations are equipped with electric typewriters, others have electronic typewriters, and three have dedicated word processors. Tanya is responsible for delegating jobs. Ten tasks to be keyboarded during a typical day are given in the following list:

1. a short telephone message originally written in shorthand
2. a 10-page report that will require extensive revisions
3. a 3-paragraph letter
4. a first draft of a brief, 2-page report
5. a 1-page agenda for a meeting
6. a letter to be sent to 20 sales representatives
7. a 500-name mailing list which will be used monthly
8. file folder labels for 3 new clients
9. a memorandum to be sent to the entire office support staff of 25 persons
10. a 6-page statistical report

**What You Are To Do:**    On a plain sheet of paper, set up three columns, headed Electric Typewriter, Standard Electronic Typewriter (no auxiliary storage), and Dedicated Word Processor. For each of the ten jobs, determine which type of equipment would be most efficient. Then place the number of that task under the appropriate heading. For example, if you think the first job — a short telephone message — should be keyed at an electric typewriter, you would place the number "1" under the first column, "Electric Typewriter."

## Gross Income by Types of Products and Services
### Comparison of Six-Months Results
#### (Dollars in Millions)

| | Current Year (6 months) | Prior Year (6 months) | Percentage Change from Prior to Current Year |
|---|---|---|---|
| **Processors:** | | | |
| Sales | 282 | 303 | ? |
| Rentals | 72 | 173 | ? |
| Total | ? | ? | ? |
| | | | |
| **Peripherals:** | | | |
| Sales | 3055 | 2507 | ? |
| Rentals | 613 | 97 | ? |
| Total | ? | ? | ? |
| | | | |
| **Office Systems / Work Stations:** | | | |
| Sales | 2828 | 2707 | ? |
| Rentals | 244 | 444 | ? |
| Total | ? | ? | ? |
| | | | |
| **Program Products** | 1088 | 854 | ? |
| | | | |
| **Maintenance Services** | 1833 | 1553 | ? |
| | | | |
| **Other:** | | | |
| Sales | 447 | 381 | ? |
| Services | 99 | 83 | ? |
| Rentals | 89 | 126 | ? |
| Total | ? | ? | ? |
| | | | |
| **Grand Total** | ? | ? | ? |

# Topic 3

## FROM FORMATTING TO STORING

When you have completed your study of this topic, you will be able to

- explain the basic formatting decisions in processing business communications

- explain basic editing procedures and processing aids

- describe how printing is done in a word/text processing system

- describe the office worker's responsibility for distribution/transmission and for storage/retrieval

This topic focuses on the remaining phases of the word/text processing cycle. As you become acquainted with formatting and editing procedures on electronic typewriters and word processing systems, you will find your general knowledge of preparing business communications at electric typewriters very useful.

Newer types of equipment make formatting and editing far easier than is possible on a standard electric typewriter. Imagine that you have prepared at an electric typewriter what you believed was a final copy of a letter. The executive reads the letter and decides that several sentences should be changed. Now you have to rekey the entire letter in order to make the changes! If you were using a text-editing system, however, the task of making the changes could be accomplished easily and quickly. First, you could recall the letter from storage. Once the docu-

ment was displayed on the screen, you could read the copy, make the needed changes, and quickly print a copy of the revised letter. You would be keying only the changes. You would delete the unnecessary words and sentences by depressing one or more keys. The time saved in making revisions makes word processing equipment very appealing to office workers.

When you key copy at an electric typewriter, each letter you strike results immediately in an imprint on the paper in your typewriter. This is not the case, however, when you key copy at many electronic typewriters or at a text-editing system. Instead of being printed immediately on paper, keystrokes (or entire documents) are saved in memory and printed only after the text has been proofread and revised.

A printer is a separate component of a text-editing system. Printers come in a variety of styles and produce varying qualities of print. You may work in an office that has different types of printers available. You may have the task of selecting the printer that is appropriate for a particular job. Your knowledge of the different types of printers and the types of jobs they are commonly used for will aid you in making these decisions.

Once a letter is printed and signed by the originator, you may be responsible for seeing that it is distributed or transmitted as directed. You also may be responsible for storing (filing) a copy of the document in order to assure prompt retrieval in the future.

## DOCUMENT FORMATTING

The arrangement of a text is referred to as its format. The process of making the proper adjustments to the machine or system in order to achieve the desired arrangement of text is called *formatting*. Many companies have procedures manuals in which you will find standard formatting instructions for the common types of documents you will be preparing. If there are no standard format examples, you will need to make formatting decisions that will result in attractive, easy-to-read documents.

### Formatting on Electric Typewriters

From your experiences in learning keyboarding, you are acquainted with the features of electric typewriters that aid you in formatting appropriately. You know how the line length is set, how spacing is established, and how tabs are set. As you know, any one of these settings can be readily changed if another document you process requires a different format.

### Formatting on Electronic Typewriters

Electronic typewriters require essentially the same operations for formatting as electric typewriters require. However, it is possible to store your formatting selections in the memory of the electronic typewriter by pressing a *code key*. For instance, you can select an option that will not require manual returning to a new line. Your typewriter will move automatically to a new writing line after the last complete word that will fit within the present writing line is keyed. You will need to use the return key only for short lines, such as the date and address of a letter and the final line in some paragraphs.

Other formatting keys on electronic typewriters were discussed in Topic 2. These special keys enable you to perform many functions automatically. For example, you can center a word or phrase, align columns of numbers at the decimal point, and indent a series of lines automatically.

**Illus. 7–20.** A wide variety of business documents must be formatted by office workers who complete word processing tasks.

### Formatting on Text-Editing Systems

Formatting on text-editing systems requires different procedures from those used on typewriters. Furthermore, there are variations among the different models of equipment in how formatting is done. Since printing is a separate function in text-editing systems, some formatting decisions may be made after all the copy has been inputted and before the printing is begun.

*Amy uses a word processor for keyboarding documents. When keying a letter for Mr. Witsenburg, she used a five-inch line, single spacing, and a nonjustified right margin. However, before printing the document, Amy changed the format instructions so that the letter was printed with a six-inch line, double spacing, and a justified right margin.*

On one system, formatting decisions are displayed below the *status line.* The information on the status line includes the identification of the document (often a number), the storage location, and where the cursor presently is located. As you can see on page 288, the document's identification (ID) is *0311,* its location is *B,* and the cursor is presently on *page 1, line 1, position 1.*

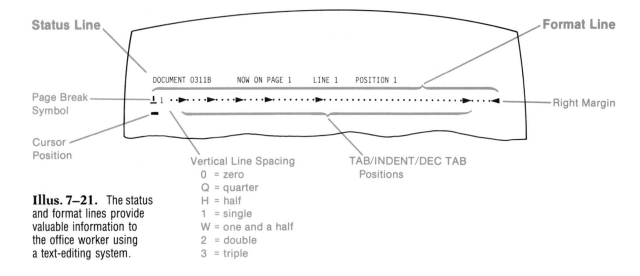

Status Line

Format Line

Page Break Symbol

Right Margin

Cursor Position

DOCUMENT 0311B        NOW ON PAGE 1      LINE 1      POSITION 1

Vertical Line Spacing
0 = zero
Q = quarter
H = half
1 = single
W = one and a half
2 = double
3 = triple

TAB/INDENT/DEC TAB
Positions

**Illus. 7–21.** The status and format lines provide valuable information to the office worker using a text-editing system.

Immediately below the status line is the *format line*, which shows the formatting decisions that will guide the inputting of copy. Such a line is a common feature of text-editing systems. Note the format line in Illus. 7–21. The format line shows that the document is to be single-spaced. It also shows the location of the tabs and the beginning and end of the writing line.

Any of these decisions can be changed. For example, you can change from single spacing to double spacing by depressing a *2* in the position where the *1* is shown in the format line on the screen. By spacing over the tab indicator, the position for a tab is eliminated. By spacing over the end-of-line indicator and continuing to space, the writing line can be extended. When the format line contains the proper specifications for the document you will process, you are ready to depress the transaction key that will cause the cursor to move from the format line to the first line where you will begin to enter text.

Many software programs provide preset format decisions called defaults. They are called defaults because if you fail to change any one of them, the preset decision stands. Commonly established defaults include line length, top margin, bottom margin, line spacing, tabs, headers, footers, page length, page number, and *pitch*. On many systems, format lines are automatically displayed at the top of each page on the screen. However, this line will not appear on the printed document.

*pitch:* number of characters or spaces per horizontal inch

You will find that a user manual for any equipment you are expected to use will have complete details for all formatting possibilities. You will need to become familiar with the procedures for choosing the range of formatting options appropriate for your word processing tasks.

## DOCUMENT EDITING

Many business documents are changed one or more times between the time they are composed and the time they are prepared in final copy. The process of making changes generally is referred to as editing. *Editing* refers both to changes the originator makes and to changes that an office assistant makes in producing a new draft of a proposed document. Drafts prior to the final copy are referred to as *rough drafts*. To make changes that any office assistant can easily understand, originators often use standard proofreader's marks. (A listing of commonly used proofreader's marks can be found in Reference Section A.)

*Steve works as a word processor in the office of the director of engineering, who prepares many reports. Steve always prepares a rough draft first because he knows that the director will use standard proofreader's marks to edit his own writing extensively. After the director gives Steve the revised report, Steve edits the document by making all the changes noted on the draft.*

### Basic Editing Tasks

When you work at a word processor, you will spend some time getting acquainted with the way in which you can easily edit copy that requires the following changes:

- correcting a word that was miskeyed
- inserting a word (or words) not in the original draft
- deleting a word (or words) now considered unnecessary

While the specific steps to be used for editing vary according to the type of equipment you are using, in all instances simply pressing the appropriate keys will quickly result in the change you desire.

### Other Edit Functions

Text-editing equipment also has been designed to accommodate more complex editing changes commonly made in the preparation of business documents. It takes slightly more time to become familiar with the steps to be followed in making changes such as these:

- moving text from one location to another
- copying text to one or more new locations, while also leaving the text in its original location
- searching through the text for words to be printed in bold type
- searching through the text to replace a word with a new word in each place where it is used

## PROCESSING AIDS

Manufacturers of word processing equipment and software have introduced a number of aids to assist operators in completing processing efficiently. Naturally, there are variations from one manufacturer to another, but some basic aids are commonly available. The more popular ones will be discussed briefly in the following paragraphs.

### Scrolling

Moving the text so that you are able to scan previous or succeeding text from any location in the document is referred to as *scrolling*. Ease in scrolling both vertically and horizontally facilitates making corrections and locating a particular line or paragraph of copy.

### Menus

A listing of available options under the specific category in which you are interested is called a menu. Note the menu in Illus. 7–22. You are able to select an option by moving the cursor to the position of the option you wish. *Submenus* are more detailed listings under each of the options in the menu.

### Prompts and Messages

Prompts and messages appear on your monitor at appropriate times to aid you in operating text-editing equipment. Their purpose is to provide guidance as you move through your processing tasks.

Prompts are usually one-line statements or questions that provide additional instructions or request specific detail before the next step can be completed. Typical prompts are:

- Copy What?
- Delete What?

- Document:
- End of Edit?

Additionally, you learned that evaluation of employees is needed in order for the manager to maintain a well-organized WP center. Evaluation of one's own performance is a valuable activity for assuring growth on the job. Steps in evaluating your performance were outlined.

May 16, 19--

Mr. Phillip H. Tobin
714 Garden City Drive
Monroeville, PA  15146-4792

Dear Mr. Tobin

Thank you very much for your inquiry concerning a position with our company as an administrative support assistant. I have just reviewed your personal data sheet, and you seem to have excellent office skills. Our administrative support assistants are promoted to those positions after they have worked in our company for a number of years and have demonstrated their ability to work efficiently within the office system.  I think you will find similar hiring policies in most companies.

No ¶ We do have several openings for text processing operators in our Text Processing Center.  If you would like to be considered for one of these positions, please complete the enclosed application and return it to James Baker, *lc* Supervisor of the Text Processing Center.

If you decide to pursue a position with our company, I think you will find that we have an excellent promotion policy for qualified employees. *very attractive working conditions and*

Yours truly,

(Mrs.) Dorothy *E.* Meyers, Personnel Director

Enclosure

ts

## KEY TERMS

| | |
|---|---|
| user departments | defaults |
| cursor | editing |
| monitor | menu |
| soft copy | prompts |
| format | messages |

**INTEGRATED CHAPTER ACTIVITIES**

## Activity 1

You are an office assistant to Ms. Renee V. Bentley, director of administrative services for a major insurance company. Ms. Bentley also is president of the National Administrative Services Association, a professional organization in which she has been active for many years. The insurance company encourages her involvement in this organization and is pleased that this year Ms. Bentley is serving as president. When you return from your afternoon break, Ms. Bentley asks you to key a final draft of a letter and an enclosure to accompany the letter.

**What You Are To Do:** • Key a final copy of the letter on page 301. Make all changes indicated on the draft. Use the letterhead provided in *Information Processing Activities* or plain paper. (The National Administrative Services Association is located at 3033 Finley Road, Downers Grove, IL 60515-3278.)
• Key a final copy of the enclosure which follows. Provide an appropriate heading for the sheet. Use plain paper. Use the current date.

Word/text processing equipment can be used to complete this activity.

## Activity 2

You work in a WP center. Bradley L. Levine, manager of Computer Services, for Current Enterprises is developing new procedures for handling software packages. The supervisor of your center gives you the rough draft of the memorandum on page 302.

**What You Are To Do:** Key a final copy of the memorandum in good form. Use the current date. Use the memorandum form in *Information Processing Activities* or a plain sheet of paper on which you key appropriate parts of the memo form.

Word/text processing equipment can be used to complete this activity.

Mr. Willard Shapiro ^President
5791 Ghirardelli Square          Shapiro Electronics (Corp.) sp.
San Francisco, 94132-4291
                    ^CA

Dear Will

           the
At ~~our~~ Board meeting following our annual convention in
Boston last week, we voted unanimously to invite you to be
the general program chairman for ~~our~~ annual meeting
~~scheduled for~~ San Francisco ~~next year.~~  next year's
          ^in        considerable
You have had ~~a lot of~~ experience in our organization ~~and~~ you
know what is required to handle this job properly.  We have
no question about your ability to do so.  You will, of
course, have the support of our staff.  At our meeting we
determined that there should be approximately 43 sessions
during the convention.  On the enclosed sheet we have
identified the general topics that the Board believes must
be ~~included in the topics of~~ the programs.  Also indicated are levels and
 ^covered by                                    formats that are to be included.
~~As you know,~~ three members of this year's committee will
continue as members of next year's committee.  The three who
are continuing are as follows:  Amy Sweeney of Sacramento,
Donald Wohland of Palo Alto, and Roger Mitliff of Berkeley.

                      that
The Board and I hope ~~the~~ you will accept our invitation to
assume this important job for the Association.

Sincerely yours

The subject areas to be covered include:

- Technology    · Training
- Management     · Productivity
- Software       · Professional Developement

Session levels ~~should include:~~  are:

- ⌈ Basic
- │ Intermediate
- ⌊ Advanced

Formats for sessions should include:

- Workshop
- Lecture          · Roundtable Exchange
                   · Panel Discussion

Use your own
judgment in
regard to arranging
this on a full sheet
of paper.
        RB

~~We believe~~ we can handle software requests in a more efficient manner if all requests within your department are approved by you before they are forwarded to my office.

To assist both you and Central Computing in requesting and evaluating software, a software Request Form has been attached to this memorandum.  As you will note, Part A ~~of this form~~ contains the minimum information that must be known about a product in order for it to be ~~investigated.~~ *considered.* Part B contains questions of a more technical nature which (can usually) be answered by the vendor or by information *(contained in* ~~secured from~~ the ~~product~~ *software* installation manual.)

Remember that acquisition of software packages is based on technical/support considerations.  Once a ~~product~~ *package* has been approved, an implementation schedule will be drawn up by our office ~~and~~ *working with* the staff member who requested ~~it~~ *the package*.  Dates will be set for initial installation, full testing, and production date.  The test period will require your full cooperation, since ~~this is the period when~~ you ~~can~~ *as* learn how to use the product, ~~noting~~ *and note* any "bugs" that need to be eliminated.

During the test period, we will develop documentation and support materials for users.

*Please send this memo to all Department Managers - the subject is Requesting New Software.*

*Bradley L. Levine*

1. Determine that the information you have received by telephone or letter is complete.
2. Identify yourself at your terminal by keying in the security ID assigned to you. Also key in the password for order processing. This is a very important step and is necessary to ensure that only persons authorized to process orders actually do so.
3. Follow the prescribed format for entering the sales order data. The prescribed format must be followed if the data you are entering are to be reviewed appropriately and accepted by the computer. Your input will be processed immediately, or as soon as possible. The first step in the processing done by the computer will be a credit check.
4. Read your terminal screen to determine if the order is acceptable. If the order has not been accepted, there will be a message of explanation on your screen. For example, the customer may not be on an approved list. Or the customer may have a balance outstanding that, when combined with this new order, would result in a balance due that is beyond the customer's credit limit. You will note such a message on the screen shown in Illus. 8–10.

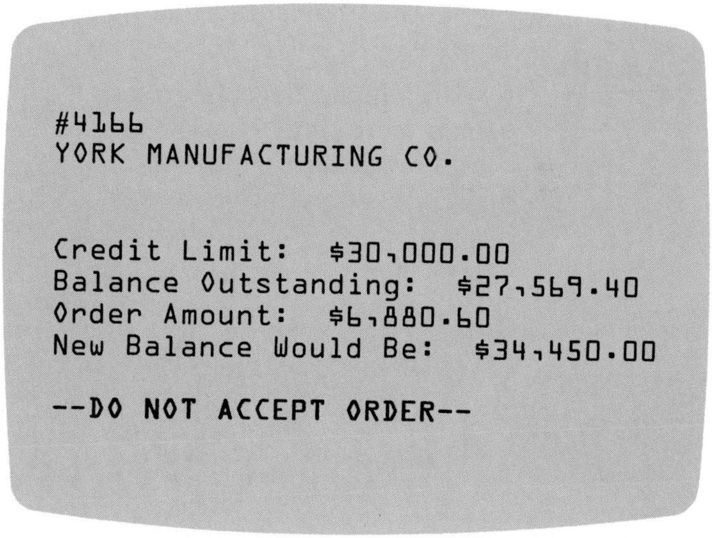

```
#4166
YORK MANUFACTURING CO.


Credit Limit:   $30,000.00
Balance Outstanding:   $27,569.40
Order Amount:   $6,880.60
New Balance Would Be:   $34,450.00

--DO NOT ACCEPT ORDER--
```

**Illus. 8–10.**
Customer credit information a worker might see on a terminal screen.

5. If the order is rejected, you will want to follow company procedures in such circumstances. You may have to prepare a letter to be sent to the customer or a memorandum to be sent to the credit department.

6. If the order is accepted, input the proper commands for completion of the processing. At this point the computer will perform all calculations required and will simultaneously transmit the necessary information to the terminals in the warehouse, the billing department, and the packing and shipping department. In each of these departments, there are printers for outputting the documents needed for completing the order processing tasks.

## DIFFERENCES IN PROCESSING

As you review the differences among the three processing methods—manual, batch and on-line—you will note that the differences are related to these factors:

- how processing is done
- how documents are prepared
- how documents are distributed

You will find these differences summarized in the table shown in Illus. 8–11. Remember, what is to be accomplished does not change as you shift from one system to another. The shift from manual to batch or from batch to on-line simply reflects the company's judgment that such a shift will result in certain advantages. These advantages are that the company's processing will be done:

- with a higher level of accuracy
- on a more timely basis
- at a far faster rate
- with less need for office workers to perform manual operations

| VARIATIONS IN ORDER PROCESSING SYSTEMS | | | |
|---|---|---|---|
| System | Processing | Preparation of Documents | Distribution of Documents |
| manual | by office employees with the aid of typewriters and calculators | by office employees | by interoffice mail or messenger |
| batch | by computer in data processing center | by computer in data processing center | by interoffice mail or messenger |
| on-line, interactive | by computer at terminals in offices throughout the organization | by computer in department where needed | by computer |

**Illus. 8–11.**
Variations in order processing systems.

# REVIEW QUESTIONS

1. Why do companies organize their order processing system carefully?
2. What departments are likely to participate in the order processing tasks?
3. Describe the information you should have at your desk if you are receiving orders by telephone in the sales department.
4. What is the responsibility of a credit department?
5. What is a packing list?
6. What is the primary task of a billing department?
7. Why is a bill of lading prepared?
8. Describe what you would do as an office worker in the sales department if your company used a batch system for processing orders.
9. Explain how documents are prepared for the various departments if you are working in an organization that has an on-line, interactive system for processing orders.
10. In what general ways do the manual, batch, and on-line systems for processing orders differ?

# INTERACTING WITH OTHERS

An office assistant in a very busy order department got a telephone call from a regular customer who ordered a long list of items. Later, when preparing a sales order, the assistant discovered that for one item there was no indication of color desired. The assistant knew that the customer wanted the order as quickly as possible. The customer had called from out of town. When the assistant attempted to reach the customer by telephone, there was no response. So as not to hold up the order, the assistant thought the best decision would be just to guess the color preference for the item. That way the order could be processed immediately.

**What You Are To Do:** Prepare brief responses to the following questions:

A. Would you have guessed the customer's preference as the office assistant did? Why? Why not?

B. What do you believe is the office assistant's responsibility in interacting with the customer who is placing an order?

C. What procedures could the assistant follow to be sure of getting all details for each item ordered?

## EXTENDING YOUR MATH SKILLS

Many companies encourage their customers to pay invoices promptly by allowing a cash discount if payment is made within 10 or 15 days of the invoice date. Assume that you are determining if customers have written checks for the correct amounts. The invoices you are checking show the details provided on the printout below. Note that 2/10, n/30 means that a 2 percent discount is allowed if payment is made within 10 days of the invoice date. The total owed is to be paid within 30 days.

**What You Are To Do:** Compute the amount that should appear on the check received from each of the following five customers.

| Customer | Invoice date | Amount | Terms | Date payment made | Amount of check |
|----------|--------------|--------|-------|-------------------|-----------------|
| E. G. Jay and Co. | 11/29/-- | $ 9,785.75 | 2/10, n/30 | 12/8/-- | ? |
| Johnson and Sanders | 11/30/-- | 4,750.25 | 2/10, n/30 | 12/9/-- | ? |
| Lannon and Sons | 11/30/-- | 21,560.59 | 2/15, n/30 | 12/14/-- | ? |
| Littleston Corp. | 11/30/-- | 8,350.00 | 2/15, n/30 | 12/17/-- | ? |
| Marsdon & Marsh, Inc. | 11/30/-- | 24,540.00 | 2/15, n/30 | 12/14/-- | ? |

## APPLICATION ACTIVITY

You work in the sales order department of Wyland Fabric & Wallcovering Company; 14 Hoosier Street; Adams, MA 01220-4351. Orders are received by letter and by telephone. Two telephone orders and two order letters follow. (**Note:** *Qty.* refers to *yards* in all cases.)

**What You Are To Do:** Complete a sales order form for each of the four orders. Use the forms in *Information Processing Activities* or prepare forms similar to the one shown in Illus. 8–4 on page 310. Number the sales orders consecutively, beginning with 5021.

*initiated:* begun; gotten underway

operations. Purchases are actually *initiated* by the various departments. An office worker in one of the departments that needs goods or supplies will fill in a purchase requisition. A *purchase requisition* is a form that describes what is to be bought. The department manager is authorized to approve purchases and to forward the forms to the purchasing department for processing.

In Illus. 8–13 you will see a purchase requisition prepared for submission to the purchasing department. You will find there are variations among different companies in the information provided.

---

**Lehigh Community Hospital** ✚          **PURCHASE REQUISITION**

Date __November 17, 19--__          Department __Central Food Services__

From __Steven Zabitz__          Location __Ground Floor, Room 310__

Date Required __Within 6 weeks, if possible__     Charge to
Account No. _____
                                                  (Accounting Use Only)

| Quantity | Description | Unit Price | Total |
|----------|-------------|-----------|-------|
| 12  doz. | Heavy white stoneware plates | 4.79 | 689.76 |
| 12  doz. | Heavy white stoneware soup bowls | 4.40 | 633.60 |
| 12  doz. | Heavy white stoneware mugs | 3.10 | 446.40 |
|          |             |           | 1,769.76 |

NOTE:   I've made some inquiries and I think these are the best prices available.  Suggest you buy from Baum Chinaware at 17 East 26th Street, New York, NY  10010-4557.

Deliver to __Steven Zabitz__          Department __Central Food Services__

Approved for Purchase by __*Emilio Ramos*__
                              Department Manager

---

**Illus. 8–13.**  A form initiated within a company to identify items that need to be purchased.

If you have the responsibility for receiving purchase requisitions, you will have to:

- review the purchase requisition to see that all the information needed is provided

- verify that the signature is that of the person in the department who is authorized to approve such requisitions
- check items listed in catalogues maintained in the purchasing department to be sure all details, including item identification number, size, and price, are correct

## Preparing Purchase Orders

If you work in the purchasing department, you will find that purchase requisitions are reviewed before you are asked to prepare purchase orders. A *purchase order* is a form used to order products from a supplier. The purchasing agent may have to make a decision about the best source for the product being ordered.

After the review by the purchasing agent, you probably will have the task of preparing purchase orders. You will find that it is common practice to use purchase order forms that are *prenumbered*, which means the numbers are printed in sequence on the supply of forms. You may be in an office that processes orders manually or one which processes them electronically.

**Illus. 8–14.** A purchase order prepared by Community Supermarkets, Inc. and sent to Modern Plastics Corporation.

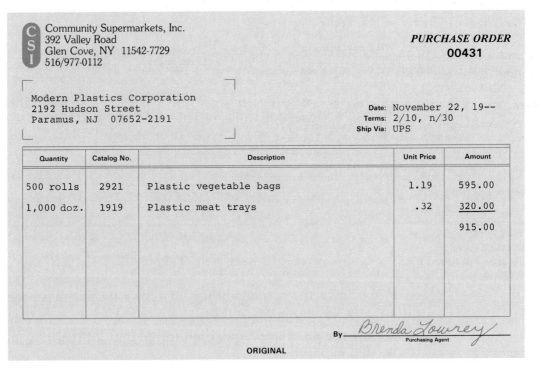

Community Supermarkets, Inc.
392 Valley Road
Glen Cove, NY  11542-7729
516/977-0112

**PURCHASE ORDER**
**00431**

Modern Plastics Corporation
2192 Hudson Street
Paramus, NJ  07652-2191

Date: November 22, 19--
Terms: 2/10, n/30
Ship Via: UPS

| Quantity | Catalog No. | Description | Unit Price | Amount |
|---|---|---|---|---|
| 500 rolls | 2921 | Plastic vegetable bags | 1.19 | 595.00 |
| 1,000 doz. | 1919 | Plastic meat trays | .32 | 320.00 |
| | | | | 915.00 |

By _Brenda Lowrey_
Purchasing Agent

ORIGINAL

If your computer system is on-line, but not interactive, you will be able to access the up-to-date listing for any item. Then you can determine what the quantity on hand is. If, on the other hand, your computer system is on-line, interactive, you will merely input your question about the particular item: "What is quantity on hand for Item No. 4567?" Then you will find printed on your screen the up-to-date quantity of the item.

*If Rachel were at work in the central stockroom for a company that had an on-line system for its total company (including the stores at the malls), managers would no longer need to call her. Instead, they would be able to use terminals at the local stores to access the information needed.*

## REVIEW QUESTIONS

1. What two principles are considered important in purchasing goods and maintaining inventories?

2. How does centralized purchasing differ from decentralized purchasing in a company?

3. Who prepares a purchase requisition?

4. What is the purpose of a purchase requisition?

5. What information is needed on a purchase order?

6. To whom are copies of purchase orders sent?

7. Describe how you prepare purchase orders if you are at work at a terminal in an on-line, interactive computer system.

8. Why does a vendor send a confirmation to a customer?

9. What are two common responsibilities of office workers who work in receiving departments?

10. What is the purpose of a physical count?

## MAKING DECISIONS

Barry, who works in the stockroom of a large department store, was surprised to see a selling department manager coming toward his workstation. Barry realized that someone apparently had left the door of the stockroom unlocked, even though the stockroom was to be locked at all times. Those who wanted goods were supposed to ring a bell to gain entrance to the stockroom. The manager said to Barry: "I need stock in a hurry; our sales are more than we anticipated today. I'll just walk around and take what I need. When I get back upstairs I'll make a list of the items I have as I put them on the shelves, and I'll send you the list."

Barry was relatively new in the position. He recalled that during his orientation, the supervisor had stated repeatedly how important it was that no merchandise leave the stockroom without a record being made on the spot. The supervisor also had said that the record had to be signed by the person taking the goods.

**What You Are To Do:**   What response would you make at this point if you were in Barry's situation?

## EXTENDING YOUR ENGLISH SKILLS

The excerpt at the top of page 339 is from a report being prepared by a manager. The excerpt has six errors in the use of plurals and five errors in the use of the possessive form.

**What You Are To Do:**   Prepare a copy of the excerpt, correcting all errors noted. Underscore the words in which you changed the form to correct an error.

## APPLICATION ACTIVITIES

### Activity 1: Purchasing Department

You work in the centralized purchasing department of the Regency hotel. The purchasing department manager has given you the purchase requisition which was received from the housekeeping department. Notes on the requisition, page 340, were made by the manager of your department. You have a file of catalogues from suppliers. When you check the catalogues for the linen and towel manufacturing companies, you find the information at the bottom of page 339.

**What You Are To Do:**   Prepare purchase orders for the goods listed on the purchase requisition from housekeeping. Use the forms provided in *Information Processing Activities* or prepare two forms similar to the one shown on page 328. Request that goods be shipped via truck.

# PRODUCTIVITY CORNER

**Blake Williams**
*OFFICE SUPERVISOR*

## HOW DO YOU LEARN A "FOREIGN" LANGUAGE?

DEAR MR. WILLIAMS:

I was elected by my two friends to ask you how we can learn a "foreign" language—the language used in the offices where we work.

My two friends and I began our first full-time jobs about a month ago. Wendy works for the chief economist at a large bank in the Wall Street area; Debbie is at a large advertising agency on Madison Avenue; I'm at the headquarters office of a brokerage house. We were together Friday night. We all said that we are stumped again and again by the language used all around us. We all decided that we could overcome this problem. We think we should understand what is going on so we can do our jobs more intelligently. Do you have any hints for us?— KATHI, FOR WENDY AND DEBBIE, TOO, FROM NEW YORK CITY

DEAR KATHI, WENDY, AND DEBBIE:

I like your spirit. Of course, you can learn the new languages you face at work.

There are a number of ways you can gain command of the new language each of you hears. Additionally, there are some sources for assistance.

1. Listen attentively to the context in which an unfamiliar word appears to determine if you can guess what the word represents.
2. Write down *every* word that is puzzling to you.
3. Think of the new words you have added each day and use the following sources to see if you can discover the proper meanings:
   - memos and other correspondence where what you heard might appear in written form and provide some clues to you
   - reference materials available to workers (magazines related to the specialization or even a dictionary)
   - specialized columns in newspapers such as the *Wall Street Journal* and *The New York Times*.

Best wishes in gaining command of your "foreign" languages.—BLAKE WILLIAMS

# Chapter 9

# Data Processing: Financial Applications

Financial information is critical to the successful functioning of any organization. For example, checks received from customers must be recorded as bank deposits and as payments in customers' accounts; records of sales must be maintained so that monthly statements can be prepared for customers who have balances outstanding.

The financial accounting system that provides the needed financial information is based on principles accepted by the accounting profession. Companies adhere to these principles so they can process financial transactions efficiently and can compare their results of operations and financial position with the results of other companies. You will learn about the reports of results of operations and financial position in Chapter 11.

In this chapter, you are introduced to several specific components of financial accounting systems and to the data processing procedures related to each. Remember that the size of an organization will influence how financial data pro-

cessing tasks are organized. For example, in a small business one office employee may take care of all financial transactions, from recording them to preparing reports. In a large business, on the other hand, many employees are needed to process just one type of transaction, such as sales to customers or payroll for employees. The method of processing—whether manual or computer-assisted—will influence the way in which you perform tasks in data processing. If you are using a manual system, payments from customers will be recorded with pen on a card or sheet. If you are using a computer-assisted system, those same payments from customers will be recorded by keying the payment at your terminal keyboard.

The objectives of this chapter are to

- introduce you to common recordkeeping procedures related to cash and accounts receivable

- help you develop an understanding of procedures for processing payments

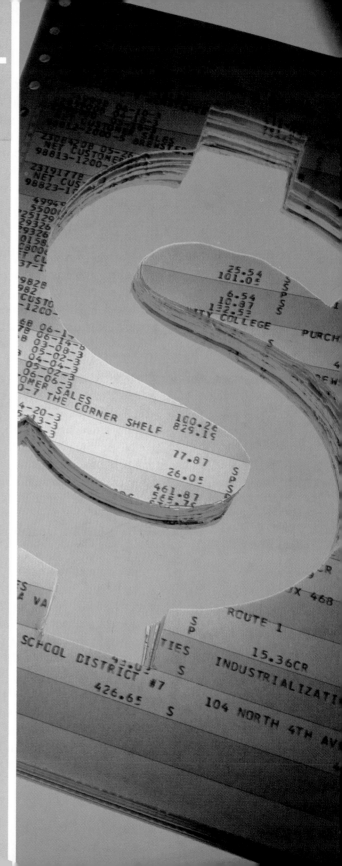

# Topic 1

## CASH AND ACCOUNTS RECEIVABLE

When you have completed your study of this topic, you will be able to

- explain the value of internal control for cash handling procedures
- prepare a deposit slip
- prepare entries for a petty cash fund
- prepare a bank account reconciliation
- describe procedures for maintaining accounts receivable

In the business world, *cash* refers both to actual cash (coins and bills) and to funds in checking accounts in banks. While some companies, such as supermarkets and retail stores, may handle large volumes of currency, in other companies virtually all transactions are paid by checks. The treasurer of the company and the departments that report to this executive are given the responsibility for managing all activity related to cash.

If you work in a small office, you are likely to have some responsibility for cash-related transactions. If you work in a large company, you may work in a department where many cash-related transactions are processed. You will find that you will comprehend your tasks if you thoroughly understand the safeguards for cash and procedures for processing cash.

As you learned in Chapter 8, many sales are made on account with payment made at some future time. The amounts of money owed a large company at any one time can be considerable. Office workers are needed to take care of customer accounts. In fact, in large companies there is an accounts receivable department. **Accounts receivable** is the accounting term for the amounts owed by customers for goods or services provided. You will find it useful to understand the basic procedures for handling accounts receivable.

## SAFEGUARDS FOR CASH

***negotiable:*** transferable from one person to another

As you know, cash is valuable. Businesses use the term *cash* to mean currency, bills, and checks. Currency and bills are easily transferred without identifying the owner. Checks can be transferred with some ease because they are ***negotiable***. Therefore businesses must carefully guard the flow of cash, regardless of its form, through their organizations.

***fraud:*** an act of misrepresentation

You will find that companies organize tasks to minimize the possibility of ***fraud*** and theft of cash. For example, in a small company, the owner may open all incoming mail, remove all checks and cash, and make all deposits at the bank. The owner also may personally sign all checks issued. Furthermore, the owner may directly supervise all the employees. This provides additional assurance that company ***assets***, including cash, are not being ***misappropriated***. The overall organization for safeguarding assets is referred to as internal control.

***assets:*** resources available for use

***misappropriated:*** used for purposes other than those anticipated

### Division of Responsibility

Of course in processing cash transactions direct supervision by the owner-manager is not possible in large organizations. You will find, therefore, that companies beyond those classified as very small have instituted procedures to safeguard cash, as well as other assets. In Illus. 9–1, note the division of tasks that aids in insuring that all checks that are mailed to the company are actually added to the company's cash account.

### Internal Audit Function

***audits:*** examinations to verify the facts reported

In many companies, you will find that there is a department overseeing that the system for safeguarding assets functions properly. Staff in such a department performs ***audits*** to determine if the procedures for control are actually being followed.

## PROCESSING OF INCOMING CHECKS

| Mailroom Clerk  | Cashier  | Accounting Clerk  |
|---|---|---|
| • opens mail<br>• sorts mail, placing all checks in one pile<br>• Prepares multiple copies of a listing of all checks<br>• forwards checks and a copy of listing to the cashier<br>• forwards a copy of the listing to the accounting office<br>• files one copy of the listing | • receives the listing of checks prepared by the mailroom clerk<br>• verifies the listing by comparing each check with the listing<br>• prepares deposit slip<br>• makes deposit in person or by mail<br>• receives a copy of duplicate deposit slip receipted by bank<br>• forwards a copy of receipted deposit slip to accounting office | • receives the listing of checks prepared by the mailroom clerk<br>• receives the copy of the receipted deposit ticket prepared by the cashier<br>• verifies the listing prepared by the mailroom by matching each check with the deposit ticket received from the cashier<br>• makes entries in accounting records |

**Illus. 9–1.** Division of responsibility for processing incoming checks.

*Jill, a staff member in the internal audit department, was assigned the task of determining the efficiency of the mailroom procedures. She arrived unannounced early in the morning just as the mail was being opened. She observed the work of two office assistants, Tom and Rica, who had the task of recording all checks received. Tom and Rica knew the procedures they were expected to follow. They adhered to the procedures at all times, so the observation revealed no problems.*

As an office worker, you at times will help the personnel responsible for internal auditing. Such employees perform a valuable service. They determine if resources are being used as planned, and they determine how well the operations of the company are functioning. Your cooperation with such personnel is critical in meeting the overall goals of the internal auditing function, and ultimately, the goals of the organization itself.

### Bonded Employees

*adhere:* stick to

To further safeguard resources, companies strive to hire persons of integrity, which means honest persons who will ***adhere*** to the policies and rules pertaining to their jobs. As further assurance that losses of assets will not be a financial loss to the company, employees are bonded. Bonding is insurance that provides payment in the event of financial loss due to an employee's theft or fraud related to company resources.

By securing references, the insurance company makes a search of the employee's past behavior. This search, which is generally more thorough than that done by the company at the time employees are hired, is considered another advantage of bonding.

**Illus. 9–2.** As a staff member in the internal audit department, this office worker has responsibility for verifying the totals of each day's sales.

**COMMON TASKS OF OFFICE WORKERS**

There are many tasks office workers perform in aiding executives and managers responsible for cash. Two of these tasks are preparing bank deposits and reconciling a bank account balance.

### Preparing Deposits

It is a common policy to deposit all checks and cash in a bank as soon as possible. In some companies, deposits are made several times a day. In other companies, there is at least one deposit on each day when there are receipts of cash and checks.

If you have the responsibility of preparing a bank deposit, your first task will be to see that all checks are properly endorsed. This means that the person authorized to endorse checks has made the appropriate endorsement. In many companies, office workers who prepare deposits also endorse the checks using a rubber stamp.

### Common Endorsements

Endorsements are signatures, and at times instructions, affixed to the back of checks. An endorsement is required before a check is transferred from the company or person to whom the check is written to another person, company, or bank. Endorsements vary. Some provide more protection than others; some provide more instruction about the disposition of the check. The most commonly used forms of endorsements are *blank*, *restrictive*, and *special*. Look closely at Illus. 9–3 as you read about each form of endorsement:

- blank:      Only the signature is used. The signature must be in ink. This endorsement provides little protection, since anyone who gains access to a check with a blank endorsement can readily transfer it to another person or to a bank. Generally, you will not want to use this endorsement unless you are in the bank and will be depositing the check immediately.

- restrictive:      The purpose of the transfer of the check is indicated in the endorsement. Note in the illustration that the check is marked *for deposit only*. Restrictive endorsements are often made with a rubber stamp.

- special:      The signature of the endorser is preceded by the name of the person or company to whom the check is being transferred. In some instances a special endorsement is referred to as an *endorsement in full*.

**Illus. 9–3.** Endorsements can be made by using a rubber stamp or by handwriting the endorsement.

*Sean Burns*

Blank endorsement

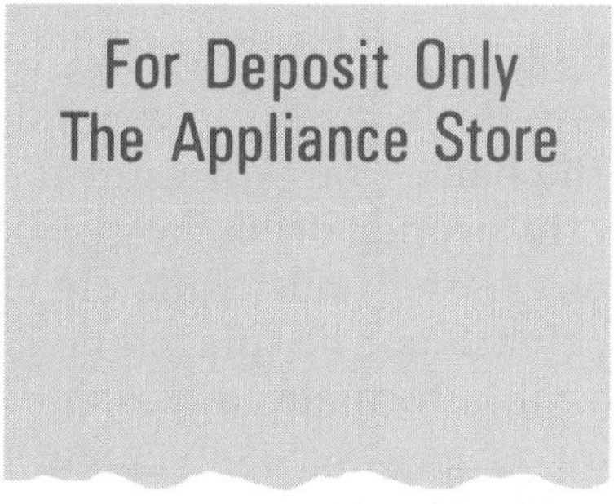

For Deposit Only
The Appliance Store

Restrictive endorsement

*Pay to the
Order of
Baylor Florists
Drew L. Westwood*

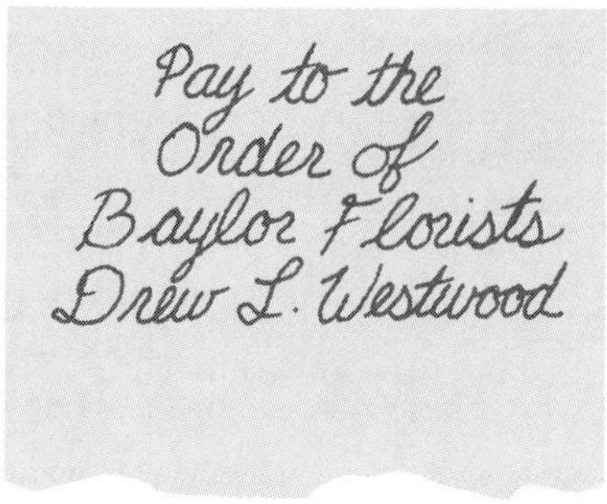

Special endorsement

To prepare checks for a rubber stamp endorsement, you should be sure they are all in reading position when face up. Then turn them over, with the left edge at the top. Stamp each carefully at the top edge. Be sure the endorsement is clearly legible.

### Deposit Slip

A deposit slip is the form which lists all items to be added to a bank account. You will need to prepare such a form for all cash and checks that are to be deposited in the bank. As you see in Illus. 9–4, you will have to record the following details:

- the date on which you are recording the items.
- each item to be deposited by amount. For each check, you will need to identify the bank on which the check is drawn. You do this by recording the bank's number, which is the upper portion of the fraction noted on each check.
- the total amount to be deposited. This amount includes all checks listed on both the front and back of the deposit slip.

To verify the accuracy of the total deposit, compute the total by going through the actual items and adding them up. Check to see if this total is exactly the same as that which you computed for the total listing on the deposit slip. If the two totals are the same, you are assured that your listing was correct and included all items.

*Consuelo works as an office assistant to the cashier in a large company. One of Consuelo's daily tasks is preparing the deposit slips for all items to be taken to the local bank. Consuelo works in a systematic fashion so that she makes no errors. She verifies that each deposit slip is correct by totaling the actual checks. She is happy that the bank has never sent the cashier a notice that an error had been made in a deposit!*

An office worker may have the additional responsibility of taking deposits to the bank on a regular basis. If your tasks include going to the bank, you will want to be sure all checks and deposit forms are in proper order before you leave your office. You will want to put these items in an envelope and carry them carefully so that they are not misplaced en route to the bank.

It is possible to make deposits electronically at teller stations at the bank or at other convenient places. Teller stations provide automatic transfer to the bank and issue a receipt when your deposit is accepted.

### Steps in Preparing a Reconciliation

You will find that the company in which you work has an established procedure for preparing bank reconciliations. Naturally, you will want to learn the specific procedures you are to follow. Assume that you are working in an office where a bank statement is received monthly and a reconciliation is prepared at that time. The steps described here are likely to be similar to the ones you will learn on the job:

1. Compare the ending balance on last month's bank reconciliation with the beginning balance on this month's bank statement. Under normal circumstances, these two balances will be identical. If there is a difference, record the two figures on a sheet of paper. You will need to investigate this difference before you complete your reconciliation.
2. Record on your reconciliation worksheet the balance in your check register as of the last day of the month. (See Illus. 9–8.)

**Illus. 9–8.**  Bank reconciliation worksheet.

| Adler Knitting Manufacturing Co. Reconciliation of Bank Statement August 20, 19__ | | |
|---|---|---|
| Balance in check register August 20, 19__ | 18711 50 | Balance on bank Statement, August 19, 19__   20596 89 |
| Deduct: | | Add: |
| Service Charge 25.00 NSF   197.50 | 222 50 | Outstanding Deposit August 20, 19__   2851 10 |
| | | Total   23447 99 |
| | | Deduct: |
| | | Outstanding Checks |
| | | No. 188   198.70 |
| | | No. 200   110.10 |
| | | No. 203   347.29 |
| | | No. 204   82.50 |
| | | No. 205   4220.40   4958 99 |
| Adjusted check stub balance, August 20, 19__   18489 00 | | Adjusted bank balance August 20, 19__   18489 00 |

3. Record the ending balance as shown on the bank statement.
4. Compare each deposit shown on the bank statement with the deposits recorded on the check register.
   A. Mark with a small check mark both places if the amount and date agree.
   B. Record on your worksheet any deposits shown in the check register that are not on the bank statement. Deposits made near the end of the month are not likely to have been processed by the bank by the date of the statement. Such deposits are referred to as *deposits in transit.*
5. Arrange in numeric order the checks returned with the bank statement. (You will skip this step if it is not the bank's policy to return checks.)
6. Compare the amount of each check with that shown on the bank statement. Use small check marks by the items on the statement to show that there is agreement. Record any differences noted. You will want to follow up on these discrepancies before preparing your final reconciliation.
7. Compare each canceled check with related information in the check register. Place a small check mark in the register if there is agreement. (See Illus. 9–9.)

| | | PLEASE BE SURE TO DEDUCT ANY PER CHECK CHARGES OR MAINTENANCE CHARGES THAT AFFECT YOUR ACCOUNT | | | | | |
|---|---|---|---|---|---|---|---|
| ITEM NO. | DATE | PAYMENT ISSUED TO OR DESCRIPTION OF DEPOSIT | AMOUNT OF PAYMENT | √ | AMOUNT OF DEPOSIT OR INTEREST | BALANCE FORWARD | |
| | | | | | | 28681 | 15 |
| 187 | 7/17 | To Taylor Brothers / For | 3750 00 | √ | | Payment or Deposit 3750 00 | |
| | | | | | | Balance 24931 15 | |
| 188 | 7/18 | To Elman and Stone Co. / For | 198 70 | | | Payment or Deposit 198 70 | |
| | | | | | | Balance 24732 45 | |
| 189 | 7/18 | To Marshall Gomez / For | 1890 25 | √ | | Payment or Deposit 1890 25 | |
| | | | | | | Balance 22842 20 | |
| 190 | 7/25 | To Leitz Mfg. Co. / For | 6590 70 | √ | | Payment or Deposit 6590 70 | |
| | | | | | | Balance 16251 50 | |
| | 7/29 | To Deposit / For | | √ | 7980 70 | Payment or Deposit 7980 70 | |
| | | | | | | Balance 24232 20 | |
| 191 | 8/1 | To Yarns, International / For | 3875 00 | √ | | Payment or Deposit 3875 00 | |
| | | | | | | Balance 20357 20 | |

**Illus. 9–9.** Check register.

8. Record on your worksheet the number, date, and amount for each check that was written but had not cleared as of the date of the bank statement. Such checks are referred to as *outstanding checks.* The total of such checks will be subtracted from the bank statement balance.

9. Review last month's outstanding checks as listed on the bank reconciliation to determine which ones are still outstanding. Also list these on your worksheet.
10. Record on your worksheet any charges shown on the statement that are not recorded in your company's records. For example, any checks returned for insufficient funds (NSF checks) must be subtracted from the balance in your check register. Bank charges also must be subtracted.
11. Complete the computations required on your worksheet. Note that the two balances are the same in the reconciliation shown on page 355. Having the same balances means that your cash account has been properly reconciled.
12. Prepare your final copy of the bank reconciliation. Use a sheet of plain paper or the reconciliation form provided on the back of the bank statement.

When you have completed a bank reconciliation, you will submit it to your supervisor for review and approval. Once it is approved, you will want to file it in the proper place so that it can be readily retrieved when you need to do the next bank reconciliation. When you receive the next bank statement, you will need to refer back to this completed reconciliation to determine which checks were outstanding and therefore should be in the next batch of canceled checks.

## Maintaining a Petty Cash Fund

There are occasions in many offices when cash is needed to pay for small expenditures, such as messenger services, postage due and taxi fares. To facilitate such payments, departments are given a small sum of money, which is called a petty cash fund. Amounts in such funds can range from $20 to as much as several thousand dollars.

*In the office of a small insurance broker, a petty cash fund of $75 is maintained to pay for taxis and special messenger services needed from time to time.*

*The sales office of a women's fashion manufacturing company has a petty cash fund of $3,500, primarily to provide money for lunch ordered at a local coffee shop for visiting buyers and for late dinners when staff members must work or entertain major buyers from around the world.*

### Establishing the Fund

The department head establishes the amount of cash that is to be maintained in the petty cash fund. Once this amount is approved by the officer responsible for payments, a check is drawn to *Petty Cash Fund* and cashed by the cashier in the treasurer's office. The cash then is given to the office worker who will serve as *petty cashier.* The office worker will keep the cash in a locked cashbox. Only the petty cashier has access to the key.

**Illus. 9–10.** Accurate records must be kept by the petty cashier.

### Making Payments

To keep control over the funds of any organization, records of the use of money are required. If you serve as cashier, you will need to keep a complete record for every payment you make from the cash box. You should be supplied with petty cash receipt forms, which you will fill in each time you give cash to an employee. Here is a procedure that is commonly followed in offices:

**reimbursement:** payment for an outlay of cash already made

1. Ask each person who seeks *reimbursement* to submit to you a sales slip, statement, or receipt that indicates what was purchased, what the price was, and that payment was made. Generally, reimbursement should not be made without some kind of document. Occasionally, cash payments are made even

though no sales slip, statement, or receipt is provided. On such occasions, the employee being reimbursed should present a brief memo describing what was spent and the purpose of the expenditure.

2. Prepare a petty cash receipt for each reimbursement and ask the person who will receive the cash to sign the receipt. Note the receipt shown in Illus. 9–11. It indicates the amount paid out, to whom payment is made, and the purpose of the payment.

3. Attach the sales slip or other document to the receipt and place these papers in the cash box.

**PETTY CASH RECEIPT**

HARDESTY SECURITY SYSTEMS

No. _42_          Date _November 17,_ 19 _- -_

Amount $ _10.75_

_Ten and ⁷⁵/₁₀₀_ _____ Dollars

For _Postage_ _____

Received by _Wanda J. Davis_

**Illus. 9–11.** A petty cash receipt is issued for each reimbursement from the petty cash fund.

### Keeping a Record

In some offices there are many transactions that require petty cash. An organized record is, therefore, justified. In some departments, a *petty cash book* is maintained for recording receipts and disbursements. A page from such a record is shown on page 360. Note the headings of the columns under which the expenditures are recorded. In each office the same types of expenditures are likely to occur again and again. Therefore, the column headings for your office may be different from the ones shown here. By classifying the expenses as indicated on page 360, the task of preparing a report at the end of the month or at the point when the fund must be *replenished* will be simplified.

*replenished:* added to to bring back to its original level

| MONTH OF November, 19__ | | PETTY CASH RECORD | | | | | | | | | PAGE 12 |
|---|---|---|---|---|---|---|---|---|---|---|---|
| | | | | | **DISTRIBUTION OF PAYMENTS** | | | | | | |
| DATE | EXPLANATION | PETTY CASH VCHR. NO. | RECEIPTS | PAYMENTS | ART SUPPLIES | BOOKS/ OTHER PUBLICATIONS | MESSENGER SERVICES | OFFICE SUPPLIES | TAXI/BUS FEES | POSTAL SERVICES | MISCELLANEOUS |
| Nov. 1 | Balance | | 250 00 | | | | | | | | |
| 6 | Books | 39 | | 12 95 | | 12 95 | | | | | |
| 8 | Taxi | 40 | | 8 50 | | | | | 8 50 | | |
| 8 | Office Supplies | 41 | | 7 70 | | | | 7 70 | | | |
| 11 | Postage | 42 | | 10 75 | | | | | | 10 75 | |
| 14 | Messenger | 43 | | 6 45 | | | 6 45 | | | | |
| 17 | Art Supplies | 44 | | 12 50 | 12 50 | | | | | | |
| 18 | Art Supplies | 45 | | 30 15 | 30 15 | | | | | | |
| 19 | Books | 46 | | 18 75 | | 18 75 | | | | | |
| 19 | Messenger | 47 | | 14 20 | | | 14 20 | | | | |
| 20 | Office Supplies | 48 | | 10 50 | | | | 10 50 | | | |
| 20 | Art Supplies | 49 | | 6 60 | 6 60 | | | | | | |
| 21 | Taxi | 50 | | 21 90 | | | | | 21 90 | | |
| 21 | Office Supplies | 51 | | 9 70 | | | | 9 70 | | | |
| 21 | Messenger | 52 | | 14 55 | | | 14 55 | | | | |
| 22 | Taxi | 53 | | 10 40 | | | | | 10 40 | | |
| 23 | Taxi | 54 | | 11 70 | | | | | 11 70 | | |
| 24 | Taxi | 55 | | 16 35 | | | | | 16 35 | | |
| 24 | Postage | 56 | | 11 45 | | | | | | 11 45 | |
| 27 | Miscellaneous | 57 | | 12 10 | | | | | | | 12 10 |
| | Totals | | 250 00 | 247 20 | 49 25 | 31 70 | 35 20 | 27 90 | 68 85 | 22 20 | 12 10 |
| | Cash Balance | | | 2 80 | | | | | | | |
| | Totals | | 250 00 | 250 00 | | | | | | | |
| 30 | Cash Balance | | 2 80 | | | | | | | | |
| 30 | REPLENISHED FUND # 3721 | | 247 20 | | | | | | | | |

**Illus. 9–12.** A petty cash book is used to record receipts and disbursements.

## Replenishing the Fund

You will need to note the amount of cash in your cash box and to replenish your fund when you do not have sufficient cash to meet expected expenditures. In some offices the petty cash fund is replenished at the end of the month as a standard procedure. In the process of replenishing the fund you also will prepare a summary report of the expenditures. Here is a procedure that is commonly used in offices:

1. Total the columns in the petty cash book. (See Illus. 9–12.) If you are not using a petty cash book, add the amounts given on all the receipts in the petty cash box.
2. Add the amount of the petty cash receipts to the amount of petty cash remaining in the cash box, as in the following example:

| | |
|---|---|
| Petty cash on hand | $ 2.80 |
| Petty cash receipts | 247.20 |
| Total of petty cash fund | $250.00 |

3. The total, in this case $250, should equal the amount of petty cash you had when you last balanced and/or replenished the petty cash fund. If the figure you arrive at does *not* equal the amount you had in the petty cash fund when you last balanced or replenished it, you have a ***discrepancy***.

***discrepancy:***
difference

4. Investigate any discrepancy. Careful attention to managing the petty cash fund will result in few, if any, discrepancies. If, after your investigation, you find that you are over or short by a few pennies, note this difference in your calculation. For example, if in Step 2, you found only $2.75 in cash, your calculation would indicate:

| | |
|---|---|
| Cash on hand | $ 2.75 |
| Receipts | 247.20 |
| Cash short | .05 |
| Total | $250.00 |

You also will indicate the shortage (the missing amount for which there is no explanation) in your summary report.

5. Prepare a report of the activity in the petty cash fund for the period beginning with the last replenishment or the last time you balanced the records. Note the portion of the report shown in Illus. 9–13 on page 362.
6. Prepare a request for a check for the amount of the receipts plus any shortage (or minus any overage).
7. Submit your report, the accompanying receipts, and your request for a replenishment check to the manager for review.
8. When the manager returns the documents to you, follow up by sending a copy of the report to the accounting department and by sending the request for a check to the proper office.
9. Exchange the check for cash in the treasurer's office or at a local bank. Immediately place the cash in the cash box.

| Petty Cash Summary Report | | | | |
|---|---|---|---|---|
| November 1 to November 30, 19__ | | | | |
| Balance, November 1 | | | | 250 00 |
| Expenditures: | | | | |
|     Art Supplies | | 49 25 | | |
|     Books/Other Publications | | 31 70 | | |
|     Messenger Services | | 35 20 | | |
|     Office Supplies | | 27 90 | | |
|     Taxi/Bus Fees | | 68 85 | | |
|     Postal Services | | 22 20 | | |
|     Miscellaneous | | 12 10 | | |
| Total Expenditures | | | | 247 20 |
| Balance, November 30 | | | | 2 80 |

**Illus. 9–13.** This petty cash summary report shows an ending balance of $2.80.

**RECORD-RELATED TASKS**

From your study of Chapter 8, you will remember that a copy of the sales invoice prepared in the billing department is forwarded to the accounts receivable department. Also, copies of credit memorandums are routed to the accounts receivable office. From the preceding topic in this chapter, you learned that a listing of all checks received from customers also is forwarded to the accounts receivable department. The listings of checks and the copies of credit memorandums are two primary sources of information that must be included in the records maintained on customers.

If you work in an accounts receivable office, you will be responsible for recording:

- all sales to customers on account
- all payments received from customers on account
- all adjustments required in customer accounts

**Illus. 9–17.** As a member of the accounts payable department, this office worker has responsibility for reviewing documents related to purchases made by the company.

## Preparation of Vouchers

In many offices a voucher system is used for payments. This is a system that requires the preparation of a voucher before a check is written. A **voucher** is a document that records the name of the vendor, the date of the invoice, the terms, and the amount owed. (See page 372.) If you have the responsibility for preparing vouchers, you generally will follow these steps:

1. Check to be sure that all the documents related to the purchase are present. Often an envelope-type file folder is used to collect all the documents for a payment. On the outside of the folder there is a listing of the documents that are included.
2. Prepare the voucher, being sure to check every detail required on the form.
3. Leave the vouchers on the manager's desk for review and signature.
4. File the vouchers appropriately. It is common to file vouchers by the dates on which they must be processed in order to meet the payment due dates. In companies where the policy is to take all cash discounts allowed, the end of the discount period determines by what date the voucher is filed.

**VOUCHER**

The Lampshade Store
426 Monroe Street
Cedar Falls, IA 50613-3467

VOUCHER NO. 4379

DATE: October 17, 19--

PAY TO: Just Shades

135 Greene Street

New York, NY 10003-4689

For the following: (All supporting documents are attached.)

| INVOICE DATE | TERMS | INVOICE NUMBER | GROSS AMOUNT | DISCOUNT | NET PAYABLE |
|---|---|---|---|---|---|
| October 17 | 2/10, n/30 | 5479 | $4,560.90 | $91.22 | $4,469.68 |

PAYMENT APPROVED

*Helen Northcutt*

**Illus. 9–18.** Many offices require that a voucher be prepared before a check is written.

## Preparation of Checks

If you are responsible for preparing checks for payments due, you generally will check your file daily to retrieve all vouchers for which checks are to be prepared. As you know, a *check* is a written order to a bank to make payment against the depositor's funds in that bank.

### Ordinary Checks

In some offices, especially small ones, a checkbook that is similar to one that an individual uses for personal check writing is the source of checks for paying business obligations. If you are responsible for writing checks using such a checkbook, these suggestions will be helpful:

1. Read carefully the name of the company or individual to whom payment is to be made as well as the amount of the check. If you are writing a check in time to take advantage of a discount, you should compute the discount using a calculator or adding machine.
2. Fill in the checkbook stub or the check register. (See Illus. 9–19 for the way in which an item is listed in a check register.)
3. Prepare the check at a typewriter or with a pen. (See Illus. 9–19.) Note that the amount is written in numbers as well as in words. Notice how the space between the name and the dollar sign and between the amount in words and the word "dollars" is filled in. This is done so that changes cannot be made easily. Notice that the purpose of the payment is shown on the face of the check.

**Illus. 9–19.** (Top) Check register. (Bottom) Check prepared at a typewriter.

| | | | | | | | |
|---|---|---|---|---|---|---|---|
| The Lampshade Store | ACP050 | | CHECK REGISTER | | | CHECK DATE: 10/25/-- PAGE 4 | |
| VENDOR NO. | VENDOR NAME | INVOICE | INV DATE | DUE DATE | GROSS | DISC + DED | CHECK NO. | CHECK AMOUNT |
| A002 | L. T. Realty Co. | 3972 | 10/15 | 10/31 | 2,000.00 | — | 2264 | 2,000.00 |
| T2161 | Barton Maintenance | 1271 | 10/20 | 10/31 | 280.80 | — | 2265 | 280.80 |
| F721 | Cheshire Co. | 791 | 10/17 | 10/27 | 81.90 | 1.64 | 2266 | 80.26 |
| L292 | Just Shades | 5479 | 10/17 | 10/27 | 4,560.90 | 91.22 | 2267 | 4,469.68 |
| M297 | Javis Air Freight | 3921 | 10/10 | 10/31 | 45.00 | — | 2268 | 45.00 |

Check Register

**THE LAMPSHADE STORE**
**426 MONROE STREET**
**CEDAR FALLS, IA 50613-3467**

October 25, 19 --   **2267**

69-439
515

**Pay to the order of** Just Shades . . . . . . . . . . . . . . . . . . . . . . $ 4,469.68

Four thousand, four hundred sixty-nine and 68/100------------------- **Dollars**

**Memo** Invoice No. 5479

⑆051504393⑆ 3 8953 4⑈ 0226

Ordinary Check

### Voucher Checks

**perforated:** having a row or series of holes through

**Voucher checks** are ordinary checks with an additional portion that gives a description of the payment. The two parts are **perforated** so that they can be separated easily. The voucher is detached before the check is deposited.

The procedures for preparing voucher checks are the same as those for ordinary checks, except that you also fill in a voucher instead of merely indicating the purpose of the check as you would on an ordinary check. You will want to be sure that all details shown on the voucher are accurate.

### Special Checks

From time to time, you may find that special checks which provide guarantee of payment are needed in your office.

- certified check: An ordinary check which the bank marks "certified" after establishing that the funds are in the account of the party drawing the check. The funds are immediately subtracted from the depositor's account.
- cashier's check: A check written by a bank on its own funds. Such a check can be purchased with cash or with an ordinary check.
- bank draft: An order drawn by one bank on its deposits in another bank to pay a third party. Such a draft can be purchased with cash or with an ordinary check.

## The Use of Electronic Funds Transfer

Payments, as well as deposits, can be made electronically. This means there is no need for a written order such as a check. Businesses, as well as individuals, use EFT for many banking transactions. For example, some businesses pay employees through EFT. A magnetic tape prepared by the business's computer is used by the bank for electronically depositing the amount of each individual's wages or salary in that individual's bank account. There is no need for a payroll check when EFT is used.

**PAYMENTS FOR WAGES AND SALARIES**

You will find that companies have carefully designed procedures for payroll. Employees expect to be paid on time and for the proper amount. To meet the expectations of all employees, office employees in payroll-related jobs keep accurate records and do their tasks on a timely basis.

You will find that the payroll in many companies is processed by computer systems. However, you will want to understand basic procedures and typical pay methods used in modern businesses.

## Methods of Payment

If you choose to work in a payroll department, you will learn the method or methods used for paying employees. In some companies, all employees are paid by the same method. However, in other companies several different methods may be used for varying groups of workers. Increasingly, payroll procedures are processed by computers. However, in order for you to fully understand what is required in processing payments to employees, you first will be introduced to basic manual procedures.

### *Salary*

*subdivided:* separated into several parts

Under this method, the employee is paid an amount that is quoted on a weekly, monthly, or yearly basis. The *gross salary*, which is the salary before any deductions, is the figure quoted. A salary quoted on a yearly basis is **subdivided** into the number of pay periods per year. A person who earns $16,500 yearly and is paid twice each month will have a gross salary of $687.50 each pay period.

**Illus. 9–20.** These office employees earn a yearly salary and are paid twice each month.

### *Hourly*

In some positions, employees are paid on the basis of a rate per hour. The hourly rate applies to the hours considered standard. The standard work week may be 35, 37½, or 40 hours. When workers paid on an hourly basis work more hours than those specified as standard for their work week, they generally earn a higher rate for the overtime hours. It is common for overtime rates to be 1.5 to 2 times the standard hourly rate. Many factory workers, as well as part-time and temporary office workers, are paid on the basis of an hourly rate.

### *Piece Rate*

In some production-type positions, workers' earnings are based strictly on what they accomplish. Payment is made per unit completed. For example, in a dress manufacturing company, workers who insert zippers are paid at a specified rate for each zipper inserted properly. People who work on their own, as *freelancers*, are paid on this basis. A freelance photographer is paid for each photograph selected to appear in the newspaper; a freelance word processor is paid for each page of manuscript completed.

**Illus. 9–21.** This office assistant works a standard 40-hour week. She is paid an hourly rate and receives a payroll check at the end of each week.

## AT WORK AT DYNAMICS: *Simulation 2*

Miss Lancaster telephoned to say that your next assignment will be in the Sales and Marketing Division of DYNAMICS. Several full-time employees are on vacation, and you are needed as a substitute for one of these employees. "I think you will enjoy working in this division," Miss Lancaster said. "There's always such a bustle of activity."

Miss Lancaster proceeded to give you a preview of what you would encounter in the Sales and Marketing Division. Since this division handles the sales and marketing functions, the major focus is the presentation and selling of products to potential customers. Here, plans are made for national advertising on television and radio. Catalog copy and newspaper and magazine advertisements also are prepared here. DYNAMICS has some exciting new products in its clothing line of warm-up suits and action sportswear. The line will soon be marketed nationwide.

An important function of this division is to provide customer services. For example, if a problem (such as the receipt of damaged merchandise) arises with an order, the Customer Service Department takes the call, determines the problem, and then proceeds to complete immediately all follow-up actions required. "We strive to keep our customers satisfied with our products and our service," said Miss Lancaster. "We pride ourselves on maintaining increasingly larger numbers of customers year after year. Naturally, the Customer Service Department prepares many letters to be sent to our customers, and it is the responsibility of our word processing workers to process these letters."

Turn to your *Information Processing Activities* workbook to learn more about your assignment in the Sales and Marketing Division of DYNAMICS.

# TIME
# AND TASK MANAGEMENT

# Chapter 10

# Activities Management

Most office workers want to be good at their jobs and to be recognized as being good at their jobs. However, you don't become a valued, respected worker by chance. Good office workers must apply all the skills they have learned:

- technical skills and knowledge, such as keyboarding documents in the approved company format

- communication and behavioral skills, such as working cooperatively with others and displaying proper work attitudes

- activities management skills, such as planning the order of work tasks

What you actually do in your office job will depend in large part on the nature of the business for which you work, the size of the business, and the geographical location of that business. You will find, however, that your job fills a specific need in that business organization. In meeting the specific requirements of your job, you may be called upon to do many different kinds of tasks. Therefore,

you will need to plan and organize your work activities carefully in order to perform efficiently and on time. You will need to learn effective use of the resources which support your work activities: your time; your workstation; office manuals; reprographic services; and the office supplies, forms, and equipment you use.

To work effectively and efficiently, you must have a safe environment. You will want to be acquainted with the critical concerns for safety and security that are the responsibility of all office workers. The objectives of the chapter are to

- assist you in developing your understanding of the importance of an organized workstation and the management of your time

- identify frequently used office reprographic equipment and procedures

- describe important safety and security procedures for the office

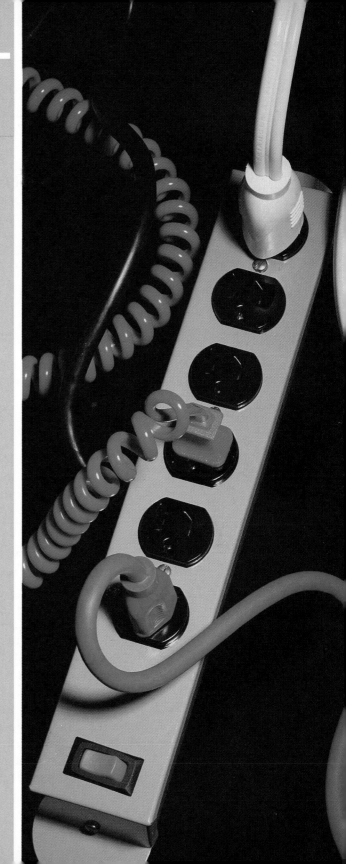

# Topic 1

## WORKSTATION AND TIME MANAGEMENT

When you have completed your study of this topic, you will be able to

- identify the function of your office workstation
- identify common office workstation equipment, supplies, and accessories
- describe how to arrange your workstation to increase your productivity
- list common office time wasters
- apply basic time analysis procedures to help you better manage your time

As an office worker, you must be able to manage your work effectively and be a productive worker. Proper lighting, sound control, climate control, and the arrangement and design of your workstation are factors which contribute to your productivity. Most companies strive to provide physically comfortable and safe environments for their office employees. It becomes your responsibility as an office employee to keep your work area well organized.

Time management is also a major factor which contributes to your productivity. Managing your time at the office is a process of choosing the most effective way to do your job. The creative use of techniques to manage time will add greatly to the quality of your work life.

In the following sections, you will read about managing your future office workstation and your time. You will learn how the proper management of these two elements will help you become more efficient in completing your work.

## FUNCTION OF THE OFFICE WORK-STATION

*modular:* constructed for flexibility and variety

Your workstation provides the physical space for you to do your job. The equipment and materials needed for your job are located at your workstation. Although the location and size of your workstation may be determined by management, the organization of your workstation generally is left to you. Many firms today are using *modular* furniture because of its design flexibility. Modular furniture permits a workstation to be designed for an individual worker's job duties, using standard components. In some work situations, workstations may be shared.

> Jamie is one of five sales assistants at the catalog counter of a large department store in a suburban shopping center. The five sales assistants have three computer terminals available to relay the customers' catalog counter sales directly to the regional warehouse.
>
> Customers have several catalogs from which they may order. Customers often will leaf through the catalogs and ask questions about the products before they place their orders. While Jamie helps a customer locate information about a desired catalog item and answers the customer's questions, another sales assistant is processing another customer's order on one of the terminals. Once Jamie's customer has finished selecting order items, Jamie inputs the catalog information into the computer at the first available terminal.
>
> The sales assistants have agreed to keep the current catalogs, ordering instructions, and the hard-copy order back-ups in the same specific location at each terminal. This procedure allows the sales assistants to process orders efficiently without wasting time trying to locate needed references.

Whether your workstation is shared or individual, you should arrange it so you can work efficiently and smoothly. An organized workstation provides the benefit of increased productivity throughout your entire day.

## EQUIPMENT, SUPPLIES, AND ACCESSORIES

Office employees use a variety of equipment, supplies, and accessories daily to do their jobs. In fact, the right resources help you perform your job better. What you need at your workstation will depend on your particular job. Not all office workers require the same equipment or supplies to perform their jobs. Also, more automated offices will have some equipment, supplies, and accessories that will differ from those used in traditional offices.

Some of the more common equipment, supplies, and accessories are shown in Illus. 10–1. Although this is not a ***comprehensive*** list, it gives you a good idea of what you may find at an office workstation. As an office employee, you will be expected to exercise good judgment in using equipment, supplies, and accessories.

***comprehensive:***
completely covering

| WORKSTATION EQUIPMENT, SUPPLIES, AND ACCESSORIES | | |
|---|---|---|
| | workstation equipment | typewriter, word processor, printer, video terminal and keyboard, dictation/transcription unit, electronic calculator, telephone |
| | basic supplies and accessories | calendar, scissors, paper clips, stapler and staple remover, pencils, pens, markers, tape and tape dispenser, writing pads, desk references, notepaper and message pads, in basket, out basket |
| | communication-related supplies | date stamp and ink pad, stationery, envelopes, forms, correction supplies, typewriter ribbons, printwheels or elements reference materials |
| | information processing supplies | floppy disks, diskette file, printwheels, software programs. computer paper, data binders, word processing ribbons, equipment/processing manuals |

**Illus. 10–1.** Here are some of the more common pieces of equipment, supplies, and accessories that you might need at your workstation.

## Using Office Equipment

Office equipment can be regarded as an investment in reducing labor costs. Since the quality of your work often depends upon the condition of your equipment, you will want to do your part to keep your equipment in top working condition. To get dependable service from your equipment, you will need to practice preventive maintenance. Preventive maintenance involves servicing equipment and replacing parts while the equipment is functioning properly in order to prevent the equipment from failing.

Fewer repairs are necessary when equipment is cared for properly on a daily basis. You will want to help cut maintenance costs by preventing the misuse and abuse of company equipment. By practicing preventive maintenance, you can help equipment perform well over a longer period of time. You will want to follow these three maintenance guidelines:

1. Know your equipment. If you are going to use the equipment, learn how to use and care for the equipment properly. Read and understand the manufacturer's operating instructions. Keep the operating manual near the equipment.
2. Inspect and clean equipment regularly. Know the basic care routines your equipment requires. Establish a regular inspection schedule. Adhere to the preventive measures (such as oiling and cleaning) recommended by the manufacturer.
3. Report problems immediately. When you spot a potential problem, report it to your supervisor. Most minor problems can be corrected before they become serious and require costly repairs.

### Using Office Supplies and Accessories

A well-stocked supply cabinet and workstation are essential to your productivity. If you run out of supplies in the middle of a critical task, you could lose valuable work time in trying to locate needed supplies. You run the risk of not completing the task on time or having to accept *inferior* supplies just to finish the task.

*inferior:* of lower quality

One of the best ways office workers can save money for their companies is to know how to use supplies properly. Here are three guidelines you will want to follow:

1. Select the quality of the supply according to the nature and importance of the task. For example, if you are preparing a rough draft copy of an important letter, don't use expensive letterhead paper. Use a lower quality paper for the rough draft and the letterhead paper for the final copy. Learn the quality of supplies required for each task. If you are uncertain, check with your supervisor. Learn to read product labels for the correct use of a product.
2. Look for ways to conserve supplies. Avoid the habit of opening a new supply item until you have finished the last one. Reuse file folders by preparing new file folder labels. Use routing forms and reusable interoffice envelopes where appropriate.

minutes discussing the latest episode of a favorite television program, a conversation which started out as productive ends up being a time waster. If this happens two or three times a day, the time lost can add up rapidly.

### Unnecessary Interruptions

In addition to the telephone, interruptions to your work can come from other sources such as drop-in visitors and even your supervisor. Discouraging the drop-in visitor may involve building barriers against interruptions. If you have a door, close it. If your workstation or desk can be turned, turn it so that you do not face an open door or common passageway. If you do not need an extra chair by your workstation or desk, remove it.

### Excessive Socializing

*abuse:* improper use

Although some socializing will help you maintain good working relations with your co-workers, too much socialization is an *abuse* of company time. Some workers have a tendency to socialize too much, and you will be wise to avoid engaging in much conversation with these workers. Workers who socialize too much on the job soon earn themselves the reputation of being *talkers*. When a talker shows up at your workstation or catches you at the water fountain and tries to involve you in idle conversation, offer a simple response like: "I'd love to talk, but I really must get back to work. Maybe we could discuss this at lunch." You will maintain good working relations while excusing yourself to continue your work. If you are consistent in your responses, the talker will soon learn that you are not distracted easily from your work.

**Illus. 10–6.** Lunch is an ideal time to socialize with co-workers.

Likewise, be careful not to mistreat your lunch time and your break times by extending them beyond the approved time periods.

### Ineffective Communication

It is quite common for office workers to communicate orally and in writing with others in the office. You will be expected to follow the written and oral instructions of your supervisor and co-workers. Likewise, you will be expected to give clear written and oral instructions to others. As you learned in Chapter 2, if the information given or received is inaccurate or incomplete, much time can be lost in doing a task wrong and correcting it. Be certain the instructions and directions you give are specific and accurate. Likewise, be sure that you understand any instructions given to you.

### Disorganization

*procrastinate:* delay intentionally

Being disorganized can be a major time waster. Searching for the paper you just had in your hands, missing important deadlines, and shifting unnecessarily from one project to another are all signs of a disorganized person. Take the time to organize your work area and prepare a daily plan for your work. You should think through and plan more complicated jobs before starting them. Group similar tasks together, and avoid jumping from one project to another before finishing the first task. Do not *procrastinate*. If unpleasant or difficult tasks are placed to the side and left for later, they become potential crises just waiting to erupt.

## Orderly Approach to Work

Using time efficiently involves developing an orderly approach to your work. You can learn to use your calendar as a work management tool to plan your work activities, set priorities, control large projects, and simplify your work. The following are some suggestions for handling your time obligations more effectively.

### Use Your Calendar as a Work Management Tool

Your calendar can become a useful work management tool if you use it to record task deadlines and reminders. A calendar can not only help you organize your daily work but also help you identify *peak* and *slack* work periods.

Once you know when to expect peak and slack work periods, you can plan your work to allow more productive use of your time and a more even work load for you. To accommodate a peak period, think ahead to determine what jobs could be completed prior to the peak period. You then will be able to free some time so that the peak period will not impose undue pressure on your schedule. Planning for the slack periods is equally important. During slack periods, you can catch up on those tasks that do not have deadlines but nevertheless must be done.

**Illus. 10–7.**

### Plan Your Work Activities

Planning your daily work activities will help you avoid forgetting tasks that need to be completed. Take five or ten minutes either at the beginning of the work day or at the close of the previous work day to plan the coming day's work. Prepare a "To Do" list, and complete the tasks according to their order of importance. Keep the list accessible as you work. Check your list frequently. This list should guide you through your daily activities. As tasks are completed, cross them off. Tasks not completed can be carried over to the next day's "To Do" list. Be alert, however, to any item that seems to be carried over too many times. Perhaps such an item should be broken down into smaller segments or perhaps you are procrastinating in completing the task.

### Set Priorities

Once you know what tasks you are facing for the day, plan to work on those tasks with the highest priority first. Rank the items on your "To Do" list, and complete the most important tasks first. To determine the priority of the tasks, ask yourself these questions:

- How important is this task?
- Is there a deadline?
- Who is responsible for completing this task?
- What will happen if this task is not completed on time?

Discuss your priorities with your supervisor to be certain that you both agree on the importance of the task. Once you set your priorities, finish the tasks in their priority order. Remain *flexible*, however, to updating your priorities as circumstances change.

*flexible:* able to adapt or change as necessary

> Before Ana Maria left work, she jotted down the tasks she needed to complete the next day at work. She checked her "To Do" list for any uncompleted tasks to be carried over to the current list. She also checked her calendar, her supervisor's calendar, and the tickler file for any *pertinent* notations. Her calendar contained a reminder notation that the national sales meeting would be held three weeks from tomorrow. Jim McPheeter, also a regional sales manager, is to accompany her supervisor to the meeting. Both her supervisor and Mr. McPheeter are to present a revised version of the standard sales contract at the meeting.

*pertinent:* significant; important; to the point

Ana Maria's "To Do" list for tomorrow is shown in Illus. 10–8. Notice that she has identified the tasks as A, B, or C. The A-level tasks are those tasks that need immediate attention or completion. If the item is a long-term project, that portion of the task that should be finished that day is listed. B-level tasks are those that can be done once the A-level tasks have been completed, such as advance preparation for the next week(s). C-level tasks have no specific deadline and are considered *fillers* — those tasks to do when A and B tasks have been completed.

### Control Large Projects

Sometimes it is difficult to start a large project even though that project may be very important. Smaller tasks can be checked off your "To Do" list with ease, whereas a large task may seem too *formidable*. Do not let the largeness of a project keep you from getting the project under control and moving toward satisfactory completion of the task. Here are several suggestions for handling a larger project:

*formidable:* causing dread or fear

- Break the large project into smaller tasks.
- Determine the steps to be taken in each of the smaller tasks.

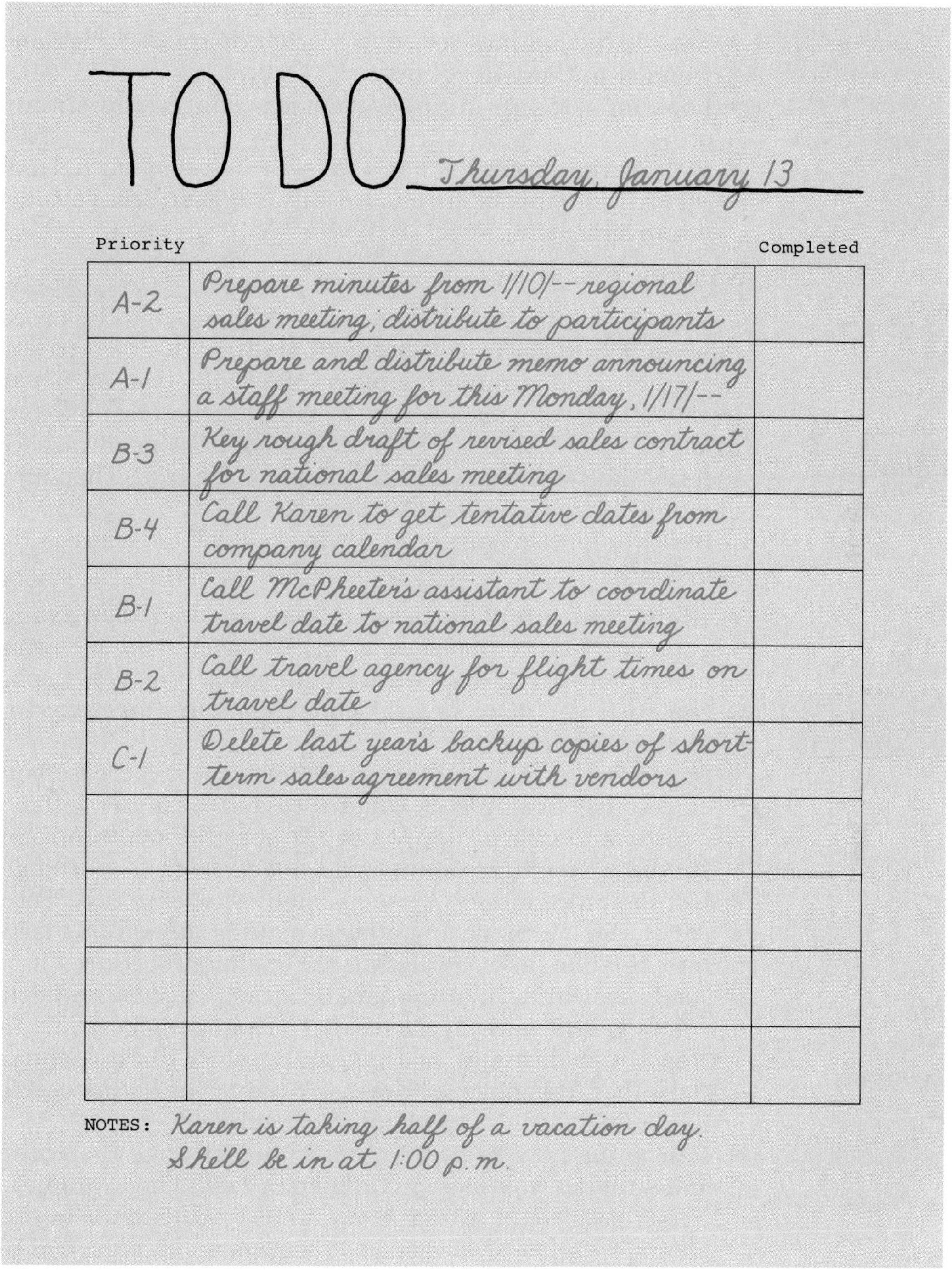

# TO DO Thursday, January 13

| Priority | | Completed |
|---|---|---|
| A-2 | Prepare minutes from 1/10/-- regional sales meeting; distribute to participants | |
| A-1 | Prepare and distribute memo announcing a staff meeting for this Monday, 1/17/-- | |
| B-3 | Key rough draft of revised sales contract for national sales meeting | |
| B-4 | Call Karen to get tentative dates from company calendar | |
| B-1 | Call McPheeter's assistant to coordinate travel date to national sales meeting | |
| B-2 | Call travel agency for flight times on travel date | |
| C-1 | Delete last year's backup copies of short-term sales agreement with vendors | |
| | | |
| | | |
| | | |
| | | |

NOTES: Karen is taking half of a vacation day. She'll be in at 1:00 p.m.

**Illus. 10–8.** Ana Maria's "To Do" list.

- Determine needed supplies and tools.
- Establish deadlines for each section or smaller task and hold yourself to those deadlines.
- Look for ways to improve your procedures and simplify the project.
- If the large project is one that will be repeated periodically, record your procedures and any suggestions you have for improvements.

### Simplify Your Work

Work simplification is the process of improving the procedures that you use to get your work done. It often involves streamlining some steps and eliminating others. Basically, you are striving to improve the way you work by looking for the most efficient way to do an essential task or series of tasks. For each task you do, identify the steps necessary to complete the task. Then eliminate any unnecessary steps and/or details.

Here are four suggestions to help you look for ways to simplify your work:

- Group and complete similar tasks together. For example, if you are to make photocopies of the letters you are preparing, make them all at once rather than making several trips to the copier. If you have several phone calls to make, try to make them in sequence.
- Be alert to combining tasks if doing so will increase your efficiency. For example, if you are to deliver a late letter to the mailroom and the supply store is near the mailroom, pick up the office supplies you intended to get the next morning.
- List the procedures you use to complete a large task. For example, if you are preparing a large mailing, divide this large task into smaller tasks by listing the major procedures involved, such as printing mailing labels, attaching labels, stuffing envelopes, and mailing envelopes. Then, if necessary, list the steps in each major procedure. Be alert to any sequence of steps that does not seem logical. Study your listing carefully to determine if any steps should be combined.
- Determine how to best organize and arrange the equipment and supplies you use to complete a task. For example, if you crisscross a room several times to use a calculator in the completion of a task, you need to reorganize the placement of the equipment and supplies to provide a smoother flow of work.

**BASIC TIME ANALYSIS PROCEDURES**

Your time is a valuable resource that you should use wisely. Time cannot be replaced. In the preceding sections of this topic, you have learned some of the ways in which you can better use your time on the job. You now know some good time management procedures, as well as some of the common ways time can be wasted. You now can analyze how you spend your time on the job.

Time analysis aids you in determining how effectively your time is used. By keeping a written account of what you do, you can determine whether or not you are using your time effectively. With this information you can then develop a plan of action to correct or redirect your use of your time.

### Keep a Time Inventory

Start by keeping a written record of what you do and how much time is used. Record all activities in your time-use log: telephone calls, meetings, discussions with co-workers, and so forth.

You may choose to keep a time-use log for a day, for several days, or even a week. The longer you keep your time-use log, the more representative it will be of how your time is spent. A partial time-use log is shown in Illus. 10–9 on page 406.

### Analyze How You Spend Your Time

When you have completed your time inventory, you are ready to analyze the results. By studying your time-use patterns, you will be able to spot problem areas and trends quickly. Be alert to the following points as you analyze your time-use log:

- During what time of the day was I most productive? When was I least productive? Why?
- How did I lose (or waste) my time? Was it because of unnecessary interruptions, visitors/socializing, crises, telephone? Who and what was involved in each case?

### Develop a Plan of Action

After you have analyzed how you spend your time, you need to determine how well the tasks you complete contribute to meeting your work goals. The tasks you actually complete should correspond to the tasks you are expected to complete.

# TIME-USE LOG

Name  *Michele Fitch*

Day 1 *Monday* Day 2 *Tuesday* Day 3 *Wednesday* Day 4 *Thursday* Day 5 *Friday*

| | | | | | |
|---|---|---|---|---|---|
| 8:45 a.m. | arrived early opened office | arrived early opened office | arrived early opened office | arrived early opened office | arrived early opened office |
| 9:00 a.m. | checked calendar, tickler & To Do list | checked calendar, tickler & To Do list | checked calendar, tickler & To Do list | checked calendar, tickler & To Do list | checked calendar, tickler & To Do list |
| 9:15 a.m. | met with supervisor | met with supervisor | keyed meeting notes and report | met with supervisor | met with supervisor |
| 9:30 a.m. | keyed report | keyed letter | | organized trip reports | memo to staff |
| 9:45 a.m. | | took notes at meeting | | keyed trip expense forms | made copies and distributed |
| 10:00 a.m. | | | | | |
| 10:15 a.m. | | | coffee | handled phone call | coffee |
| 10:30 a.m. | coffee break | | checked supplies and completed requisition form | coffee break | talked to Nancy |
| 10:45 a.m. | telephone call to confirm Wed. travel | mail arrived | mail arrived | mail arrived | filed |
| 11:00 a.m. | mail arrived | opened/sorted/ distributed | opened/sorted/ distributed | opened/sorted/ distributed | |
| 11:15 a.m. | opened/sorted/ distributed | coffee | talked to Nancy | keyed report | mail arrived |
| | | | | | opened/sorted/ |

**Illus. 10—9.**   Michele's record of how she used her time each day, Monday through Friday.

**maximize:** to increase to the greatest extent possible

For each activity you have listed in your time-use log, ask yourself if that activity contributed to the satisfactory completion of your job requirements. If not, you need to develop a plan of action to **maximize** the effective use of your time. Use the techniques discussed in this topic as a basis for increasing your time-use effectiveness and as a foundation for developing an orderly approach to your job.

## REVIEW QUESTIONS

1. What is the function of the office workstation?

2. Discuss the usage guidelines an office worker should follow when working with office equipment, supplies, and accessories.

3. What is the guiding principle you should follow in planning the arrangement of any workstation?

4. Define the term "functional work area."

5. Describe how you can organize your workstation (both surface areas and drawers) to increase your productivity.

6. Define time management. Why is time management important to the office worker?

7. Identify and describe common time wasters in the office.

8. Describe the procedures you can use to handle your time obligations effectively.

9. Describe the procedures you can use to simplify your work.

10. What steps do you take to complete an analysis of how you spend your time?

## MAKING DECISIONS

Ana Maria arrived at the office a few minutes early and began to review her "To Do" list for the day. (**Note**: Take time now to review Ana Maria's "To Do" list on page 403.) Her supervisor arrived shortly and asked her to come into his office immediately. Ana Maria picked up her notepad and her "To Do" list and followed her supervisor into his office.

Her supervisor told Ana Maria he had received a call at home last night that the sales meeting scheduled three weeks from today at the national headquarters had been moved to the day after tomorrow because of an emergency. The supervisor and Jim McPheeter will need to fly to the sales meeting tomorrow and will need 20 copies of the new sales contract form to take with them.

Ana Maria took notes as her supervisor discussed these changes. She also added making the 20 copies of the sales contract form to her "To Do" list.

Ana Maria said to her supervisor: "This definitely changes the priorities for today. Let's go over them to be certain we're not overlooking anything."

**What You Are To Do:**   Your teacher will divide you into groups to discuss the changes Ana Maria needs to make in her priority list. As a group, decide the new order of priorities needed to reflect the change in her supervisor's schedule. Use a sheet of plain paper to prepare a revised "To Do" list.

## EXTENDING YOUR ENGLISH SKILLS

In this exercise, you will be reviewing adjectives. Identify all the adjectives in the customer form letter on page 409. This letter is sent to all first-time customers of the Raleigh Corporation, a manufacturer of modular business furniture.

**What You Are To Do:**   • Using plain paper, write the adjectives you find in the order in which they occur in the customer form letter. Remember to include the articles *a, an,* and *the* in your adjective list.
• Your teacher may wish to review the identification and use of adjectives with you.

## APPLICATION ACTIVITY

As you have learned in this topic, managing your time on the job and developing an orderly approach to your work are important elements in your job productivity. Learning how to use your time effectively and to approach your work in an orderly fashion are important to you right now as well. You can begin now to develop the habits of proper time management and orderly arrangement of your work. This will be beneficial to you as you continue your education and also will be helpful in any occupation you choose. In this activity you will complete a daily time log. When you have charted your activities, you will use your chart to help you determine your most productive time periods.

**Illus. 10–15.**  A form used to request reprographic services.

**REQUEST FOR REPROGRAPHIC SERVICES**

DEPARTMENT _Advertising_

ACCOUNT CODE _0341_

DATE SUBMITTED _3/14/--_

DATE NEEDED _3/16/--_

PRIORITY COPY _____

SUBMITTED BY _Amy Santos_ _____ ROOM NO. _418_ EXT. _5174_

APPROVED BY _Cory Roe_

JOB NO. _____

TOTAL ORIGINALS _____

TOTAL COPIES _____

TOTAL CHARGE _____

(For use by Reprographics Dept.)

| Number of Originals | Description | Paper Size | | Duplex | Tot. Copies Per Orig. | TOTAL COPIES |
|---|---|---|---|---|---|---|
| | | Letter | Legal | | | |
| 1 | Letter | ✓ | | | 150 | 150 |
| 12 | Report | ✓ | | ✓ | 150 | 1800 |
| | | | | | | |
| | | | | | | |
| | | | | | | |

_____ Colored Paper: _____ Canary __✓__ Buff _____ Blue _____ Green _____ Pink

_____ Colored Cover Stock: _____ Buff _____ Blue _____ Green

__✓__ Collate _report_

__✓__ Staple (No. of Staples __1__ ; Location _upper left corner_ _____ )

__✓__ Call when ready for pick-up

_____ Return by interoffice mail

_____ SPECIAL INSTRUCTIONS _Use buff cover stock for front and back covers of the report._

## Copy Log

A common copier control procedure is the copier log book. When a copier log book is used, you are expected to record information pertaining to your copy job in a log similar to the one shown in Illus. 10–16 on page 420. To complete the log, you would:

1. record your name as the person making the copy
2. record the name of the person/department for whom the copies are being made
3. record the number of originals
4. record the number of copies per original
5. record the total copies made
6. record any special features used

**Illus. 10–16.** Page from a copier log book.

| COPY LOG | | | | | Machine *Copier 2* |
|---|---|---|---|---|---|
| Name | Person/Department | Number of Originals | Number of Copies Per Original | Total Copies | Special Features |
| J. Talbert | Customer Service | 4 | 5 | 20 | sorter |
| J. Talbert | Customer Service | 20 | 10 | 200 | duplex sorter |
| C. Krane | Accounting | 1 | 23 | 23 | shift left |
| K. Lyle | President Votaw | 2 | 25 | 50 | book mode |

## Individual User Guidelines

Another way to control copying is to establish procedures and guidelines for individual employees who use copiers. As a responsible employee, you should make it your practice to follow these five general guidelines:

1. Follow company policy regarding the maximum number of copies to be made at convenience copiers. Larger copier needs are best handled through centralized reprographic services, when available.
2. Be cost conscious when planning to use the copier:
   - Use the economy features of the copier, such as duplexing, to save file space, postage costs, and work time.
   - Never run off more copies than you need or rerun copies to see if you can get a better one.

*explicitly:* clearly

3. Comply with copyright laws. Copyright laws list *explicitly* those documents that cannot be copied. These documents include money, postage stamps, United States securities, birth certificates, passports, draft cards, drivers' licenses, automobile registrations, and certificates of title.
4. Do not make copies for personal use.
5. Practice good housekeeping rules and common courtesy when using the copier. Always clean up the area after you have completed your copying project. If you have a long copy job and another worker needs a priority copy, stop at a convenient point and let the other person have access to the machine.

Likewise, if you need a few copies and someone else is near the end of a long copying job, wait until the other person is finished to make your copies.

**COPY PREPARATION PROCEDURES**

To obtain attractive copies, care must be taken when preparing copy to be reproduced. The following guidelines will help you achieve professional-looking copies.

### Originals

Even the most attractive format can be ruined if you do not give attention to the actual preparation of the original on your typewriter or word processor. The print wheel, printing element, or keys should be clean to produce clear, sharp characters. Use white bond paper with a dark ribbon (preferably a carbon ribbon). Handle your original carefully. Smudges and smears can show up on the copy. Unless your copier reproduces to the edge of an original, leave at least a one-fourth-inch margin on all sides of your original.

Proofread the copy carefully. One mistake on an original from which you make 100 copies magnifies that mistake a hundred times. If you do not have a typewriter with a correction ribbon, make corrections using white-out or correction tape. When using liquid white-out, make sure the fluid is thin enough that it will not mound up when it dries. Allow the fluid time to dry before making the correction. Correction tape can be used to cover entire lines of copy and can be typed upon immediately after its application. Correction tape comes in several widths to cover entire lines of copy.

### Paste-Up Materials

When long reports are prepared, the wording of a paragraph often is changed or portions of the report are moved from one section to another. Also, entire sections may be deleted or graphic materials may be inserted into the copy. If you are using a typewriter rather than a word processor to prepare and revise copy material, one quick revision *technique* is to cut and paste. Key the corrected copy onto a separate sheet of paper and then cut it out. Paste the cut section onto the original right over the paragraph to be replaced. This procedure eliminates keying the entire page over.

*technique:* method

One primary caution in using cut and paste is to guard against the pasted copy becoming wrinkled or puckered. Use rubber cement or paper glue that does not tend to wrinkle. If you are not certain about the procedure or the products, practice first on paper of identical quality. Good photocopies cannot be made from wrinkled originals. Use guide marks to align the pasted copy so that it does not run at an angle to the other lines on the copy.

Transparent tape or double-sided tape will work as well as rubber cement or glue. However, all pasted or taped edges should be secured. On older copier models, a loose edge may appear as a line on the photocopy.

## Equipment Checks

To achieve excellent copies, you must keep the equipment operating at peak performance. Know your copier and follow the directions for using it. If the copies are too light or too dark, adjust the darkness indicator. If your copier does not have an automatic feed, position the original carefully so that copies do not appear to be run at an angle. If spots appear on your copies, check the glass surface to see if it is clean. Do not remove paper clips and staples over the machine, because they may fall into a machine opening.

**Illus. 10–17.** An occasional paper jam is easily remedied by an employee knowledgeable about the equipment.

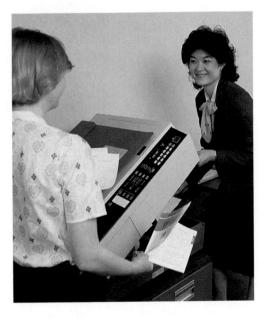

## EMERGENCY OFFICE PROCEDURES

Learn emergency procedures immediately upon beginning a new job. If your office does not have established procedures, do what you can to help initiate practices such as those described in the following paragraphs. The safety of you and your co-workers is too important to leave to chance.

### Emergency Telephone Numbers

Emergency telephone numbers should be placed on each telephone or posted beside the telephone. *Emergency telephone numbers* are those telephone numbers you can use to seek help for an immediate, dangerous situation. The primary emergency telephone numbers are the police, fire department, ambulance, operator, and sometimes a general emergency number, such as 911.

### First Aid Procedures

First aid kits should be located conveniently within the office. They should be inspected frequently and restocked whenever supplies are used from the kit.

Some firms will send an employee from each floor or work group for first aid training and/or CPR (cardiopulmonary resuscitation) classes. These courses are given periodically by the American Red Cross. Each employee should know who has completed first aid training and who is qualified to help in the critical first minutes of an emergency. First aid posters can be put in ***conspicuous*** places to further assist employees.

*conspicuous:* easily seen

**Illus. 10–21.** It is important to identify those employees who are trained in first aid and CPR.

### Fires

As an office employee you should know the locations of the nearest fire exit, fire alarm box, and fire extinguisher. Large office buildings generally have the fire alarm boxes and fire extinguishers in the same location patterns on each floor, with additional boxes and extinguishers located in high-risk areas. Learn how to use the fire extinguisher and know the type of fire it is intended to put out. Never attempt to fight a fire alone. Always have someone report the fire to the proper agency.

### Building Evacuation Plans

*evacuation:* leaving

Learn the established escape routes and *evacuation* procedures. Emergency exit routes should be posted in conspicuous places throughout the building.

Employees should know their individual responsibilities during a drill or evacuation. Who, for example, is responsible for assisting a handicapped office worker? Who is responsible for checking conference rooms, rest rooms, and other areas where the alarm may not be heard?

## PERSONAL SECURITY ON THE JOB

*vigil:* watch

Protection of yourself and your property requires a continuous *vigil* on your part. Concern for security, like concern for safety, cannot be turned on and off as the mood strikes. Most businesses strive to provide a safe and secure work environment for their employees. To complement the company's effort in providing for your safety and security on the job, you should always use good common sense.

### Protecting Personal Property

A purse left at a workstation, a jacket slung over the back of a chair or left in an unoccupied office, cash left out in plain sight—all are invitations to a would-be thief. Keep personal belongings out of sight and locked up in a drawer, file cabinet, or employee locker or closet. The key to this drawer or other receptacle should be issued only to the employee who is assigned its use.

### Working Alone

Sometimes you may find it necessary to stay late at the office or to come in early. If your company has established security measures, follow the company procedures for being in the building during the non-working hours.

If no after-hours procedures exist, establish your own security routine and stick to it. Small offices normally do not have security forces. Be alert to the following security procedures when you work alone:

- Always work near a phone and keep emergency telephone numbers handy.
- When working late, lock all doors to your work area. Do not open the door to anyone you are not expecting or cannot identify.
- Get to know the custodial staff and when to expect them.
- If someone else is working late, establish a check procedure with that person and check at regular intervals. The security force in a larger building often provides this checking function.
- If you use the elevator to leave the building, do not enter the elevator if anyone is in it whom you have reason to suspect. Stand next to the control buttons.
- Avoid using even a locked restroom if you are the only one working late.
- Park your car near the building entrance and/or near a parking lot light. Check the parking lot visually before leaving the building. Keep your car keys in your hand ready to use. In some organizations, security personnel are available to escort you to your car.

## BUILDING AND OFFICE SECURITY

*safeguards:*
protection

Building and office security measures are necessary *safeguards*. Casual consideration of security measures today has been replaced by a more serious approach to planning and analyzing security needs. Crime and fire are the two major security concerns of a business.

### Controlling Outsider Access

Protecting the office from access by unauthorized outsiders can be a major concern. Although businesses cannot operate without being open to the public, the public does not need open and uncontrolled access to all parts of most office buildings.

Businesses use varied security means to safeguard their personnel and assets. In large metropolitan areas, for example, the presence of a highly visible, centrally located security guard or security station in the lobby has proved effective.

Some firms require a visitor to sign a log and give his or her name, address, and the name of the person or office being visited.

Other firms find it more convenient to send an employee to the lobby to escort the visitor back to the office. In smaller offices, the receptionist may be the controlling agent simply by being present in the front office.

**Illus. 10–22.** The purpose of office security is to provide protection for office workers and office property. This security guard makes sure all visitors sign the visitors' log.

### Controlling Employee Access

Many medium- and large-sized businesses gain positive identification of those employees who should have access to the buildings and grounds through the use of *identification (ID) cards*. The trend in employee identification is the photo ID. Your cooperation in wearing your ID helps assure your personal safety and security on the job.

Some firms use magnetically coded badges that can be sensed by electronic readers, referred to as *proximity readers*. As the wearer approaches a controlled access point, the electronic reader reads the code on the badge and transmits the information to a computer. This information provides a record of who entered and left designated areas, the time of entry, and in some instances, the time of exit—all valuable security information.

Businesses which must restrict employee entry into selected areas of a building often use magnetically coded cards as a substitute for keys. A magnetically coded card carried by the employee can be inserted into a magnetic card reader to gain access. If the card is authorized for entrance, the door opens.

**Illus. 10–23.** Some firms issue ID cards or access cards to their employees.

*Olivia looked up to see a repairman coming through the doorway. "I'm here to check your computer. Here's the order," he said as he flashed a copy of a repair order in front of Olivia. "Apparently, you had a large electrical surge last night, and we have to check any micros that might be damaged. This will take a few minutes — why don't you just take a short break."*

*Olivia got up from her terminal, but she was puzzled. She hadn't heard of an electrical surge. "Besides," she thought, "we have switches to protect the equipment." Olivia felt she should check this with her supervisor, Ms. Calibre.*

*Ms. Calibre was not aware of an electrical surge either. "Let me check on this before we do anything," she said.*

*Olivia stepped back into her office to see the repairman disconnecting the computer:*

*Repairman:   Looks like I'll have to take your computer back to the shop for repairs.*

*Olivia:        You'll have to wait until my supervisor receives authorization for you to take the computer.*

*Repairman:   Well, I have several other computers to check. Why don't I just come back after I've checked them and pick this one up.*

*The repairman left hurriedly, and a minute or so later Olivia's supervisor appeared at the door: "I think we may have a problem — no one authorized a computer repair check. We had better report this."*

*Ms. Calibre called the police immediately to report the incident. The police sergeant told her that several businesses had lost computers and typewriters during the past two months. "You're lucky to have an alert employee," the sergeant told Ms. Calibre. "None of the others questioned an unexpected repair check. When the employees returned from their 'little breaks,' their equipment was gone."*

### Detection Systems and Alarms

After a detailed study of security needs and an analysis of the building and the surrounding area, firms often choose a combination of approaches to secure their facilities. In addition to the methods discussed previously, detection systems and alarms help complement a firm's security measures. A *detection system* consists of *monitoring* devices and alarms that sense and signal a change in the condition of an area being protected. Some detection systems detect entry into the area while others are designed to detect movement in the area.

*monitoring:* warning; watching

Detection systems and alarms are designed to reduce a firm's reliance on an on-site security guard. Even if a firm has security officers, the officers cannot be at all stations at once. Closed circuit television can be used to provide continuous monitoring of corridors, entrances, or other sensitive areas. When used with a video tape recorder, closed circuit television provides the firm with a record of significant events for review.

**Illus. 10–24.** A closed-circuit television monitoring device.

# REVIEW QUESTIONS

1. Describe how an accident-prevention approach can help control office accidents.

2. What are the safety practices you should follow in maintaining your own workstation?

3. What are the safety practices you should follow with regard to office furnishings and electrical equipment?

4. What are the safety practices you should follow with regard to general office equipment and video monitors?

5. Describe the emergency office procedures you should learn immediately upon starting a new job.

6. Describe some of the precautions you may take as an office worker to protect your personal property on the job.

7. How can you help assure your personal security when you are working alone?

8. How can a firm control an outsider's access to the business?

9. Explain some of the procedures businesses use to control employee access.

10. Explain how detection systems and alarms complement a firm's security measures.

# MAKING DECISIONS

Your supervisor, Mr. Petersen, is reading a memo when you enter his office. He shakes his head and says: "This is the second memo the managers have received about security leaks. One of our competitors has just introduced a new product, and it's identical to a product we have been working on. Apparently they discovered our plans. The president wants our thoughts on how to improve our product security. In addition to the main shredder in the reprographics center, he is suggesting a shredder for each office. Well, I'm just glad everyone on *my* staff can be trusted."

As you hear this, you remember several situations you have observed in the office:

- You have seen poor photocopies—even photocopies of confidential material—discarded in the wastebasket.
- Computer printouts with product-testing results are left stacked next to files rather than being locked in the files.

- Workers often talk about current projects during their breaks.
- Workers have a habit of using the offices of other workers who are out of town or on vacation.
- Workers too freely give out unnecessary information to callers, such as telling a caller exactly where the individual is.

"Tell me," Mr. Petersen says, "Do you think we need a shredder?" How do you respond to him? Do you tell him what you think he wants to hear, or do you use your observations as a basis for your response? How can you use this question as an opening to discuss security procedures in your office? What suggestions can you make for tightening general office security?

**What You Are To Do:**   Prepare a response to the questions.

## EXTENDING YOUR ENGLISH SKILLS

In this exercise, you will practice spelling correctly some frequently misspelled words.

Word/text processing equipment can be used to complete this activity.

**What You Are To Do:**   Set your margins for a 70-space line. Set your first tab 19 spaces from your left margin. Set the second tab 38 spaces from the left margin. Set your third tab 57 spaces from the left margin. Leave a 2-inch top margin and double-space the entire exercise. On a sheet of plain paper, center the title: FREQUENTLY MISSPELLED WORDS.

Key the words as shown at the left margin. Tab to the second column and key the word again while looking at the correct spelling in your textbook. Tab to the third column and key the word without looking at the word either in the textbook or from your keyed copy. Tab to the fourth column and repeat the spelling practice. After you have practiced each word following this procedure, remove your paper and use standard proofreader's marks to correct your copy. Give your corrected copy to your teacher. Refer to Reference Section A for standard proofreader's marks.

# PRODUCTIVITY CORNER

**Blake Williams**
*OFFICE SUPERVISOR*

## SAFETY FIRST—ALL THE TIME!

DEAR MR. WILLIAMS:

My supervisor arrived this morning and found the coffee pot left plugged in. Last week, someone forgot to lock up an expensive calculator at the end of the day. My employer is becoming concerned that the safety and security practices of our office are too lax.

Although we have no formal safety program, we do try to practice good work habits. We are all very busy and we won't have a lot of time to listen to lectures on safety and security. Do you have any suggestions for us?— FRED IN TULSA

DEAR FRED:

Safety and security instruction should not be left to lectures alone. Try the following ideas:

- Establish a safety committee. Rotate membership to get maximum involvement from all employees. Get first-aid training for committee members to increase their value to the employees.

- Use bulletin boards, posters, brochures, booklets, films, checklists, and the company newspaper to communicate safety messages.
- Use a checklist with specific safety and security pointers so that employees know exactly what is expected of them.
- Assign particular duties, such as unplugging the coffee pot or locking up the calculator, to specific individuals. Post the list of assignments.
- Hold periodic fire drills. With over 18,000 office fires a year, according to the National Safety Council, this can be time well spent.
- Designate specific employees to help handicapped workers in an emergency. Devise an evacuation plan and practice it together.
- Write the National Safety Council, 444 North Michigan Avenue, Chicago, IL 60611, for information on office safety and security.

Good luck in developing a sound program for your office.—BLAKE WILLIAMS

# *Chapter 11*

# Management Support Activities

Today's office assistant is an important part of the management team. Much of the decision making and processing of information required of business executives is based upon the input they receive from their staffs. Likewise, many of an executive's business responsibilities, such as conducting a meeting or traveling, are facilitated by the executive's staff. Tasks supporting the executive's activities often are delegated to responsible and trustworthy workers. As an office worker, you may be involved in a wide range of support activities which facilitate executive decision making, processing of information, and other responsibilities.

In this chapter, you will learn about the management support activities which you as a future office worker may expect to handle. You will learn about reminder systems, such as calendars and tickler files, that are used to schedule office activities. You will also learn to apply correct procedures for maintaining these systems.

Assisting with meetings and making travel arrangements are two important support activities. Your knowledge of how to handle these activities will contribute significantly to a smoothly operating office.

One of the more challenging support activities is assisting with business reports. Your responsibilities may vary from gathering information for business reports to formatting and keying the reports.

Management support activities provide you with an opportunity to utilize your creativity and resourcefulness in the office. As you perform these duties successfully, you demonstrate the accomplishment of your professional skills and allow others to see you as a responsible assistant—truly an important member of the management team.

The objectives of this chapter are to provide you with the background and skills to

- help you understand your role in using common reminder systems, assisting with business meetings, and making travel plans

- help you understand your role in assisting with business reports

# Topic 1

## CALENDARS, BUSINESS MEETINGS, AND TRAVEL

When you have completed your study of this topic, you will be able to

- identify proper procedures for maintaining calendars and tickler files
- describe the office assistant's duties in helping with business meetings
- prepare documents related to business meetings
- describe the major forms of business travel
- identify proper procedures for completing business travel arrangements

Knowing what to do, when to do it, and how to do it are important factors in your ability to be of assistance to executives or managers. The more knowledgeable you are about the details of calendars, tickler files, business meetings, and travel, the more help you can provide the executive or executives for whom you work.

Reminder systems such as calendars and tickler files are used in offices to assist you in scheduling office activities. **Reminder systems** consist of a group of devices designed to bring to mind events, tasks, and other office-related activities. The purpose of reminder systems is to allow scheduling these activities for the most efficient use of time and resources.

**449**

Business meetings bring people together in order to communicate information and make decisions. Increasingly, however, more meetings are not face to face. Technological developments allow executives or managers in many different locations—even on different continents—to conduct meetings without leaving their offices. Well-organized meetings, whether face to face or by electronic means, are necessary if businesses are to function smoothly.

Because a significant portion of an executive's time during the day is spent in meetings, most executives recognize the importance of meetings that are well planned. You can do much to help your employer plan and conduct meetings efficiently and effectively. In this topic, you will learn how to handle meeting arrangements.

Many executives must travel to meet their business responsibilities. As an assistant to a traveling executive, you will be expected to be knowledgeable about the major methods of business travel. In this topic, you will also learn proper procedures for completing basic travel arrangements.

## CALENDARS AND TICKLER FILES

As an office assistant, you may have the responsibility for keeping track of appointments, meetings, travel dates, and deadlines. Perhaps the most widely used device for keeping track of such items is the calendar. The tickler file (so named because it "tickles" your memory) is a companion to your calendar because it provides a convenient place to keep notations of tasks to be performed on specific dates.

### Calendars

It is very likely that you will have your own calendar to maintain, as well as that of any executives for whom you make appointments and schedule meetings. In order to maintain the calendars properly, you will need to clarify the following points with the executive or manager:

- To what extent do you have authority to make appointments?
- When should you check with the manager before making appointments?
- Are there times when the manager prefers that you not make appointments, such as the first half-hour of the day, the day before or after a trip, or the day before a deadline?

**Illus. 11–1.** Since a calendar on your desk can be viewed by others, avoid writing confidential entries on it.

The extent of authority delegated to you for making appointments will depend in great part on the nature of the business. For example, if you are keeping the appointment book for a doctor, most of the appointment requests will be from patients. In this case, you will be expected to schedule appointments without having to verify each appointment with the doctor. On the other hand, you may work in a general office where both you and the executive make appointments. Therefore, you both must agree on procedures which will allow you to operate effectively.

### Guidelines for Making Appointments

1. Do not schedule overlapping appointments. Try to determine the amount of time needed for each appointment. Also, the executive may prefer that some time be left unscheduled to return telephone calls or prepare for the next appointment.

2. Keep a neat calendar. Use legible handwriting to record names, telephone numbers, and other *pertinent* information kept on your calendar. Avoid crossing out entries and rescheduling over scratched-off entries. Many assistants keep their appointments in pencil to prevent such problems.

3. As appointments are confirmed, place a check by each appointment (see page 452). Office assistants who maintain electronic calendars often devise their own means of identifying appoint-

*pertinent:* related to the point at hand

ments as confirmed. For instance, they may underline the individual's name (see page 453).

4. If the executive does not keep a calendar of appointments, provide a daily listing of appointments and reminders at the beginning of the workday. This listing should be typed and should list the appointments for the day in *chronologic* order. If you maintain an electronic calendar, simply provide the executive with a printout of the day's calendar, such as the one shown in Illus. 11–3.

*chronologic:*
arranged in order
by time

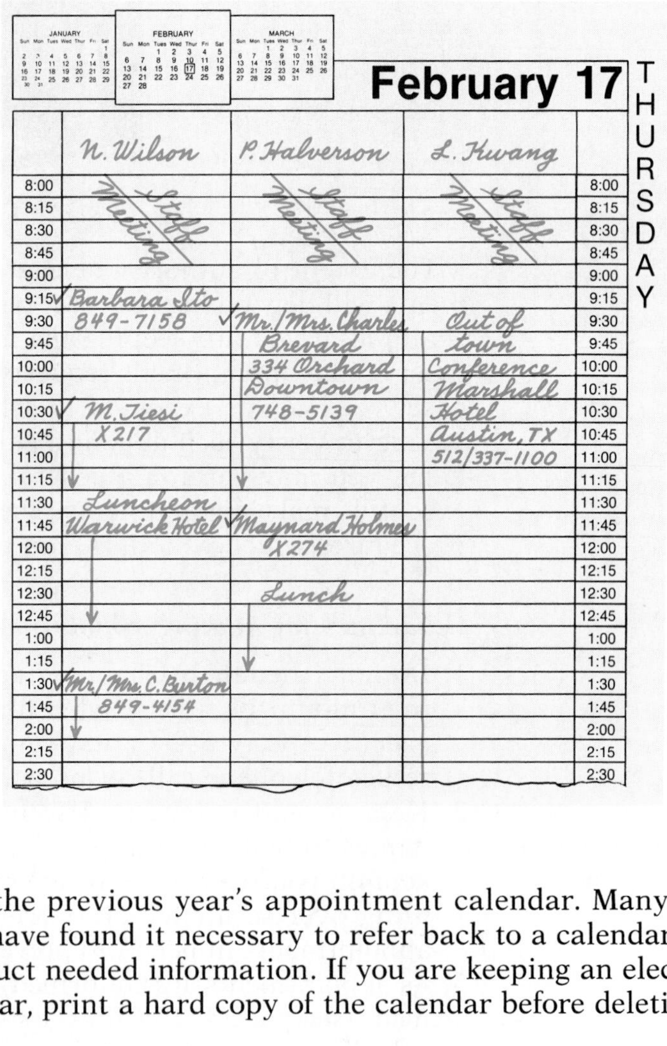

**Illus. 11–2.**  An office assistant responsible for scheduling appointments for more than one executive often uses a group appointment calendar, like the one shown here.

5. Keep the previous year's appointment calendar. Many assistants have found it necessary to refer back to a calendar to reconstruct needed information. If you are keeping an electronic calendar, print a hard copy of the calendar before deleting the data.

```
                          NATHAN WILSON

                SCHEDULE FOR MONDAY, MARCH 28, 19--

 NO    START    FINISH  LENGTH    WITH         REMARKS

  1    08:00    08:30     30      Staff        Meeting to discuss week's
                                               priorities; Conference Room A.

  2    08:30    09:00     30      Nancy        Initial budget review planning
                                               session to determine documents
                                               needed for 1:30 meeting.

  *    09:00    10:00     60      FREE         Reminder: Check with Dave (X2221)
                                               about trip to Simms Plant

  3    10:00    12:00    120      Blondelle    Meeting to discuss system designs
                                  Webb         for Simms Plant
                                  (887-5667)

  *    12:00    01:30     90      FREE

  4     1:30    03:30    120      Mat          Meeting to discuss quarterly budget
                                  Hastings     review; Marketing Department.
                                  (X5321)      Conference Room C.
                                  John
                                  Baker
                                  (X3444)
                                  Nancy

  *    03:30    04:00     30      FREE         Review management articles

  5    04:00    05:00     60      Dave         Planning session for trip to Simms
                                  Tokuda       Plant, Conference Room B.  Check
                                  (X2221)      with Nancy for backup materials.
```

**Illus. 11–3.** An office assistant who maintains an electronic calendar provides an executive with a printout of the day's schedule. Notice that all appointments have been confirmed (confirmed appointments are underlined).

**Illus. 11–4.** This medical assistant uses a computer to maintain a listing of appointments.

### Responding to Appointment Requests

People will request appointments in different ways: in person, by telephone, by letter or memorandum, or by electronic message. Although the manner in which you respond to these requests changes slightly according to the ***medium*** of communication used, the basic information you gather about the appointment will still be the same:

***medium:*** means

- WHO:      name and telephone number of the individual requesting the appointment/meeting
- WHEN:    date, time, and approximate length of appointment/ meeting
- WHERE: location, if other than the executive's office

***backup materials:***
related documents

In some instances, the executive may also ask you to determine the purpose of the meeting and identify all ***backup materials*** needed.

When you receive a request for an appointment, check your calendar to determine that the date and time requested are available. If the requested time is not available, you can suggest alternative appointment dates and times. If requests for appointments have to be approved, obtain the executive's approval before confirming the appointment.

### Entering Recurring Items

You will find that some meetings and tasks are performed periodically, perhaps weekly, monthly, quarterly, or annually. As you are setting up your calendar at the beginning of the year, enter the recurring meetings and tasks on both your desk calendar and the executive's calendar. If you block out the times for these recurring items, both you and the executive will know what time is available for scheduling other appointments.

### Coordinating Calendars

If both you and the executive schedule appointments, you need to coordinate both appointment calendars so that they are consistent and up to date. This usually is done at the beginning of the workday or at the end of the previous workday. Adjustments to schedules (such as confirming tentative appointments, rescheduling appointments, deleting cancelled appointments, and changing time allotments), are reviewed by the executive and assistant at that time.

## Tickler File

A **tickler file** is a chronologic file divided into 12 monthly divisions with 31 daily parts for the current month, as shown in Illus. 11–5. Tickler files can be set up using cards, a pocket file (an accordion-like file), or a file drawer with file folders. A tickler file also can be maintained on a computer.

Store in a tickler file items requiring future action. For example, an executive may say to you, "Mr. Flanigan from the home office will be visiting here next Friday. Please call a local restaurant on Monday and make a luncheon reservation for us." You would write a personal reminder to make the reservation and place the sheet of paper behind the proper guide in the tickler file.

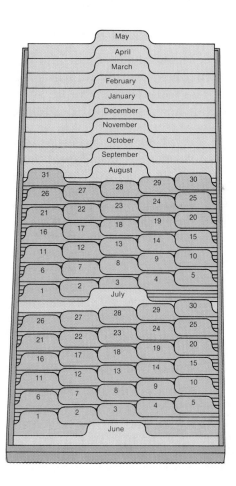

**Illus. 11–5.** A tickler file provides a convenient place to keep notations of tasks to be performed on specific dates.

As soon as you become aware of a deadline or of a detail that needs to be checked again in the future, place a notation in your tickler file under the relevant day. Check your tickler file each morning and remove those items filed for the current day. Complete the appropriate action for each item. Between your tickler file and your calendar, you should be able to schedule most of your work smoothly.

## BUSINESS MEETINGS

Meetings provide an important communication link within the business. Without meetings, it would be difficult for employees to keep up to date on company matters. Meetings may range from an informal meeting in the executive's office to a formal board of directors' meeting in the company board room. Your duties in assisting with these meetings will vary, depending upon the formality, function, size, and location of the meeting.

### Informal and Small Group Meetings

Many of the meetings in which executives or managers are involved will be informal discussions and small group meetings. The following example shows how one office employee carried out her responsibilities for setting up a meeting:

> *The manager called Jana on the intercom. "Jana, see if you can get the four Hansville Project engineers together tomorrow at three o'clock for about an hour . . . and see if the conference room is available." As the manager spoke, Jana wrote down the instructions. She noted the materials she had to prepare for the meeting, as well as the arrangements she needed to make for special equipment. Immediately after taking all of the instructions, Jana verified the availability of the conference room and telephoned each of the engineers. She told them the time, place, and approximate length of the meeting. She then arranged for the necessary equipment and photocopied the materials needed for the meeting. The next day, Jana checked the conference room before the meeting to see that everything was in order.*

### Formal Business Meetings

A formal meeting follows a definite order of business, which frequently is called an agenda. An agenda is a list of the topics to be discussed during the meeting. You may have responsibilities before, during, and after a formal meeting.

**Illus. 11-6.** Informal, small group meetings are held frequently in many organizations.

### Before the Meeting

The following suggestions will be helpful to you in your planning. You may not use all the suggestions for each meeting. However, these guidelines will be helpful to you in planning most business meetings.

*Establish a Meeting Folder.* Once you are aware that a meeting will take place, set up a folder for that meeting. Use this folder to collect items related to the meeting, such as the list of attendees, the agenda, notes, and copies of materials to be distributed.

*Reserve the Meeting Room.* When you are given the date, time, and location of the meeting, check immediately to see if the desired meeting room and time are available.

*Use Your Reminder Systems.* Mark your calendar and the executive's calendar with the meeting time and place. Use your tickler file to help you control the planning details which must be completed. For example, if you must prepare 20 copies of a report for the meeting, place a note in the tickler file to remind you of this responsibility.

*Notify the Meeting Participants.* Participants should be notified as soon as possible of the time, place, approximate length, and purpose of the meeting. They also should be told about any materials they should bring to the meeting.

*Prepare the Agenda.* All participants and the recording secretary should receive a copy of the agenda prior to the meeting. The agenda typically contains the items shown in Illus. 11–7.

*Obtain Equipment.* With the help of the executive or manager, determine what equipment is needed for the meeting. Follow through by arranging for the equipment that is needed.

*Organize Meeting Materials and Handouts.* You may be expected to gather certain materials such as extra notepads, pencils, file folders, and courtesy identification badges. Also organize any materials and handouts such as reports, letters, and statistical data, that will be distributed at the meeting.

```
                        AGENDA

              RIVERTON IMPROVEMENT COUNCIL

                     June 30, 19--

  1.  Call to Order:  Nancy Hollingshead, Improvement Council
                      President

  2.  Roll Call:  Troy Canfield, Secretary

  3.  Reading of the Minutes:  Troy Canfield, Secretary

  4.  Treasurer's Report:  Shawn Petersen, Treasurer

  5.  Committee Report:

           Recognitions Committee:  Harold King, Chairperson

  6.  Unfinished Business:

           Telecommunications Improvement Project

  7.  New Business:

           East Riverfront Drive Improvement Project

  8.  Date of Next Meeting

  9.  Adjournment
```

**Illus. 11–7.** An agenda is a list of the topics to be discussed during a formal business meeting.

*Prepare the Meeting Room.* Be sure that the temperature is comfortable and that the room is arranged to fit the meeting style. Also, make sure any equipment requested is available and working properly.

**Illus. 11–8.** If a meeting is to run smoothly, a lot of planning and organization must be done before the meeting begins. Here, the office assistant is preparing the meeting room.

### During the Meeting

The degree to which you participate during the meeting will depend upon where the meeting is held and the tasks to be done. The following pointers relate to duties you may be asked to perform:

*Take Minutes.* **Minutes** are the official record of a meeting. The minutes detail the action taken by the group, and they provide the reader with a concise presentation of factual information about the meeting. The minutes should not be a *verbatim* transcript of the meeting, but you must record all pertinent information. Thus, the minutes must give a clear, accurate, and complete accounting of the happenings of the meeting. Although various reporting formats are acceptable for recording minutes, the following items appear in most minutes:

*verbatim:* word for word

- name of group, committee, organization, or business holding the meeting
- time, date, place, and type of meeting (for example, weekly, monthly, annual, called, special)
- name of presiding officer
- members present and absent (In a large organization, only the number of members present needs to be recorded to verify that a *quorum* was present.)

*quorum:* minimum number of members necessary to conduct business

- reading and approval of the minutes from the previous meeting
- committee or individual reports (for example, treasurer's report, standing committees, special committees)
- unfinished business (includes pertinent discussion and action taken)
- new business (includes pertinent discussion and action taken)
- time, date, and place of next meeting
- time of adjournment
- signature of the secretary/recorder or individual responsible for the minutes

The following suggestions will be helpful to you when it is your responsibility to record the minutes of a meeting:

1. Have at the meeting a copy of the meeting agenda, a copy of the minutes of the previous meeting, and a copy of any report or document that might be referred to during the meeting.

*parliamentary procedure:* guides for conducting meetings

2. If you record and transcribe minutes frequently, a ***parliamentary procedure*** reference source (such as *Robert's Rules of Order Revised*) will help you to better understand the meeting proceedings and the correct terminology to use when taking and preparing minutes.

3. Record the important points of discussion during the meeting and identify the individual making a comment. Often, only the action taken or the conclusion reached is presented in the minutes.

4. Record the name of the person making a motion and the name of the person seconding the motion. Motions should be recorded verbatim and a statement should be made in the minutes as to whether or not the motion was adopted.

*Correct Minutes.* Sometimes it is necessary to make corrections in the minutes at the following meeting, before they can be approved. If only a few words are affected, lines may be drawn through the incorrect words and the proper insertions made above them. If more than a few words are affected, lines may be drawn through the sentences or paragraphs to be corrected and the corrections written on a new page. The page number of each correction should be indicated on the original minutes. The minutes should not be rewritten after they have been read and approved at the meeting.

```
                    RIVERTON IMPROVEMENT COUNCIL
                          Meeting Minutes
                          June 30, 19--
```

| | |
|---|---|
| Time and Place of Meeting | The regular weekly meeting of the Riverton Improvement Council was held on Tuesday, June 30, 19--, in the Meeting Chambers at City Hall. The meeting was called to order by President Nancy Hollingshead at 7:30 p.m. |
| Attendance | Present were Improvement Council members: Elizabeth Clark, Roger Addock, Douglas Ivey, Laura Johnston, Steve Munesada, Harold King, Shawn Petersen, Troy Canfield, and President Nancy Hollingshead. Absent was Emily Pierce. |
| Approval of Minutes | The minutes of the June 23, 19--, meeting were read and approved. |
| Treasurer's Report | Treasurer, Shawn Petersen, reported that with the receipt of the State Improvement Funds check, the Improvement Projects account has a balance of $359,450. |
| Report of Recognition Committee | Harold King, chairperson, submitted the committee report (attached to the minutes) recommending that the name of Jane Ann Adams be submitted to the City Council as a candidate for Employee of the Month. Ms. Johnston moved and Mr. Munesada seconded that the committee report be accepted. President Hollingshead directed the secretary to prepare the Resolution of Recognition for submission (attached to the minutes). |
| Unfinished Business | President Hollingshead reported that the three recorded bids for the Telecommunications Improvement Project have been forwarded to the city engineering department for evaluation. |
| New Business | East Riverfront Drive Improvement Project. Purchase of the Martin Victor Wolfe property at 1232 Riverfront Drive. |
| | City Manager, John Byrd, reported that the city has negotiated with the property owner to acquire the property as part of the East Riverfront Drive Improvement Project for the sum of $150,000. The property has been |
| | profits from the resell of the house be returned to the Improvement Project Fund. Mr. Addock seconded the motion. All members voted aye. President Hollingshead directed the treasurer to prepare a check to the City of Riverton for $150,000 for the acquisition of the property. |
| Date of Next Meeting | President Hollingshead declared the next regular meeting of the Improvement Council of Riverton to be held on July 7, 19--, at 7:30 p.m. in the Meeting Chambers at City Hall. |
| Adjournment | Mr. Ivey moved and Ms. Johnston seconded the motion that the meeting be adjourned. The motion carried, and President Hollingshead declared the meeting adjourned at 8:45 p.m. |

*Troy Canfield*
Troy Canfield, Secretary

*Nancy Hollingshead*
Nancy Hollingshead, Improvement Council President

**Illus. 11–9.** Minutes are the official record of a meeting.

### *After the Meeting*

Your work does not end when the meeting ends. Once the meeting is over, you will need to complete certain follow-up activities. Place notations on your calendar and the executive's calendar regarding any item from the meeting that will require future attention.

*Prepare and Distribute the Minutes.* Prepare the minutes as soon as possible. Preparing the minutes will be easier if you do it while the details of the meeting are fresh in your mind. Use examples of previous minutes for appropriate format. The chairperson will proofread the typed minutes before they are distributed to be sure there are no omissions or errors.

*Complete Related Correspondence.* Complete any correspondence associated with the meeting, such as thank-you letters to speakers or resource persons or letters requesting information. All these letters will be signed by the executive, but you may prepare them.

## TELECONFER-
## ENCES

*audio:* sound

*video:* picture images

A teleconference is a meeting of three or more individuals in different locations communicating by means of a telecommunications system. The telecommunications system may involve only *audio* exchanges among the participants, as in a telephone conference. Or it may be more sophisticated, as a *video* exchange system. *Videoconferencing* permits people to meet at two or more different locations, but have visual contact (through television cameras and monitors) almost as if they were in the same room.

You may play a part in preparing for a teleconference. Your role may include the following duties:

1. Reserve the conference room and necessary equipment.
2. Notify the participants of the date, time, length, and purpose of the meeting. Include a telephone number and the name of a contact for participants in the event of technical difficulties.
3. Prepare and distribute any related materials well in advance of the meeting. If several documents are to be sent, use different paper colors to copy different reports. That way, it will be easy to identify reports during the teleconference.
4. Prepare and distribute to the participants the on-line agenda well in advance of the teleconference. The on-line agenda is a listing of the events and topics of discussion planned for the teleconference, with the estimated time that each item will require.

**Illus. 11–10.** A teleconference is a meeting of people who are geographically separated but who are connected by a telecommunications system. This video conference permits voice, text, and video communication.

## BUSINESS TRAVEL

Travel arrangements are made in accordance with company policy. Large firms may have a travel department to handle travel arrangements. Smaller firms, however, may rely on the services of a travel agency or the office assistant to make the travel arrangements. In addition, some companies have special agreements with travel agencies, hotels, and transportation companies for designated services. You will be given instructions to follow in completing any travel arrangements you are assigned.

To complete such arrangements, you will need to be knowledgeable about the major forms of business travel. There is frequently some opportunity to choose the *mode* of travel, the time of departure and arrival, and the kind of accommodations. When such choices are available, you will need to know the executive's personal preferences in order to make travel plans effectively.

*mode:* manner or way of doing something

### Commercial Air Travel

Time is money for the busy executive, and the popularity of air travel among business people reflects this point. Often, the only way to manage a tight schedule is through air travel. To meet this demand in the United States, there is an extensive network of airline routes provided by major national, regional, and commuter airlines.

### Schedules and Flight Information

If the manager is a frequent flyer on one particular airline, an updated airline timetable provides a convenient way to determine travel information such as:

- arrival and departure times
- flight numbers
- days of the week the flight is available
- services offered (meals, snacks, movies)
- toll-free reservation numbers

Airline schedules are available free of charge at ticket counters in airports, at airline offices in major cities, at large hotels, and from travel agents.

If the manager uses several different airlines, you will find the *Official Airline Guide* to be a valuable source of information. It provides schedules and flight information for all airlines. The company for which you work may have a copy of this publication for your reference. If not, a travel agent can provide you with the same information.

### Reservations and Tickets

You may make reservations by calling a travel agent or by calling the airline directly. While you are on the telephone, the agent or airline representative will access a computer and tell you at once if seating is available. If seating is available on the flight(s) you request, the reservations can be confirmed at that time.

Airline tickets frequently are printed by commands from a computer. If you use the service of a travel agent, a computerized printout schedule of the flight itinerary and invoice, as well as a boarding pass, may be received with the airline tickets.

## Other Forms of Business Travel

The rental car and train provide alternative forms of executive travel. You may have occasion to make travel arrangements for the executive using one of these forms of transportation.

### Rental Car

For short trips, particularly in a local area, many business people prefer to rent cars. A rental car may also be suitable when an executive flies into a city and has appointments in outlying areas. Rental cars are available at most airports and other convenient locations for the traveler.

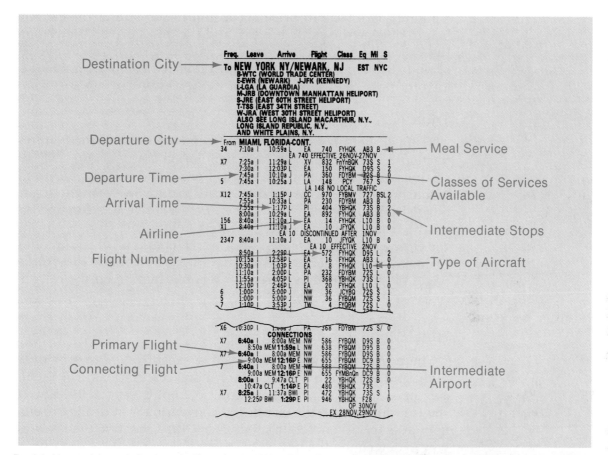

Destination City —

Departure City —

Departure Time —

Arrival Time —

Airline —

Flight Number —

Primary Flight —

Connecting Flight —

— Meal Service

— Classes of Services Available

— Intermediate Stops

— Type of Aircraft

— Intermediate Airport

| Freq. | Leave | Arrive | Flight | Class | Eq | MI | S |
|---|---|---|---|---|---|---|---|

**To NEW YORK NY/NEWARK, NJ   EST NYC**
B-WTC (WORLD TRADE CENTER)
E-EWR (NEWARK)   J-JFK (KENNEDY)
L-LGA (LA GUARDIA)
M-JRB (DOWNTOWN MANHATTAN HELIPORT)
S-JRE (EAST 60TH STREET HELIPORT)
T-TSS (EAST 34TH STREET)
W-JRA (WEST 30TH STREET HELIPORT)
ALSO SEE LONG ISLAND MACARTHUR, N.Y.,
LONG ISLAND REPUBLIC, N.Y.,
AND WHITE PLAINS, N.Y.

From **MIAMI, FLORIDA-CONT.**

| Freq | Leave | Arrive | Airline | Flight | Class | Eq | MI | S |
|---|---|---|---|---|---|---|---|---|
| 34 | 7:10a | 10:59a L | EA | 740 | FYHQK | AB3 | B | |
| | | | EA 740 EFFECTIVE 26NOV-27NOV | | | | | |
| X7 | 7:25a | 11:29a L | XV | 832 | FnYnBQK | 73S | S | 1 |
| | 7:30a | 12:03P L | EA | 150 | FYHQK | D9S | S | 2 |
| | 7:45a | 10:10a J | PA | 360 | FDYBM | 72S | B | 0 |
| 5 | 7:45a | 10:25a J | LA | 148 | PCY | 767 | S | 0 |
| | | | LA 148 NO LOCAL TRAFFIC | | | | | |
| X12 | 7:45a | 1:15P J | CC | 970 | FYBMV | 727 | BSL | 2 |
| | 7:55a | 10:33a L | PA | 230 | FDYBM | AB3 | B | 0 |
| | 7:55a | 1:17P J | PI | 404 | YBHQK | 73S | B | 2 |
| | 8:00a | 10:29a L | EA | 892 | FYHQK | AB3 | B | 0 |
| 156 | 8:40a | 11:10a J | EA | 14 | FYHQK | L10 | B | 0 |
| X1 | 8:40a | 11:10a J | EA | 10 | JFYQK | L10 | B | 0 |
| | | | EA 10 DISCONTINUED AFTER 1NOV | | | | | |
| 2347 | 8:40a | 11:10a J | EA | 10 | JFYQK | L10 | B | 0 |
| | | | EA 10 EFFECTIVE 2NOV | | | | | |
| | 8:50a | 2:29P L | EA | 572 | FYHQK | D95 | L | 2 |
| | 10:15a | 12:58P L | EA | 16 | FYHQK | AB3 | L | 0 |
| | 10:30a | 1:03P E | EA | 8 | FYHQK | L10 | L | 0 |
| | 11:10a | 2:00P L | PA | 232 | FDYBM | 72S | L | 0 |
| | 11:55a | 4:05P L | PI | 368 | YBHQK | 73S | L | 1 |
| | 12:10P | 2:46P L | EA | 20 | FYHQK | L10 | L | 0 |
| 6 | 1:00P | 5:00P J | NW | 36 | JCYBQ | 72S | S | 1 |
| 5 | 1:00P | 5:00P J | NW | 36 | FYBQM | 72S | S | 0 |
| 7 | 1:10P | 3:53P J | TW | 4 | FYQBM | 72S | L | 0 |

| | | | | | | | | |
|---|---|---|---|---|---|---|---|---|
| X6 | 10:30P | 1:05a J | PA | 368 | FDYBM | 72S | S/ | 0 |
| | | | **CONNECTIONS** | | | | | |
| X7 | **6:40a** | 8:00a MEM | NW | 586 | FYBQM | D9S | B | 0 |
| | 8:50a MEM | **11:59a** L | NW | 638 | FYBQM | D95 | B | 0 |
| X7 | **6:40a** | 8:00a MEM | NW | 586 | FYBQM | D9S | B | 0 |
| | 9:00a MEM | **12:16P** E | NW | 655 | FYBQM | DC9 | B | 0 |
| 7 | **6:40a** | 8:00a MEM | NW | 588 | FYBQM | 72S | B | 0 |
| | 9:00a MEM | **12:16P** E | NW | 655 | FYMBnQn | DC9 | B | 0 |
| | **8:00a** | 9:47a CLT | PI | 22 | YBHQK | 72S | B | 0 |
| | 10:47a CLT | **1:14P** E | PI | 480 | YBHQK | 73S | | 1 |
| X7 | **8:25a** | 11:37a BWI | PI | 472 | YBHQK | 73S | S | 1 |
| | 12:25P BWI | **1:29P** E | PI | 946 | YBHQK | F28 | | |
| | | | OP 30NOV | | | | | |
| | | | EX 28NOV,29NOV | | | | | |

**Illus. 11–11.** Listing from the *Official Airline Guide.* If you departed from Miami on the 12:10 p.m. flight, at what time would you reach New York's LaGuardia Airport?

**Illus. 11–12.** Some businesses prefer to have all travel arranged through a designated travel agency.

Rental cars vary in price according to the size of the car, the length of time the car is needed, and the miles driven. Determine the executive's preference before contacting a car rental agency or your travel agent. Follow any established company guidelines for renting a car.

### *Train*

Train travel may be possible in some sections of the country, particularly in areas with high population concentrations. Train stations are located in the centers of cities and can provide an alternative to air travel on certain rail routes. Overnight trains have sleeper services which allow the executive to sleep and eat on the train. If the executive is interested in rail service, consult the *Official Guide of the Railways,* which contains schedules of all railroad lines. Check with a travel agent or check the yellow pages of your telephone directory for information on the railway lines serving your area.

## Hotel/Motel Accommodations

There may be times when traveling executives must stay overnight and ask you to make hotel or motel reservations. The executive may specify a particular hotel or motel, especially if he or she is familiar with the city or if a convention or meeting is being held at a specific hotel. In other cases, the executive may rely on you to determine the best place to stay.

The *Hotel/Motel Red Book* is an excellent source of information about accommodations. It provides names, addresses, telephone numbers, room rates, and other information about hotels and motels throughout the United States. Also included are maps for selected cities and listings for hotels and motels in more than sixty countries. The company for which you work may have a copy of this publication. If not, a travel agent can provide you with the same information.

## Procedures for Arranging Travel

Traveling executives must be able to meet their business obligations scheduled away from their offices. They must arrive at meetings on time and with the necessary supporting materials. You will find that carefully planned travel arrangements are crucial to the success of the business trip.

### Initial Trip Planning

As soon as you learn that the executive is making a trip, you probably will become involved in the planning of that trip. As an office assistant, you will be responsible for gathering accurate and timely information for the executive on the many details relating to the trip.

*Prepare a Travel Folder.* A travel folder (or trip file) will help you organize the details of an upcoming trip. A folder should be used to collect background information and details about the trip, such as notes on reservations, tickets, accommodations, and meeting or appointment confirmations.

*Plan the Trip.* Planning for the trip probably will revolve around meetings already scheduled and around meetings which the executive needs to schedule during the trip. If you are responsible for scheduling the meetings, you will need the names and titles of the persons to be scheduled as well as the company names, addresses, and telephone numbers of the individuals.

**Illus. 11–13.** At large airports, rental car agencies provide shuttle service to and from car rental lots and the airport terminal.

### Completing Travel Arrangements

Once the travel plans are approved, you will be responsible for making final arrangements for appointments and for making the travel and accommodations reservations. In addition, you will be responsible for assembling the travel documents and related business materials for the meetings.

*Confirm Appointments.* Call each individual with whom the executive plans to meet and confirm the appointment time, date, and purpose.

*Make Reservations.* You already will have much of the information needed to make reservations. If you are working with a travel agent or with a travel department within the firm, you can give the travel details to the appropriate personnel. However, if you are making the reservations yourself, you will contact the airline, car rental agency, and hotel or motel to communicate the travel details.

If you are making reservations yourself, use toll-free telephone numbers whenever possible. Ask for written confirmations if there is enough time to receive such confirmations before the trip. Some reservations are in the form of a *confirmation number.* Record the confirmation number and repeat it to the reservation clerk to assure the accuracy of the number. The confirmation number should be included on the executive's itinerary.

*Prepare an Itinerary.* The itinerary is a detailed plan of a trip which serves as a guide for the executive while he or she is away from the office. The itinerary includes travel arrangements, appointments, hotel or motel reservations, and reminders or special instructions. The itinerary should be in an easy-to-read format which gives the executive his or her day-by-day schedule for the complete trip.

Check with the executive to determine if anyone in the company other than you should have a copy of the itinerary. The executive will need several copies: a copy to carry, an extra copy to be carried in the baggage, and possibly a copy for family members.

*Gather Supporting Items.* The following items represent various supplies, documents, and supporting materials the executive may expect you to assemble:

- travel tickets, itinerary, and travel funds
- hotel or motel confirmations
- supporting correspondence, speeches, reports, and files for each appointment/meeting
- forms for recording expenses

### While the Executive Is Away

Keeping the office running smoothly while the executive is out of town may seem like a formidable task for the beginning office worker. However, you can do much toward meeting this responsibility by following the procedures on page 470.

```
                    ITINERARY FOR CHARLES R. STAFFORD
                         May 17 to May 19, 19--

WEDNESDAY, MAY 17       Atlanta to Dallas

    9:43 a.m.           Leave Hartsfield Atlanta International
                        Airport on Delta Flight 17.  Breakfast
                        served.

   10:50 a.m.           Arrive Dallas/Ft. Worth International
                        Airport.  Pick up rental car keys at Sun
                        Rentals Counter; confirmation number:
                        3840576.

                        Hotel reservations at Fairmont Hotel,
                        1717 N. Akard St. (214-748-5454).
                        Confirmation number:  3K4895F.

    2:30 p.m.           Meeting with Mr. Thomas Thatcher, Vice
                        President Marketing, Fabric Wholesalers,
                        1314 Gaston Avenue, 214-630-1958, to
                        discuss fabric purchase agreement.

    7:00 p.m.           Dinner with staff at hotel to review
                        plans for Apparel Fair.

THURSDAY, MAY 18        Dallas to San Diego

   12:02 p.m.           Leave Dallas/Ft. Worth International
                        Airport on Delta Flight 443.  Lunch
                        served.  Drop rental car keys at Sun
                        Rentals counter at airport.

   12:55 p.m.           Arrive at Lindbergh Field International
                        Airport.  Mr. Stanley (619-235-6687)
                        will meet you at the airport and drive
                        you to the Naples plant for the tour and
                        return you to your hotel.

                        Hotel reservations at the Seven Seas
                        Lodge, 411 Hotel Circle South,
                        619-291-1302.  Confirmation number:
                        38T2684.

FRIDAY, MAY 19          San Diego to Atlanta

    7:55 a.m.           Leave San Diego Lindbergh Field
                        International Airport on Delta Flight
                        860.  Breakfast served.

    3:52 p.m.           Arrive Hartsfield Atlanta International
                        Airport.
```

**Illus. 11–14.**  A comprehensive itinerary contains relevant travel details, as shown here.

- Keep up your regular duties and use your time wisely.
- Keep an itemized listing of incoming mail.
- Answer any routine mail that you can.
- Keep a log of telephone calls and office visitors.
- If possible, avoid making appointments for the first day the executive is back in the office.

### When the Executive Returns

Certain follow-up activities should be completed as soon as possible after the trip is completed. One common follow-up activity is handling the correspondence generated by the executive's trip. He or she will need to send several follow-up letters and thank-you letters as a result of the business contacts and activities encountered on the trip. Another important follow-up activity is the completion of reports that the executive needs to submit regarding the trip.

### Office Assistant's Procedures

If you assist a manager by recording shorthand notes for letters and other communications, you will want to follow procedures that simplify the processing of those notes. Among the procedures that will be helpful to you are the following:

- Keep a shorthand notebook readily available for all your notetaking.
- Date the first page of the day's dictation. A date placed in the bottom right-hand corner of the first page will be easy to locate if you must find your notes later.
- Number each item (letter, memorandum, report, etc.) dictated to you.
- Use only one column of your notebook to record your notes. Use the second column for instructions and changes made in the course of the dictation.
- Keep a small notepad handy for recording any questions that arise while you are taking dictation.
- Use any pauses in dictation to read your notes, making any corrections that will assure correct reading when you begin processing copy.
- Organize any correspondence or material related to the dictation that the manager gives you. That way you will be able to refer to these documents as you begin to transcribe the dictation.

## REVIEW QUESTIONS

1. What points should you clarify with the executive or manager in order to be able to maintain calendars effectively and efficiently?

2. What guidelines should you follow in scheduling appointments?

3. Describe the duties of the office assistant prior to a formal business meeting.

4. What items generally appear in minutes of a meeting?

5. What guidelines should an office assistant follow when taking minutes during a meeting?

6. After the meeting, what duties will the office assistant be expected to complete?

7. What duties might an office assistant be asked to complete in order to prepare for a teleconference?

8. Identify and describe three common forms of executive travel.

9. Identify and describe the procedures an office assistant should follow to complete travel arrangements for the executive.

10. What are the office assistant's duties while the executive is away from the office? when the executive returns?

## MAKING DECISIONS

Megan's employer, Mr. Burrell, is meeting with union labor leaders to discuss delicate labor-management relations pending the renewal of the employees' contract. The meeting has been going on for about half an hour when Mr. Burrell's brother appears in the office and asks to speak to Mr. Burrell. Even after Megan tells him that Mr. Burrell is in a very important meeting, the brother still insists on speaking with him. He is becoming upset with Megan for attempting to prevent him from entering his brother's office.

**What You Are To Do:** Write a paragraph explaining how Megan might handle this situation.

## EXTENDING YOUR ENGLISH SKILLS

In this exercise, you will be reviewing pronouns. The following are sentences taken from reports keyed by an office assistant.

1. The filing cabinet (who, that) is against the left wall is full of inactive correspondence.

2. Neither Jack nor Jim feels that (his, their) workstation should be replaced.

3. The executives said that (they, them), along with a group from another company, would attend the seminar in Paris.

4. All office workers need dictionaries available to (them, they).

5. The committee has promised to have (its, their) findings ready for review early next week.

6. Honesty is a quality that employers evaluate when interviewing candidates for positions in (its, their) companies.

7. The executive and her associate were uncertain as to what (she, they) should do at such a moment.

8. The members of the group want (its, their) opinions aired before the final vote is taken.

9. The workstation (that, who) was placed in the modular office will be there for only a short time.

10. Joy and Wendy reviewed the report and (it, they) was sent to the word processing department for final preparation.

**What You Are To Do:** Key the sentences, selecting the proper pronoun. Your teacher may wish to review the identification and use of pronouns with you. Basically, pronouns are words that serve as substitutes for nouns. They take the place of nouns. They must agree with their *antecedents* (nouns for which they stand) in person, number, and gender.

## APPLICATION ACTIVITIES

### Activity 1

As the assistant to Ms. Moyer, planning director for the city, you are responsible for scheduling appointments. Ms. Moyer is preparing a briefing that she must give tomorrow at the state capital. She has asked not to be interrupted except for previously scheduled appointments or for any critical business that requires her official input. "Just take my messages, but bring in the mail after you've opened it," she says as she closes the door to her office.

Word/text processing
equipment can be used to
complete this activity.

**What You Are To Do:** On a plain sheet of paper, center the heading HANDLING APPOINTMENT REQUESTS. Key a short paragraph telling how you would handle each appointment situation. Number each paragraph to match the situation numbers given. Ms. Moyer prefers to confirm all appointments. She does not like to have appointments before 9 a.m., because she likes to plan her day and attend to critical issues early in the day.

### WEDNESDAY, OCTOBER 1

**The following situations arise during the day:**

**1** 8:30 a.m. You open a letter from the City Beautification Council asking Ms. Moyer to speak at its luncheon five weeks from today.

**2** 9:45 a.m. The mayor's secretary telephones to set a time for Ms. Moyer to meet with the mayor when she returns from tomorrow's briefing at the state capitol. The meeting will be held in the mayor's office down the hall. You check your calendar and note that Ms. Moyer does not have an appointment scheduled until 1 p.m. on Friday when she returns.

**3** 10:25 a.m. A staff member comes by to set up an appointment. "I'd like to see her sometime tomorrow, if possible. We need to discuss the Riverfront Development Project. If tomorrow isn't convenient, then it will have to wait until next week when I return from my Baltimore trip."

**4** 11:10 a.m. Ms. Moyer buzzes you and asks you to reschedule her 3:15 p.m. appointment with Mr. Bellevue for the same time next week. "By the way, do I have any messages?" she asks.

**5** 1:30 p.m. A staff member comes by to see Ms. Moyer about arranging neighborhood group meetings to discuss the new city zoning plan. "No rush," she says to you. "Anytime within the next two or three days is fine. If she likes the idea, our meeting could take about an hour."

**6** 3:45 p.m. A salesperson without an appointment wants to see Ms. Moyer about a new office copier.

## Activity 2

You work in Atlanta as an office assistant to Ernest L. Fogg, Director of Marketing. Mr. Fogg is in the process of finalizing arrangements for a teleconference with regional marketing vice presidents located in five different regional offices. The teleconference will originate in Atlanta.

Mr. Fogg hands you an edited copy of the on-line agenda for the teleconference and says, "Please key this agenda in final form. Open up the spacing as I've indicated and list the participants in alphabetic order according to city. Proofread very carefully. It's vital that all times and telephone numbers are correct."

Word/text processing equipment can be used to complete this activity.

**What You Are To Do:**  Use plain paper to key the final agenda. Follow Mr. Fogg's oral and written instructions.

```
                          TELEconference

              Regional    Edgewater Plastics
                        ^ Marketing Vice Presidents

   #    DATE:  May 14, 19--
   #    On-Line Time:  1:00 p.m., EST
   #    Call-in Number:  404/765-0494
   #    Disconect number:  404/765-0490 (Sandra Leland)
             n        =                    Ernest Fogg
        Participants/Locations:  Stacey Shelton (Atlanta)
                                   404/765-0936
                                 Sharon Cottrell (Ft. Worth)  817/336-7744
                                 Dorcas Windeler (Portland)
                                   503/228-2583
                                 Coleman Ward (Denver)
                                   303/696-3470            Cincinnati
                                 Christin Sheehan (Denver)
                                   513/765-0495
                                 Helder Barreto (Boston)
                                   616/567-4117
                                                7
   * On-Line Agenda:  00:  Participants on line;
                            Identification of participants
                      03:  Conference guidelines
                      05:  Meeting purpose;
                           (Review agenda)
                      07:  Product announcement report
                           (blue copy)
                      15:  Quarterly budget report
                           (yellow copy; note highlighted
                            figures on page 2) 3
                      25:  Meeting summary  and conclusions
                      30:  Meeting ends   ^

   * Reminder:  Identify yourself and your location when you
                speak.
```

# Topic 2

## BUSINESS REPORTS

When you have completed your study of this topic, you will be able to

- identify the parts of a formal business report and describe the function of each part

- identify and explain two vital financial statements used by businesses

Business reports represent an important method of communication for a business. They are a source of information for many of the decisions affecting a business organization. For example, if the owners of a firm are considering expanding their firm's product markets, much of the information they need to have in order to make this decision will be presented to them in the form of a report. Other reports, such as those including financial statements, are of interest to outsiders. A potential stockholder, for example, will spend time studying the financial reports of the business before investing money in that business.

In this topic you will be introduced to the formal business report and to some commonly prepared financial reports. The extent of your involvement in the preparation of business reports will vary. It will depend not only on the size and type of your organization, but also on the nature of the report. Generally the smaller the organization, the more likely you are to be involved personally with developing, preparing, assembling, and distributing business reports. Whatever your depth of involvement, as an office worker you will want to have a basic understanding of the business reports your employer prepares.

You are already familiar with the short, informal business report from your study of Chapter 6. In this topic, you will study the function and purpose of both the formal business report and the major financial reports used to measure the economic health of a business.

A formal business report includes standard parts that readers find valuable in understanding such a report. Generally there is an explanation of the reason the report is being presented, the type and source of information used, the meaning of the information, and the conclusions. In this topic, you will be introduced to the parts of a formal report and to your role in helping to prepare such reports.

## Parts of the Formal Business Report

The common parts of a business report that are covered in this topic are:

- title page
- table of contents
- body

- references
- appendices

A formal business report may contain all or some of the common report parts. An informal business report may contain only a heading and the body of the report. Several acceptable formats are available for keying a business report. However, your company may have a preferred format which you can determine from previous reports or from the company procedures manual. The formats presented to you in this topic represent acceptable business report formats for keying documents.

Business reports may be single- or double-spaced. Double spacing provides copy that is easier to read. Single spacing, however, reduces the volume of paper required. Report formats are identified as unbound, leftbound, or topbound:

- The unbound report is fastened together (generally in the upper left-hand corner) with a fastening device such as a paper clip or staple. No extra space is provided in the margin of the unbound report for fastening the report together.
- The leftbound report format moves the left margin a half inch beyond the margin for the unbound report, making the left margin one and one-half inches. This allows room to bind the report at the left. All other margins are the same as those of the unbound report.
- The topbound report format moves the top margin down approximately a half inch below the top margin for the unbound report. This allows room for the report to be fastened at the top of the pages.

### Title Page

The title page contains the report title, the writer's name, the name of the organization, and the report date (month, day, and year). To facilitate keyboarding the title page at the video terminal, all lines are double-spaced, as shown in Illus. 11–15.

### Table of Contents

The table of contents presents an overview of the material covered in the report by listing chapter titles or main topics with their page numbers. (Refer to Illus. 11–15.) The final copy of the table of contents is keyed after the entire report has been completed. This allows you to verify the titles and page numbers, particularly if any last-minute changes were made in the report.

The heading, CONTENTS, is centered according to the format you have selected (unbound, leftbound, or topbound). Double-space after the title and key the word *Page* at the right margin. Then double-space to the first entry.

Leaders (periods and spaces alternated) extend across the page to guide the reader in finding the page number. The periods in the leaders are aligned vertically (each directly over the other) by keying all periods at either the even or odd numbers on the horizontal line scale.

### Body

In longer reports, the body of the report will be divided into chapters or sections. The main heading of each of these divisions should begin on a new page with the word "Chapter" or "Section" typed in all capital letters, followed by the Roman numeral for that division. (Refer to page 478.) Double-space before and after all side heads. Underscore all side heads and all paragraph heads. Page 479 summarizes information regarding margins and page numbers in formal reports.

It may be necessary for your supervisor to quote from sources of information used to prepare the report. *Quotations*, which are excerpts from other sources, are identified in the body of the report. A quotation of more than three lines is set off from the rest of the text. Single-space the quotation, and indent it five spaces from the left and right margins. The process of giving credit to the sources of information used in a report is called documentation. Common methods of documentation are footnotes, endnotes, and textual citations.

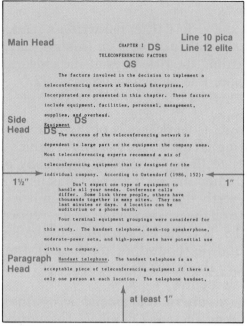

**Leftbound, page 1**

**Leftbound, page 2**

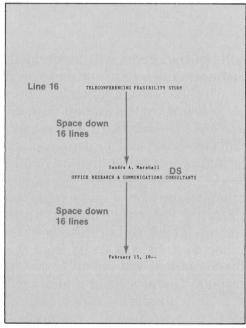

**Leftbound, Title Page**

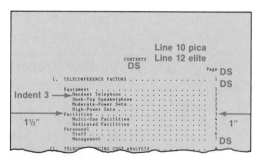

**Leftbound, Contents page**

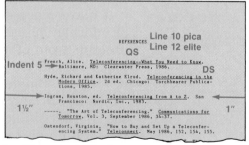

**Leftbound, References**

**Illus. 11–15.** Report formats.

**Illus. 11–16.** Guidelines for setting up formal business reports.

## FORMAL BUSINESS REPORTS

| Report Format | Top Margin | Bottom Margin | Left Margin | Page Number |
|---|---|---|---|---|
| **Unbound** | | | | |
| First page or major page division | line 10, pica line 12, elite | 1" | 1" | Not numbered (If numbered, line 62.) |
| All other pages | line 8 | 1" | 1" | Line 6 at right margin |
| **Leftbound** | | | | |
| First page or major page division | line 10, pica line 12, elite | 1" | 1 1/2" | Not numbered (If numbered, line 62.) |
| All other pages | line 8 | 1" | 1 1/2" | Line 6 at right margin |
| **Topbound** | | | | |
| First page or major page division | line 12, pica line 14, elite | 1" | 1" | Not numbered (If numbered, line 62.) |
| All other pages | line l0 | 1" | 1" | Centered at bottom on line 62 |

*Footnotes.* The footnote method requires the use of a superior (raised) reference figure at the appropriate point in the copy with a matching numbered footnote at the bottom of the page. The footnote reference appears on the same page as the footnote number.

Random access devices, however, can go directly to the data without having to read all the other data in front of it.[1]

[1] James F. Clark and Judith J. Lambrecht, Information Processing Concepts, Principles, and Procedures (Cincinnati: South-Western Publishing Company, 1985), p. 94.

*Endnotes.* The **endnote method** uses the superior (raised) reference figure at the appropriate point in the copy, the same as the footnote method does. The matching numbered references, however, are listed at the end of the report. The endnote method of documentation relieves the office worker of having to estimate footnote placement at the bottoms of individual pages.

```
Random access devices, however, can go directly to the data

without having to read all the other data in front of it.¹
```

*Textual Citations.* When the **textual citations method** is used, the source information is placed in parentheses within the text. This information includes author(s), date of publication, and page number(s).

```
Random access devices, however, can go directly to the data

without having to read all the other data in front of it

(Clark and Lambrecht, 1985, 94).
```

If the source is identified by name or author within the report copy, only the publication date and page number are used.

```
According to Clark and Lambrecht (1985, 94), random access

devices can go directly to the data without having to read

all the other data in front of it.
```

Textual citations are receiving increased use with word processing equipment. This is because many word processors cannot "raise" the superior figure as required in the footnote and endnote methods.

### References

*paraphrased:*
expressed in another
form

The reference section follows the body of the report. The reference section identifies the sources used in preparing the report. These include all direct quotes and *paraphrased* sources, as well as sources your supervisor used to obtain ideas or background information.

The title and format of the reference section depend upon the methods of documentation used in the body of the text:

- For footnotes, title the reference section BIBLIOGRAPHY. Place the footnote references in alphabetic order and in appropriate format for a bibliography. Consult a style manual, an office handbook, or a previously prepared report which you know has an acceptable format.
- For endnotes, title the reference section ENDNOTES. Number and list each endnote in the footnote reference format in the order presented in the body of the report.
- For textual citations, title the reference section REFERENCES. Place the textual citations in alphabetic order by the authors' surnames. If a reference does not show the author's name, list it alphabetically by the first important word in the title. Illustration 11–15 on page 478 shows one acceptable form of sequence, capitalization, punctuation, and spacing for textual citation references.

### Appendices

An appendix provides more detailed data (usually in the form of a chart, graph, table, or text) to support the recommendations made in the body of the report. The appendix (or *appendices* if several are included) is placed at the end of the report for the benefit of interested readers. If more than one appendix is included, number or letter each in sequence.

Center the heading APPENDIX (plus the appropriate number or letter, if needed) according to the format you have selected for the body of the report (unbound, leftbound, or topbound).

## Guidelines for Increasing Your Effectiveness

A responsible office worker can be a helpful assistant in preparing a report. If you are asked to assist with a report, you will be expected to locate and process information quickly, accurately, and with attention to detail. Following are some guidelines that will help you work efficiently:

1. Use note cards for recording information.
2. Photocopy material (such as tables) to be sure the details are accurate and to save time.
3. Record complete source details for all information you locate. (For example, title of publication, author, publisher, date, and page.)

**Illus. 11–17.** This office assistant is helping with the preparation of a report. He is careful to record complete source details for all information he locates.

## FINANCIAL REPORTS

Many reports relate to financial aspects of businesses. Some financial reports are for internal use only. Others are provided to those outside the company, including shareholders in publicly owned corporations. In this section you will examine two commonly prepared financial reports—the balance sheet and the income statement. You will also be given guidelines for keying these important financial reports (also known as *financial statements*).

*resources:* available wealth

Financial statements provide information about a company's economic *resources* and results of operations. Publicly owned companies must provide financial statements to shareholders at the end of each quarter and at the end of the fiscal year.

## Balance Sheet

A balance sheet is a report that presents the financial condition of a company as of a specific date. The balance sheet reports the assets, liabilities, and owner's equity or capital. You are already familiar with assets and liabilities from your study of Chapter 9. You will recall that the *assets* of a company include all the goods and property owned by the firm as well as the amount due the company from others. *Liabilities* are the debts of the company — what the company owes. The owner's equity or *capital* is the owner's share or the worth of the firm — the excess of assets over liabilities. On every balance sheet, the total assets must equal the total liabilities plus the owner's equity. Thus, the accounting formula

$$\text{Assets (A)} = \text{Liabilities (L)} + \text{Owner's Equity (E)}$$

applies to every balance sheet, whether the balance sheet is for a giant corporation or a small, individually owned business.

### *Standard Report Format*

    *Samantha is the office assistant to Sandy and Dan Burke, the owners of SandyDandy's Delights. SandyDandy's cookies and baked goods are sold in most local supermarkets, and the Burkes are planning to expand soon into nearby states. One of Samantha's duties is to key the final copy of each financial statement prepared at the end of the fiscal year (refer to Illus. 11–18 on page 484). Note the format and contents of the balance sheet keyed by Samantha.*

## Income Statement

*revenues:* earnings realized for goods and services

An income statement is a financial report that details the results of operations for a specified period of time. In this report you will find *revenues,* expenses, and the net income or net loss of a business for the reporting period. An income statement answers the question, "How successful was the business during the time period?"

The income statement lists the amounts and sources of revenues, as well as expenses, for the reporting period. A *net income* results if revenues are greater than expenses. A *net loss* results if expenses are greater than revenues. Illustration 11–19 on page 485 shows SandyDandy's income statement for the recently ended fiscal year.

```
                        SandyDandy's Delights
                           Balance Sheet
                         December 31, 19--

                                QS

                              Assets
                               DS
             Current Assets
                Cash                          $12,000
                Petty Cash                        300
Indent 3 ──────▶Accounts Receivable             3,500
                Baking Supplies Inventory        2,000
                Office Supplies                    200
                    Total Current Assets                  $ 18,000
             Fixed Assets
                Delivery Van                   $ 7,000
                Baking Equipment                 5,000
                Building and Land               70,000
                    Total Fixed Assets                      82,000
                       Total Assets                       $100,000
                               DS
                            Liabilities
                               DS
             Current Liabilities
                Notes Payable                  $ 1,500
                Accounts Payable                 1,000
                Salary and Wages Payable         2,500
                    Total Current Liabilities             $  5,000
             Fixed Liabilities
                Long-term Note Payable         $ 5,000
                Mortgage Payable                50,000
                    Total Fixed Liabilities                 55,000
                       Total Liabilities                  $ 60,000
                               DS
                          Owner's Equity
                               DS
             Sandy and Dan Burke, Capital     $40,000
                 Total Owner's Equity                     $ 40,000
                    Total liabilities and
                    Owner's Equity                        $100,000
```

**Illus. 11–18.**   Balance sheet.

```
                          SandyDandy's Delights
                            Income Statement
                     For Year Ended December 31, 19--

                                   QS

        Sales                              $200,000
          DS
        Cost of Goods Sold                   50,000
          DS
        Gross Profit on Sales                          $150,000
          DS
        Operating Expenses
Indent 3 ──►Advertising Expense          $   5,000
        Delivery Expense                     1,000
        Miscellaneous Expense                  500
        Office Supplies Expense              1,000
        Payroll Taxes Expense                2,000
        Salaries Expense                    36,000
        Utilities Expense                    4,500
Indent 6 ────────►Total Operating Expenses         $ 50,000
        Net Income from Operations                     $100,000
          DS
        Other Expenses
        Interest Expense                                  3,000
        Net Income Before Income Tax                   $ 97,000
        Less Income Tax                                  37,000
        Net Income After Income Tax                    $ 60,000
```

**Illus. 11–19.** Income statement.

## Guidelines for Preparing Financial Statements

Look over the following guidelines. They will help you to prepare financial statements accurately and with confidence.

### Study the Report Formats

Before you attempt to prepare financial statements, study the formats of earlier copies of the balance sheet and income statement. Continuing to use the same report formats helps executives compare data from year to year. You may find format guidelines in the company's procedures manual.

### Check Calculations

Check the accuracy of all calculations before preparing the statements. Use a calculator or your computer to check the addition and subtraction required on the statements.

### Use Acceptable Report Format

Although the financial statement formats may vary somewhat, the following guidelines represent the generally accepted style of presenting financial statements:

- Leave at least a one-inch margin at the top and bottom and on both sides.
- Center the lines in the statement heading—company name, statement name, and the date(s) covered by the statement.
- Double-space before and after headings in the body of the statement.
- Key headings and titles in upper- and lowercase letters.
- Use a single line (extending the width of the longest item in the column) typed underneath the last figure to indicate addition or subtraction.
- Use double lines underneath the final figure in a column.
- Use leaders, if necessary, to guide the reader's eye from the explanation column to the first column of amounts.
- Use the dollar sign with the first figure listed vertically in each amount column and with every figure which has double lines typed directly underneath it.

### Proofread the Copy

Proofread slowly and carefully. Give attention to detail. If another worker is available to help you, proofreading can be made easier with one person reading aloud from the original document while the other person proofreads the prepared copy. In addition to the words and figures, the person reading aloud should indicate details such as capitalization, punctuation, underscores, vertical spacing, indentions, and dollar signs. Be particularly alert to *transposing* figures (for example, keying $1,245,385 for $1,254,385). As a final phase of your proofreading, you should recalculate or *prove* all totals.

*transposing:* changing the order of

*prove:* check the correctness of

**MICRO-COMPUTER ASSISTANCE**

You will find your microcomputer to be a valuable tool as you prepare business reports. You are familiar with using a microcomputer to process text. Additionally, various software packages are available which allow the user to develop graphs to include in formal and informal business reports. When color is available, graphs can be in color both on the screen and on the printout. Software packages also enable you to use electronic worksheets to help perform calculations and analyze data to be included in reports.

**Illus. 11–20.** One effective method of proofreading is to have one person read aloud from the original document while the other person proofreads the typed copy.

## Graphics

You are familiar with graphs found in newspapers, magazines, and textbooks. Graphs help to make the copy more interesting, and in some cases they are easier to interpret by the reader than are columns of figures or blocks of text. Therefore, several graphic forms are used in many business reports to display supporting information.

As an office assistant, you may be expected to keyboard or assemble documents which require the preparation of graphics. Three commonly used illustrations are discussed here: the *line graph*, the *bar graph*, and the *circle graph*. Refer to Illus. 11–21 as you read about each type of graph.

### *Line Graph*

*plotted:* marked

The line graph is used to display trends that emerge over a period of time. Monthly sales, for example, are frequently represented in line graph form. The line graph shown in Illus. 11–21 indicates changes in the quantity of items produced over a six-week period. The weekly production quantities are **plotted** on the graph and the points are connected by lines. In preparing such a graph, place the time categories across the bottom and the amounts along the side.

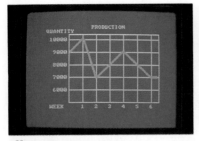
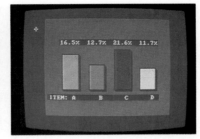
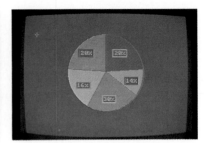

**Illus. 11–21.** (From left to right) A line graph, bar graph, and circle graph prepared using a computer.

### Bar Graph

A bar graph can be used to show comparisons from one period to another. For example, the total sales of the current year could be compared to the total sales of the past three years. The bar graph shown in Illus. 11–21 compares items A, B, C, and D.

In preparing a bar graph, use bars of equal width. Space the bars equally across the graph. If you are using a graphics software package, the spacing probably will be determined automatically for you from the graphic specifications you entered into the computer.

### Circle Graph

The circle graph (also called a *pie chart* because of the way in which the graph itself is divided into wedges which look like pieces of a pie) is used to show how part of something contributes to the whole. In Illus. 11–21, a circle graph is used to divide data into five parts. The whole circle represents 100 percent, and each wedge represents a portion of the whole.

Software programs are available which will take the figures you key into the system (or the data already in the system), convert the figures into percentages, and prepare the pie chart for you. Whether you are using a graphics software package or preparing the graph by hand, be sure each wedge is identified with an appropriate label, color, or pattern.

## Guidelines for Preparing Graphics

The following general guidelines will be helpful to you as you keyboard and assemble a business report which contains graphics:

1. Study previous reports from the company to determine style preferences.

2. If the graph is half of a page or less in size, include it in the body of the text. Leave enough space before and after the graph to separate it visually from the text. Position the graph as near as possible to the portion of the text in which it is mentioned, ideally on the same page.
3. If the graph is larger than half of a page, place it on a separate page. That portion of the text in which the graph is mentioned should include a reference to the specific page on which the graph can be found.
4. Center the graph title in capital letters at the bottom or top of the graph.

## Spreadsheets

A spreadsheet is an electronic worksheet made up of columns and rows of data. Some spreadsheet programs contain hundreds of columns and rows to accommodate the needs of business. Once the information is displayed on the screen, calculations can be made and results can be analyzed. Decisions can then be made based upon the projections made by the computer. For example, an executive might use a spreadsheet program to forecast sales over the next five years or to determine whether to rent or buy new equipment.

Spreadsheets can be used for administrative tasks as well as for executive decision making. For example, you might be asked to use a spreadsheet program to calculate figures for a report your supervisor is submitting.

*Mr. Koebel, Audrey's supervisor, stopped at her workstation and said, "Please figure 7-percent, 10-percent, and 12-percent price increases for our 10 varieties of Valentine's Day candy boxes. Once I have that information, I can complete my report and have it in the sales manager's hands by Friday morning."*

*Audrey used her spreadsheet software program to determine the projected price increases for the ten types of candy, (The data that appears in red in Illus. 11–22 on page 490 was entered by Audrey. The computer automatically made the calculations that resulted in the information shown in blue.) Within minutes, Audrey was able to produce a computer printout showing the needed information. Mr. Koebel then was able to complete his report.*

```
    ¦ A ¦¦  B  ¦¦  C  ¦¦  D  ¦¦  E  ¦¦  F  ¦¦  G  ¦

  1                         ZAMBERNELLI CHOCOLATES
  2                             Price Increases
  3
  4   ======================================================================
  5
  6    Candy      Current
  7     ID         Price
  8    Number     (Pound)     7%         10%         12%
                            Increase    Increase    Increase
  9
 10   ======================================================================
 11
 12    1041       4.89        5.23        5.38        5.43
 13    1050       3.45        3.69        3.80        3.86
 14    1053       2.25        2.40        2.48        2.52
 15    1057       5.15        5.51        5.67        5.78
 16    1063       5.98        6.40        6.58        6.70
 17    1075       6.50        6.96        7.15        7.28
 18    1147       3.98        4.26        4.38        4.46
 19    1148       2.22        2.38        2.44        2.49
 20    1150       5.49        5.87        6.04        6.15
 21    1151       5.51        5.90        6.06        6.17
```

**Illus. 11–22.** Using a spreadsheet software program, Audrey entered the data that appears in red. The computer automatically made the calculations that resulted in the information shown in blue.

## Windowing

You learned in Chapter 7 that integrated software packages are available that combine word processing with other applications such as database management, spreadsheet, graphics, and communications. The windowing feature allows the user to divide the screen into sections side by side or one on top of the other so that two or more displays are seen at the same time (See Illus. 11–23.). Windowing is a visible sign that the operator is using more than one application at a time. When the cursor is moved into one of the windows, that application is being accessed. For example, you may be keying a technical report when you find it necessary to call up a spreadsheet to verify some figures or to access an on-line database in order to get up-to-date information.

**Illus. 11–23.** Windowing enables the computer user to perform several different applications or to view several different documents simultaneously.

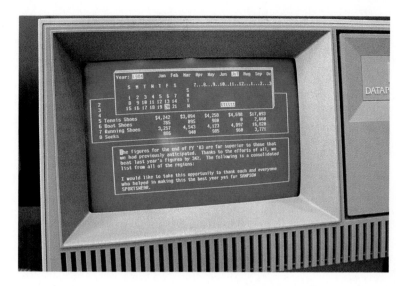

## REVIEW QUESTIONS

1. Name five common parts of a formal business report.

2. Describe the formats of unbound, leftbound, and topbound reports.

3. What is report documentation? Name the three common methods of report documentation.

4. Describe how the titles and formats of the three report documentation methods differ in the reference section of a business report.

5. What guidelines should you follow to increase your effectiveness as you assist with locating and processing information to be included in a report?

6. Identify and describe two common financial reports.

7. What format guidelines should you follow when preparing financial statements?

8. Identify three common graphic illustrations. What is the primary function of each kind of graph?

9. What is a spreadsheet? Describe one way an office worker might use a spreadsheet.

10. What is the purpose of the windowing feature in an integrated software package?

# INTERACTING WITH OTHERS

Mary Beth is the new office assistant to Mr. Stanhope, supervisor of the Customer Service Division. This morning Mr. Stanhope called Mary Beth into his office and asked her to arrange for dinner reservations for himself and two clients at a local restaurant. When Mary Beth returned from Mr. Stanhope's office, she looked upset. "I don't think I was hired to be a social secretary," she said. "I guess rank has all the privileges. Doesn't it seem that way to you?"

**What You Are To Do:**   Prepare a brief response to Mary Beth's question.

# EXTENDING YOUR MATH SKILLS

As an office worker, you will be expected to deal with common measurements (such as seconds, hours, feet, yards, ounces, and pounds). Sometimes you may be asked to convert measurements into their equivalent values in another measurement form. For example, a project is scheduled to be completed in 217 days. How many weeks will it take to complete the project? The following exercise requires you to convert measurements into equivalent values.

**What You Are To Do:**   On plain paper, number from 1 through 15. Convert the measurements in Column A into the equivalent measurements requested in Column B. (Use scratch paper for figuring.) Write the answers on your numbered paper and show any remainder as a fractional part.

| Column A | Column B | | Reference |
|---|---|---|---|
| 1. 390 seconds = | 6 1/2 | minutes | 60 seconds = 1 minute |
| 2. 1,230 minutes = | ? | hours | 60 minutes = 1 hour |
| 3. 1,008 hours = | ? | days | 24 hours = 1 day |
| 4. 371 days = | ? | weeks | 7 days = 1 week |
| 5. 1,095 days = | ? | years | 365 days = 1 year |
| 6. 723 months = | ? | years | 12 months = 1 year |
| 7. 728 weeks = | ? | years | 52 weeks = 1 year |
| 8. 485 pints = | ? | quarts | 2 pints = 1 quart |
| 9. 628 quarts = | ? | gallons | 4 quarts = 1 gallon |
| 10. 528 dozen = | ? | gross | 12 dozen = 1 gross |
| 11. 88 ounces = | ? | pounds | 16 ounces = 1 pound |
| 12. 10,500 pounds = | ? | tons | 2,000 pounds = 1 ton |
| 13. 768 inches = | ? | feet | 12 inches = 1 foot |
| 14. 105 feet = | ? | yards | 3 feet = 1 yard |
| 15. 26,400 feet = | ? | miles | 5,280 feet = 1 mile |

## APPLICATION ACTIVITY

Your supervisor hands you the two handwritten drafts on page 494 and says, "Please prepare final copies of these two financial statements. I've checked the totals once, but you'd better verify them before you begin to keyboard."

**What You Are To Do:**

1. Use a calculator or paper and pencil to prove the totals on both financial statements. (Refer to Reference Section D for instructions for verifying totals.)

2. Using sheets of plain paper, key final copies of the balance sheet and income statement for Energy Enterprises. Use the format guidelines presented on pages 484–486.

3. Clip together the final copy of the balance sheet and the final copy of the income statement. Also include the paper tape or sheet of paper showing the verification of the totals (if a paper form was used).

## CHAPTER SUMMARY

In this chapter, you were introduced to the importance of your role as an office assistant in management support activities. Much of the executive's decision making is based upon information received from the support staff. As an office worker, you can help the executive complete his or her responsibilities by your efficient and responsible handling of reminder systems, business meetings, travel arrangements, and the preparation of business reports.

The office calendar is the most widely used reminder system for scheduling the activities and resources of the business office. You will be expected to maintain office calendars and to manage appointment requests. The tickler file aids you in completing tasks on a timely basis.

Handling the arrangements for business meetings and business travel is an important management support activity. Executives spend a significant portion of their time in meetings and traveling on business. Your ability to complete meeting and travel arrangements efficiently and accurately adds to the executive's effectiveness. Such arrangements typically involve procedures that must be completed before, during, and after the event.

Business reports represent an important form of communication within a business. In this chapter you learned about formal business reports and financial reports. You also learned about your role in helping to complete business reports and how a microcomputer can assist you with the preparation of business reports and graphics.

| ENERGY ENTERPRISES BALANCE SHEET DECEMBER 31, 19-- | | |
|---|---|---|
| Assets | | |
| Current Assets | | |
| Cash | 15 230 00 | |
| Accounts Receivable | 25 500 00 | |
| Merchandise Inventory | 85 490 00 | |
| Total Current Assets | | 126 220 00 |
| Plant Assets (Net) | | 251 000 00 |
| Total Assets | | 377 220 00 |
| Liabilities | | |
| Current Liabilities | | |
| Notes Payable | 3 270 00 | |
| Interest Payable | 373 00 | |
| Accounts Payable | 19 540 00 | |
| Federal Income Tax Payable | 4 500 00 | |
| Total Current Liabilities | | 27 683 00 |
| Long-term Liability | | |
| Mortgage Payable | | 15 480 00 |
| Total Liabilities | | 43 163 00 |
| Owner's Equity | | |
| Capital | 334 057 00 | |
| Total Owner's Equity | | 334 057 00 |
| Total liabilities and Owner's Equity | | 377 220 00 |

| ENERGY ENTERPRISES INCOME STATEMENT FOR YEAR ENDED DECEMBER 31, 19-- | | |
|---|---|---|
| Operating Revenue | 328 500 00 | |
| Cost of Merchandise Sold | 203 470 00 | |
| Gross Profit on Operations | | 125 030 00 |
| Operating Expenses | | |
| Delivery Expense | 4 530 00 | |
| Sales Salary Expense | 23 820 00 | |
| Warehouse Supplies Expense | 15 170 00 | |
| Office Salary Expense | 22 800 00 | |
| Administrative Expense | 3 290 00 | |
| Total Operating Expenses | | 69 610 00 |
| Net Income from Operations | | 55 420 00 |
| Other Expenses | | |
| Interest Expense | | 400 00 |
| Net Income Before Income Tax | | 55 020 00 |
| Less Income Tax | | 19 257 00 |
| Net Income After Income Tax | | 35 763 00 |

## KEY TERMS

| | |
|---|---|
| reminder systems | documentation |
| tickler file | footnote method |
| agenda | endnote method |
| minutes | textual citations method |
| teleconference | appendix |
| on-line agenda | balance sheet |
| itinerary | owner's equity |
| unbound report | income statement |
| leftbound report | spreadsheet |
| topbound report | windowing feature |

**INTEGRATED CHAPTER ACTIVITY**

Word/text processing equipment can be used to complete this activity.

You work as an office assistant for East Coast Office Consultants. Mrs. Nelda B. Mashuda, your supervisor, is in the process of preparing a report on legal documents. She comes to your workstation and says, "Although this report is far from complete, I'd like you to key a draft of the title page and the first chapter. That way, I'll have some idea of how it will look in final form."

**What You Are To Do:**  Keyboard the leftbound report on page 496 using plain paper. Refer to page 478 for proper document format. Prepare a title page that gives (a) the title of the report, LEGAL DOCUMENTS; (b) your supervisor's name; (c) the name of the company; and (d) the current date. Then prepare the pages for Chapter I of the report. Side heads are indicated by an underscore. There are no paragraph heads.

CHAPTER I
PREPARING LEGAL DOCUMENTS

(P) Legal documents are official papers which may be keyed by office assistants. Typical documents include contracts, powers of attorney, affidavits, wills, and acknowledgments. While each legal document has its own requirements, there are some general guidelines which apply to most documents. Legal Papers Legal documents may be prepared using standard 8 1/2 by 11-inch paper or special legal-size paper which is 8 1/2 by 14 inches. This paper may have printed left and right margin lines. Preprinted Legal Forms Some legal documents are prepared by keying the necessary information on a printed legal form. Standard forms for bills of sale, deeds, leases, mortgages, and wills may be purchased from office supply stores. However, important legal documents, even though they are on a printed form, should be checked carefully by a lawyer. Legal Backs or Covers A single backing sheet (called a legal back or cover) is used to protect a legal document. The sheet is usually a high-grade, heavy-quality paper that is wider and longer than the legal document itself. According to Tilton, Jackson, and Popham (1987, 644), backing sheets may be color coded to differentiate types of documents. Margins Minimum margins of two inches at the top and one inch at the bottom are usually allowed. When typing on legal paper with printed margin rules, margin stops are set so that margins of the typewritten material will be one or two spaces within the printed rules. If paper without margin rules is being used, a 1 1/2-inch left margin and a 1/2-inch right margin is allowed. Spacing and Paragraphs Legal documents are usually double-spaced, and paragraphs are indented ten spaces. Acknowledgments and quoted material are single-spaced. Erasures and Corrections A legal document states the rights or privileges or obligations of the parties who sign it  and later may be submitted in a court of law as evidence. Therefore, it is imperative that there be no erasures or corrections on key details (such as names, amounts, and dates). Such corrections are forbidden in most states. Errors of only one or two letters in a relatively unimportant word are usually allowed. If the legal document has already been signed when an error is discovered, the change on that page must be initialed by the signers. Signature Lines Signature lines for the maker or makers of the document should be placed on the right side of the page. Lines for the signatures of witnesses (if any) are placed on the left side of the page. The first signature line is placed a quadruple space below the last line of the document. If there is more than one line, double spacing is used. The actual lines should be approximately three inches in length.

# PRODUCTIVITY CORNER

**Blake Williams**
*OFFICE SUPERVISOR*

## IS IT ANY OF MY BUSINESS?

DEAR MR. WILLIAMS:

I have been worrying about something that happened last week, and I still am not sure what I should have done. You see, I work as an assistant in the office of one of the division managers in our company. One of the staff members asked me to prepare a draft of the monthly income statement. I left the draft on the staff member's desk. A few hours later, the division manager called me into his office. He said, "I've just reviewed the figures in this draft. These revenues aren't right; the profit isn't high enough. Some of these figures must be changed. Please prepare another draft." I said nothing. I took the draft and changed the figures as indicated.

Now I wonder what I should have done. Did the division manager dishonestly change numbers to reflect false profits? Should this have been done? Did I have any responsibility?— LYNN IN LITCHFIELD

DEAR LYNN:

As an office assistant, it was your job to prepare the drafts as instructed. From what you say, I am guessing that you did not keep the records from which the staff member prepared the initial income statement. Therefore, it is possible the staff member had to use some *estimates* for the figures because final figures for the month were not available. The division manager may have had access to the final figures and used this information to revise the estimated numbers. The figures you were asked to use in the revision may have given a more accurate presentation of the month's activity than the figures you had keyed initially. Of course, there is the possibility that the manager was deliberately distorting the figures in order to show a more favorable performance record.

I would advise you not to worry about having done the wrong thing. You were not in a position to challenge the manager. However, in the future:

- Become familiar with your company's ethical standards. There may be a printed code of ethics available to all employees. Ask about such a code and read it carefully to determine its application to your job.
- Be careful to understand a situation fully before you make judgments about the ethical behavior of others.
- Always strive to reflect high ethical standards in all aspects of your own work.

Lynn, companies need employees with high ethical standards. Your sensitivity to such matters is a valuable trait.—BLAKE WILLIAMS

# RECORDS ADMINISTRATION AND TECHNOLOGY

**Illus. 12–1.** An efficient records management system provides for the proper storage of records. Filing cabinets are ideal for storing paper records.

## Outlining Procedures for Filing

Filing is the process of storing office records in an orderly manner within an organized system. The procedure you follow to file records will vary according to the storage media used and the manner in which the files are organized. Chapter 13 will present specific filing procedures.

You may file records alphabetically according to name, subject, or geographic location. Or you may file them by number or date. Topic 2 of this chapter explains these systems in more detail.

## Developing an Efficient Retrieval Procedure

You need an orderly way to retrieve records. An efficient retrieval procedure will include specific instructions for removing or *charging out* records. Charging out a record usually means that the following information is taken down when the record is removed from the file: the name of the worker who is taking the record, the department, the date the record was retrieved, and the date the record will be returned. This information is kept on file in case someone else must locate the record. A retrieval procedure also would indicate whether all workers had free access to the records or whether only designated staff members could retrieve the records. Chapter 13 will explain retrieval procedures in more detail.

## Setting Up a Record Retention and Destruction Policy

*policy:* rule

Most records are not kept forever. A records management system should include a statement of the *policy* on how long records are kept and how they are to be destroyed. Most companies use a *retention schedule*, which lists how long each type of record should be kept. You should keep the files free of outdated or unnecessary records so that you can work efficiently. Later in this topic, you will learn more about this area of records management.

An effective records management system benefits the company in two ways. First, workers are more productive. Second, customer *goodwill* is maintained.

**BENEFITS OF AN EFFECTIVE RECORDS MANAGEMENT SYSTEM**

### Greater Productivity

*goodwill:* positive relationship

*compile:* put together

To make an intelligent decision or complete a task well, you need accurate, current information. To *compile* a monthly sales report, you need to have the sales figures for each sales representative. Before you pay an invoice, you should check your records to be sure the charge is correct. Before you can mail a package, you need to know the recipient's complete address.

**Illus. 12–2.** Because current information is readily available, this medical assistant can perform office tasks without wasting valuable time.

You must be able to access needed records easily and quickly. An effective records management system will enable you to be more productive since you will not waste valuable time searching for information that should be easily available.

### Customer Goodwill

Customers and business associates usually do not fully appreciate efficient records management in your company even though they like the results of such management. They are pleased when you retrieve pertinent information quickly. Yet they usually take the smooth operation of the records management system for granted.

Imagine a customer's reaction if he or she called to ask a question, and after several minutes the receptionist reported that there was no record of the account! The customer would be furious and probably would tell others about this frustrating event. Customer goodwill would have been *eroded*.

*eroded:* made less; worn away

On the other hand, if a customer called and received a prompt and courteous response to questions, he or she would be pleased. Goodwill between the customer and the business would be maintained.

An effective records management system will specify procedures for accessing records quickly and for keeping records current. If you follow these procedures, the records management system will help you maintain customer goodwill.

## STORAGE MEDIA FOR RECORDS

Businesses typically store records on a variety of media. The most common storage medium is paper, even in modern offices. But businesses are also beginning to record more and more information on magnetic media and microfilm because less space is required to store the records and because the records can be accessed more quickly.

### Paper

Each time you print a file copy of a letter, record an address on an index card, complete a telephone message form, or command the computer to print out a statistical report or complicated graph, you are recording information on paper. These paper records are referred to as *hard copy.*

The advantage of paper is that you can immediately read the information recorded. With magnetic media, on the other hand, you need a display screen or printer to read the information recorded. Two disadvantages of storing records on paper are that paper records take up a great deal of space and that they can easily be misfiled.

**Illus. 12–3.** (Left) A variety of paper records.

**Illus. 12–4.** (Right) A variety of records stored on magnetic media.

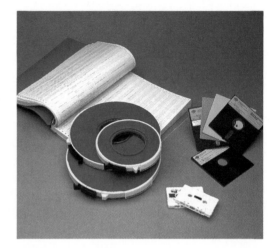

## Magnetic Media

You have been introduced to magnetic media in Chapter 5. You will recall that magnetic media are reusable media that store information electronically. The most frequently used forms of magnetic media are flexible (floppy) disks, hard disks, and tape.

### *Advantages of Using Magnetic Media*

There are four major advantages to the use of magnetic media:

- Records can be retrieved quickly and easily.
- The storage space required for housing records on magnetic media is much less than that required for paper media.
- Records stay in the same sequence on the magnetic media even after being retrieved several times.
- Records can be updated easily.

### *Disadvantages of Using Magnetic Media*

There are three disadvantages to using magnetic media to store records:

- An output device such as a VDT screen or printer is needed to read the information recorded on the magnetic media.

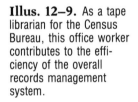

*conservative:* not
wasteful

cost of maintaining a records management system. Proper care of equipment and *conservative* use of supplies on your part will help control costs.

## Storage Space

Businesses usually lease their office space by the square foot. The company pays for the space occupied by records every time it writes a rent check. By keeping the space required to house records to a minimum, the space available for work is increased. Using microfilm to store records is one way to reduce the amount of space required to house records.

## Personnel

Workers are a key element in an effective records management system. Efficient procedures are worthless unless they are put into practice by workers. The salaries a company must pay personnel to manage records are a cost factor of records management.

**Illus. 12–9.** As a tape librarian for the Census Bureau, this office worker contributes to the efficiency of the overall records management system.

Large companies often have an entire staff of records management personnel. There may be a records manager who is in charge of the records management department. The staff may include a records management analyst, a records center supervisor, and several records clerks. Since records management is a field growing in importance, more and more businesses are looking for workers who specialize in managing records. Records management is a major career opportunity.

## Use of Cost-Saving Techniques

Professional office workers eagerly search for ways to reduce costs. Even as a beginning office worker, you can be on the lookout for ways to improve the existing records management system. Three techniques you might use are as follows:

*streamline:* make
more efficient

- Identify ways to *streamline* the filing and retrieval process.
- Analyze ways to cut down on the storage space required for records.
- Make it a habit to be cost-conscious.

## RECORD LIFE CYCLE

Records that a company needs come from many sources. Some records originate from outside the organization (industry surveys; forms; and correspondence from other businesses, for example). Other records originate within the organization (interoffice memorandums; records of sales and purchases; and copies of outgoing correspondence, for example).

Each record has a life cycle, in that its usefulness has a beginning and an end. The phases of the record life cycle are the same regardless of whether the records are kept on paper, magnetic media, or microfilm. A record life cycle is shown in Illus. 12–10. Refer to this illustration as you read the following brief description of each phase.

### Phase 1: Collect the Records

The cycle begins when you collect the records. The two arrows at the top of Illus. 12–10 indicate the source of the records— either from outside the company or within the company.

### Phase 2: Categorize the Records

*categorize:* assign to
a group on the basis of
certain characteristics

Next, you need to *categorize* the records as to how important they are to the operation of the company. A company records management policy will help you do that. How records are categorized will affect how you store the records and how long you keep them. Refer to Illus. 12–11 on page 514.

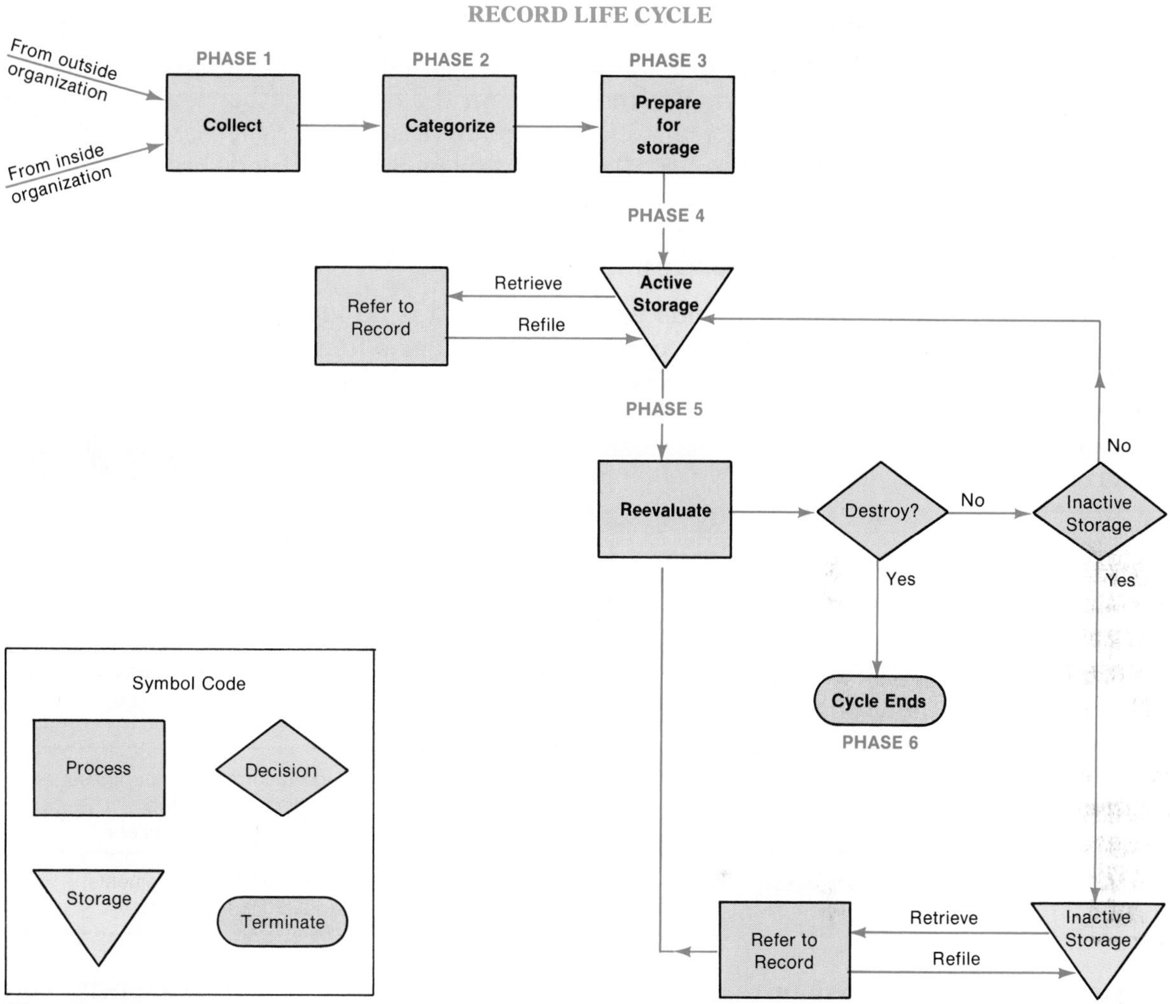

## RECORD LIFE CYCLE

From outside organization

From inside organization

PHASE 1 — **Collect**

PHASE 2 — **Categorize**

PHASE 3 — **Prepare for storage**

PHASE 4 — **Active Storage**

Refer to Record — Retrieve / Refile

PHASE 5 — **Reevaluate**

**Destroy?** — No — **Inactive Storage** — No

Yes — **Cycle Ends** — PHASE 6

Inactive Storage — Yes

Refer to Record — Retrieve / Refile — **Inactive Storage**

### Symbol Code

Process

Decision

Storage

Terminate

**Illus. 12–10.** These six phases make up the life cycle of records, whether the records are kept on paper, magnetic media, or microfilm.

## Phase 3: Prepare the Records for Storage

The procedure you use in this phase will vary. The specifics of the procedure will depend on whether the record is on paper, magnetic media, or microfilm. You also need to know whether the record should be filed alphabetically, numerically, or chronologically.

## Phase 4: Maintain the Records in Active Storage

When a record is in active storage, you probably will file and retrieve it many times. A good records management system will specify procedures for retrieving records and for returning them to the files efficiently.

## Phase 5: Reevaluate the Records

As a record becomes older, you need to reevaluate its importance. You may remove it from the file altogether and destroy it, or you may transfer it to inactive storage. When a record is in inactive storage, it still is retrieved and refiled, but not as frequently as when it was in active storage.

## Phase 6: Destroy the Records

The cycle ends when the record is no longer useful to the company. When a record is outdated or no longer needed, you remove it from storage and destroy it to make room for current records.

**Illus. 12–11.** Records must be categorized as to their importance to the company. Into which category would cancelled checks fall?

| RECORD CATEGORIES | | |
|---|---|---|
| **Category** | **Description** | **Examples** |
| Vital Records | Essential for the company to survive | Original copies of: deeds, copyrights, mortgages, trademarks |
| Important Records | Needed for business to operate smoothly; expensive to replace | tax returns, personnel files, cancelled checks |
| Useful Records | Convenient to have, yet replaceable | correspondence, purchase orders, names and addresses of suppliers |
| Nonessential Records | Has one-time or very limited usefulness | meeting announcements, advertisements |

**REMOVING RECORDS FROM ACTIVE STORAGE**

When records are outdated, or needed only infrequently, you should remove them from the active storage area. An effective records management system will include a policy for removing records from active storage.

## Retention Schedule

A retention schedule, shown in Illus. 12–12, is a valuable records management tool that identifies how long you should keep particular types of records. You will notice that the retention schedule has columns for a description of the type of record, the retention period (how long the record should be kept), and the authority who regulates how long the record should be kept. Government authority dictates how long you should keep certain

# Topic 2

## PAPER FILING SYSTEMS

When you have completed your study of this topic, you will be able to

- identify the components of a filing system
- describe four alphabetic filing systems
- explain how a numeric filing system is organized
- explain how a chronologic filing system is organized

In Topic 1 you learned that each record has a life cycle. In this topic you will become acquainted with systems for organizing paper files while the records are in the storage phase of the record life cycle. Systems for organizing magnetic media and microfilm files will be presented in detail in Chapter 13. In this topic you will concentrate on filing systems for paper files.

In a filing system for paper records, you store individual records in folders. The folders are labeled and organized alphabetically according to names of individuals or businesses, subjects, or geographic locations. You also can organize files numerically and by date. As a beginning office worker, you probably will not be responsible for establishing a filing system. But you will be expected to understand the existing filing system so you can file and retrieve records efficiently.

Some companies use only one filing system for all their paper records. Other companies may use more than one. For example, purchase orders may be filed numerically by order number, while records about customers are filed alphabetically. In this topic you will learn how each type of filing system is organized and used.

A filing system requires equipment, procedures, and supplies. You will need to understand the various types of each.

### Equipment

Various types of equipment—cabinets and shelves—are used to **house** paper records. Lateral file cabinets like those shown in Illus. 12–13 are used in many offices. In this topic we will assume that all records in your company are stored in a lateral file cabinet. Chapter 13, Topic 1, describes other equipment used in a paper filing system.

**Illus. 12–13.** Lateral files are frequently used to store medical records.

### Procedures

Before placing records in folders, you should index and code each record. Chapter 13 will explain procedures for indexing, coding, and filing in detail. However, a brief introduction is included here to help you understand why these procedures are an important component of a filing system.

### Indexing

Indexing is the process of deciding how to identify each record you need to file—by which specific name, subject, geographic location, number, or date. In a name file, for example, you would index a record by a specific individual or company name. In a numeric file, on the other hand, you would index a record by a specific number.

### Coding

Coding is the process of marking a symbol or other identification on the record to indicate how it was indexed. Colored pencils often are used for coding.

You may code a record by circling the appropriate name, subject, geographic location, or number which appears on the record. Or you may write the identification in the upper right corner of the record.

As you learned in Topic 1, you may retrieve and refile a record many times while it is in active storage. By coding a record, you help ensure that the record will be filed correctly each time it is returned to the files.

## Supplies

Each drawer in a file contains two different kinds of filing supplies: guides and file folders. The *guides* divide the drawer into sections and serve as *signposts* for quick reference. They also provide support for the folders and their contents. File folders hold the papers in an upright position in the file drawer and serve as containers to keep the papers together. *Labels* are attached to file folders to identify the contents of the folders. Labels are also attached to file cabinet drawers to identify the contents of each drawer.

### Guides

Guides are heavy cardboard sheets which are the same size as the folders in a file. A *tab* extends over the top of each guide, and a notation is marked or printed on the tab. This notation on the tab of a guide is called a caption. By reading the captions, you can quickly identify divisions within the file. For example, a guide may carry the caption A, which tells you that only material starting with the letter A is found between that guide and the next one.

Guides are classified as primary or special. *Primary guides* indicate the major divisions, such as letters of the alphabet, into which the filing system is separated. *Special guides* indicate subdivisions within these major divisions. Illus. 12–16 on page 525 shows how primary and special guides are arranged in an alphabetic filing system. Behind primary guide "C" you may have a special guide such as Cooper Temporaries. Try not to have more than 10 folders behind a guide, and try to have only about 15 to 25 guides in a file drawer.

### *Labels*

You need labels on file drawers so you can identify the contents of each drawer without opening the drawer. You also need labels on file folders.

*Drawer Labels.* The information on the drawer label should be specific, easy to read, and current. When the contents of a cabinet are changed in any way, the drawer label must be corrected immediately.

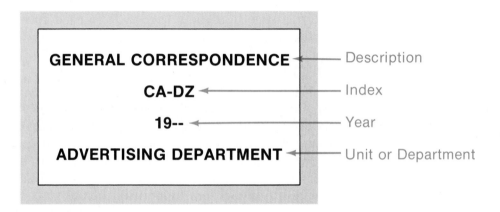

*Folder Labels.* Folder labels are strips of paper you attach to the folder tabs. The caption on the label identifies the contents of the folder. It is important for you to format the captions in a consistent manner.

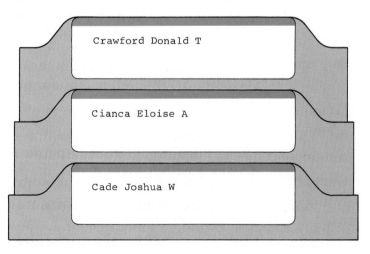

*Color-Coded Labels.* Many companies use color-coded labels to improve filing efficiency. There are several ways to use color-coded labels. One way simply involves assigning each alphabetic or numeric section of the files a specific color. On page 525 notice that all the fourth/fifth position folders in the drawer labeled CA-DZ have labels coded with the same color.

A more complex coding system is shown in Illus. 12–14. You can see the color pattern formed by the labels. Such a pattern helps you file and retrieve records quickly and accurately. If a folder were misfiled, you could know immediately because the color pattern would be interrupted.

**Illus. 12–14.** A color-coded filing system is designed to help office workers file and retrieve records efficiently. Can you see the pattern formed by the folder labels?

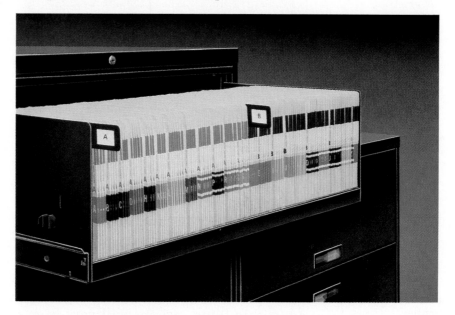

## Folders

A folder is made of strong, durable paper called *manila.* Folders are larger than the papers they contain so that they will protect the papers. Standard folder sizes are designed for papers that are 8½″ × 11″ and for papers that are 8½″ × 13″ or 8½″ × 14″.

*Folder Cuts.* Folders are cut across the top so that the back has a tab that projects above the top of the folder. You attach labels to the folder tabs to identify the contents of the folders. Folder tabs vary in width and position, as shown on page 524. Sometimes the tab is the full width of the folder. This is called a full-cut folder. Half-cut tabs are half the width of the folder and have two possible positions. Third-cut folders have three positions, each tab occupying a third of the width of the folder. Another standard tab has five positions and is called a fifth-cut folder. Some folders hang from metal frames placed inside the file drawer. Removable tabs can be attached to these folders at appropriate positions.

**Illus. 12–15.** Standard folder cuts. Notice that the folder tabs vary in width and position.

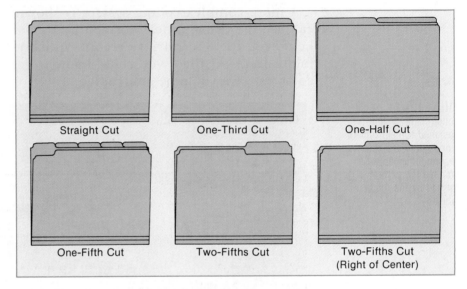

Straight Cut          One-Third Cut          One-Half Cut

One-Fifth Cut          Two-Fifths Cut          Two-Fifths Cut
(Right of Center)

## Position of Guides and Folders

There exists in offices today a variety of filing systems. Some systems (especially color-coded systems) are purchased from commercial manufacturers of filing supplies; other systems are developed *in-house*. Therefore, the positioning of guides and folders within filing systems will vary from company to company. Regardless of the system used, the guides and folders should be arranged in such a way that they are easy to see and in a logical order. You can see that the arrangement in Illus. 12–16 allows your eye to move easily from left to right.

*in-house:* within the company

### Primary Guides

When you open a file drawer, you look first for the appropriate primary guide. Since you read from left to right, the tab on the primary guide should be at the far left (*first position*) where it will be easy to locate. Usually companies use guides with fifth-cut tabs. Tabs on primary guides are most often in the first position.

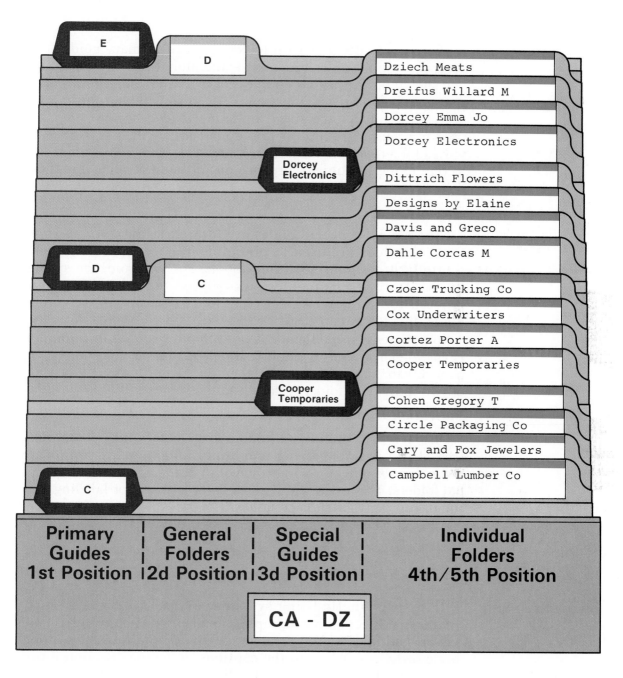

Dziech Meats
Dreifus Willard M
Dorcey Emma Jo
Dorcey Electronics

Dittrich Flowers
Designs by Elaine
Davis and Greco
Dahle Corcas M

Czoer Trucking Co
Cox Underwriters
Cortez Porter A
Cooper Temporaries

Cohen Gregory T
Circle Packaging Co
Cary and Fox Jewelers
Campbell Lumber Co

| Primary Guides 1st Position | General Folders 2d Position | Special Guides 3d Position | Individual Folders 4th/5th Position |

CA - DZ

**Illus. 12–16.** Portion of a name file. Notice the positions of the guides and folders.

### General Folders

There is usually a general folder for each primary guide. This second position folder bears the same alphabetic caption as the one shown on the primary guide. For example, the general folder that goes behind the primary guide "C" also will bear the caption "C." These folders are given the name *general* because they are used to accumulate records that do not justify the use of an individual folder. When you accumulate five or more records relating to one name or subject, prepare an individual folder for those records.

### Special Guides

On page 525, special guides are located in the *third position*. Special guides are used to pinpoint the location of a specific *fourth/fifth position* individual folder. For example, the special guide "Dorcey Electronics" was added because of frequent requests for the Dorcey Electronics folder. Because of the special guide, this folder can easily be located.

Sometimes a special guide is used to pinpoint the location of a single folder or a series of folders relating to a specific subject. On page 529 for example, the special guide "Film" marks the location of two individual folders relating to the subject, film.

### Individual Folders

On page 525, individual folders are located in the combined *fourth/fifth position*. Using individual folders helps you locate records more quickly. Notice the width of the tabs on the individual folders. This extra width allows ample space for labeling personal, company, or subject names.

**ALPHABETIC FILING SYSTEMS**

In an alphabetic filing system, you use letters and words (names, subjects, or geographic locations) as captions on the guides and folders. You arrange the guides and folders in alphabetic order according to the captions. Reference Section F presents rules for filing alphabetically. You will refer to Reference Section F when you complete the end-of-topic activities.

Four common alphabetic filing systems use name, subject, a combination of name and subject, and geographic location.

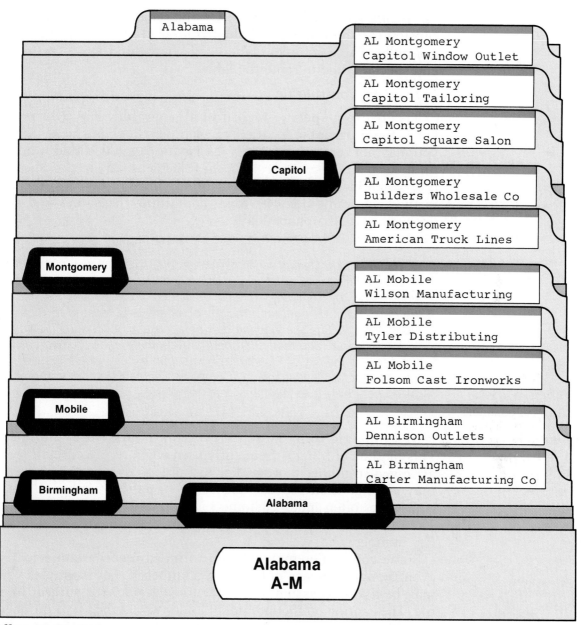

Alabama

AL Montgomery
Capitol Window Outlet

AL Montgomery
Capitol Tailoring

AL Montgomery
Capitol Square Salon

Capitol

AL Montgomery
Builders Wholesale Co

AL Montgomery
American Truck Lines

Montgomery

AL Mobile
Wilson Manufacturing

AL Mobile
Tyler Distributing

AL Mobile
Folsom Cast Ironworks

Mobile

AL Birmingham
Dennison Outlets

AL Birmingham
Carter Manufacturing Co

Birmingham

Alabama

**Alabama
A-M**

**Illus. 12–20.** Portion of a geographic file. Notice that the primary guides identify the largest geographic divisions.

You need a general folder behind each location name guide. In the illustration, the general folder and the location name guide bear the same caption (Alabama). When you prepare labels for individual folders, give the geographic location on the first line

(*AL Birmingham*, for example). On the second line, indicate the caption for the individual folder (*Carter Manufacturing Co*, for example). These complete labels tell you behind which primary and special guide to refile the folder.

### Index Card Control File

To retrieve a specific record in a geographic file, you must know the geographic location of each person or business. Since you may not remember all this information, you will find it helpful to keep an *index card control file*. This is usually a 5″ × 3″ card file, which includes a card for each individual or business record in the geographic file. The cards containing the names and addresses are filed alphabetically.

> *The firm where Carlota works uses a geographic filing system based on states. This morning her supervisor needed a record pertaining to Wonderland Toy Company. To retrieve the record, Carlota first checked the card index. She learned the toy company was located in Richmond, Virginia. She scanned the drawer labels and opened the drawer labeled Virginia. She then searched through the primary guides until she came to the city of Richmond. It was then easy to locate the individual folder for Wonderland Toy Company. Carlota's supervisor appreciated her ability to locate the record so quickly.*

## NUMERIC FILING SYSTEMS

In a numeric filing system, records are indexed by number. This method of filing is frequently used when records are already arranged in numeric order. For example, insurance companies may arrange their records according to policy number. Utility companies often index customers' accounts by account number. The Internal Revenue Service indexes tax returns by social security number.

Some companies may ask you to index records numerically even though they are not already numbered. For example, you may be asked to assign a number to each name or subject in a file. The caption on the individual folder would then be a number (i.e. 3877 for Global Security Systems or 8551 for West Coast Development Project) rather than a name or a subject.

### Guides

The guide captions in a numeric system are numbers instead of letters or words. Look at the numeric file shown in Illus. 12–21.

Notice how the numbered special guides highlight divisions within the primary guide category. This helps you retrieve records quickly.

**Illus. 12–21.** Portion of a numeric file. Insurance companies, for example, often arrange their records according to policy number.

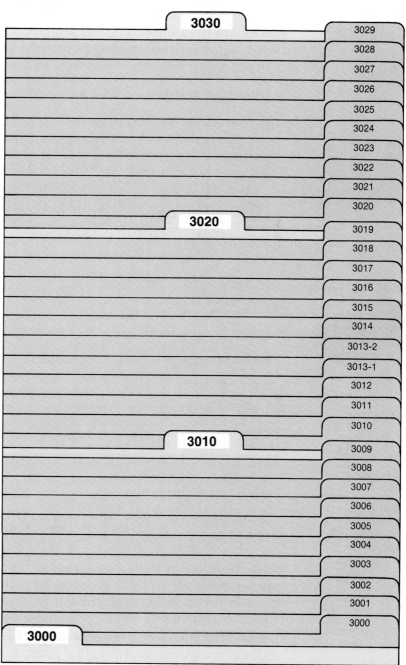

Records Administration and Technology

## General Folders

In a numeric system you do not provide a general folder behind each numeric guide. Instead, you maintain a separate *alphabetic general file*. Records that do not have an individual numeric folder are filed in the general alphabetic file by name or subject. When you collect enough records related to one name or subject, you create an individual numeric folder.

## Individual Folders

To set up an individual folder, you first refer to the accession book. An **accession book** is a record that lists in numeric order the file numbers already assigned and the name or subject related to each number. In Illus. 12–22 you can see that the last number, 3877, was assigned to Global Security Systems. The next number you assign will be 3878. By keeping an accession book, you avoid assigning the same number to more than one name or subject.

**Illus. 12–22.** Portion of an accession book. Can you identify the file number assigned to the Joseph E. Fuline Co.?

| NUMBER | NAME | DATE |
|--------|------|------|
| 3873 | Payroll Register | Jan. 1, 19-- |
| 3874 | Joseph E. Fuline Co. | Jan. 3, 19-- |
| 3875 | Monthly Production Reports | Jan. 3, 19-- |
| 3876 | Rogers Collection Agency | Jan. 4, 19-- |
| 3877 | Global Security Systems | Jan. 10, 19-- |
|  |  |  |
|  |  |  |

## Index Card Control File

After you have assigned a number to an individual folder, you need to record both the name or subject of the folder contents and the folder number on a 5″ × 3″ card. Just as you need an alphabetic index with a geographic file, so you need one with a numeric file as well. It is extremely difficult to remember the number for each name or subject in the files. When you must retrieve a record, you refer to the index card control file to learn the correct file folder number. Illus. 12–23 shows how the card index corresponds to individual records.

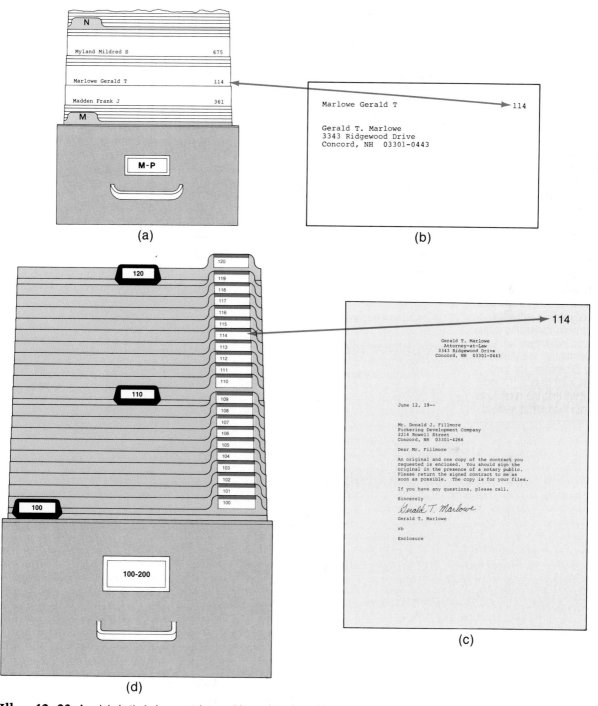

**Illus. 12–23.** An alphabetic index must be used in conjunction with a numeric file. (a) index card control file, (b) individual alphabetic index card, (c) incoming letter with numeric code, and (d) numeric file.

You also should prepare a 5″ × 3″ card for each name or subject in the general alphabetic file. Instead of including a folder number on the card, type the letter "G" as shown in Illus. 12–24. The G indicates you filed the record in the general alphabetic file instead of in an individual numeric folder.

An advantage to a numeric system is that it helps you keep records confidential. Scanning the numeric captions on folders will not tell an intruder much about the contents.

*Today is Carlos' first day of work. Miss Dibbern, Carlos' supervisor, briefed him on the filing system they use: "Carlos, the records in our department are confidential. We use a numeric filing system so unauthorized people cannot locate specific records easily. To keep these files secure, we have a policy which allows only workers in our department to have access to the index card control file and the accession book."*

**Illus. 12–24.** If a name or subject has been assigned an individual numeric folder, the alphabetic index card will have the number recorded on it. Otherwise, the card will only have a "G" indicating that the record has been filed in the general folder.

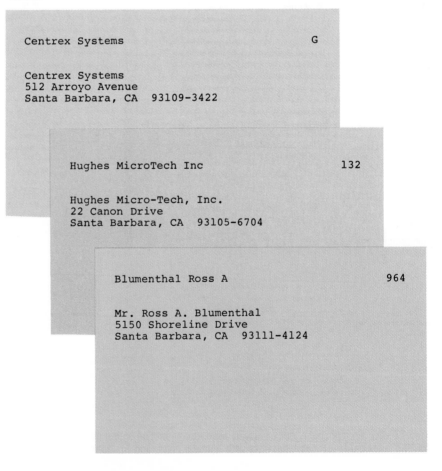

```
Centrex Systems                                       G


Centrex Systems
512 Arroyo Avenue
Santa Barbara, CA   93109-3422
```

```
Hughes MicroTech Inc                                132


Hughes Micro-Tech, Inc.
22 Canon Drive
Santa Barbara, CA   93105-6704
```

```
Blumenthal Ross A                                   964


Mr. Ross A. Blumenthal
5150 Shoreline Drive
Santa Barbara, CA   93111-4124
```

## CHRONOLOGIC FILING SYSTEMS

In a chronologic filing system you file according to date. A few companies may choose to use a chronologic system for filing all records. But most often you will use a chronologic file to help you keep track of tasks you need to complete each business day.

As you learned in Chapter 11, a desk calendar and a tickler file are two kinds of chronologic files.

## REVIEW QUESTIONS

1. What are the three components of a filing system?
2. What are two methods of coding a record?
3. Why is coding helpful?
4. Why are guides used in a filing system?
5. What is a caption?
6. Describe an advantage of using color-coded labels.
7. What are four frequently used alphabetic filing systems?
8. Why do you need an index card control file in a geographic filing system?
9. What is an accession book?
10. When would you most often use a chronologic file?

## MAKING DECISIONS

For three months, you have worked in the office of Davis-Rider, Inc. — a company with 12 employees. When you began the job, your supervisor, Mr. Davis, told you that you would be "generally in charge of the files" as well as having transcribing and light bookkeeping duties. While everyone has access to the files, he explained that you need to make sure the files are neat and that materials do not stack up.

Although the task seemed simple when Mr. Davis explained it to you, it has become a source of frustration. Some employees remove records and do not return them for several weeks. Other employees open file drawers and place folders on top of the other folders instead of inserting them in their proper places. Needless to say, the files are not being managed well.

Since you are "generally in charge of the files," you are being held account-able for the situation.

**What You Are To Do:**   Remembering that you are a relatively new em-ployee, how would you approach Mr. Davis about the problem? Prepare a written description of the ap-proach you would take.

## EXTENDING YOUR ENGLISH SKILLS

Knowing when to use "it's" (contraction) and when to use "its" (posses-sive) can be difficult. To help you know which term to use, ask yourself: "Could I substitute the words 'it is' or 'it has' in the sentence and have it make sense?" If you can, use "it's"; if not, use "its."

**What You Are To Do:**   Rewrite the following eight sentences, inserting ei-ther "it's" or "its," whichever is appropriate.

1. You need to put the folder back in _____ place.
2. _____ time to remove the inactive files from active storage.
3. He replied, "_____ necessary to charge out each record."
4. This folder has lost _____ label.
5. _____ been returned to the files.
6. Please let me know when _____ ready.
7. The company improved _____ image.
8. _____ on the top shelf of the bookcase.

## APPLICATION ACTIVITY

You work for a management consulting firm in Miami, Florida. In order to keep the records confidential, a numeric file system is used. You find that enough records have accumulated in the general files to necessitate creat-ing individual folders for the following Miami businesses:

Rosewood Import Company, 2699 South Bayshore Drive, 33133-0630

Peninsula Savings & Loan, 100 South Biscayne Boulevard, 33131-1221

Fuline's Delivery Service, 10039 Little River Drive, 33147-0330

Nico's Fine Seafood Restaurant, 1502 Coral Way, 33129-1202

Gomez, Jackson & Associates, 1680 Meridian Avenue, 33139-0930

Trade Winds Travel Agency, 2121 Ponce De Leon Boulevard, 33134-3056

# PRODUCTIVITY CORNER

**Blake Williams**
*OFFICE SUPERVISOR*

## LOOKING TO THE FUTURE

**DEAR MR. WILLIAMS:**

I recently graduated from high school and found a job at a local insurance agency. A good deal of my time on the job is spent filing and retrieving customer records. From my experience, I see that management puts a high priority on maintaining good records. I wonder, therefore, if there would be any future for me in the records management field?—KARLA IN PORTLAND

**DEAR KARLA:**

You have made a good observation. Even though you are a new employee, you are able to see the value of the customer records you handle each day. Records management is a vital part of *every* company, not just the insurance agency for which you work. If a business is to operate efficiently, up-to-date records must be available when needed.

I heartily recommend that you pursue your interest in the records management field. The practical experience you are getting on the job today will provide a firm foundation upon which to build a career in this rapidly growing field.

There are several professional organizations for records management personnel that you might wish to contact for additional information. One organization is the Association of Records Managers and Administrators (ARMA). Another is the Institute for Certified Records Managers (ICRM). The ICRM administers a professional exam. If you pass the exam and meet the qualifications, you earn the title of Certified Records Manager.

Approximately 90 percent of all office workers perform some records management tasks. So, whether or not you plan to pursue a records management career, your interest in maintaining good records and your desire to learn more about the field of records management will be a definite aid to you on this job or any job you hold in the future. Best wishes.—BLAKE WILLIAMS

# Chapter 13

# Managing Records

As you learned in Chapter 12, office records are stored on a variety of media. These storage media include paper, magnetic media (such as floppy disks, hard disks, and magnetic tape), and microfilm. Some companies use only one storage medium for records. Most offices, however, use a combination of several different media. For example, a small accounting firm may store tax returns on paper in file folders but keep customer account records on hard disks. A large bookstore may keep its inventory records on microfiche but maintain other records on paper or magnetic media.

With technology becoming more affordable to businesses, it is very probable that you will work in an office that uses a variety of media for storing records. Different media have different storage requirements. For example, magnetic media must be protected from other magnetic sources that could erase or change the stored information. Therefore, equipment and supplies specially designed to protect magnetic media should be used. Special storage equipment and supplies also are available for microfilm files as well as for paper records.

The trend now is to store together (whenever possible) all records that relate to a particular topic, regardless of the storage media used. For example, a floppy disk containing a project proposal, as well as the paper correspondence relating to the project, is placed in a file folder that is stored in a file cabinet.

This chapter explores the procedures, equipment, supplies, and technologies available to help you manage various forms of records efficiently.

The objectives of the chapter are to

- help you understand principles and procedures for managing paper storage systems

- help you understand principles and procedures for managing records stored on magnetic and micrographic media

# Topic 1

## MANAGING PAPER FILES

When you have completed your study of this topic, you will be able to

- explain how to prepare records for filing
- apply efficient filing procedures
- list three charge-out procedures
- describe how inactive files are transferred and stored

Wherever you work—whether it be in a small advertising agency or in a large manufacturing company—you probably will store some records on paper. Even in offices where magnetic media and microfilm are used extensively, there may still exist a need for certain paper (hard copy) records.

*Kerry works for O'Roark & Sullivan, a law firm of four attorneys. Kerry keeps form documents such as leases and wills on floppy disks. But for a legal transaction to be valid, the document must be signed. These signed paper documents are stored so that the signatures can be kept on file.*

Because paper is still the major medium for storing records, it is important that you understand how to maintain paper files. Once you have a clear understanding of the principles and procedures for managing paper files, you can easily adapt this knowledge to maintaining records stored on other media.

You already know how to organize records alphabetically, numerically, and chronologically. In this topic you will learn about preparing individual records for storage. You will learn methods for locating and removing individual records as well as entire folders. You also will become acquainted with the equipment used to store paper records.

## PREPARING RECORDS FOR STORAGE

Before you file a record for the first time, you need to prepare it properly for storage. By doing so, you speed the actual filing process and insure that you file the record correctly. The five steps you should take to prepare paper records for storage are:

1. Collect the records.
2. Inspect the records.
3. Index/code the records.
4. Cross-reference the records.
5. Sort the records.

**Illus. 13–1.** In order to file and retrieve records, this office worker must be thoroughly familiar with the procedures for managing paper files. Here, he is preparing records for storage.

### Collect Records

*designated:* set apart for a specific purpose

Throughout the work day, you will accumulate records that need to be filed. Instead of preparing and filing each record as you are finished with it, collect the records in a ***designated*** place such as a tray labeled *TO BE FILED*. Then at scheduled times, such as after lunch or at the end of the day, you can prepare a batch of records for storage at one time. You will not need to

**Illus. 13–9.** This executive is removing a file folder from a mobile file. The file sections are mounted on rollers and can be moved quickly and quietly.

## Printout Storage

With the increasing use of computer information processing, more and more computer printouts are being generated. Printouts vary in size, but they usually are too bulky to store in traditional filing cabinets. Most companies prepare printouts for storage by placing them in binders made of pressboard or plastic. The binders have thin, flexible metal posts that fit through the holes on the sides of the printouts. When the posts have been threaded through the printout, the remaining portion is folded over so the binder can be closed. Binders can be stored in several ways:

- They can be placed on shelves horizontally.
- They can be hung on racks or cabinets. In this case, binders with special hooks or handles are used.
- They can be filed in a frame which accommodates hanging binders.

Some storage units for printouts are mobile in that they can be rolled from one location to another. Most binders are indexed by tabs or labels that attach to the binder. Color-coded binders frequently are used to help you locate specific groupings of printouts.

**Illus. 13–10.** (Left) A variety of card files, like those shown here, are used in many offices.

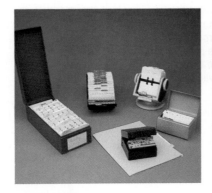

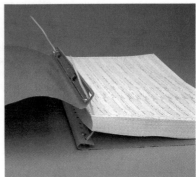

**Illus. 13–11.** (Right) Bulky materials such as computer printouts are often stored in binders like the one shown here.

## RETRIEVING RECORDS

In Chapter 12, you learned about the record life cycle. Once records are in active storage, you may retrieve and refile them many times. An effective records management program will include charge-out procedures that help you keep track of records when workers remove them from the files.

### Requisition Cards

Many companies that use central files have a staff of trained records management personnel to file and retrieve records. In companies using this arrangement, other office workers do not have direct access to the files. To retrieve records, you must fill out a requisition card. A requisition card is a card that has space for all the charge-out information needed. A member of the records management staff will read the information on the card and retrieve the record for you.

If you work in the central files, you will keep a copy of each requisition card in a card tickler file. When a record has not been returned by the expected date, you need to take appropriate follow-up action. Taking such action is an important part of an effective records management program. A records manager also may use requisition cards to analyze how often the files are used and which records are most active.

### Out Guides

When you remove a record from the files, you must replace it with a record of the charge-out information. This can be accomplished by using an out guide. An out guide is a sheet of thick cardboard, called pressboard, that has the word OUT printed on the tab. On some out guides, you write the charge-out information on ruled lines. On other out guides, there is a pocket where you insert the completed requisition card. You usually use out guides when individual records within a folder are removed.

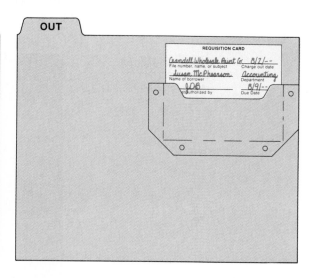

| OUT | | | |
|---|---|---|---|
| **NUMBER, NAME, OR SUBJECT** | **CHARGE OUT DATE** | **NAME OF BORROWER** | **DUE DATE** |
| Forest Park Florist | 4/22/-- | Ruth Carson | 5/1/-- |
| Spanish Village Apartments | 5/6/-- | Jerry Ahmed | 5/14/-- |
| | | | |
| | | | |
| | | | |
| | | | |
| | | | |
| | | | |
| | | | |
| | | | |
| | | | |

OUT

REQUISITION CARD

Crandell Wholesale Paint Co. 8/7/--
File number, name, or subject    Charge out date

Susan McPhearson    Accounting
Name of borrower    Department

JDB    8/9/--
Authorized by    Due Date

**Illus. 13–12.** (Left) Ruled out guide and (Right) out guide with pocket containing a requisition card.

## Out Folder

An out folder is used when an entire folder is removed from the file. When an out folder is used, you may temporarily file additional records in the out folder until the regular folder is returned.

*When Marcy removed the Brandon-Mills folder from the files, she provided the charge-out information on the printed lines of an out folder. Later, when Peter was filing, he placed two letters in the Brandon-Mills out folder. If Marcy had not provided the out folder, Peter would not have been able to file the two letters. This way, Peter could file the records. Marcy then would insert those records into the Brandon-Mills folder when she returned it to the files.*

**REMOVING RECORDS FROM ACTIVE STORAGE**

An efficient records management system will have a retention schedule that identifies which records should be removed from active storage and on which dates. Records that are kept in inactive storage usually are kept in cardboard or fiberboard storage files rather than metal cabinets. The boxes are sturdy and provide a place to identify the contents. Some storage boxes are stackable, which saves space. Color-coded storage boxes can help you locate inactive records quickly.

Some companies store inactive records in off-site locations. These locations range from rented storage space to underground vaults.

**Illus. 13–13.** An off-site location for storing inactive records.

**REVIEW QUESTIONS**

1. List the five steps involved in preparing paper records for storage.

2. What is the purpose of a release mark?

3. How would you code a record indexed by name?

4. Why is it necessary to cross-reference some records?

5. Give two reasons for sorting records before filing them.

6. How should you arrange records in an individual folder?

7. What is a special folder and how might it be used?

8. What is an advantage of mobile files?

9. Under what circumstances might a requisition card be used?

10. What is the difference between an out guide and an out folder?

## Identifying Individual Files

One company stores its mailing list for the city of Austin, Texas, on a floppy disk. This mailing list is considered to be a file, and it must be assigned a name so that it can be identified and accessed when needed. Many word/text processing systems and computer systems limit the length of the name you can assign a file. Any combination of letters, numbers, and/or symbols (with some exceptions) can be used for a file name. Naturally you will want to assign a name that reflects the type of information stored in the file. For example, the name assigned to the Austin mailing list file could be *AUSTINML.*

A directory of the files that you store on magnetic media is easily accessed and displayed on the screen. If you are using a microcomputer system, you key a command that causes a directory of files stored on secondary storage media to be displayed on the screen. A command is a word or abbreviated word that instructs the system to perform a function or operation.

Common commands are DIR (for directory), FILES, and CATALOG. Page 566 shows a list of the files stored on the floppy disk presently in disk drive B of a microcomputer system. The operator keys the proper command, and the names of files saved on the floppy disk are displayed. The name assigned to each file in this case is the last name of the individual who created the document, plus the number assigned to the document.

### *Prompts and Menus*

Application software programs are available which perform records management tasks. Some software programs provide *prompts* which aid you in assigning names to files and in storing files automatically on secondary storage media. The prompt may be in the form of a directive (for example, "Enter file name: _____") or a question (for example, "Delete what?"). Other software programs provide a series of *menus.* Once the menu is displayed on the screen, you select from the options listed the specific activity you wish to complete. Page 567 shows a typical menu for creating and maintaining a mailing list.

As you can see, the menu in the illustration offers you several options. You can view a directory of all the files, create a new file, add to an existing file, read/print a file, change/delete a record, or return to the records management menu. If you select option 2

(Create New File), you can, for example, create a new mailing list. The system prompt "Enter file name: _____" will appear on the screen, and you then will key in the name of the new file.

**Illus. 13–15.** A directory of the files stored by an office assistant on the diskette currently in disk drive B of a microcomputer system. Notice that the name assigned to each file in this case is the last name of the individual who created the document (Douglas, for example), plus a document number (08, for example).

```
Displaying Directory!
                                               !Ext 340-B!

        Drive: B              Available: 9%
        Directory:
   ID   NAME       EXT     SIZE      DATE         TIME
   a    DOUGLAS    08      19456     01-01-87     00:18:16
   b    ADAMS      23      5120      01-01-87     00:02:28
   c    HART       02      3072      01-01-87     10:20:08
   d    SWETTS     12      7680      01-01-87     00:30:52
   e    ADAMS      24      4096      01-01-87     00:24:24
   f    ADAMS      25      3584      01-01-87     02:09:12
   g    HART       03      16904     01-01-87     04:12:18
   h    HART       04      4096      01-01-87     00:36:16
   i    HART       05      759       01-01-87     00:35:12
   j    SWETTS     13      10240     01-01-87     01:53:48
   k    SWETTS     14      3072      01-01-87     00:06:28
   l    ADAMS      26      1408      01-01-87     00:13:52
```

Next, you will see on the screen the prompts asking for specific information regarding the names, addresses, and telephone numbers of the individuals to be included on the new mailing list. (Refer to Illus. 13–17.) You respond to each prompt by providing the necessary information.

After all data has been keyed, you will be given an opportunity to make any necessary corrections or changes. The information then is stored automatically on the magnetic medium under the file name that you selected. A new prompt then will appear on the screen, asking you if additional records are to be entered. If you respond by entering *Y* for *yes*, a new record can be keyed. If you enter *N* for *no*, the Mailing Lists menu again will be displayed.

As you can see from this brief illustration, applications software programs provide prompts and menus designed to help you in carrying out records management tasks.

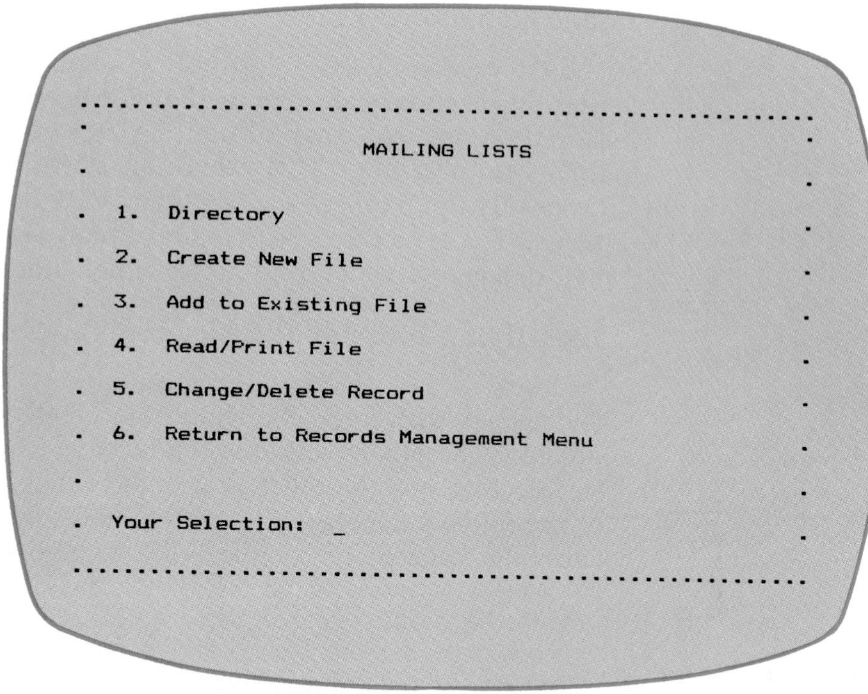

**Illus. 13–16.** A typical menu for creating and maintaining a mailing list.

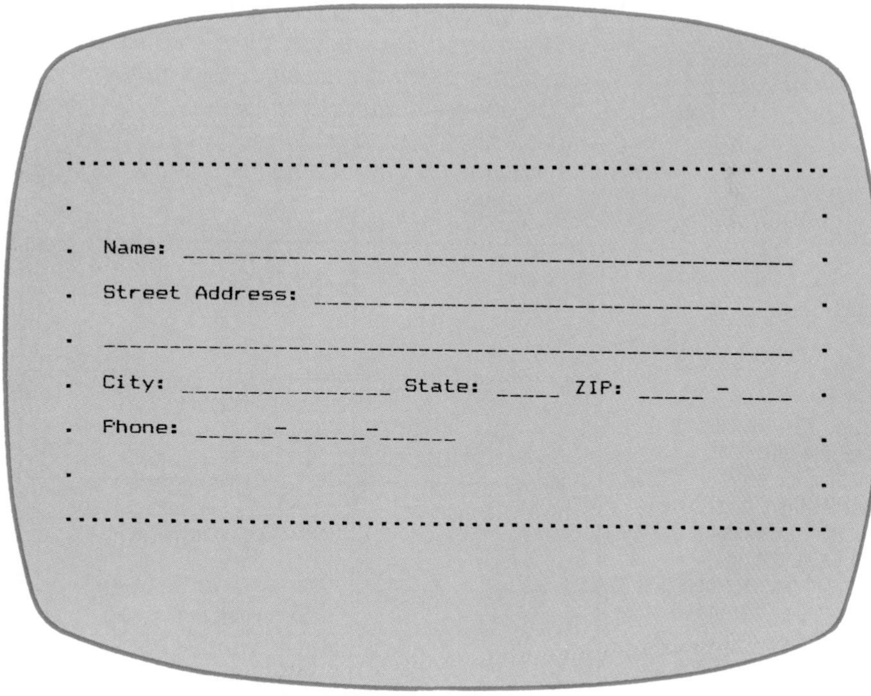

```
..................................................
.                                                .
.                    MAILING LISTS               .
.                                                .
.   1.   Directory                               .
.                                                .
.   2.   Create New File                         .
.                                                .
.   3.   Add to Existing File                    .
.                                                .
.   4.   Read/Print File                         .
.                                                .
.   5.   Change/Delete Record                    .
.                                                .
.   6.   Return to Records Management Menu        .
.                                                .
.                                                .
.   Your Selection:  _                           .
.                                                .
..................................................
```

**Illus. 13–17.** The screen prompts shown here aid you in providing information about individuals to be included on the mailing list.

```
..................................................
.                                                .
.   Name:  _____  .
.   Street Address:  _____  .
.                                                .
.   _____  .
.                                                .
.   City: _____ State: _____ ZIP: _____ - ____  .
.   Phone: _____-_____-_____                  .
.                                                .
.                                                .
..................................................
```

### Policies and Procedures

Businesses must develop policies and procedures for storing files on secondary storage media. For example, will all letters be stored on one diskette? All mailing lists on another? All business forms on another? Will documents be stored in chronologic order? By the name of the originator? By the name of the department? The type of records management system a company uses will determine which files go on which storage medium.

## Identifying Individual Disks and Tapes

Magnetic media can be organized alphabetically or numerically. Each disk and tape should be labeled so you can locate it quickly. The labels you use should have captions that are as descriptive as possible, just as a folder label caption is descriptive of the folder's contents. Often, the labels are color coded to indicate how long the data on the disk or tape should be *retained*.

*retained:* kept

*The Petro-Davis Company has classified all information placed on its floppy disks as permanent, semi-permanent, or temporary in nature. The chart shown in Illus. 13–18 further describes these categories. The disks in each category are stored in a different location. To aid in distinguishing the disks by their retention category, disk labels are color coded. Permanent disks are labeled with a red felt-tipped pen; semi-permanent, with blue; and temporary, with green. Look at the disk shown in Illus. 13–19. Label A identifies the type of information that will be placed on the disk. Label B tells (1.) what Disk Operating System (DOS) and computer program were used and (2.) the retention category.*

**Illus. 13–18.** Just as there is a retention schedule for paper records, there must be a retention schedule for records stored on magnetic media. Notice, for example, that the balance sheet and income statement are classified as permanent records.

| Retention Category | Label A<br>Information on Disk | Label B<br>Disk Operating System<br>Computer Program<br>Retention Category |
|---|---|---|
| Permanent | Balance Sheet 12/31/--<br>Income Statement 12/31/-- | DOS 3.1<br>WordText<br>Permanent |
| Semi-Permanent | Expense Forecast 5/8/--<br>Alcorn Proposals 5/l0/-- | DOS 3.1<br>MaxiCalc<br>Semi-Permanent |
| Temporary | Correspondence | DOS 3.1<br>WordText<br>Temporary |

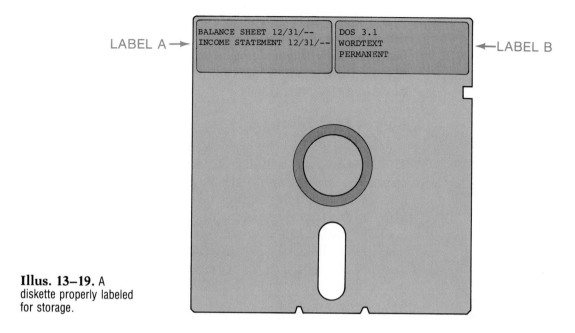

LABEL A → | BALANCE SHEET 12/31/-- | DOS 3.1
INCOME STATEMENT 12/31/-- | WORDTEXT
PERMANENT | ← LABEL B

**Illus. 13–19.** A diskette properly labeled for storage.

## Making Backup Copies

It is a good practice to make a *backup* (duplicate) copy of each disk or tape if the loss of the disk or tape or the accidental erasure of the data would have serious consequences. *Backing up a tape or disk* means making a copy of the data on another tape or disk. *Backing up a file* means making a copy of an individual file on a different tape or disk. Most word/text processing systems and computer systems provide easy-to-follow procedures for automatically making backup copies of tapes and disks. On many systems, the command COPY begins the backup process. Prompts and messages then appear on the screen to tell you what to do next.

It is common practice to make a backup copy of all applications software, such as software designed to handle databases, records management, spreadsheets, and text processing. Applications software is fragile and expensive to replace. Backup copies are also made of important files such as customer, payroll, and personnel records. Can you imagine the difficulties that would arise if a company lost all of its customer records? Backup copies of tapes and disks should be stored in a separate, safe location.

## STORING MAGNETIC MEDIA

You know that magnetic media require special care to protect the valuable information they contain. You will want to become familiar with the wide variety of equipment and supplies available so that you can adequately protect the media that you handle and organize.

### Floppy Disk Storage

Floppy disks can be organized and stored in a variety of ways. The way selected will depend on the number of disks you need to store, the size of the disks (standard, mini, or micro), the frequency with which you use the disks, and the storage space available. Many companies color code their floppy disk labels to *expedite* the storage and retrieval process. The protective covers for floppy disks also are available in various colors. Some examples of floppy disk storage are explained in the following paragraphs.

*expedite:* speed up

#### *Floppy Disk Containers*

Floppy disks often are filed in plastic boxes, cases, or trays designed to protect the disks. Within the case are guides to aid you in filing and retrieving the floppy disks.

Floppy disks also are stored in pockets that are attached to a stationary post or a disk stand. The disks are stored and retrieved easily by rotating the pockets around the center post.

Floppy disks also are stored in plastic pockets punched to fit a ring binder. The floppy disk slips into the clear plastic pocket,

**Illus. 13–20 and 13–21.** Floppy disks are a very popular storage medium. They are easily stored in plastic trays (left) and binders (right).

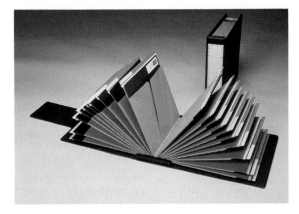

where it is protected. Each pocket has space for some type of disk identification. Some plastic pockets can hold hard copy as well as the floppy disk. Other pockets are designed so that you can file floppy disks in a standard file drawer.

### Minidisks and Microdisks

*Minidisks* and *microdisks* are smaller versions of the standard floppy disk. They frequently are used as storage media in word/ text processing. These smaller disks can be filed in containers and pockets similar to those used for floppy disks. In some cases, two minidisks or microdisks are filed in the same pocket.

### Reel Tape Storage

Reels of tape are stored in round, protective cases. These cases usually are hung for easy access or are stored on wire racks. Sometimes the cases have handles or hooks that allow the reels to be attached to frames or cabinets. Other times, the cases rest on a backward-slanting shelf. Labels on the protective cases of tapes can be color coded for easy reference.

**Illus. 13–22.** Magnetic tapes are stored in protective cases. Notice the color-coded numbering system used by this company.

**RETRIEVING
FILES ON
MAGNETIC
MEDIA**

Files stored on secondary storage media are considered to be *off line* when they are removed from the disk drive or tape drive of the word/text processing system or computer system. In order to access the information on a secondary storage medium, the medium must be returned to the disk drive or tape drive so that it is once again *on line* with the system.

You must complete the following three steps in order to retrieve a file stored on a secondary storage medium:

1. Locate the proper disk or tape in its storage facility by reading the labels.
2. Insert the disk into the disk drive or mount the tape on the tape drive.
3. Select the appropriate menu option or initiate the proper command to access the file.

### Security Procedures

Much of the information in the files of a company is confidential and vital to the continued operations of the organization. Therefore, companies are careful to protect their interests. Security of information stored on magnetic files is of particular concern because an ***unscrupulous*** person can quickly and easily:

***unscrupulous:*** lacking respect for legal or moral considerations

- access information
- copy information (Hundreds of pages can be copied in less than a minute!)
- transmit information
- alter information

To avoid these and other potential security problems, companies establish security procedures and limit access to files to authorized employees who need the information to perform their jobs. For example, an employee in the inventory department would not need access to company personnel records or accounting records.

Two common security measures are access logs and access codes or passwords. An access log is a computer-generated record of each time an authorized user retrieves information from a file and/or completes any type of processing. An access log also records any attempt by an unauthorized operator to access a file. An access code or password is a preassigned number or term designed to keep unauthorized people from accessing files. For example, if you select the *read a file* option from a Mailing

Lists menu and indicate the name of the file you want to access, the monitor might display a prompt like the one shown in Illus. 13–23.

**Illus. 13–23.**
Companies frequently assign passwords or access codes as a security precaution. In order to access certain files, an office worker must be able to enter the proper password or access code when the prompt is displayed.

Enter Access Code: ##########

If you were able to enter the requested access code, you would be able to access information from this file. If you were not able to enter the required code, you would not be given access to the file. In addition, on many systems your attempt to enter a *secured file* (a file which requires a code or password to be entered) would be logged and an alert might be sounded at the computer center to indicate that an attempt had been made from your workstation to enter a secured file.

## Databases

You know that a database is any collection of related items stored in computer memory. Databases are useful to businesses because a manager or office assistant can search through thousands of files in only a few seconds in order to locate the specific information needed. If you had to search through the same number of files stored on paper, the search would be overwhelming! Also, the use of a database helps remedy the problem of having information filed in several different departments within the company. Many computer software programs exist that allow a company to ***devise*** its own database designed to meet the needs of that particular organization.

*devise:* make up

*premises:* grounds

Advancements in technology have made it possible for businesses to use databases not located on their ***premises*** as sources of additional information. The information available covers a wide range of topics, including airline schedules and price quotations on stocks and securities. There are several companies which, for a fee, provide a wide variety of database services. Sometimes these companies which sell information services are called *information utilities.* One such service organization is The Source Telecomputing Corporation (often shortened to *The Source*). It provides over 1,000 services to thousands of subscribers. It is easy to access The Source by telephone from over 350 metropolitan areas throughout the country.

## ADVANCED COMPUTER TECHNOLOGY

*innovations:* changes

Computer manufacturers continue to research and develop new products in order to satisfy the ever-changing needs of business and industry. Sometimes the technological breakthroughs are so rapid that businesses find it difficult to keep up with the latest ***innovations***! One recent technological development that has affected records management is the use of optical disks as an alternative way of storing large amounts of text or pictures and sound.

### Optical Disks

An optical disk looks like a long-playing record with a special coating. Laser technology is used to record information on the disk. One of the major advantages of optical disks is their large storage capacity. The storage capacity of an optical disk begins at the level of approximately four *gigabytes.* (One gigabyte represents one billion bits of storage.) In contrast, hard disk storage capacity ranges from one *megabyte* to over three hundred megabytes. (One megabyte represents one million bits of storage.) About 60,000 document pages can be stored on an optical disk. It would take approximately seven reels of microfilm to equal the storage capacity of one optical disk.

Once information has been recorded on an optical disk, it cannot be erased. Therefore, optical disks are used for archival storage and for storage of large databases of information such as those used in government, banking, and insurance. Hospitals also use optical disks to keep patients' medical records. The major disadvantage of optical disk storage is that it is expensive.

**Illus. 13–24.** Laser technology has made it possible to store records on optical disks. This relatively new storage medium holds great promise for highly automated offices.

## CREATING MICROFILM FILES

You will recall from your study of Chapter 12 that the space required to keep records on microforms is greatly reduced from the space needed to keep the same number of records on paper.

You also will recall that images on microfilm can be created in two ways:

- Paper records are photographed and are developed as images on roll microfilm, microfiche, or aperture cards.
- A computer is used to convert information stored on magnetic media into images on microfilm. Microfilm produced by computer is *computer output microfilm*, usually referred to as COM. The most common form of COM is microfiche.

### Photographing Records

A company that chooses microfilm as a storage medium may purchase photographic equipment so the microfilm can be produced in-house. Large companies that store many records on microfilm often decide to purchase their own equipment. Some businesses offer micrographic services and will photograph a company's records for a fee.

Special cameras are used to reduce records onto film. **Reduction ratio** is a term used to describe how small the microimage is compared to the original record. For example, if the reduction ratio is 48:1 (also written as 48×), the microimage is 48 times smaller than the original record.

## Computer Output Microfilm (COM)

You learned in Chapter 12 that computers are also used to create microfilm files. By using a COM recorder in *conjunction* with a computer, information stored on magnetic media is converted directly into readable images on roll microfilm or microfiche. Illus. 13–25 shows how records on computer-produced magnetic tape are converted into images on microfiche. When a record is needed, it can be retrieved quickly and viewed on a microfilm reader.

**Illus. 13–25.** Can you follow the path of the computer-produced magnetic tape as it is converted into images on microfiche?

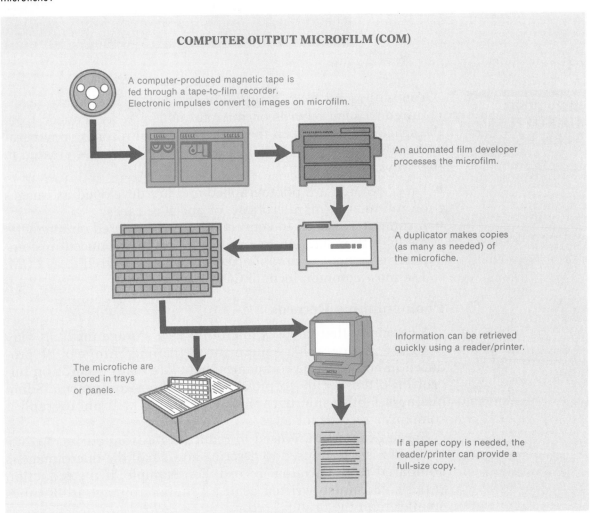

**COMPUTER OUTPUT MICROFILM (COM)**

A computer-produced magnetic tape is fed through a tape-to-film recorder. Electronic impulses convert to images on microfilm.

An automated film developer processes the microfilm.

A duplicator makes copies (as many as needed) of the microfiche.

Information can be retrieved quickly using a reader/printer.

The microfiche are stored in trays or panels.

If a paper copy is needed, the reader/printer can provide a full-size copy.

## ORGANIZING MICROFORMS

In a paper system, you file individual records in folders. You label each folder so you can identify the contents of the folder and file the folder alphabetically, numerically, or chronologically with other folders. A microform is similar to a folder because it contains many records. It is important to label and organize microforms alphabetically, numerically, or chronologically so that they can be retrieved easily. How you label and organize the microforms will depend on the particular filing system used in your company.

### Organizing Microfiche

You will recall that a microfiche is a transparent sheet of film containing several rows of microimages. At the top of each microfiche (or *fiche*) is space to label the contents of that particular microform. The caption on a microfiche is similar to the caption used on a folder in a paper filing system. Microfiche labels are frequently color coded for easy retrieval.

Microfiche is the microform commonly used for active (frequently used) storage. Fiche can be stored efficiently in panels. A panel is a page of paper or vinyl that has several slots into which you insert the microfiche. The slots are deep enough to protect the fiche, yet shallow enough to allow the microfiche caption to be read easily.

**Illus. 13–26.**
Microfiche are easily stored in plastic trays (left) and in packets attached to a rotary stand (right).

Microfiche can also be stored in trays where guides and color-coded labels are used to organize the media, just as in a diskette tray or card file.

## Organizing Roll Microfilm

Roll microfilm is kept in protective cases or boxes. A label is attached to the case or box to identify that particular roll of microfilm. The roll is filed alphabetically, numerically, or chronologically with other rolls in a drawer or cabinet.

## Organizing Aperture Cards

You will recall that the most commonly used aperture card contains only one microrecord or image. Because identifying information can be printed along the top edge of the card, you may file and retrieve aperture cards much as you would file and retrieve paper records. Aperture cards are often housed in trays.

**Illus. 13–27.** An aperture card labeled for storage.

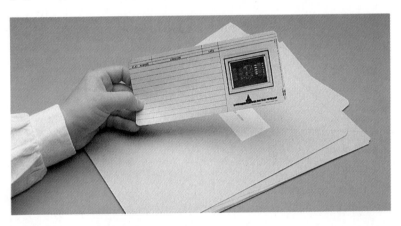

## RETRIEVING RECORDS ON MICROFILM

When you find it necessary to refer to a record on microfilm, you must know on which roll, fiche, or aperture card the record is stored. If the record is on roll microfilm or microfiche, you also must know the specific location of the record on the film. An index provides you with the information you need by listing an *address* for each microfilm record. Therefore, the first step in retrieving a specific record is to consult the index to determine the exact location of that record. You then would use a reader to view the record. If a hard copy of the record is needed, many readers are equipped with printers that allow you to make a full-size copy of the record.

**Illus. 13–28.** This office worker is using a microfilm reader/printer.

## Computer-Assisted Retrieval (CAR) Systems

Computer-assisted retrieval (CAR) is the process of locating records on film by using computer-stored indexes. A CAR system may be very simple or very sophisticated.

### Simple CAR System

A simple CAR system uses an off-line computer and a reader/printer. When you need to refer to the index, you command the computer to print the index on paper, display it, or print it on film. Then you consult the index and manually locate and load the proper microform into the reader.

### Database Indexes

Some CAR systems use computer software to maintain an index that is similar to a database. You will recall that a database is a collection of related information or data maintained in computer memory. A database can be accessed in many ways. An advantage of a database index is that you can search for a record by name, subject, or date. The address of the needed record will be displayed on the screen. Then you place the microform into the reader/printer and view the record. Some CAR systems automatically locate the correct image and display it on the reader screen.

**Illus. 13–29.** An
advanced computer-
assisted retrieval system.

### *Advanced CAR Systems*

More advanced CAR systems are created as new technologies become available and as existing technologies are integrated with one another. For example, when the ability to transmit data over telephone lines was combined with the need to view microimages from a **remote** location, an advanced CAR system became available. The following steps outline the way in which you would use an advanced CAR system to view from a remote location a record stored on microfilm.

*remote:* distant

1. Use the computer keyboard to access the database index; search the index for the appropriate record address.
2. Then use the computer to command the film autoloader to load the proper roll of film and scan the film until the specific image you need is located. The *film autoloader* is a piece of equipment that not only loads and scans the film but also houses the microfilm rolls until they are needed.
3. While the image is being scanned, it is being converted into electrical impulses which travel through a *local area network* (LAN) or over telephone lines to your remote computer terminal. You then can view the enlarged image on the terminal screen.
4. If a hard copy of the record is needed, a printer can quickly produce one.

**INTEGRATED CHAPTER ACTIVITY**

At the end of Topic 1, you completed an application activity that involved indexing names of individuals and organizations and placing them in correct alphabetic order. That application activity dealt with Rules 1–7 of Reference Section F. The names presented in this activity relate mainly to Rules 8–14. You will need thirty-five 3″ × 5″ cards or thirty-five pieces of plain paper cut to that size.

**What You Are To Do:**

1. Key each name at the upper left corner of a card, placing the units in correct indexing order (see the sample card in Topic 1, page 562). Refer to Reference Section F, Rules 8–14. Also key the number of each name in the upper right corner of the card. (These numbers will help your instructor check your work.)

2. Arrange the cards alphabetically, combining them with the cards you prepared in Topic 1.

(26) North Side Florist Shoppe
(27) McCullum Printing Co., Augusta, Georgia
(28) Collin County Department of Human Services
(29) Lightner & Bagwell, Inc.
(30) 39 and Holding Club
(31) Republic National Bank
(32) Louann D. Grayson
(33) The First Bank of Topeka
(34) Parker-Smith Real Estate
(35) Northside Dry Cleaners
(36) Saint John's Hospital
(37) Omaha Savings and Loan
(38) California Department of Public Safety
(39) Bonny Brite Industries
(40) Carl Michael Collin
(41) Carrollton Department of Engineering and Planning
(42) East Texas State University
(43) North Trails Inn
(44) Strickland-Hall Photography

(45) United States Government Department of Labor
(46) X-Cel Interiors
(47) Lou Ann Grayson
(48) Health Science Center
(49) 16th Street Cafe
(50) Anderson Paint Store, Paris, Tennessee
(51) McCullum Printing Co., Atlanta, Georgia
(52) American Institute of Architects
(53) Clarence C. Bonner
(54) 16th and Grand Shoe Repair
(55) City of Richardson Department of Parks & Recreation
(56) E-Z-Rest Motel
(57) 18th Avenue Apartments
(58) McCullum Printing Co., Savannah, Georgia
(59) 39 Palms Hotel
(60) Anderson Paint Store, Paris, Texas

**Blake Williams**
*OFFICE SUPERVISOR*

## HALTING HACKERS

**DEAR MR. WILLIAMS:**

I am a computer operator for a large chemical company that manufactures prescription drugs. My supervisor constantly stresses the need to keep the files confidential. Each week we use a different password to access the files. Only those that are authorized to use the files are told the new password.

Recently on the news I've been hearing about hackers—those who gain access to computer files without permission. What other types of security measures besides passwords are available to keep hackers out? —ERNEST IN SANTA FE

**DEAR ERNEST:**

You might be surprised at the variety of security systems that are used. For example, an access control may use fingerprints, voice recognition, or even palm geometry to verify your identity.

One interesting access control is referred to as Random Personal Identification. Stored with the computer are personal history questions about each authorized user. When you try to access files, the computer will randomly choose several personal history questions to ask such as, "Where did you live in 1983?" "What is your mother's maiden name?" or "When did you begin working for the company?" It is very unlikely that someone other than the person seeking access could successfully answer these questions.

Another access control is an *error lockout*, which means that after a certain number of unsuccessful attempts to gain access, the terminal's power shuts off. A company may also choose a *time lock*. A time lock restricts the use of the computer to regular office hours.

These are only a few of the security control measures available. As technology advances, even more sophisticated methods of security control probably will be invented. But the best security "device" of all is people who recognize and respect the need for companies to maintain confidential files. I'm glad *you* realize the importance of protecting your company's files! —BLAKE WILLIAMS

## AT WORK AT DYNAMICS: Simulation 3

Miss Lancaster telephoned to say that your next assignment will be in the Finance and Administration Division of DYNAMICS. This division prepares the financial and managerial reports necessary for planning, budgeting, reviewing, and reporting purposes. Because this time of the year is always a peak period for the Finance and Administration Division, several temporary employees are being called to help out.

"As a temporary worker in this division," Miss Lancaster said, "you will find that two qualities are very important to getting the work done: *flexibility* and *cooperation*. The employees in the Finance and Administration Division all gladly pitch in to help one another whenever possible." Miss Lancaster further explained that this division handles all the accounting, management information services, business planning, and purchasing. "Fortunately, we have a satellite word processing

center to support the various departments within this division," she said.

A key component of the Finance and Administration Division is the Management Information Services Department. This department is responsible for all computer operations within the company. Additionally, the creative people in this department develop software to meet the information needs of the total company. "Your experiences in the Finance and Administration Division will be varied, and you will find that all phases of the company's activities are involved in what you do. I know you will find your work challenging," said Miss Lancaster.

Turn to your *Information Processing Activities* workbook to learn more about your assignment in the Finance and Administration Division of DYNAMICS.

pouch, alphabetized expanding folder, lightweight mail basket, or mail cart as you make your rounds through the office. You should arrange the bundles according to the route you will take.

*When Brad is finished sorting the mail, he places rubber bands around each stack, creating a separate bundle for each worker. Then he places the bundles in a mail cart in the order he will deliver them. Since Mrs. Wesley's workstation is his first stop, Brad places her mail bundle at the front of the cart. Using this procedure, Brad can distribute the mail quickly.*

### In Large Companies

Many companies have mailrooms to take care of the large volume of incoming mail often received several times each day. A mailroom is a designated area easily accessible to postal workers who deliver the mail to the company. Here you are likely to find specialized equipment to aid mailroom workers in following procedures for opening, sorting, and delivering the mail. Such equipment typically includes electric envelope openers, sorting units, and automated delivery systems.

Procedures and equipment for processing incoming mail are described here. In Topic 2, you will learn about procedures and equipment for processing outgoing mail.

**Illus. 14–2.** This mailroom worker is sorting incoming mail from the post office and from private mail services.

### Opening Envelopes

In some companies, mailroom workers open all the mail (except envelopes marked *Personal* or *Confidential*), before delivering it. An electric envelope opener often is used for this task.

An electric envelope opener trims a narrow strip off one edge of each envelope. The amount trimmed off is very small so that there is little risk that the contents of the envelope will be damaged. To reduce the chances of cutting the contents, tap each envelope on the table before placing it in the opener, so the contents will fall away from the edge that you are trimming.

### Sorting Mail

A wide variety of bins and compartments is used to sort the mail. Each bin or compartment is labeled with the name of an individual or department within the organization. To sort the mail, you place each piece of mail in the appropriate container.

Companies with a huge amount of incoming mail have found that they can save time and energy by using a rotary unit. The unit turns easily, and the worker can remain in one place as he or she sorts the mail.

### Distributing Mail

Once the mail has been sorted, it is ready for distribution. Procedures for delivering mail within the organization vary from company to company. For example:

- A worker from each department comes to the mailroom to pick up the department's mail.
- A mailroom employee carries the mail in a basket or cart from the mailroom to the departments.
- An **automated** delivery system transports mail to the various departments.

*automated:* automatic

**HANDLING INCOMING MAIL FOR YOUR SUPERVISORS**

Some executives ask office workers to process their incoming mail further—after the mail is sorted and before it is distributed. Some supervisors prefer to process their own mail.

*Becky is the receptionist in a small real estate office. For each of her supervisors she opens the mail, removes the contents, and stamps the date and time on each item.*

*Todd works in a florist shop where he only sorts and distributes the mail. His supervisors then process their own mail.*

**Illus. 14–3.** Some large companies use mobile mail carts like the one shown here to distribute the mail. This robot-like cart follows a chemical path on the floor and is programmed to stop at certain locations throughout the building. Employees can then pick up incoming mail and deposit outgoing mail.

Typical procedures for processing incoming mail are described next. Your supervisors will tell you which procedures they want you to follow.

## Opening the Mail

If the mail is not opened when it reaches you, use a letter opener to open all envelopes except those marked *Personal* or *Confidential*. If you mistakenly open an envelope marked *Personal* or *Confidential*, write on the envelope, "Sorry, opened by mistake," and add your initials. Check the outside of each envelope carefully before you open it so you will not make that error often.

If your supervisor wants you to remove the contents from the envelopes, be sure to verify that all enclosures referred to in the correspondence are actually enclosed. If an enclosure is missing, you should note the *omission* in the margin of the letter. You may need to keep a record on file of the missing enclosure if it is a check, money order, cash, or stamps.

*omission:* something left out

Check each letter for the signature and the address of the sender before you discard the envelope. If either is missing on the letter, attach the envelope to the letter, since the envelope usually has a return address on it. Sometimes the envelope is stapled to a document because the mailing date may be important.

### Dating and Time-Stamping

Each incoming mail item should be marked with the current date and time. You can do this with a pen or pencil, a rubber stamp, or a time-stamp machine.

**Illus. 14–4.**

### Separating Mail

As you inspect the mail, put aside the letters that you can answer or handle yourself if your supervisor has instructed you to do so. These would include communications that could be answered by a form letter, circular, or advertisement. Requests for catalogs or price lists can usually be handled this way. However, *inquiries:* questions  your supervisor may wish to see all ***inquiries*** that are received.

### Underlining and Annotating

If your supervisor prefers, you may further assist in handling correspondence by underlining and ***annotating***. However, good *annotating:* writing comments  judgment is necessary here, since too many markings can be annoying.

First of all, underline the key words and phrases in the correspondence that will help your supervisor understand the content quickly. Note the key phrases underlined in Illus. 14–5.

Secondly, determine the answers to questions you can answer and to which your supervisor must respond. Where appropriate, make related comments on the letter. Write the clearly worded answers and/or comments in the margin in legible handwriting. Note the annotations in the margin of the letter shown in Illus. 14–5.

**Illus. 14–5.** The date-time stamp, underlined words and phrases, and annotations indicate that this incoming letter is ready for presentation to the supervisor.

COTTON COOPERATIVE
FIBER SALES & SEED DELINTING    Route 27
Levelland, TX 79336-4081

MAR 19, 19-- 11:30 a.m.

March 17, 19--

Miss Louanne Crecelius
Western Computers, Inc.
680 Polk Avenue
Houston, TX  77002-9602

Dear Miss Crecelius

Our new computer was installed March 14, and we were
impressed with the efficiency of your installation
team. The hardware is installed and working well.

*Copy sent to Mr.
Edwards of
Installation Dept.*

Mr. Ardis, your installation supervisor, advises that
one more terminal be added to maximize the use of the
computer. Please add another X3-11042 component to our
order.

*Order prepared
March 19
Invoice # A41043*

Mr. Ardis also reminded me to make plans for our unit
supervisor, Mary Ann McKay, to attend your New Owner
Workshop April 2-5. Ms. McKay is eager to attend, and
we know this additional education will improve our
utilization of the new equipment. Please send
registration forms to Ms. McKay in the Information
Processing Department.

Sincerely

*Paul W. Adono*

Paul W. Adono
Operations Director

br

*Registration forms sent.
Reservations for Ms. McKay
made March 19.*

## Attaching Related Materials

Copies of previous correspondence, reports, and other related documents may help your supervisor respond to the mail. For example, you may attach the file copy of a letter written to Ms. McKay to the reply you receive from her. Or you may place related items where your supervisor can find them easily. For example, you might retrieve from the files a folder related to an inquiry and place it with the incoming letter on your supervisor's workstation.

### Recording Expected Mail

If your supervisor prefers that you remove the contents from the envelopes and process the mail further, you may learn of promises by senders to mail materials under *separate cover* (in another envelope or package). You should keep a record of these expected items to be sure that you receive them. One type of record for separate cover mail is shown in Illus. 14–6. Notice that the entry on the first line was made on August 2 (Date of Entry). The article promised was a report from Reid Brothers. The correspondence indicated that the report was mailed on August 1 (Date Sent) to A. Weir (For Whom). It was received on August 4 (Date Received). Notice on the last line of the "register" that the tickets mailed on September 22 have not been received yet.

Check the record at least twice a week to see which items have not been received. That way, you can take follow-up action on delayed mail. Workers in the mailroom usually do not keep such records since they do not read the contents of the mail.

**Illus. 14–6.** Register of mail expected under separate cover.

| EXPECTED MAIL | | | | | |
|---|---|---|---|---|---|
| Date of Entry | Article | From Whom | Date Sent | For Whom | Date Received |
| 8-2 | Report | Reid Bros. | 8-1 | A. Weir | 8-4 |
| 8-5 | Micro-cassettes | Foxworth Supply | 8-3 | J. Tyler | 8-10 |
| 8-15 | Computer Printouts | Lehman & Bennett | 8-12 | A. Weir | 8-18 |
| 9-3 | Catalog | Cole Mfg. Co. | 9-1 | H. Rice | 9-7 |
| 9-25 | Benefit Tickets | Jack Hill | 9-22 | H. Rice | |

### Documenting Receipt of Important Mail

Whether you process incoming mail in a small firm or in the mailroom of a large company, you should document the receipt of mail sent by special postal services. For example, you should record the receipt of special delivery, insured, registered, or Express Mail. You may use a form similar to that shown in Illus. 14–7.

| | |
|---|---|
| June 1 | A letter from Fletcher Waggoner refers to computer printouts he sent to Susan Alonso on May 28. |
| June 1 | In a letter dated May 28, Joan Murray states she mailed a catalog to Larry Pokowski. |
| June 3 | In her June 1 letter, Meagan Czander states she sent five copies of a marketing research analysis in another package to Roger Wilcox. |
| June 4 | A letter dated May 30 from Stanley Johnson states he returned a briefcase by parcel post to Elizabeth Koenig. |
| June 5 | The computer printouts from Fletcher Waggoner arrived. |
| June 5 | The marketing analysis from Meagan Czander arrived. |
| June 8 | A letter from Roy Almondson states he sent twelve copies of his company's annual report to Nico Mirandos on June 2. |
| June 10 | The briefcase from Stanley Johnson arrived. |
| June 10 | A notice dated June 6 from Jerrod's Office Supply states that supplies were shipped by parcel post on the same day to Larry Pokowski. |
| June 10 | A letter dated June 7 from Ulin Mitchell states he sent three copies of this year's budget in another envelope to Susan Alonso. |
| June 10 | The annual reports from Roy Almondson arrived. |
| June 11 | The budgets from Ulin Mitchell arrived. |

# Topic 2

## OUTGOING MAIL PROCEDURES

When you have completed your study of this topic, you will be able to

- prepare outgoing mail for delivery by the United States Postal Service
- identify the classes of domestic mail
- explain the various services provided by the USPS
- arrange for courier service
- send materials through an interoffice mail system

Throughout a working day, much communication is sent to those outside the company. For example, you may be asked to send purchase orders to customers, letters to business organizations, and advertisements to potential customers. It is important that outgoing mail be properly prepared.

You have prepared letters for mailing and are acquainted with addressing envelopes, inserting documents, and affixing proper postage. However, you will find that companies have developed specific procedures for completing these tasks in order to handle outgoing mail efficiently.

The way outgoing mail is processed will depend on the size of your company and the procedures designated by the company. If you work in a small office, you probably will be responsible for all the details involved with processing outgoing mail. However, if you work in the mailroom of a large company, you may weigh and seal, apply postage to, and mail envelopes that have been prepared and stuffed by workers in other departments.

The *United States Postal Service* (USPS) processes over 360 million pieces of mail each day! Businesses all across the country use its varied services to send such items as letters, financial reports, computer printouts, architectural drawings, invoices, manuscripts, newsletters, and merchandise to their intended destinations. In some cases, the items are destined for delivery in the same city; in other cases, delivery is to be made to an individual or an organization in a city halfway around the world.

*courier:* messenger

Although most outgoing mail is sent through the USPS, there also are local, national, and worldwide *courier* services available that deliver envelopes and packages. Most courier services guarantee their delivery times. You also may send some mail, though, through the *interoffice mail system* — mail delivered within the company. As an office worker, you need to be acquainted with the mailing options available to you. This topic will help you learn about procedures for processing outgoing mail efficiently.

## PROCESSING OUTGOING MAIL IN A SMALL ORGANIZATION

In a small organization you may be responsible for processing all the outgoing mail, as well as handling other office tasks.

*Linda is the receptionist in a small real estate office. On her workstation is an out basket where all the workers place their outgoing mail. A postal carrier usually picks up and delivers the mail about 10:30 a.m. At 10:00 a.m., Linda prepares an envelope for each item in the out basket. Then she stuffs the envelopes, seals them, weighs them, and applies the appropriate postage. By 10:30 a.m., the mail is ready to be picked up by the postal carrier.*

**Illus. 14–10.** This office worker places outgoing mail in a small mail rack on her desk. The mail is then collected by a mail clerk making regularly scheduled pickups and deliveries.

*drop box:* mail box

The USPS picks up and delivers mail to some organizations twice a day. In other organizations, a postal carrier may come in the morning, but an office worker may take outgoing mail to a post office or *drop box* in the afternoon. You need to know the scheduled times for pickup so you can have the mail ready on time. The USPS recommends mailing as early in the day as possible for the fastest service.

## Folding and Inserting Mail

Once a document is ready to mail, it is a good idea to give it a final check before inserting it in the envelope. Be sure that:

- copies are prepared for mailing, if necessary
- your initials appear below your supervisor's signature on any letter you have signed for your supervisor
- any enclosures noted at the bottom of a letter are actually enclosed in the envelope
- the address on the envelope agrees with the letter address on the letter
- the ZIP Code appears on the last line of both the envelope address and the return address

You usually will insert documents into standard or window envelopes. Folding business documents correctly to fit into envelopes is a simple task. You should take care that the creases are straight and neat. A document should be inserted in an envelope in such a way that it will be in a normal reading position when it is removed from the envelope and unfolded.

### Standard Envelopes

The most common sizes of standard envelopes are 9½″ × 4⅛″ (No. 10) and 6½″ × 3⅝″ (No. 6¾). Illus. 14–11 shows how to fold a letter and insert it into a No. 10 envelope.

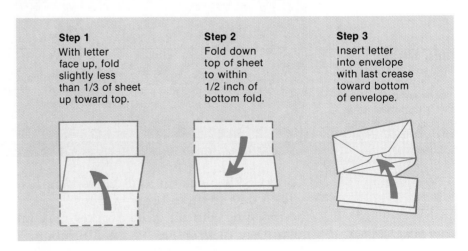

**Step 1**
With letter face up, fold slightly less than 1/3 of sheet up toward top.

**Step 2**
Fold down top of sheet to within 1/2 inch of bottom fold.

**Step 3**
Insert letter into envelope with last crease toward bottom of envelope.

**Illus. 14–11.** Follow these steps to fold an 8½″ × 11″ letter to insert into a No. 10 envelope.

## HANDLING VOLUME MAILINGS

Sending the same items to many people at the same time is a **volume mailing**. For example, a marketing research company may send a questionnaire to all residents in a city to determine their preferences with regard to particular products, such as televisions or breakfast cereals.

### Mailing Lists

*current:* up to date

Mailing lists for volume mail may contain addresses for customers, prospective customers, subscribers, or those who live in certain geographic areas. For a mailing list to save you time, it should always be *current*. That means you should delete, correct, and add addresses as soon as you learn about the changes. The post office recommends having the words ADDRESS CORRECTION REQUESTED printed on all envelopes. When this is done, the post office will *forward* to the proper address the mail addressed to the now-out-of-date address. Then, for a small fee, the post office will send you a card giving the correct address.

*forward:* send on

As companies expand their mailing lists, many are choosing to keep their lists on computer storage media. Some of the advantages of using computer-generated mailing lists are:

- You can quickly retrieve, change, or delete addresses.
- You can easily eliminate duplicate addresses.
- Most software allows you to search and select addresses from a master mailing list to create a smaller list of those to receive a special mailing.
- Some software allows you to use the information stored on computer disks or tapes to print not only the address labels but also the letter address and salutation on form letters.

### Preparing Labels

One method of preparing labels is to type all the addresses on paper in a format that will allow you to photocopy the addresses onto sheets of labels. Each time you have a mailing, you simply photocopy the addresses, peel the labels off the backing sheets, and apply them to the envelopes.

Some companies use computers to print address labels. On page 612, you can see an efficient addressing/labeling/folding/inserting system. With such a system, addresses stored on a diskette can be printed onto sheets of pressure-sensitive labels. *Pressure-sensitive labels* can be peeled from a backing sheet and affixed to an envelope, using light pressure. Some printers can print as many as 7,000 addresses per hour.

You can apply computer-generated address labels to envelopes either manually or automatically, using an automatic labeling device.

**Illus. 14–18.** Large companies may have an addressing/labeling/folding/inserting system to speed up the processing of volume mail.

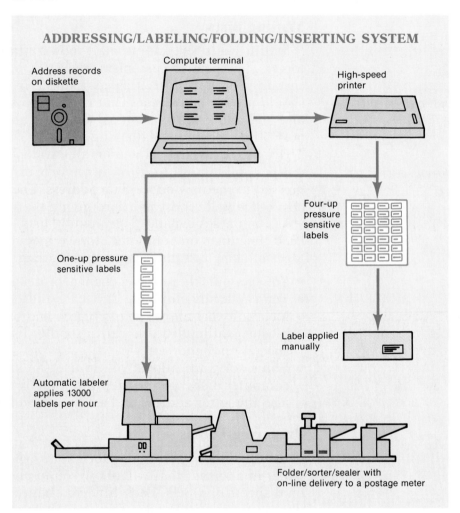

ADDRESSING/LABELING/FOLDING/INSERTING SYSTEM

Address records on diskette

Computer terminal

High-speed printer

Four-up pressure sensitive labels

One-up pressure sensitive labels

Label applied manually

Automatic labeler applies 13000 labels per hour

Folder/sorter/sealer with on-line delivery to a postage meter

## ADDRESS REQUIREMENTS FOR AUTOMATED MAIL HANDLING

The USPS uses automated mail-handling equipment in many of its large postal centers in order to speed mail to its destination. This automated equipment includes optical character readers and bar code sorters. An **optical character reader** (OCR) is electronic equipment that quickly "reads" the address on first class mail and prints a bar code at the bottom of the envelope. During the sorting process, the bar codes are "read" by a bar code sorter and the mail is quickly routed to its proper destination. Not all postal centers are equipped with OCR equipment and bar code sorters; therefore, not all mail you receive will have a printed bar code on the envelope.

If the optical character reader is unable to read an address, the envelope is routed to a manual letter-sorting machine. This, of course, increases the processing time. Some of the reasons why an OCR may be unable to read an address are listed here:

- The address is handwritten.
- The address is not printed or typed in the proper format.
- The envelope may be too small or too large for the OCR equipment to handle. (To avoid this problem, use rectangular envelopes no smaller than $3\frac{1}{2}'' \times 5''$ and no larger than $6\frac{1}{8}'' \times 11\frac{1}{2}''$.)
- The address is not within the OCR read area.
- The complete address is not visible through the panel of a window envelope.

## Address Format

The address should be typewritten or machine printed on the envelope or label. It is very important that the characters be dark, even, and clear. As you learned in Chapter 6, the address is typed or machine printed according to the following format:

- Use all capital letters.
- Block the left margin of the address.
- Omit all marks of punctuation (except the hyphen in the ZIP Code).
- Use the standard two-letter abbreviation for the state (See Reference Section E for a list of these abbreviations.).
- Leave two spaces between the state abbreviation and the ZIP Code.

The post office has an approved list of abbreviations for cities and other words commonly used in addresses. You should use these approved abbreviations if the address is too long to fit on a label.

**Illus. 14–19.** Proper address format for mailing labels as recommended by USPS.

```
MS EMMA JO BERMAN
APARTMENT 6A
132 CANNON GREEN TOWERS
SANTA BARBARA CA  93105-2233


MR ARTURO FUENTES
VICE PRESIDENT MARKETING
ROSSLYN WHOLESALE COMPANY
1815 N LYNN STREET
ARLINGTON VA  22209-6183


MR THOMAS W THIESEN
BATES MICROWAVE COMPANY
4025 EASTWAY DRIVE
CHARLOTTE NC  28205-2736
```

## ZIP Codes

To assure prompt delivery of your mail, always use ZIP Codes. You are already familiar with the five-digit ZIP Code. The first three digits indicate a major geographic area or post office, while the last two digits designate a local post office.

ZIP + 4 is a nine-digit ZIP Code now being used by some businesses. A hyphen and four digits are added to the existing five-digit ZIP Code to help the post office sort the mail more specifically. The first two digits after the hyphen indicate a delivery *sector*. A sector is several blocks within a city, a group of streets, several office buildings, or another small geographic area. The last two digits represent a delivery *segment*, which can indicate one side of a street, one floor in an office building, or specific departments in a firm. ZIP + 4 is a voluntary program.

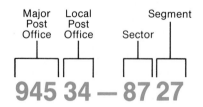

ZIP Code directories for both the five-digit and nine-digit codes can be purchased from the post office. If a directory is not available in the office where you work, you can call the post office to obtain a particular ZIP Code.

## CLASSES OF DOMESTIC MAIL

Domestic mail is distributed within the United States and its territories (such as Puerto Rico, the Virgin Islands, and Guam.) Domestic mail is divided into general classes, which are described in the following paragraphs.

### First-Class Mail

*expeditiously:*
quickly

The USPS requires that you send the following items first-class. That means you pay first-class postage and the post office will handle and transport it *expeditiously*.

- personal correspondence
- handwritten and typewritten messages, including copies
- bills and statements of account
- post cards (privately purchased mailing cards which require postage) and postal cards (cards sold by the post office with postage imprinted on them)
- canceled and uncanceled checks
- printed forms filled out in writing
- business reply mail

**Illus. 14–20.** Various classes of domestic mail must be sorted by postal workers each day.

There is a minimum charge for all first-class mail weighing up to one ounce. An additional charge is made for each additional ounce or fraction of an ounce. If you are sending material in an oversized envelope that does not bear a pre-printed FIRST CLASS notation, be sure to print or stamp FIRST CLASS on the envelope. First-class mail cannot be opened without a federal search warrant.

### First-Class Zone Rated (Priority) Mail

First-class mail that weighs over 12 ounces is referred to as *Priority Mail*. The maximum weight for priority mail is 70 pounds. Priority mail is usually delivered within two to three days. The amount of postage for priority mail is based on the weight of the item and its destination.

### Second-Class Mail

Second-class mail consists of publications such as newspapers and periodicals. To mail material second class, you need authorization from the USPS and must pay a special fee. Second-class mail must bear a notice that it is second class, and it must be mailed in bulk lots. A special single-piece rate is available when a single copy of a publication is mailed.

### Third-Class Mail

Third-class mail is material that is not classified as first-class mail or second-class mail and that weighs less than 16 ounces. Advertising brochures and catalogs often are sent third class. Third-class mail sent in 200-piece quantities or in 50-pound batches may be eligible for reduced postage rates. Third-class mail that is sealed must bear the notation THIRD-CLASS MAIL.

### Fourth-Class Mail (Parcel Post)

Fourth-class mail is also known as *parcel post*. It includes packages, printed matter such as books, and all other mailable matter that weighs 16 ounces or more and is not included in first-, second-, or third-class mail. Parcel post rates are based on the weight of the item and the distance it must travel to be delivered.

A *library rate* may be used by some mailers who send books, printed music, academic papers, and other similar items. The material must be clearly labeled LIBRARY RATE. Library rate is usually used by organizations such as schools, libraries, nonprofit organizations, and veterans' groups.

## Mixed Classes of Mail

Sometimes it is better to send two pieces of mail of different classes together as a single mailing to make sure they both arrive at the same time. For example, you may attach a first-class invoice to the outside of a large package sent fourth class, or you may enclose a first-class letter in a large envelope or parcel. When a first-class letter is *attached*, the postage is affixed to each part separately. When a first-class letter is *enclosed*, its postage is added to the parcel postage on the outside of the package. You should write or stamp the words FIRST-CLASS MAIL ENCLOSED below the postage and above the address. A piece of mixed mail is not treated as first-class mail. The class of mail that the larger piece falls into determines how the mixed mail is handled.

## SPECIAL POSTAL SERVICES

In addition to the regular delivery of first-, second-, third-, and fourth-class mail, special postal services also are available. You must pay a small fee for each of these special services. As a worker who processes outgoing mail, you need to know the different services that are available so you can choose the one best suited to your mailing needs.

## Express Mail

Express Mail offers the fastest delivery service. It guarantees delivery the next day, and sometimes even the same day. All Express Mail travels by regularly scheduled airline flights; therefore, only cities with airports are able to participate in the Express Mail service.

You may send any mailable item weighing up to 70 pounds by Express Mail. Express Mail rates are based on the weight of the item and the distance it must travel. The rates include insurance coverage, record of delivery, and a receipt. If the item is not delivered on time, the sender receives a refund.

### Express Mail Next-Day Service

To obtain Express Mail Next-Day Service, you must take the letter or package to the post office by the time authorized by the postmaster. Tell the postal clerk whether the item should be sent to the destination post office or delivered to the addressee. The postal clerk then fills in a customer receipt. If the item is to be sent to the post office, it will be available for pickup there by 10 a.m. the next day. If it is sent to the addressee, it will be delivered by 3 p.m. the next day.

**Illus. 14–21.** The United States Postal Service, as well as many private courier services, offer guaranteed delivery by a certain day or specific time.

### Express Mail Custom-Designed Service

Many companies that send important mail regularly to the same locations take advantage of the Express Mail Custom-Designed Service. For example, many large companies use the Custom-Designed Service to send payrolls to branch offices. The mail is sent in special pouches and delivery is guaranteed within 24 hours. When you use this service, a customer-service representative from the post office will work with you to design a convenient pickup and delivery procedure.

### Express Mail International Service

Express Mail service is available between cities in the United States and several major foreign countries. An official at the post office can give you details about this service.

## Special Delivery and Special Handling

Special delivery mail is handled with the same promptness given to first-class mail. In addition, it is given immediate delivery within prescribed hours and distances. The fees charged are in addition to the regular postage and vary according to the weight of the letter or parcel. The mail must be marked SPECIAL DELIVERY and is available for all classes of mail.

For a fee in addition to regular third- or fourth-class postage, packages may receive a *special handling* service. Packages marked SPECIAL HANDLING travel with first-class mail between cities. At the post office, special handling packages are processed before regular third- and fourth-class mail, but after priority mail. They are delivered on regularly scheduled trips.

## Registered Mail

Mail can be *registered* to give protection to valuable items such as money, checks, jewelry, stock certificates, and bonds, as well as important items including contracts, bills of sale, leases, mortgages, deeds, wills, and other vital business records. All classes of mail may be registered, but the first-class rate must be paid.

Mail may be registered for any amount. The post office, however, will only pay claims up to $25,000, regardless of the amount for which the package was registered.

You will be given a receipt showing that the post office has accepted your registered mail for transmittal and delivery. For an additional fee, you may obtain a *return receipt* to prove that the mail was delivered.

## Insured Mail

*reimburse:* pay back

Third- or fourth-class mail may be insured for up to $500 against loss or damage. A receipt is issued to the sender of insured mail. You should keep the receipt on file until you know that the insured mail has arrived in satisfactory condition. If an insured parcel is lost or damaged, the post office will **reimburse** you for the value of the merchandise or the amount for which it was insured, whichever is smaller.

## Certificate of Mailing

An inexpensive way to obtain proof that an item was taken to the post office for mailing is to purchase a *Certificate of Mailing*. The certificate is *not* proof of delivery; it serves only as proof that the item was mailed.

## Certified Mail

If any first-class mail (such as a letter, a bill, or an important notice) has no dollar value of its own, yet you want proof of mailing and delivery, send it by *certified mail*. Certified mail provides a receipt for the sender and a record of delivery. However, no insurance coverage is provided for certified mail.

**Illus. 14–22.** Certified mail receipt. From whom was the item sent? Where specifically was the item delivered?

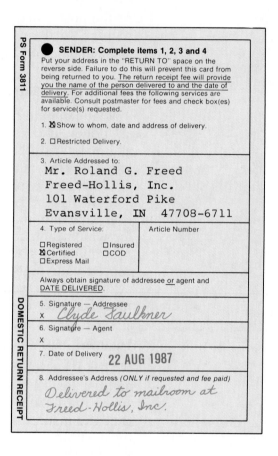

## COD Mail

As a seller of goods, a company may send an order to a buyer and collect payment for the item when it is delivered. Mail sent in this manner is referred to as COD — *collect on delivery*. The seller may obtain COD service by paying a fee in addition to the regular postage. Since fees and postage must be ***prepaid*** by the seller, the seller often specifies that the total COD charges to be collected from the buyer include the postage and the collect-

***prepaid:*** paid in advance

want you to process his or her mail more extensively than just sorting and distributing it. The role you take in processing incoming mail is determined by the size of the company, the volume of incoming mail, and the preferences of your supervisor.

It is important to process outgoing mail as efficiently as incoming mail. There are several options for sending outgoing mail. Companies typically have an interoffice mail system which allows you to send messages to workers *within* the company. To send mail to those *outside* the company, you may be instructed to use a courier service. A courier usually will guarantee a delivery time. There are local as well as nationwide courier services.

The most frequently used option for sending outgoing mail is the United States Postal Service (USPS), which provides a wide range of postal services. Mail must be properly prepared to ensure prompt and accurate delivery by the postal service. Your role in preparing outgoing mail will be affected by whether you work in a small or a large company.

---

### KEY TERMS

mailroom                                         optical character reader

postage meter                                    ZIP + 4

volume mailing

---

**INTEGRATED
CHAPTER
ACTIVITY**

You work as an office assistant at Chaparral Cheese Company. Your supervisor gives you a handwritten list of names and addresses. Your supervisor says, "Here is a list of this month's new mail-order customers. When you key the names and addresses, please group them by state. Use alphabetic order to arrange the customers within each state. Use the all-caps format recommended by the USPS, and be sure to include the appropriate two-letter state abbreviations. "

Word/text processing
equipment can be used to
complete this activity.

**What You Are To Do:**   Key the following customer list. Use the labels provided in *Information Processing Activities* or an 8½″ × 11″ sheet of plain paper. Refer to Reference Section E for a listing of standard two-letter state abbreviations and if necessary, refer to page 614 for an example of the address format recommended by the USPS.

Mail=Order Customers

Mr. Jerry M. Osterman
1906 N. Market Street
Shreveport, Louisiana 71107-4568

Mr. Robert J. Caldwell
373 Pleasant Valley Road
Harrisonburg, Virginia
22801-6624

Miss Linda A. Wood
301 Rue Dauphine
New Orleans, Louisiana 70112-4688

Ms. Debe M. Behun
61 Jefferson Avenue
Newport News, Virginia
23605-7124

Mr. Richard C. Wiegand
12 Roderick St.
Morgan City, Louisiana 70380-1233

Mr. Darryl M. Brandon
50 Sand Dunes Drive
Monterey, California
93940-4524

Mrs. Sherri E. Sempf
101 Pinckney Place
Howell, Michigan 48843-2638

Miss Karen S. Bentz
2563 La Paz Road
Laguna Beach, California
92653-4179

Ms. Sandra B. Sholl
301 Centerville Road
Sturgis, Michigan 49091-8244

Dr. Diane C. Arnold
111 Colorado Ave.
Santa Monica, California
90401-3679

Mrs. Susan A. Curlovich
927 Mt. Royal Circle
Apartment 16-G
Roanoke, Virginia 24014-7634

Miss Judi W. Nalitz
1911 St. Armonds Way
Sarasota, Florida
33577-3912

Ms. Kiki L. Mashusa
555 Sailfish Drive
St. Augustine, Florida
32084-1143

Dr. Ralph D. Narcissi
95 Staples Mills Road
Richmond, Virginia 23230-4433

**Illus. 15–1.** When you answer the telephone, it is important to remember that you represent the company for which you work.

### Communicate Positively

*animated:* full of life

*monotonous:* one tone

How do you communicate positively with your voice? The easiest way is to speak with enthusiasm. An *animated* voice reflects interest in the caller. A *monotonous* voice suggests indifference and inattention.

## Your Speech Patterns

*project:* send out

Your speech patterns affect the impression you *project* to callers. While you may have a pleasant tone of voice, communication is difficult if the caller cannot understand your words. Follow these suggestions for good telephone speech:

### Pronounce Each Word Distinctly

Try not to mumble or run words together. For example, say "what do you" instead of "whaddaya."

### Speak at a Proper Speed

You have probably called a company where the receptionist said the company name so quickly that you wondered whether or not you had reached the correct number! Speak slowly enough so that the caller can understand what you are saying. This is especially true if you are giving detailed or technical information.

### Your Vocabulary

State your ideas in simple terms and use standard English to express yourself. Choose words that are tactful and positive. When you do not understand a caller, do not respond with "Huh?" Instead, ask the caller, "Would you please repeat your last statement?"

### Your Attitude

You learned in Chapter 4 that a positive attitude is a key to success. Your success in being able to handle incoming calls courteously will depend on your ability to maintain a positive attitude. If one of your main responsibilities is to answer the telephone, do not regard the phone as an interruption. Instead, view it as an opportunity to be helpful, thereby giving callers a favorable impression.

## PROPER TELEPHONE TECHNIQUES

You have seen how your voice, your speech patterns, your vocabulary, and your attitude all affect a caller's impression of you and your company. To strengthen that positive impression still further, you should use the telephone techniques described in the following paragraphs.

### Answer Promptly

Answer all incoming calls promptly and pleasantly. If possible, answer the telephone after the first ring. At the same time you reach for the receiver, reach for your pen or pencil and a notepad or message form. You must be ready to take messages immediately.

### Identify Yourself

A telephone conversation cannot begin until the caller knows that the correct number has been reached. Immediately identify your company, department or office, and yourself:

*Not Proper:*   *"Hello," or "Yes?" (These greetings do not give any identification.)*

*Proper:*   *"Skyway Airlines, Linda Perkins." (Use this greeting when you are answering an outside line.)*

Proper: "Baggage Claim, Ben Sorrells speaking." (Use this greeting when you are answering in a company where all calls are routed through a switchboard operator or a receptionist who has already identified the company.)

Proper: "Mrs. Turner's office, Pat Wells speaking." (Use this greeting when you are answering the phone for a supervisor.)

**Illus. 15–2.** Always be prepared to take a message when you answer the telephone.

## Assist the Caller

Your job is to help the caller as efficiently as you can. Be careful not to *assume* you know what the caller wants. Instead, listen attentively to the caller's questions and comments. If you believe it will take more than a minute or two to find the information the caller needs, do not keep the caller waiting. Ask if you may call back after you locate the information. It is important that you *conscientiously* follow through on any promise you make to return a telephone call.

**conscientiously:** with a sense of duty

Make sure that you give accurate information to callers. If you do not know the answer to a question, admit that you do not know. Then either transfer the call to someone who can answer the question or tell the caller that you will obtain the information and call back.

**Illus. 15–3.** This office worker is assisting the caller by providing accurate information in response to the questions asked.

### Conclude the Call

As a general rule, the person who places a call is the one who should end it and hang up first. By following this rule, you avoid making the caller feel as if the conversation were "cut off" before he or she was ready to hang up.

It is also a good habit to use the caller's name as you end the conversation. For example: "Yes, Mrs. O'Sullivan, I'll be sure to put the catalog in the mail today," or, "Thank you for calling, Mr. Salzen. I'll be sure to give Ms. Driscoll the information." Such a practice personalizes the conversation.

## EFFECTIVE TELEPHONE PROCEDURES

As you answer incoming calls, you may find it necessary to screen calls, give information, take messages, transfer calls, place callers on hold, or handle a disconnected call. Effective procedures for managing each of these situations are presented here.

### Screening Calls

In some offices, you may be asked to *screen* the incoming calls. Screening is a procedure used to determine who is calling and, at times, the purpose of the call. Screening can save you and the caller time because you will be able to transfer the call immediately to the proper person. You can learn the caller's name by asking questions such as:

*May I say who is calling?*    *May I tell Ms. Grayson who is calling?*

Sometimes callers refuse to give their names. If it is the policy of your company to identify each caller by name before transferring the call, you must be courteous, yet firm:

| | |
|---|---|
| *Office Worker:* | *"Hartford, Grayson, and Thatcher — Mary Timms speaking."* |
| *Caller:* | *"I want to speak to Ms. Grayson."* |
| *Office Worker:* | *"May I say who is calling?"* |
| *Caller:* | *"My name is* **irrelevant**. *I just want to talk with Cora Grayson."* |
| *Office Worker:* | *"I'm very sorry, sir, but I am unable to transfer a call without first identifying the caller."* |
| *Caller:* | *"I understand. I'm Jess Evans, Cora's uncle."* |

**irrelevant:**
unimportant

## Giving Information

There may be times when executives are out of the office for several days. In these situations, you must tactfully communicate to the caller that the executive is not available:

| | |
|---|---|
| *Caller:* | *"May I please speak with Mr. Lesinski? This is Henry Robbins from Central Realty."* |
| *Office Worker:* | *"I'm sorry, Mr. Robbins, but Mr. Lesinski is out of the office until Friday. I'm Mr. Lesinski's secretary. Perhaps I could help you, or may I have him call you when he returns?"* |

When executives are unavailable to receive calls, give the caller enough information to explain the executive's absence without revealing unnecessary details. If you give the caller too many details, you may be providing a competitor with valuable information or *divulging* personal information to customers:

**divulging:** revealing

| | |
|---|---|
| *Proper:* | *"Mr. Hollis is in a meeting now, but he should be available this afternoon. May I take a message or have him return your call?"* |

*Not Proper:*     "Mr. Hollis is in a meeting with the board of directors right now. Since they're trying to decide whether or not to sell the Ohio plant, it should take all morning. May I take a message or have him return your call later this afternoon?"

*Proper:*     "Mrs. Cibulas will be in tomorrow morning. May I ask her to call you then?"

*Not Proper:*     "Mrs. Cibulas has taken the afternoon off to play golf. May I take a message or have her call you tomorrow?"

**Illus. 15–4.** It is quite common for an executive to be in a meeting and unable to take a call. When this occurs, ask the caller if you can take a message or have the executive return the call.

## Taking Messages

You probably will have a pad or printed message forms for recording telephone messages. When you record a message, be sure that it is accurate and complete. Verify names and telephone numbers with the caller. Write the message in legible handwriting so you do not waste time rewriting it later. Each message should include the following:

- the date and exact time of the call
- the name of the caller and the caller's company (Check the spellings of any names about which you are uncertain.)
- the telephone number, including the area code if it is a long distance call (Repeat the number to verify it with the caller.)
- the details of the message
- the initials of the person who wrote the message

Receptionist A: "Can I tell Ms. Clausen who is calling?"

Receptionist B: "I am very sorry that Mr. Nielson ain't here. Him and Miss Wenloff are downtown at a meeting."

Receptionist C: "Copies of the report were sent to them who was at the meeting."

Receptionist D: "I don't know nothing about the equipment on the fourteenth floor."

Receptionist E: "Between you and I, we should be able to key and print the five tables in time for the conference."

Receptionist F: "Yes, I understand what you want; I just don't know to who to give the request."

Receptionist G: "He is the one which planned the meeting."

Receptionist H: "It's me! Don't you recognize my voice?"

Receptionist I: "All of the group is going."

Receptionist J: "It will be necessary for each employee to report what they spent."

## APPLICATION ACTIVITY

You work for Bateman-Humphries, Inc., a company which provides financial planning services to individuals and businesses. In addition to the company officers (Juanita Bateman and Martin Humphries) and one administrative assistant, there are two general office assistants and a word processing specialist. As one of the general office assistants, you answer incoming calls for Miss Bateman and Mr. Humphries when the administrative assistant is unable to do so.

At 9:00 a.m. you are told that Miss Bateman and the administrative assistant are attending an integrated office information systems seminar. The seminar ends at noon, and they should be back in the office by 1:00 p.m. Mr. Humphries is in conference with a client and expects to be unavailable until at least 10:00 a.m. Mr. Humphries has asked that you record the figures Jim Stevens will provide when he calls.

What You Are To Do: Use the message forms provided in *Information Processing Activities* or prepare forms similar to the one shown on page 637. Record the messages for Miss Bateman and Mr. Humphries, which follow. Be sure the messages are accurate and that your handwriting is legible. Use the current date.

9:15 a.m.  Caller:  "I need to speak with Miss Bateman, please."

You:  "Miss Bateman is out of the office now. May I take a message?"

Caller:  "This is Ben Ivey with Hughes Development Company. Please ask her to call me when she returns."

You:  "May I take your number?"

Caller:  "556-6341."

You:  "Thank you, Mr. Ivey. I'll give Miss Bateman your message."

9:30 a.m.  Caller:  "I'd like to speak to Martin Humphries. This is George Rosen."

You:  "I'm sorry, Mr. Humphries is with a client right now. May I take a message?"

Caller:  "No . . . tell him I'll call back around four this afternoon."

You:  "May I take a number where you can be reached in case he is able to return your call before four o'clock?"

Caller:  "No, I'm calling from a pay phone at the airport. My flight leaves within an hour. Just tell him that I called about the Symonds Account and will call back this afternoon."

9:55 a.m.  Caller:  "This is Jim Stevens from Hittner Accountants in Chicago. Martin Humphries called yesterday and asked for interest figures that I did not have readily available. He said I could call today and give the figures to you."

You:  "Yes, Mr. Stevens, that is correct. I was told you would be calling."

Caller:  "Good. Here are the figures: We earned $5,051 in interest from First American Bank, $997 from Fidelity Savings and Loan, and $2,690 from the Stevens Children's Trust. We paid $3,273 in interest to Buckeye Mortgage Company and $514 in interest to Bright Savings and Loan."

You:  (You verify all amounts by repeating the figures to Mr. Stevens.) "May I have your number in case Mr. Humphries has any questions?"

Caller:  "Of course. It's Area Code 312, 555-8067, Extension 211."

10:45 a.m.  Caller:  "This is Karen Sumida with Brinson & Associates. I'd like to speak with Miss Bateman, please."

You:  "I'm sorry, Miss Bateman is out of the office. May I take a message?"

Caller:  "Please ask her to call me as soon as possible. My number is 745-9988. Tell her that I want to discuss plans for refinancing the corporate loan that we discussed last week."

# OUTGOING TELEPHONE COMMUNICATIONS

When you have completed your study of this topic, you will be able to

- describe the kinds of telephone directories you will find useful
- place local and long-distance domestic calls
- place international calls

Workers in a company make outgoing calls for a number of reasons. Calls often are placed to request information, confirm an appointment, or give instructions. Placing a telephone call to a co-worker or another business is often less time-consuming than writing a letter.

Local telephone service frequently is provided by a Bell operating company, although there are also other companies offering local telephone service. Long-distance calls outside the service area of the local telephone company may be handled by a long-distance company, the largest being AT&T. Other companies such as MCI, LDS, and Sprint, offer similar services. Therefore, businesses today have an opportunity to select the long-distance company that can best meet their needs.

As an office worker, you sometimes may need to place outgoing calls. Perhaps you must arrange with a courier to have a package picked up. You might need to obtain flight information for an executive. Maybe you have been asked to check on an order for office supplies. You also may place local and long-distance calls to customers. You may even be asked to place international calls to companies or individuals overseas.

In order to make outgoing calls efficiently and economically, you should be aware of the many services offered by the telephone company or companies that provide local and long-distance service to your office. You should also be aware of the kinds of information contained in printed telephone directories so you can locate what you need quickly.

## TELEPHONE DIRECTORIES

Local telephone companies usually provide directories to their customers free of charge. If your office makes frequent calls to certain large cities, you also may have access to some out-of-town directories. Most directories include a *Customer Guide,* complete with a table of contents. You should become familiar with this contents page so that you can find needed information rapidly. You may also keep a personal directory or a listing of frequently used telephone numbers.

These directories are valuable references. You should keep them close at hand so that you can use them efficiently.

### Local Telephone Directory

You will use this directory when you want to find the telephone number of a business or individual in your local area. Unless a local business or individual has an unlisted number or has recently moved into the area, you should be able to find the number listed. Otherwise, you may call the operator for assistance.

### *White Pages*

This directory lists in alphabetic order the names and telephone numbers of individuals, businesses, and government agencies. In some cities, the white pages may be divided into two sections. The first section lists personal names and numbers only, while the second section lists only business names and numbers. Sometimes these sections are each contained in separate books. When personal and business numbers are divided, another section called the *Blue Pages* may also be included. The Blue Pages serve as an easy reference for locating telephone numbers of government offices and other helpful numbers such as those of the chamber of commerce, consumer protection, and weather service.

Government agencies are listed in the directory according to their level of government—federal, state, county, and city. For example, to find the telephone number for the Environmental Protection Agency, you would first turn to *U.S. Government.* There, you would find listed alphabetically the various departments, bureaus, and agencies of the federal government. To locate a state agency, you would first look under the name of the state, as in *Florida, State of.* County and city government telephone numbers are listed under the appropriate county or city name, as in *Allegheny, County of* and *New York, City of.*

**Illus. 15–7.** Government agency listings from a local telephone directory.

**U.S. GOVERNMENT**

**Justice Dept Of—**
**Bureau Of Prisons** U S Post Ofc & Ct Hse ....... 424-2603
**Drug Enforcement Admin** Fedl Ofc Bldg ........ 424-3671
**Immigration & Naturalization Serv Information**
Fedl Ofc Bldg................................ 424-3781
**U S Marshal** U S Post Ofc & Ct Hse............. 424-3594
**US Attorney E Dist**
Fedl Ofc Bldg.............................. 321-3184
**US Attorney So Dist**
U S Post Ofc & Ct Hse ..................... 424-3711
**Labor Dept Of—**
**Office Of Administrative Law Judges**
U S Post Ofc & Ct Hse ..................... 424-3252
**Office Of Labor Management Standards**
(OLMS) 4th & Penn ........................ 321-3121
**Office Of Pension & Welfare Benefit Programs**
5225 Lincoln Way .......................... 321-3125
**Apprenticeship & Training Bureau Of**
Fedl Ofc Bldg.............................. 424-2112
**Consumer Price Index—**
Recorded Message.......................... 424-2349
**Occupational Safety & Health Admin (OSHA)**
Fedl Ofc Bldg............................. 424-3784
OSHA Lab.................................. 424-3721
**Wage & Hour Div** Fedl Ofc Bldg ............... 424-2942
**Occupational Safety & Health Admin (OSHA)**
Toll Free-Dial 1 And Then .................. 800-753-1708

## Yellow Pages

The Yellow Pages contain an alphabetic listing of businesses only. The businesses are arranged according to the services they provide or the products they sell. For example, to find a telephone number for a company that repairs computers, you would look under *Computers—Service and Repair*. If you wanted to find the names and telephone numbers of businesses in the area that might **cater** your company's 50th anniversary dinner, you would look under *Caterers* (as shown on page 646). To find a listing for a company which sells briefcases, you would look under *Luggage*.

*cater:* supply food

Included in the Yellow Pages is an index that lists the headings under which all businesses are categorized. The Yellow Pages can be in the same directory as the white pages or in a separate directory.

## Directory Assistance

If you are unable to locate a telephone number, call the directory assistance operator for help. Turn to the "Directory Assistance" section of your directory to find the operator's number. Be sure to have a pad and pencil ready to record the information the directory assistance operator will give you. Be prepared to tell the operator the city, exact name and street address (if known) of the person or business you need information about.

**Illus. 15–8.** The Yellow
Pages can help you find
out where to obtain a particular product or service.

**Illus. 15–8.** The Yellow Pages can help you find out where to obtain a particular product or service.

## Personal Directory

To save the time it would take to look up numbers in a bulky telephone directory, you might consider keeping a personal directory of frequently used telephone numbers. This is also a good place to record emergency numbers, such as those of the fire department or the police. If you have only a few numbers to record, you may wish to tape the list to the telephone or post it at your workstation. If your list is more *extensive*, you may prefer to use a card file or a small directory with tabs for the letters of the alphabet.

*extensive:* far-reaching

**LONG-DISTANCE SERVICE**

**Long-distance calls** are calls made to numbers outside the service area of your local telephone company. Several factors determine the cost of long-distance service, including the time of day the call is placed, the type of call, and the length of the conversation. To place calls efficiently and economically, you must be familiar with the various long-distance services available.

Several types of long-distance service are available from AT&T and other carriers such as MCI and Sprint. Four common services (direct-dial calls, operator-assisted calls, wide-area telecommunication service, and 800 service) are described here.

## Direct-Dial Calls

Direct-dial calls are those placed without assistance from an operator. To make a direct-dial call, first dial *1*, which gives you access to a long-distance line. Then dial the area code and the number you are trying to reach. (In some places, it is not necessary to dial the area code if it is the same as yours.) If, for example, you work in Lincoln, Nebraska, and wish to call Barkley Distributors in Sacramento, California, you dial 1-916-555-3094:

*1* (for a long distance line)
*916* (the area code for Sacramento)
*555-3094* (the telephone number for Barkley Distributors)

Charges for direct-dial calls begin as soon as the telephone is answered. If you make a direct-dial call and the person you need to speak with is unavailable, your company will still be charged for the call.

## Operator-Assisted Calls

Calls that require the help of an operator to complete them are known as operator-assisted calls. These calls are more expensive than those you dial direct. Person-to-person calls, collect calls, and conference calls are all types of calls which require the assistance of an operator. Each of these is explained here.

**Illus. 15–9.** In addition to helping you place operator-assisted calls, telephone operators can also be of help when problems arise. For example, an operator can credit your account if you accidentally reach a wrong number or call the police in case of an emergency.

### Person-to-Person Calls

**Person-to-person calls** are the most expensive type of operator-assisted calls. To place a person-to-person call, dial 0 (operator), the area code, and the telephone number of the individual or business you are calling. When you have finished dialing, the operator will come on the line:

*Operator:*   *"How may I help you?"*

*Caller:*   *"I want to make this a person-to-person call to Andrew Verreng. The last name is spelled V as in Victor, e-r-r-e-n-g."*

*Operator:*   *"One moment, please."*

Charges for the call begin only after the person you have asked for comes on the line. If that individual is not available, you will not be charged for the call. If you wish, you may ask the operator to continue trying to complete the call. Once the party is on the line, the operator will call to inform you that your call can be completed.

### Collect Calls

The charges for a collect call are billed to the telephone number being called, not to the number from which the call was placed. To place a collect call, dial the operator, the area code, and the number you are calling. When the operator comes on the line, state that you want to place a collect call and give your name. The operator will complete the call and ask the recipient if she or he will accept the charges.

Traveling executives frequently make collect calls to their offices. In some cases, businesses will give their customers or clients permission to call collect.

### Conference Calls

A conference call is placed when it is necessary to talk simultaneously with persons at several different locations. Such calls must be arranged in advance with a *conference operator.* Dial the operator and state that you want to place a conference call. The operator will connect you with a conference operator, who will arrange the call. Be prepared to give the conference operator the names, telephone numbers, and locations (city and state) of the persons who will participate in the call. Be sure to give the exact time the call is to be made. At the designated time, the conference operator will call you and indicate that the other parties are on the line.

Bank vice president in **Washington** whose bank is financing the PARAGON MALL PROJECT.

Advertising executive in **San Diego** whose company is planning the major campaign to announce the PARAGON MALL PROJECT.

Executive in **New York City** who is in charge of the PARAGON MALL PROJECT and who initiated the conference call.

**Illus. 15–10.** Because of the ever-increasing expense of travel, conference calls are being used to replace face-to-face meetings.

## Wide Area Telecommunication Service (WATS)

A company that makes many long-distance calls may find it economical to lease one or more WATS lines. Instead of charging a regular long-distance rate for each call placed, the telephone company charges a set monthly fee plus a discounted rate for each outgoing call. The geographic service area covered will vary.

## 800 Service

*interstate:* between two or more states

*intrastate:* within one state

As a convenience to customers who call long distance, a company may subscribe to 800 Service. This discounted service applies to incoming calls only, and there is no charge to the caller. 800 Service is available on either an **interstate** or **intrastate** basis. For example, a company which services customers from Maine to Florida may subscribe to 800 Service that includes all the states along the East Coast. A company with customers in California only may subscribe to 800 Service for that one state. To determine whether a company in the United States has an 800 number, dial 800 directory assistance at 1-800-555-1212.

## DIFFERENCES IN TIME ZONES

It is important that you be aware of time zone differences when placing long-distance calls. The continental United States and parts of Canada are divided into four standard time zones: *Eastern, Central, Mountain,* and *Pacific* (See Illus. 15–11). As you move west, each zone is one hour earlier. For example, when it is 1 p.m. in Washington, D.C. (Eastern zone), it is noon in Dallas (Central zone), 11 a.m. in Denver (Mountain zone), and 10 a.m. in Los Angeles (Pacific zone). If you are in San Diego and need to speak to a co-worker in the New York regional office, you will need to place the call before 2 p.m. Pacific time (which is 5 p.m. Eastern time). Otherwise, the New York office may be closed.

## INTER-NATIONAL CALLS

Satellites and undersea cables make it possible to place calls to most countries. There are 24 time zones throughout the world. You need to be aware of time differences when placing international calls, just as you do when placing long-distance calls within the United States.

International calls that you dial yourself are less expensive than calls placed through an overseas operator. Additional information about placing international calls can be found in the "Directory Assistance" section of some local directories or by dialing 1-800-874-4000.

# Topic 3

## TELECOMMUNICATIONS TECHNOLOGY

When you have completed your study of this topic, you will be able to

- identify types of telephone equipment and services

- explain how data and images are transmitted

- describe an integrated communication system

In Topics 1 and 2 you learned about voice communication. For years, workers have been using telephones to exchange information orally both with co-workers and those outside the company. But technology also makes it possible for equipment (such as teletypewriters, facsimile machines, word processors, and computers) to exchange information through telephone lines. The most advanced telecommunications systems allow a worker to use a single terminal rather than several pieces of equipment to transmit and receive information in the form of voice, text, data, and images.

Microwaves and satellites are used to transmit information over great distances at high speeds. For example, satellite communications make it possible for you to watch a live television news broadcast originating from across the world.

Telecommunications technology will play an important role in office operations during the coming decade. As costs are reduced and equipment is refined, more and more businesses will look to modern telecommunications technology in order to reduce the amount of time it takes to communicate. The use of telecommunications in any one particular company will be determined by that company's communication needs and its budget.

Major changes are taking place in today's offices as businesses find new and better ways of solving their communications problems. As an office worker, you will need to understand the technology, equipment, and procedures involved in transmitting information from one location to another. You must be adaptable and flexible as new equipment is acquired and procedures are revised.

## TRANSMITTING INFORMATION

When you call someone on the telephone, your voice travels through the telephone wires as electronic *analog signals.* The telephone "understands" analog signals and is able to translate them into voices. On the other hand, machines such as teletypewriters and computers, which send and receive data and images, "understand" electronic *digital signals.* This equipment translates the digital signals into words and images that can be either displayed, printed, or stored. Digital signals are clearer and transmit faster than analog signals. In the future, it is expected that all equipment will transmit only digital signals. Voice, text, data, and images can be transmitted by electrical impulses through copper wires or as light signals through thin fiberglass cables called *fiber optics.* Fiberglass cables transmit signals faster and clearer than copper wires so they are replacing copper wires for transmitting information.

Suppose you want to send data from one computer to another via telephone lines. First, the data at the sending station must be converted from digital signals (which the computer understands) into analog signals (which the telephone understands). The data can then travel through the telephone lines to the receiving station. At the receiving station, the analog signals must be converted back into digital signals so the receiving computer can understand the data. A modem is a device used to convert one type of signal to another. A modem can be a separate device (such as that shown in Illus. 15–13) or it can be installed inside the computer.

**Illus. 15–13.** Information is easily transmitted from one computer to another via telephone lines.

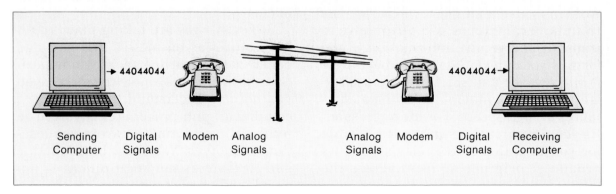

| Sending Computer | Digital Signals | Modem | Analog Signals | | Analog Signals | Modem | Digital Signals | Receiving Computer |

are a speedy and economical way to send longer messages. Charges are based on groups of 50 words. A mailgram is less expensive than a telegram, and delivery is guaranteed by the next day.

**Illus. 15–20.** Mailgrams are used for longer messages. Mailgrams are popular because they are faster than sending a letter through the USPS, yet less expensive than a telegram.

## Teletypewriters

A teletypewriter is a keyboard input device that sends data to remote locations via telephone lines, fiber optic cables, microwave dishes, and space satellites. Western Union uses teletypewriters to input telegrams. Individual businesses sometimes prefer to have their own private-line teletypewriters. A major advantage of owning a private-line teletypewriter is that a company can send and receive information, regardless of the time of day, from its own offices. A private-line system, for example, might be used by a large company with branch locations throughout the country or all over the world.

Companies may also subscribe to a worldwide teletypewriter service called Telex. This service, available through Western Union, makes it possible to transmit and receive information from other Telex subscribers and to access information from Western Union's *InfoMaster* computer system.

If a company is a Telex subscriber, a worker can use the teletypewriter in the office to keyboard and send a telegram directly to Western Union. Telegram rates are lower because a Western Union operator did not have to key the message.

## Facsimiles

Facsimile (or *FAX*) is a popular and relatively inexpensive form of electronic mail. Because facsimile machines transmit not just the text of a message or document, but also photographic images, they are often referred to as *telecopiers*. FAX technology is easy to understand. The sending facsimile machine scans a page and encodes (electronically "takes a picture of") the information to be sent. The information is transmitted over telephone lines to a receiving facsimile machine in less than a minute. The receiving unit then reproduces the page, including text, drawings, logos, and signatures.

As long as the machines at the sending and receiving ends are compatible, businesses can use the facsimile equipment to communicate with each other. Businesses with branch locations find this form of communication convenient, because communication is maintained less expensively than by telephone and more speedily than by regular mail.

*Luisa works for an engineering design firm that has branch offices located in 14 states. Luisa is the FAX operator at her branch office. This morning she received a typical assignment. One of the engineers needed to get a copy of several design changes to a supervisor at another branch office as soon as possible. The engineer also had a handwritten note explaining the changes that was to be sent along with the design changes. Using the facsimile equipment, Luisa was able to send both the design changes and the handwritten note to the supervisor at the other branch office within minutes.*

**Illus. 15–21.** FAX technology enables documents to be transmitted within the same building or around the world! A portable facsimile machine is shown here.

## Communicating Word Processors

Word processors can be electronically connected within a network to send and receive information. For example, a document can be keyed in one location and transmitted electronically to another location, where it can be edited, printed, and stored for future reference. Some word processors can also communicate with teletypewriters.

## Computer-Based Messaging Systems

*Computer-based messaging,* also known as *electronic messaging,* is similar to voice messaging because workers have electronic "mailboxes." Instead of hearing a voice message, however, the recipient views a screen where the message is displayed. A blinking light at the computer terminal signals a worker that a message is in the mailbox. The recipient may view the message, forward it, or erase it. Common computer-based messaging system options are listed in Illus. 15–22.

**Illus. 15–22.**
Computer-based messaging systems provide the user with a variety of options.

| BASIC COMPUTER-BASED MESSAGING OPTIONS | | | |
|---|---|---|---|
| Compose | Sender keys a simple message using a computer keyboard. | Read | Receiver views message using a computer terminal and has the option to print a hard copy, if desired. |
| Edit | Sender revises the message before transmission. | | |
| Send | Message is transmitted to one or more "mailboxes." | Store | User files message for a short time or stores message permanently. |
| Scan | Receiver checks messages for sender's name, subject, and time stamp. | Retrieve | User recalls message from storage. |

A major benefit of using an electronic messaging system is that paperwork is reduced and messages are transmitted quickly. To send a message, you use a computer keyboard. A series of prompts and menus on the screen guide you through the process of sending an electronic message. The message is then transmitted in a matter of seconds to the intended recipient's electronic mailbox.

## TELECONFER-ENCING

In Topic 2, you learned about the simplest form of teleconferencing—a conference call, or *audio conference*. You will recall that while the participants in a conference call can hear one another's voices, they cannot see one another, nor can they exchange documents or images of any kind. In Chapter 12, you learned about the management tasks related to a video conference. A *video conference* enables the participants both to see one another and to use visual aids.

A technique used in conjunction with teleconferencing is the *electronic blackboard*. Images drawn on a special board can be transmitted to a screen or terminal in another location. Highly advanced electronic blackboards have a device which scans the images and prints hard copies of the information presented on the board.

**Illus. 15–23.** An "electronic blackboard" sends blackboard writing to remote TV screens or terminals.

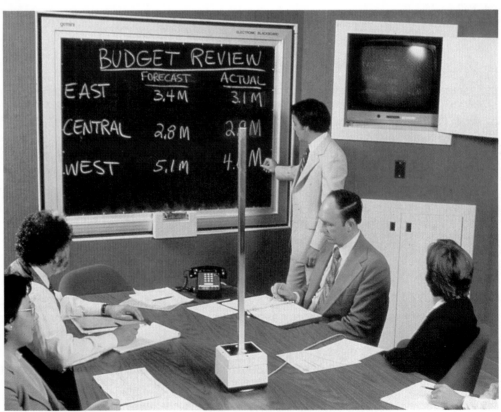

## KEY TERMS

| | |
|---|---|
| telecommunications | wide area networks |
| screening | voice mail |
| long-distance calls | electronic mail |
| direct-dial calls | teletypewriter |
| operator-assisted calls | Telex |
| person-to-person calls | facsimile |
| modem | IVDT |
| local area network | |

**INTEGRATED CHAPTER ACTIVITIES**

To complete the following role-playing activities, you will need the assistance of a classmate. Your teacher will divide your class into learning teams of two students each. Once the assignments have been made, decide who will play the role of the caller and who will play the role of the person who answers the call in each of two telephone situations.

**What You Are To Do:**

A. You and your learning partner will work together to create a script for each of the two telephone situations that follow. Key the dialogue on plain paper. Both you and your learning partner should have a copy.

B. Role-play the first situation, following the script.

C. Evaluate your partner's telephone techniques. Use the forms provided in *Information Processing Activities* or follow your teacher's instructions for writing your comments on plain paper. (**NOTE:** While you are evaluating your partner, your partner will be evaluating you.) Then exchange evaluation sheets and review the evaluation of your telephone techniques.

D. Role-play the second situation, following the script. Complete the evaluation process as you did in Step C. Have you improved any poor techniques that were identified while role-playing the first situation?

Word/text processing equipment can be used to complete this activity.

## Situation 1

*The receptionist at Shuman Brothers department store receives a call from Timothy Wolinsky, who wishes to speak to Miss Holthaus, the store manager. The receptionist is aware that Miss Holthaus is visiting several departments throughout the store and is not in her office. The receptionist also knows that Mr. Wolinsky works for Lee, Wolinsky, and Jones — the accounting firm that handles the department store's tax records. The receptionist puts Mr. Wolinsky on hold while she uses the in-house paging system to try to locate Miss Holthaus. Another employee answers the page and informs the receptionist that Miss Holthaus has left the store, but will return after 2:00 p.m. Mr. Wolinsky says he will call back at 2:30 p.m.*

## Situation 2

*The order clerk in the order department of the Seal-Rite Packaging Company receives a call from Mr. Adam Foster of Sandalwood Breakfast Foods. Mr. Foster wants to know if the order he placed on October 5 has been shipped yet. He had expected to receive the shipment last week. The order clerk checks the records and finds that the order was shipped on October 8 and should have arrived at Sandalwood Breakfast Foods by now. The order clerk relays that information to Mr. Foster and suggests that he call back if the order does not arrive within another week. It may be necessary for Seal-Rite to replace the shipment. Mr. Foster is not happy with the delay, but he is willing to wait another week with the hope that the shipment will arrive.*

# PRODUCTIVITY CORNER

**Blake Williams**
*OFFICE SUPERVISOR*

## THE TELEPHONE'S RINGING —AGAIN!

DEAR MR. WILLIAMS:

Last month I was hired as an office worker in an auto parts supply store. My duties include keying invoices and correspondence, keeping the books, and answering the phone. I am interrupted <u>often</u> by the phone. To compound the problem, my supervisors always seem to misplace the messages I leave. Mr. Parra is especially bad about losing messages. More than once he has said something like, "Sylvia, I can't find that message from Peter Torres. Please look up his number in the phone book." So I'm interrupted twice about the same matter! — SYLVIA IN SHREVEPORT

DEAR SYLVIA:

Did you notice the contradiction in your letter? You said that your job <u>includes</u> answering the telephone, but then you said that you are <u>interrupted</u> by the telephone. Remember, answering the telephone contributes to the smooth functioning of your office just as much as the other tasks you perform. If you regard telephone calls as interruptions, you probably feel annoyed each time the phone rings. You may even communicate that annoyance through your voice while you talk with a caller. Feeling annoyed also can reduce your willingness to work efficiently. Your overall productivity suffers as a result.

Suppose you are keying a letter when the telephone rings. Instead of resenting the call, remember that answering the telephone is a high work priority for you. The telephone does not keep you from doing your job — it <u>is</u> your job! Giving attention to incoming calls is an important task. When the telephone rings, mentally note where you are with the letter you are keying. Then, switch your full attention to the caller. When you have completed the conversation, return to keying the letter you had put aside.

You must be helpful when your supervisors request information about a particular telephone message. Consider buying a spiral-bound pad of telephone message forms that includes duplicate-copy forms. Each time you record a message, you also record a copy of it. When you give the original to your supervisor, a copy remains in your spiral pad. If one of the supervisors loses a message, you can quickly refer to your own copy. — BLAKE WILLIAMS

# PERSONAL AND CAREER DEVELOPMENT

# Chapter 16

# Advancing Your Career

In this final chapter, the spotlight shifts to you and to the tasks of job seeking and career planning. In addition to valuable office skills, your personality goes with you when you enter the office as an employee. Knowing your own personality, including your strengths and weaknesses, will be of critical importance to you as you consider job possibilities.

You learned how important good human relations are in the office when you studied Chapter 4. You learned that your behavior contributes to the atmosphere of the office in which you choose to work. In this chapter, you will be asked to step back and think of yourself in a somewhat more basic manner. You will be asked to consider the value of self-acceptance, the process of self-assessment, and the nature of mature behavior. Knowing your-self and your potential for growth will be invaluable strengths as you enter the world of work on a full-time basis.

Attention also will be given to the practical tasks of developing a career strategy and getting a job. Common job application procedures will be outlined for you. Job-seeking knowledge will help you make decisions about your job choice with confidence and competence. Also, you will be introduced to how you can guide your own professional growth on the job.

The objectives of this chapter are to

- aid you in understanding and assessing your own personality

- introduce you to the practical tasks of career planning and job hunting

# Topic 1

## FOCUS ON YOU

When you have completed your study of this topic, you will be able to

- explain why self-acceptance is important to personal growth
- describe the value of self-assessment
- identify key components of one's personality
- explain the value of a mature personality

Psychologists talk of a person "becoming" as a way of emphasizing the limitless possibilities for personal growth. The unique complex of characteristics that distinguishes one person from another is called personality. You are undoubtedly aware of your own ability to change your personality. Possibly, from your efforts to change, you know that there is nothing absolutely fixed about who you are, what you believe, and how you behave. There is perhaps no more magical characteristic of human beings than that which allows them to shape their own personalities.

You may recognize, then, that you *can* change your personality. There are others, though, who deny the possibility of change. You have probably heard comments such as, "Well, that's just the way I am; I can't change me," or "I wish I could be different, but it is too late now to try to change."

679

Such comments are made by individuals who do not realize the power they have to make changes or who, in truth, do not want to change. Individuals who insist that change is beyond their control are not likely ever to become the persons they are capable of becoming. On the other hand, individuals who know that they possess the power to change can quietly and sensibly modify their attitudes, beliefs, and behaviors to attain their own goals for a satisfying life. Human beings can make deliberate efforts to improve aspects of their personalities.

## SELF-ACCEPTANCE

*scornful:* filled with disrespect

At the core of your mental health is your attitude toward yourself. When you accept yourself, you have respect for yourself as a person. You are not *scornful* of who you are or what you do. It is generally believed that individuals cannot have a positive view of the world if they do not accept themselves.

### Perceiving Yourself

To learn self-acceptance, you must first have a proper perception of yourself. People who accept themselves have adopted certain basic attitudes that help them understand themselves. To learn self-acceptance, you must:

*deceive:* keep hidden, lie

- be honest with yourself, and not *deceive* yourself about what you really believe
- understand that while you are a unique individual, you also share many of the same wants, needs, and fears with other persons
- develop a deep-seated belief in your own worthiness

### *Being Honest With Yourself*

There is no way for you to accept yourself if you are unable to view yourself honestly. You are behaving in a mature manner when you can face yourself honestly, admitting your weaknesses as well as your strengths.

*Don believed that he was a hardworking student who studied carefully before every examination. When he performed poorly on an examination, however, he blamed the teacher for giving an unfair examination. He had convinced himself that he was hardworking and was unwilling to admit that he simply had not studied for the examination.*

*Kevin wanted to be a good student, but he knew that from time to time he didn't apply sufficient effort to his studies. When he did poorly on an examination, he admitted that he had neglected studying. He concluded that if he really wanted to be a good student, he would have to change his study habits.*

Can you guess how Don's performance differed from Kevin's on later examinations? Don continued to blame others for his poor grades while maintaining the false belief that he was hardworking. Kevin, on the other hand, began to behave like a hardworking student. Don's performance never improved; Kevin earned a high grade in the course.

**Illus. 16–1.** You must be willing to be completely honest with yourself—to identify your strengths as well as your weaknesses—if you are to grow personally and professionally.

### *Being Aware of Others*

It is very easy to believe that you are the only person in the world with deficiencies or weaknesses. Others sometimes don't seem to have the problems that you face. Such thoughts, however, will not solve your problems. Besides, they are usually mistaken.

*Marie was deeply unhappy because she always felt so shy. She resented how her classmates talked with one another and answered questions the teacher raised in class. She wondered why it was so easy for them to interact. She could not understand her fear of others and thought life was unfair.*

*Elsie had suffered from shyness; but by talking with others, she learned that she was not alone in being shy. She also noted that others did not give in to their shyness—they reached out to people. Elsie decided to put aside thoughts of her own shyness and began thinking of others instead. She soon found it much easier to talk with people.*

An awareness that others face problems and overcome them can help you accept yourself. You are not likely to impose unrealistic standards on yourself when you understand that everyone has both strengths and weaknesses in their personalities.

### Being Aware of Your Own Worthiness

Self-acceptance means that you are willing to live with yourself, faults and all. With such a basic belief, you are able to feel confident and secure. Good emotional health depends, to a considerable extent, on your sense of worthiness as reflected in your confidence and feelings of security.

**Illus. 16–2.** When you accept yourself, you respect yourself as a person. Self-respect gives you a sense of confidence and security when dealing with others.

*Carol is highly self-critical and anxious. She feels worthless and conveys her feelings through her unkind behavior toward others. Carol often complains that no one can be trusted, that people aren't nice, and that others reject her.*

*Betsy, on the other hand, believes that every person is valuable, including herself. She assumes that others are as trusting, secure, and confident as she is. Her behavior toward others reflects these attitudes. In most cases, other persons respond with a reflection of the same attitudes as those Betsy has.*

How you behave toward others influences how others behave toward you. Your own sense of worthiness seems to be a basic factor in determining your behavior. You should strive to develop a realistic, yet positive, attitude about yourself.

## Recognizing Your Separateness

When you accept yourself, you become an individual with choice-making opportunities. You have a *sense of person* — you are able to make choices uninfluenced by pressures from others. This does not mean that you have a closed mind to what others suggest or recommend. It means that although you consider what others are saying, in the end you come to an independent decision that you believe is best. An individual with a sense of person does not justify a decision or a choice by saying, "Well, everyone else was doing it and I didn't want to be different from others." You are able to develop your own awareness of what is right and what is wrong.

*gait:* manner of walking

*Four friends were seated on a park bench one afternoon after school. An elderly man, who was having difficulty walking, came into sight. Three in the group began to laugh at the man's strange **gait**. The fourth one was surprised at the laughter and thought it was unjustified. She did not laugh, and she did not think it was proper for her friends to poke fun at the elderly gentleman. She turned to her three friends and said, "Why are you laughing? That man should be admired, not ridiculed. He is trying to get someplace despite his problem."*

*The young woman did not feel the need to follow the group. She took a risk when she communicated her feelings to the others. In this instance, the three friends listened and realized that their behavior could have been different. However, they could have judged their friend's comment to be ridiculous.*

*authentic:* genuine

You must think for yourself. It is likely that in many instances your beliefs will match those of your friends and acquaintances; in other instances, they will not. Nevertheless, you must treasure your own individuality so that you have a clear sense of who you are. Others generally respect **authentic** persons.

## SELF-ASSESSMENT

*paradox:* contradiction

It may seem something of a **paradox** that you are told that you must accept yourself and then told that you must assess yourself. Remember, though, that accepting yourself does not mean that you will make no further effort to improve aspects of your personality. In fact, accepting yourself is necessary before you can profit from a self-assessment.

### The Value of Assessing Yourself

As you know, you must give conscious attention to anything you want to accomplish. This also applies to changing yourself in ways that will make you happier. You are undoubtedly familiar with the common American tradition of making New Year's resolutions, but have you ever thought about their significance? Frequently, they deal with the hope of improving one's personality. A typical resolution might be, "I am going to be more considerate of my brother and sister this year," or "I am never going to disappoint a friend by overlooking a promise I made," or "I am going to be fair to my friends and not talk behind their backs." Resolutions demonstrate that individuals are unhappy with past behavior, that they believe they can do better, and that they want to establish, in effect, a contract with themselves to change their behavior. Determining what aspects of yourself need your attention is a critical step in the process of making efforts to change. Furthermore, clearly identifying what you do not like gives you clues as to what you must do. Self-assessment implies that you care about how you behave and are willing to make changes.

### Components to be Assessed

There are many components to one's personality. Only a few of the key components, as related to one's behavior at work, will be discussed here.

#### Disposition

One of the most basic components of personality is disposition. **Disposition** is the combination of attitudes that influence the nature of an individual's behavior. Have you ever characterized a friend as having a "sunny disposition"? What you undoubtedly meant was that your friend tends to see the bright side of any situation. In general, individuals at work prefer to associate with those who have good dispositions. If you try to discover what is meant by "good," you may elicit such comments as these:

*moody:* sullen, gloomy

*"A person with a good disposition is calm, friendly, and not **moody** when interacting with me at work."*

*"I think a good disposition means that you enjoy associating with others and can consider other persons' points of view."*

**Illus. 16–3.** You have within yourself the power to shape your own personality. You can make dramatic changes in your attitudes and behavior patterns if you truly want to do so.

### Confidence

A firm belief in oneself and one's abilities is what is meant by *confidence.* It is very important that you strive to develop confidence in yourself. Of course, the self-confidence must be based on realistic assessment, not fantasy.

*Ken studies for all of his courses in a very thorough manner. One day, a teacher asked him to explain to the class some techniques for using time wisely when studying. Ken was so frightened at the teacher's request that he responded, "I'm sorry, I do not know any time management techniques." The teacher was surprised because she knew that Ken was an excellent student. She sensed that Ken did not feel confident when he had to talk before the class. After class, the teacher found a chance to talk with Ken privately. She tried to convince Ken that he did know what he was asked to discuss. After some discussion, Ken promised to speak before the class very soon. The teacher said to Ken, "We must build up your confidence. You are cheating yourself if you don't face life with confidence."*

*Margarita studies in much the same fashion as Ken but does not have Ken's problem. When she is asked to speak to the class, she quickly assesses her knowledge of the topic. If she decides that she has studied the topic carefully, she accepts the teacher's offer to speak to the class. Margarita has confidence when she talks because she has learned to make an accurate evaluation of her own level of knowledge.*

Isn't Ken robbing himself of an opportunity to participate in class? Is he being fair to himself? He undoubtedly knew something worthwhile to communicate to his fellow students. Would he not feel happier if he could respond positively to his teacher's request?

Margarita is fortunate to have self-confidence, which she bases on an accurate assessment of her knowledge. Margarita has developed an objective way of viewing herself and is able to determine whether or not she can manage her teacher's requests.

### *Character*

**integrity:** soundness of character

The basic values and principles that are reflected in the way you live your life are referred to as *character.* Basic values, such as *integrity,* honesty, and sincerity, are implied when someone speaks of a "person's character." A person of good character is one who observes the ethical standards of society. For example, an employee whose work hours end at 5 p.m. is expected to continue working until 5 p.m. even if the supervisor or manager is out of the office. An office worker who leaves the office at 4:30 because the manager is out of town and will not know what has happened would be considered a person of questionable character. A person of good character is one who knows the difference between right and wrong when situations require a judgment. Persons of good character can be trusted because their behavior reflects what they actually believe.

> *Sandy and Eileen became good friends by working together in the same office. When Sandy was asked, "Why do you consider Eileen your best friend?" Sandy answered, "Eileen never lies to me. She is always truthful. She is a good person, and I like knowing her and being her friend."*

### Achievement

Interest and behavior that is guided by a wish to accomplish something is what is meant by *achievement*. Your personality is markedly influenced by your attitude toward achievement. If you have an **intrinsic** wish to do something well, you are likely to develop some key characteristics of a good employee. Among the key characteristics are:

*intrinsic:* basic, natural

- willingness to take initiative
- acceptance of responsibility
- persistence in maintaining high standards

**Illus. 16—4.** Set high, yet realistic standards for yourself. Work hard to achieve your goals and take pride in a job well done.

Persons who choose *not* to achieve encounter many problems. For example, students who fail to give attention to their studies are unsuccessful in passing courses. If they accept jobs, they are often dismissed because they cannot meet the minimum requirements for employment. Furthermore, such persons often become very unhappy because they seem to be failing in many ways. A serious assessment of their own attitudes, though, can sometimes aid in redirecting their behavior.

## How to Assess Yourself

It is a common human reaction to reflect on something you said or did and make a judgment about your behavior. It is also a common human reaction not to face your own evaluation — to hide from or ignore it — when it is not favorable. You will find it valuable, though, to make a deliberate effort to think about your behavior from time to time. You may choose to reflect on those specific aspects of your behavior that you might want to change in some way. A simple strategy to help you change your behavior follows:

1. Identify something that is less than satisfactory in your own personality.
   Example: I wish I were more interested in doing better in class. I don't use the most efficient techniques to complete assignments and study for exams.

2. Think of circumstances or situations that give you clear evidence of the problem.
   Example: I submitted two assignments late. I didn't study for the last test and I failed it.

3. Think of the reasons why you behaved as you did.
   Example: I had a shortsighted view of how I wanted to spend my time. I thought it was more important to spend time with my friends.

4. Think about the different ways you could have behaved.
   Example: I could have begun the assignments earlier if I had refused to go to the ball game. I could have turned down the invitation to play tennis by explaining that I had to study for a test.

# Topic 2

## FOCUS ON YOUR CAREER

When you have completed your study of this topic, you will be able to

- devise a career plan
- prepare a resume
- compose job application letters
- participate in job interviews confidently
- plan how to advance in your career

In Chapter 2, you became aware of the wide variety of job opportunities available to office workers. You will recall that the demand for employees in office occupations is projected to continue at a high level for the next decade. In this topic, attention will be given to the practical tasks of developing a career strategy, getting a job, and advancing in your career. You will learn specific techniques and procedures to follow as you plan your career and search for a job. You also will learn how to project a polished, professional image as you grow professionally and advance in your career.

While there may be many job openings available to you, there may also be many candidates applying for the same position that you want. Therefore, you must convince a prospective employer that you are the best person for the job. Basically, employers want to hire workers who:

- have the ability (skills and knowledge) to do the job
- have the desire (dedication, initiative, and enthusiasm) to do the job
- are able to interact cooperatively with co-workers and others with whom they come in contact
- have a positive attitude toward work
- can adjust to changing work demands

You will want to keep these important characteristics in mind as you explore job possibilities and market your strengths to prospective employers.

Throughout your work life, you may change jobs several times. You may be promoted within the same company or you may be employed by several different companies. Since you may spend most of your adult life in the workforce (about 45 years), begin now to develop the skills and attitudes needed to make intelligent career decisions. To be successful in your career, you must remain flexible and adaptable as advancements in technology bring about changes in the workplace.

## MARKETING YOUR STRENGTHS

How does a prospective employer judge whether or not you possess the qualifications needed for a job? Since the employer may not know you personally, he or she can only make an evaluation based on how well you sell yourself—how effectively you market your strengths. You can highlight your strengths by using a resume, a letter of application, an employment application, your appearance, and your personality. By following the suggestions presented here, you will be prepared to cope with the possible stress of job hunting.

### Develop a Career Strategy

A career strategy involves skillful management of your career. It involves identifying a career goal (for example, owning your own company) and devising a plan to reach that goal. Having a career strategy helps you make career decisions: "Yes, I will apply for this job because it fits into my career strategy." "No, I will not apply for this job because it takes me in a career direction I do not want to go."

#### Set a Career Goal

Your career goal sets the direction for your career strategy. For example, if your ultimate goal is to own your own company, your career plan should prepare you to reach that goal. Actually write down your career goal and refer to it regularly. This keeps the goal foremost in your thoughts and motivates your actions.

#### Devise a Career Plan

Devise a plan to reach the career goal you set. For example, assume that you are a word processing specialist and have set a goal of being promoted to an administrative assistant in three years. Your plan might include taking courses at a community college, reading periodicals that relate to your field, volunteering to perform tasks usually assigned to an administrative assistant, and requesting an appointment with your supervisor to discuss promotion possibilities.

**Illus. 16–6.** You will want to have a career goal in mind and devise a plan to reach that goal. For example, this library assistant wants to become a librarian some day.

### Review Your Career Strategy

Devising a career strategy is not a one-time event. As you achieve each goal, set a new one with a new plan. Achieving goals you set for yourself reinforces your self-confidence. Strong self-confidence improves your attitude, and a positive attitude is what ***propels*** you on to the next goal.

*propels:* pushes forward

Your career strategy may be affected by personal decisions (such as getting married, raising a family, or moving to another city) or by changes in the workplace. You will need to review your career goal and career plans periodically to keep your career strategy ***viable***.

*viable:* workable

## Plan Your Job Search

Once you have a career strategy, you are better prepared to begin your job search. Obviously, one of your career goals includes finding the "right" job. A plan to reach that goal should involve the following steps:

1. Decide which type of job (data entry operator, receptionist, word processing operator, etc.) and which field (law, advertising, medicine, etc.) you would enjoy.
2. Prepare a resume.
3. Search for job opportunities that interest you.
4. Send letters of application and resumes to prospective employers.
5. Interview with companies and take appropriate follow-up action.
6. Begin your new job!

## PREPARING YOUR RESUME

A resume (also called a data sheet or vita) is a concise, well-organized presentation of your qualifications for a job. The prospective employer usually will see your resume before interviewing you. Your resume should make the best possible impression. Proofread your resume carefully. You may have it duplicated on a high-quality copier or an offset press. Whichever method you use, however, be sure that the copies are clean and sharp.

### Categories of a Resume

A resume usually has six categories: career goal, personal information, work experience, education, extracurricular activities, and references. You may include additional categories, such as of-

*competencies:* skills

fice **competencies** and scholastic honors, if appropriate. There is no standard resume format. Therefore, a prospective employer may consider your resume to be a representation of your organizational ability. You may wish to prepare several variations of

*appropriate:* fitting

your basic resume, each one highlighting information **appropriate** for the job you seek. A general guideline is to list the most important information first. Refer to page 698 as you read about common resume categories.

### *Career Goal*

Carefully state your present career goal so a prospective employer can assess whether or not the position available will help you to achieve your ambitions.

### Personal Information

*marital:* relating to marriage

List the mailing address and telephone number where you can be reached. You need not provide information such as age, date of birth, or *marital* status. However, you may volunteer such information if you choose to do so.

### Work Experience

List in chronologic order the jobs you have had, beginning with the most recent job. For each job, list the name and address of the company, your job title, a brief description of the tasks you performed, and the dates of your employment.

At this stage in your career, your job experience may be quite limited. If you have had no work experience, list any volunteer work you may have done.

### Education

Give the name and address of the high school you attended and the year you graduated. List the courses you took (such as accounting and office procedures) that will highlight your qualifications for the job you are seeking. Also list any scholastic honors or awards, and include any workshops and community classes you may have attended.

### Extracurricular Activities

Extracurricular activities are non-classroom activities, such as participation in a club or community organization. This information reflects your interests and your willingness to do more than just what is required of you.

### References

*credible:* reliable

References are those people who know your academic ability and/or work habits and are willing to recommend you to a prospective employer. A friend in the business community is also a *credible* reference. Before you list anyone on your resume as a reference, however, ask for his or her permission. Provide the reference's name, your relationship to the reference (teacher, employer, etc.), and the reference's address and telephone number. Three references are sufficient. Instead of actually listing their references, some job applicants simply include the statement "Furnished upon request" on their resumes.

```
                                RESUME
                         CONCETTA A. AMELIO


   Career Goal                       A word processing position in a dynamic
                                     environment with a growth-oriented
                                     company.


   Personal Information

   Address                           2113 Sand Road
                                     Albuquerque, NM  87112-0341
   Telephone Number                  505/263-8997

   Work Experience

   New Mexico Beverage               Part-time receptionist; duties include
   2313 Avenue F                     entering data using microcomputer,
   Albuquerque, NM  87112-3723       greeting visitors, and answering the
   (September 19-- to present)       telephone

   Desert Ice Cream Company          Part-time office assistant; duties in-
   3424 Highway 85 NW                cluded conducting tours, operating cash
   Albuquerque, NM  87112-3424       register, and filing
   (May 19-- to August 19--)

   Attendance Office                 Part-time student assistant; duties
   Hayes Junior High School          included recording attendance, operating
   3100 Mountain Road NW             switchboard, and filing
   Albuquerque, NM  87104-3131
   (August 19-- to May 19--)


   Education

   Southwest High School             Diploma pending; graduation, May 30, 19--
   5401 Ferrales Lane NW
   Albuquerque, NM  87104-5401

   Grade Average                     B (3.2)
   Class Standing                    62 out of 572 students

   Business Subjects                 Accounting, cooperative office education,
                                     keyboarding, office procedures

   Machines Operated                 Electronic typewriter, microcomputer,
                                     transcribing machine, calculator


   Extracurricular Activities

   Office Education Association       Member (19-- to present)
                                     Vice president (19-- to present)
   National Honor Society            Member (19-- to present)
   Chorus                            Member (19-- to present)
   Hobbies                           Water and snow skiing; jogging

   References                        Furnished upon request
```

**Illus. 16–7.** A resume tells a prospective employer a lot about you — not only by the information given but also by the overall appearance of the resume and how the information is organized.

### *Plan to Make a Good First Impression*

Since your appearance makes such a vivid impression on an interviewer, you should take time before the interview to plan what you will wear and to handle personal grooming responsibilities. Choose conservative, businesslike attire, even though you may know that some employees wear casual clothing—you are not an employee yet! Women should choose a business dress, conservative suit, or coordinated skirt, blouse, and jacket. Men should choose a dark suit or dress slacks and appropriate jacket.

The night before the interview, spend the necessary time it takes to be sure the clothes you want to wear are clean and in good repair. Try to get a good night's rest so you will look healthy and feel energetic the next day.

### *Learn about the Company*

Find out as much as possible about the company. What is the company's primary product or service? Does the company have branch offices? Does the company sponsor community events? If you are unsure about the proper pronunciation of the company name or the name of the interviewer, call ahead of time and ask for clarification.

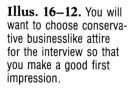

**Illus. 16–12.** You will want to choose conservative businesslike attire for the interview so that you make a good first impression.

### Anticipate Questions

During the interview, you will be asked many questions. You will want to listen carefully to each question and answer it thoughtfully. Therefore, it is wise to anticipate probable questions and be ready with appropriate responses. Some questions interviewers frequently ask are:

- Why does this job opening interest you?
- What do you know about this company and its products or services?
- Why do you want to work for this company?
- What are your strengths as a potential office worker? your weaknesses?
- Do you enjoy working alone or with others? Why?
- What are your career goals?
- Why should we hire you?

In our country, laws have been established to safeguard your right to an equal opportunity for employment. Therefore, questions regarding age, marital status, ethnic background, religious beliefs, and physical and emotional disabilities (unless job-related) are considered illegal. If you encounter questions on these points, you are not legally required to answer. However, you are free to answer if you like.

It is a good idea to rehearse or *role play* the interview by having someone ask you questions. Role playing gives you an opportunity to practice responding and to evaluate those responses. You should be much more relaxed and confident in the real interview situation if you take the time to anticipate questions and rehearse your responses.

### Prepare Questions

Interviewers usually ask, "Do you have any questions about the company or the position?" Therefore, before the interview you should prepare a list of appropriate questions you might ask. Some of the questions would naturally pertain to the job for which you are applying: "What would my specific duties be? Is a training program available? What opportunities are there for advancement?" Other questions could cover a broad range of subjects, such as the company's product line and fringe benefits provided by the company. Do not, however, make salary and other benefits the **focal point** of your questions. If you do, the interviewer may think you are interested only in what you will receive from the company instead of what you can contribute to it.

*focal point:* center of attention

You may want to take the list of questions with you to the interview. Place the list in a folder where you can easily refer to it.

### Be on Time

*frenzied:* wild and disorderly

Better yet, be *early*. Arriving late for a job interview will probably ruin your chances of being hired. Plan to arrive early enough so you can relax and gather your thoughts before the appointment. A calm, composed job applicant will make a better impression than a rushed, *frenzied* one. Go to the interview *alone*; do not take friends or relatives with you.

**Illus. 16–13.** The interviewer, by talking with you, forms an opinion of you as a prospective employee. In some companies, you complete an application form and see an interviewer during the same visit.

## During Your Interview

It is natural to be nervous before a job interview, especially your first one. But instead of dwelling on how apprehensive you may be, think instead about the measures you have taken to prepare for the interview. By keeping a positive attitude, you will increase your confidence and have a better interview. Concentrate on the information the interviewer gives you and the questions you are asked. Remember that the interview is a two-way communication process. The interviewer is learning more about you, and you are learning more about the company. Be sure to follow the job interview "Dos and Don'ts" shown on page 708.

**Illus. 16–14.** There are specific things that you want to do, as well as things you do not want to do, during an interview.

| JOB INTERVIEW DOS AND DON'TS | |
| --- | --- |
| **DO** | **DON'T** |
| Dress appropriately. | Bring a friend or relative to the interview. |
| Greet the interviewer with a smile and a firm handshake. | Display nervousness by tapping a pencil on the desk, twirling your hair, or any other annoying habit. |
| Remain standing until you are asked to have a seat. | Slouch in your chair. |
| Use good posture when standing or sitting. | Answer questions with "yeah," "nope," or "uh huh." |
| Listen attentively. | Lie about your strengths or your accomplishments. |
| Answer questions honestly and clearly. | Smoke, chew gum, or complain. |
| Use good grammar. | Criticize past employers or your teachers. |
| Exhibit a positive attitude. | Ask questions only about the company's benefit package (what the company will do for you). |
| Ask questions about the company, its products, and your role in the company, as well as about the benefits. | Stand at the door after the interview is over and continue to talk. |
| Keep good eye contact with the interviewer. | |

Do not expect a job offer during the interview. Most of the time, a company will interview other applicants before deciding whom to hire. It is reasonable, though, to expect the interviewer to tell you when you can expect a letter or telephone call regarding the decision made.

Some companies administer *pre-employment tests*. Such tests often give you an opportunity to exhibit your competencies in keyboarding, spelling, or calculating. If you are to be tested on a piece of equipment such as a typewriter, word processor, or calculator, ask for time to practice briefly on the machine. Remain calm and follow all instructions. Do not be afraid to ask questions. If you have time, review your work before returning the completed test.

### Following Up Your Interview

Review the interview in your mind and jot down notes to yourself that will help you in future interviews. Take time to write the interviewer a brief follow-up letter. This extra effort will demonstrate your willingness to follow through on a job, thereby enhancing the impression you made during the interview.

If the interviewer does not communicate with you within the time period mentioned in the interview, call the interviewer to express your continued interest in the job. If you receive a job offer and decide to take the job, accept the offer in writing. If you interviewed with other companies, inform them that you have accepted another position.

**STARTING OFF RIGHT**

Make just as favorable a first impression on your new co-workers as you did on the interviewer. Report to work on time. Listen carefully to instructions and suggestions offered by supervisors and co-workers. Take notes. Make a concentrated effort to learn co-workers' names as quickly as possible. It may take you a few weeks to feel totally comfortable around the other workers. But, if you exhibit a genuine desire to learn and improve, you will be accepted into the work environment.

**ADVANCING IN YOUR CAREER**

To advance in your career, you must continue to learn and to grow professionally. Not only must you be prepared for advancement, you must project an image that convinces others that you deserve a promotion.

### On-the-Job Growth

Take advantage of opportunities available to you every day to learn and to improve. Keep informed about new office procedures and products. Be flexible and willing to adapt to the changes taking place in offices today. Be open to new ideas and suggestions that can increase your productivity. Learn as much as you can about your job, the company, and the business environment.

There are many organizations, publications, and courses available to help you grow professionally.

**Illus. 16–15.** Attending a trade show or an equipment exhibition such as the one shown here is one way to learn about new technologies.

### Professional Organizations

A professional organization consists of individuals with similar job positions or interests. For example, *Professional Secretaries International* (PSI) is a professional organization whose members are secretaries and other administrative office workers.

The purposes of a professional organization usually are to set standards for professional performance and salaries, to provide a *forum* for exchanging ideas, and to serve as a source of encouragement and support for its members.

*forum:* a place for discussion

### Professional Periodicals

Read periodicals that will keep you up to date about technological developments in the office and suggest ways to improve your work.

### Courses and Seminars

Take your career seriously and continue learning about your field of interest. Here are four sources for updating your skills and knowledge:

- classes offered by community colleges and private business schools in specific subjects such as computer programming, word processing, and business law
- one- and two-day seminars presented by schools or training/ management organizations
- in-house seminars sponsored by your company
- degree programs offered by colleges and universities

### Professional Certificates of Proficiency

*criteria:* standards

*rigorous:* difficult

Some professional associations (PSI, for example) have programs that certify an individual's level of knowledge and experience. The **criteria** for being certified vary for each association. Work experience, or a combination of formal education and work experience, is a common requirement. You also may be required to pass a **rigorous** examination.

## Projecting a Professional Image

To advance in your career, your employers must perceive you as someone who is competent, who is an asset to the company, and who is able to work well with others. You want your image to match these qualities. Following are four suggestions for projecting a professional image as you perform your assigned tasks.

**Illus. 16–16.** It is important to project a professional image at all times. You want others to recognize that you are capable, responsible, and persistent in maintaining high standards.

### Document Your Work

Documenting your work means keeping a record of your major accomplishments, including a description or sample of the work, letters of commendation, and any other pertinent information. This documentation will benefit you in several ways:

- It gives you an accurate account of your accomplishments.
- It provides specific evidence of your worth to the company when your progress is reviewed.
- It allows you to update your resume easily and accurately.

Marlene and Jeremy work for Anderson & Associates. Employee performance is reviewed and evaluated every six months. During lunch, Marlene and Jeremy were discussing their upcoming reviews:

Jeremy:   Do you think Mr. Rissinger will recall all of the work I have done? I don't know if I could recall all of my work myself!

Marlene: Don't you keep a personal profile folder?

Jeremy:   What is a personal profile folder?

Marlene: It is a folder in which you can keep a complete record of all you do, as well as evidence of any major accomplishments. For example, when I do an especially complicated job that takes extra time and very intensive effort, I keep notes about it and put my notes in my personal profile folder. Also, any letters from customers or memos from supervisors or co-workers who thank me for a job well done are filed in the folder. I've always believed that if my accomplishments were challenged (if I didn't get an anticipated promotion, for example), I would share the contents of my folder with the person evaluating me. To date, though, I have never had to do that.

Jeremy:   I like the idea of keeping a personal profile folder. I'll begin mine today.

### Inform Your Supervisor

As opportunities present themselves throughout the week, describe simply and briefly the work you have accomplished and the plans you have for completing other work.

17. **Before a short, informal, direct quotation.**

> Mr. Collins asked, "Will Diane accept the position?"

18. **To separate elements which might be misread if the comma were omitted.**

> Though I called, Anne had left her desk.

## DASH (--)

In keyboarding, the dash consists of two hyphens placed together, with no space preceding or following them. The dash is used

1. **To indicate a change in the sense or construction of a sentence.**

> When the executive arrived--she had almost missed her flight--the meeting began.

2. **Instead of a comma, semicolon, colon, or parentheses, when strong emphasis is desired.**

> His suggestion--and I think it is the most sound--is the best option.

## HYPHEN (-)

The hyphen is used

1. **To divide a word between syllables at the end of a line.**

The supervisor indicated that everyone would have to work overtime if the project was to be completed on time.

2. **To show compound words.**

> She ordered single-sided, double-density diskettes.

## PARENTHESES ( )

Parentheses are used

1. **To enclose figures or letters that mark a series of enumerated elements.**

He made these points: (1) our profit margin is too low, (2) our gross sales have decreased, and (3) our distribution system is inadequate.

2. **To enclose figures confirming a number which is written in words.**

> fifty (50) dollars                    eighty-seven dollars ($87)

3. **To enclose material that is indirectly related to the main thought of a sentence.**

> The schedule (as it stands now) is incomplete.

4. **To enclose matter introduced as an explanation.**

> The microcomputer software (software for our 256K machines) arrived this morning.

## PERIOD (.)

The period is used

1. **After a sentence that makes a statement or gives a command.**

> There are basic guidelines for spacing after punctuation marks.
> Complete it now.

2. **After initials in a name.** Space once after each period.

> N. R. Evans                                    Robin E. Cook

3. **Within some abbreviations.** Do not space after these periods.

> p.m., Ph.D., M.D.

4. **After many abbreviations.**

> St., Co., Inc.

The following abbreviations usually are written without periods:

(a)   News and broadcasting organizations: KDKA, UPI, NBC
(b)   Business abbreviations: IBM, YWCA, COD
(c)   Data processing terminology: BASIC, LED, VDT
(d)   Geographic abbreviations: USA, USSR, NM, NC, CA
(e)   Government agencies: FBI, CIA, IRS
(f)   Shortened words: memo, photo

5. **In decimal numbers, and between dollars and cents when expressing figures.** Do not space after a period that is used as a decimal point.

> $18.33, 5.8%, 16.227

## QUESTION MARK (?)

The question mark is used

1. **After a direct question, but not after an indirect question.**

> Will you accept the position?
> She asked who was hired for the position.

**It is not necessary to use a question mark after a polite request.**

> Will you please take these materials to Mr. Jones.

2. **After each question in a series, if special emphasis is desired.** When the question mark is used in this way, it takes the place of the comma, and each element in the series begins with a lowercase letter.

> What is the scheduled starting date? the duration? the completion date?

## QUOTATION MARKS (" ")

Quotation marks are used

1. **To enclose direct quotations.** Single quotation marks are used to enclose a quotation within a quotation.

The supervisor said, "This report must be completed by 2:30 p.m."
Andrea whispered, "I heard the director say, 'Don't be late'; then she left the office."

2. **To enclose the titles of articles, lectures, reports, and so forth; and the titles of sections of publications (parts, chapters, and so forth).** The titles of books and periodicals are not enclosed in quotation marks, but are italicized, underscored, or keyed in all capital letters.

The chapter was titled "Effective Letter Writing."

3. **To enclose unusual, peculiar, or slang terms.**

The television "news blurb" interrupted the regularly scheduled programming.

4. **To enclose words used in some special sense, or words to which attention is directed in order to make a meaning clear.**

The word is "picture," not "pitcher."
The "efficient" secretary lost the executive's report.

*Quotation Marks with Other Punctuation*

At the end of quoted material, a quotation mark and another mark of punctuation often are used together. The rules governing the placement of these marks are not entirely logical, but since they are well established and generally accepted, you should follow them.

1. **A period or comma should *precede* the closing quotation mark, even though it may not be a part of the quotation.**

"I'll be back in ten minutes," he said, "and will sign the letters then."

2. **A semicolon or colon should *follow* the closing quotation mark, even when it is part of the quotation.**

Susan Hutchinson was named "Employee of the Month"; Dennis Jacobs was named "Employee of the Year."

3. **Other marks of punctuation should precede the closing quotation mark if they apply to the quotation only, and should follow the mark if they apply to the sentence as a whole and not just to the quotation.**

Mr. Stern asked, "Have you completed the report?"
Did you read the article "Controlling Office Expenses"?

# SEMICOLON (;)

The semicolon is used

1. **Between closely related independent clauses not joined by a conjunction.**

This is an excellent report; the president will be pleased.

2. **Before a conjunction joining two independent clauses, if either clause contains internal punctuation.**

Since it was 5 o'clock, most of the office staff had gone home; but Frances stayed to keyboard the report.

3. **Before a connective joining two independent clauses.** (A comma follows the connective only if the connective is to be emphasized.) Some commonly used connectives are *consequently, however, in fact, nevertheless, therefore,* and *thus.*

   Our earnings were up 15 percent in March; however, our earnings were down 5 percent in April.

4. **Before such words and abbreviations as** *e.g., i.e., for example,* **and** *namely,* **when they introduce a long list of terms.** A comma precedes the list.

   Many different typewriter fonts are available; for example, italic, prestige elite, and letter gothic.

5. **Between punctuated elements of a series.**

   Ann Dorazio, Miami, Florida; Jennie Lewis, Niles, Ohio; and Ted Martinez, Lubbock, Texas, were accepted into the program.

# Section C: CAPITALIZATION

Capitalization (the use of uppercase letters) is used primarily to indicate the importance of certain words. Unnecessary capitalization should be avoided. When in doubt about a specific capitalization principle, consult a dictionary or other reference book.

## BASIC RULES

1. **Capitalize the first word of a sentence.**

   > He was eager to begin work as a receptionist.

2. **Capitalize proper nouns (names of particular persons, places, or things) and proper adjectives derived from these nouns.**

   | | | |
   |---|---|---|
   | Monica | West Virginia | the Liberty Bell |
   | America (n.) | | American (adj.) |

3. **Capitalize the first word of the salutation of a letter and the first word of the complimentary close.**

   > Dear Mr. Stevensen          Sincerely yours

4. **Capitalize the days of the week, the months of the year, and holidays.**

   > Friday          February          Christmas

5. **Capitalize all significant words in the names of companies, organizations, and main government agencies.**

   | | |
   |---|---|
   | Delta Air Lines | Future Business Leaders of America |
   | the Utah Tax Commission | Department of Justice |

6. **Capitalize the first word of a direct quotation.**

   > The sales manager stated, "We will honor our commitment."

7. **Capitalize principal words in the titles of books, articles, magazines, newspapers, reports, and so forth. Do not capitalize articles (*a, and,* and *the*), short prepositions (*of, in, to,* and *but*), or short conjunctions (*and, but, or,* and *nor*).**

   | | |
   |---|---|
   | <u>An Introduction to Computers and Data Processing</u> | *Time* |
   | "The Key to Success with Graphics" | *The New York Times* |

## BUSINESS TITLES AND POSITIONS

1. **Capitalize titles when they immediately precede individual names and are directly related to them.**
   Generally, titles that follow personal names are not capitalized. When known, it is always correct to follow the preferences of specific companies.

   > It was Ambassador Young who delivered the proposal.
   > Janet Turner was appointed president of Woodrow College.

2. **Do not capitalize business titles when they do not refer to specific persons.**

A regional manager of the company spoke to us.
The chairperson will be appointed at the next meeting.

## GEOGRAPHIC NAMES

1. **Capitalize the names of countries, regions of countries, cities, and sections of cities. The names of mountains, islands, bodies of water, and other such geographic places and sections are also capitalized.**

Egypt                                   Appalachian Mountains
Paris                                   Bahama Islands
Montego Bay                             the East Coast
Mississippi River                       Greenwich Village

2. **A geographic term such as *river, ocean, country, city,* and *street* that precedes a proper name, or a geographic term that is used in the plural and follows a proper name, should not be capitalized.**

the river Thames                    the Antarctic and Indian oceans

**NOTE:** If the term is part of the legal name, it should be capitalized.

the City of New York

3. **Capitalize points of the compass designating specific geographic sections of the country.**

the North                               the South
the Northeast                           the Southwest

**Points of the compass used to indicate direction are not capitalized.**

Miami is south of Atlanta.          The storm moved west to east.

4. **Capitalize proper names denoting political divisions.**

Allegheny County                        Sixth Precinct

## INDIVIDUAL NAMES

1. **Capitalize all units in the name of an individual (except some surname prefixes such as *du, de, van,* and *von,* which are capitalized or left lowercase according to the practice of the individual).**

DeKoven                                 deGaulle
Demille                                 deSoto

2. **When a surname with a prefix that is usually lowercase begins a sentence, capitalize the prefix.**

DeGaulle was known for his speeches.

## HYPHENATED WORDS

1. **Capitalize only the parts of hyphenated words that you would normally capitalize if the word were written alone.**

The mid-January sale ends tomorrow.
The up-to-date references were hard to locate.

2. **When a sentence begins with a hyphenated term, capitalize the first word.** All other words in the hyphenated term follow Rule one.

Mid-January computer reports are due tomorrow.
Up-to-date references will be required.

# *Section D:* MATH

Numbers are used by almost everyone who works in offices. This math review covers basic math skills and will help you complete the Extending Your Math Skills activities included in this text.

## ADDITION

1. **In addition, two or more numbers (called addends) are combined to get a sum, or total.**
2. **If the sum of one column exceeds 9 (6 + 7 = 13), carry the excess digit (1) to the next column; then add the digits in that column (1 + 2 + 5 = 8).**

$$
\begin{array}{r}
1 \quad \leftarrow \text{carry} \\
26 \left.\right\} \text{addends} \\
+\ 57 \\
\hline
83 \ \text{sum (total)}
\end{array}
$$

3. **Decimal points must be aligned one above the other before addends can be added correctly.**

| Decimals Not Aligned | Decimals Aligned |
|---|---|
| 71.16 | 1 1  ← carry |
| 9.5 | 71.16 ⎫ |
| + .872 | 9.5 ⎬ addends |
|  | + .872 ⎭ |
|  | 81.532  sum (total) |

4. **Prove the sum (total) of an addition problem by calculating the addends in opposite directions.**

Add Down
$$
\begin{array}{r}
71.16 \\
9.5 \\
+\ .872 \downarrow \\
\hline
81.532 \ \text{sum (total)}
\end{array}
$$

Add Up
$$
\begin{array}{r}
81.532 \ \text{sum (total)} \\
\hline
71.16 \uparrow \\
9.5 \\
+\ .872
\end{array}
$$

## SUBTRACTION

1. **In subtraction, one number (the subtrahend) is deducted from another number (the minuend) to get a difference.**
2. **If a digit in one column (the 4 in 24) is too large to be subtracted from a digit in the same column, (the 2 in 62), borrow 10 from the next column to the left (60 − 10 = 50, and the 2 becomes 12).**

$$
\begin{array}{r}
{}^{5}\ {}^{1} \\
\cancel{6}2 \ \text{minuend} \\
-\ 24 \ \text{subtrahend} \\
\hline
38 \ \text{difference}
\end{array}
$$

3. **Prove a subtraction problem by adding the subtrahend to the difference; the total should be the minuend.**

$$
\begin{array}{r}
1 \\
38 \ \text{difference} \\
+\ 24 \ \text{subtrahend} \\
\hline
62 \ \text{minuend}
\end{array}
$$

# Section E: TWO-LETTER STATE ABBREVIATIONS

The United States Postal Service has authorized the use of two-letter abbreviations for use in conjunction with the ZIP Code System.

| U.S. State, District, Possession, or Territory | Two-Letter Abbreviation | U.S. State, District, Possession, or Territory | Two-Letter Abbreviation |
| --- | --- | --- | --- |
| Alabama | AL | North Carolina | NC |
| Alaska | AK | North Dakota | ND |
| Arizona | AZ | Ohio | OH |
| Arkansas | AR | Oklahoma | OK |
| California | CA | Oregon | OR |
| Canal Zone | CZ | Pennsylvania | PA |
| Colorado | CO | Puerto Rico | PR |
| Connecticut | CT | Rhode Island | RI |
| Delaware | DE | South Carolina | SC |
| District of Columbia | DC | South Dakota | SD |
| Florida | FL | Tennessee | TN |
| Georgia | GA | Texas | TX |
| Guam | GU | Utah | UT |
| Hawaii | HI | Vermont | VT |
| Idaho | ID | Virgin Islands | VI |
| Illinois | IL | Virginia | VA |
| Indiana | IN | Washington | WA |
| Iowa | IA | West Virginia | WV |
| Kansas | KS | Wisconsin | WI |
| Kentucky | KY | Wyoming | WY |

| U.S. State, District, Possession, or Territory | Two-Letter Abbreviation | Canadian Province, Possession, or Territory | Two-Letter Abbreviation |
| --- | --- | --- | --- |
| Louisiana | LA | | |
| Maine | ME | | |
| Maryland | MD | | |
| Massachusetts | MA | Alberta | AB |
| Michigan | MI | British Columbia | BC |
| | | Labrador | LB |
| Minnesota | MN | Manitoba | MB |
| Mississippi | MS | New Brunswick | NB |
| Missouri | MO | Newfoundland | NF |
| Montana | MT | Northwest Territories | NT |
| Nebraska | NE | Nova Scotia | NS |
| Nevada | NV | Ontario | ON |
| New Hampshire | NH | Prince Edward Island | PE |
| New Jersey | NJ | Quebec | PQ |
| New Mexico | NM | Saskatchewan | SK |
| New York | NY | Yukon Territory | YT |

# Section F: ALPHABETIC INDEXING RULES

Many organizations use the indexing rules developed by the Association of Records Managers and Administrators, Inc. (ARMA). Adaptations of these rules are presented immediately following the alphabetizing procedures. Alphabetizing procedures are necessary in order to determine the proper location of a name in relation to other names in a file.

## ALPHABETIZING PROCEDURES

1. **Alphabetically compare the Key Unit (Anderson in Elizabeth Anderson) of one filing segment (a complete name such as Elizabeth Anderson is a filing segment) with the Key Unit (Brown in Thomas Brown) in another filing segment.** File Anderson before Brown because A is before B in the alphabet. An underscore is placed below the letter that determines the filing order.

   | Key Unit | Unit 2 |
   | --- | --- |
   | Anderson | Elizabeth |
   | Brown | Thomas |

2. **Alphabetically compare parts in the same filing unit of two names.** File Anderson before Andress because alphabetically the e in Anderson is before the r in Andress. All punctuation is disregarded when indexing personal and business names.

   | Key Unit | Unit 2 |
   | --- | --- |
   | Anderson | Elizabeth |
   | Andress | M |

3. **When the first unit of two names being compared are identical, determine the filing order by comparing the next unit in the filing order.** The first filing unit, Anderson, is identical for both names. Anderson, Elizabeth is filed before Anderson, Thomas, because the E in Elizabeth is before the T in Thomas in the alphabet.

   | Key Unit | Unit 2 |
   | --- | --- |
   | Anderson | Elizabeth |
   | Anderson | Thomas |

4. **When a name is the same as the first part of a longer name, the shorter name is filed first. In filing, "nothing comes before something."** When comparing Anders and Anderson, there is nothing after the s in Anders which precedes the something (o-n) in Anderson.

   | Key Unit | Unit 2 |
   | --- | --- |
   | Anders | Elizabeth |
   | Anderson | Elizabeth |

Other applications of the "nothing before something" rule are:

| Key Unit | Unit 2 | Unit 3 |
|----------|--------|--------|
| Anderson | T | |
| Anderson | Thomas | |
| Anderson | Thomas | L |
| Anderson | Thomas | Lawrence |

# INDEXING RULES

## Rule 1: Order of Indexing Units

**A. PERSONAL NAMES. A personal name is indexed in this manner: (1) the surname (last name) is the key unit, (2) the given name (first name) or initial is the second unit, and (3) the middle name or initial is the third unit. Unusual or obscure (often foreign) names are indexed in the same manner. If it is not possible to determine the surname in a name, consider the last name as the surname. Cross-reference unusual or obscure names by using the first written name as the key unit.**

### Index Order of Units

| Name | Key Unit | Unit 2 | Unit 3 |
|------|----------|--------|--------|
| Elizabeth Anderson | Anderson | Elizabeth | |
| Elizabeth R. Anderson | Anderson | Elizabeth | R |
| M. M. Andress | Andress | M | M |
| Thomas James Ansley | Ansley | Thomas | James |
| John Anthony | Anthony | John | |
| Ann B. Arthur | Arthur | Ann | B |
| J. Brett Austin | Austin | J | Brett |
| Isheanyl Awambu | Awambu | Isheanyl | |

**B. BUSINESS NAMES. Business names are filed *as written*\* using letterheads or trademarks as guides. Business names containing personal names are indexed as written. Newspapers and periodicals are indexed as written. For newspapers and periodicals having identical names that do not include the city name, consider the city name as the last indexing unit. If necessary, the state name may follow the city name.**

\*"As written" means the order of the words or names *as written or printed* on the person's, organization's, or publication's signature, letterhead, or title.

### Index Order of Units

| Names | Key Unit | Unit 2 | Unit 3 |
|-------|----------|--------|--------|
| Action Appliance Store | Action | Appliance | Store |
| Dallas Morning News | Dallas | Morning | News |
| Evening Times (Duluth) | Evening | Times | (Duluth) |
| Evening Times (Houston) | Evening | Times | (Houston) |
| John Baker Company | John | Baker | Company |

## Rule 2: Minor Words in Business Names

Each complete English word in a business name is considered a separate indexing unit. Prepositions, conjunctions, symbols, and articles are included; symbols (&, ¢, $, #, %) are considered as spelled in full (and, Cent, Dollar, Number, Percent). All spelled-out symbols except "and" begin with a capital letter.

When the word "The" appears as the first word of a business name, it is considered the last indexing unit.

### Index Order of Units

| Name | Key Unit | Unit 2 | Unit 3 | Unit 4 |
|------|----------|--------|--------|--------|
| The Baker Company | Baker | Company | The | |
| Baker $ Store | Baker | Dollar | Store | |
| For You Shop | For | You | Shop | |
| John Baker & Sons | John | Baker | and | Sons |
| John the Baker | John | the | Baker | |

## Rule 3: Punctuation and Possessives

All punctuation is disregarded when indexing personal and business names. Commas, periods, hyphens, and apostrophes are disregarded, and names are indexed as written. (For example, Smith's Playhouse would be filed after Smiths' Bakery.)

### Index Order of Units

| Name | Key Unit | Unit 2 | Unit 3 | Unit 4 |
|------|----------|--------|--------|--------|
| Samuel B. Church | Church | Samuel | B | |
| Church, Wilson, and Jones | Church | Wilson | and | Jones |
| Church's Fried Chicken | Churchs | Fried | Chicken | |
| Church-Town Bookstore | ChurchTown | Bookstore | | |

## Rule 4: Single Letters and Abbreviations

A. **PERSONAL NAMES.** Initials in personal names are considered separate indexing units. Abbreviations of personal names (Wm., Jos., Thos.) and brief personal names or nicknames (Liz, Bill) are indexed as they are written.

B. **BUSINESS NAMES.** Single letters in business names are indexed as written. If there is a space between single letters, index each letter as a separate unit. An acronym (a word formed from the first, or first few, letters of several words) is indexed as one unit. Abbreviations are indexed as one unit regardless of punctuation or spacing (AAA, Y M C A, Y.W.C.A.). Radio and television station call letters are indexed as one word. Cross-reference spelled-out names to their acronyms or abbreviations if necessary. For example: American Automobile Association SEE AAA.

| Name | Key Unit | Unit 2 | Unit 3 |
|------|----------|--------|--------|
| A M Motors | A | M | Motors |
| Billy Bob Adams | Adams | Billy | Bob |
| J. B. Adams | Adams | J | B |
| Robt. Adams | Adams | Robt | |
| KLYO Radio | KLYO | Radio | |
| PAWS Assoc. | PAWS | Assoc | |
| SHOWS, Inc. | SHOWS | Inc | |

## Rule 5: Titles

**A. PERSONAL NAMES.** A personal title (Miss, Mr., Mrs., Ms.) is considered the last indexing unit when it appears. If a seniority title is required for identification, it is considered the last indexing unit in abbreviated form, with numeric titles (II, III) filed before alphabetic titles (Jr., Sr.). When professional titles (D.D.S., M.D., CRM, Dr., Mayor) are required for identification, they are considered the last units and filed alphabetically as written. Royal and religious titles followed by either a given name or a surname only (Father Leo) are indexed and filed as written. When all units of identical names, *including titles,* have been compared and there are no differences, filing order is determined by the addresses.

**B. BUSINESS NAMES.** Titles in business names are filed as written. See Rules 1 and 2.

Index Order of Units

| Name | Key Unit | Unit 2 | Unit 3 | Unit 4 |
|------|----------|--------|--------|--------|
| Miss Anila Armstrong | Armstrong | Anila | Miss | |
| Mrs. Mason's Bakery | Mrs | Masons | Bakery | |
| Travis Parker, II | Parker | Travis | II | |
| Travis Parker, Jr. | Parker | Travis | Jr | |
| William Porter, M.D. | Porter | William | MD | |
| A. B. Price, Mayor | Price | A | B | Mayor |
| Princess Margaret | Princess | Margaret | | |
| Sister Jeanice | Sister | Jeanice | | |
| Rev. Charles Tyson | Tyson | Charles | Rev | |

## Rule 6: Married Women

A married woman's name is filed as she writes it. It is indexed according to Rule 1. If more than one form of a name is known, the alternate name may be cross-referenced. For example: Atwill Doris C Mrs SEE Atwill James T Mrs.

Note: A married woman's name in a business name is indexed as written and follows Rules 1B and 5B.

Index Order of Units

| Name | Key Unit | Unit 2 | Unit 3 | Unit 4 |
|------|----------|--------|--------|--------|
| Mrs. Karen Lynn Cole<br>*(Mrs. Keith J. Cole) | Cole | Karen | Lynn | Mrs |
| Mrs. Kathy Jones Cole<br>*(Ms. Kathy Jones) | Cole | Kathy | Jones | Mrs |
| Mrs. Keith J. Cole | Cole | Keith | J | Mrs |
| Ms. Kathy Jones | Jones | Kathy | Ms | |
| Karen Cole's Jewelry | Karen | Coles | Jewelry | |

*These names are the alternate names and are also listed at their alphabetic locations as cross-references.

## Rule 7: Articles and Particles

**A foreign article or particle in a personal business name is combined with the part of the name following it to form a single indexing unit. The indexing order is not affected by a space between a prefix and the rest of the name, and the space is disregarded when indexing. Examples of articles and particles are: a la, D', Da, De, Del, De la, Della, Den, Des, Di, Dos, Du, El, Fitz, Il, L', La, Las, Le, Les, Lo, Los, M', Mac, Mc, O', Per, Saint, San, Santa, Santo, St., Ste., Te, Ten, Ter, Van, Van de, Van der, Von, Von der.**

Index Order of Units

| Name | Key Unit | Unit 2 | Unit 3 |
|------|----------|--------|--------|
| Mary M. D'Andro | DAndro | Mary | M |
| D'Anglo's Dairy | DAnglos | Dairy | |
| Andrew Del Gado | DelGado | Andrew | |
| A. D. du Boise | duBoise | A | D |
| Duboise Medical Inc. | Duboise | Medical | Inc |
| Sharon Fitz Henry | FitzHenry | Sharon | |
| John A. MacGeorge | MacGeorge | John | A |
| George Saint Thomas | SaintThomas | George | |

## Rule 8: Identical Names

**When personal names and names of businesses, institutions, and organizations are identical, filing order is determined by the addresses. Cities are considered first, followed by states or provinces, street names, house numbers or building numbers in that order.**

   **Note 1  When the first units of street names are written as figures, the names are considered in ascending numeric order and placed together before alphabetic street names.**

   **Note 2  Street names with compass directions are considered as written. Numbers after compass directions are considered before alphabetic names (East 8th, East Main, Sandusky, SE Eighth, Southeast Eighth).**

   **Note 3  House and building numbers written as figures are considered in ascending numeric order and placed together before spelled-out building names (The Charter House). If a street address and a building name are included in an address, disregard the building name. ZIP Codes are not considered in determining filing order.**

   **Note 4  Seniority titles are indexed according to Rule 5 and are considered *before* addresses.**

## Index Order of Units

| Name | Key Unit | Unit 2 | Unit 3 | Unit 4 | Address |
|------|----------|--------|--------|--------|---------|
| *Names of cities used to determine filing order* | | | | | |
| Abington School<br>  Harrisburg, Pennsylvania | Abington | School | | | Harrisburg<br>  Pennsylvania |
| Abington School<br>  Lancaster, Pennsylvania | Abington | School | | | Lancaster<br>  Pennsylvania |
| *Names of states and provinces used to determine filing order* | | | | | |
| First Federal Bank<br>  Decatur, Georgia | First | Federal | Bank | | Decatur Georgia |
| First Federal Bank<br>  Decatur, Illinois | First | Federal | Bank | | Decatur Illinois |
| Gould's Clothiers<br>  Windsor, Connecticut | Goulds | Clothiers | | | Windsor Connecticut |
| Gould's Clothiers<br>  Windsor, Ontario | Goulds | Clothiers | | | Windsor Ontario |
| *Names of streets and building numbers used to determine filing order* | | | | | |
| Saving Markets<br>  3204 14 Street<br>  Salem, Oregon | Saving | Markets | | | 3204 14 Street |
| Saving Markets<br>  6062 14 Street<br>  Salem, Oregon | Saving | Markets | | | 6062 14 Street |
| Saving Markets<br>  7832 Abbott Ave.<br>  Salem, Oregon | Saving | Markets | | | 7832 Abbott Ave |
| Saving Markets<br>  5403 East Abbott Ave.<br>  Salem, Oregon | Saving | Markets | | | 5403 East Abbott Ave |
| *Seniority titles used to determine filing order before addresses* | | | | | |
| Dennis B. Davis<br>  5207 Vicksburg<br>  Boise, Idaho | Davis | Dennis | B | | |
| Dennis B. Davis II<br>  1607 Albany Avenue<br>  Des Moines, Iowa | Davis | Dennis | B | II | |
| Dennis B. Davis III<br>  1001 University Avenue<br>  Des Moines, Iowa | Davis | Dennis | B | III | |
| Dennis B. Davis, Jr.<br>  1001 University Avenue<br>  Des Moines, Iowa | Davis | Dennis | B | Jr | Des Moines Iowa |
| Dennis B. Davis, Jr.<br>  4420 Marshall Drive<br>  Ogden, Utah | Davis | Dennis | B | Jr | Ogden Utah |

## Rule 9: Numbers in Business Names

Numbers spelled out in a business name are considered as written and filed alphabetically. Numbers written in digit form are considered one unit. Names with numbers written in digit form as the first unit are filed in ascending order before alphabetic names. Arabic numerals are filed before Roman numerals (2, 3; II, III). Names with inclusive numbers (33-37) are arranged by the first number only (33). Names with numbers appearing in other than the first position (Pier 36 Cafe) are filed alphabetically within the appropriate section and immediately before a similar name without a number (Pier and Port Cafe).

Note: In indexing numbers written in digit form which contain *st, d,* and *th* (1st, 2d, 3d, 4th), ignore the letter endings and consider the digits (1, 2, 3, 4).

### Index Order of Units

| Name | Key Unit | Unit 2 | Unit 3 | Unit 4 |
|---|---|---|---|---|
| 2 By 4 Lumber | 2 | By | 4 | Lumber |
| 2 Circle Ranch | 2 | Circle | Ranch | |
| 2-20 Circle Shopping Center | 2 | Circle | Shopping | Center |
| 2d Street Cafe | 2 | Street | Cafe | |
| 4 Seasons Restaurant | 4 | Seasons | Restaurant | |
| IV Seasons Motel | IV | Seasons | Motel | |
| Four Seasons Shop | Four | Seasons | Shop | |
| Four-Hundred Club | FourHundred | Club | | |
| Fourth Street Shops | Fourth | Street | Shops | |
| Route 40 Motel | Route | 40 | Motel | |
| Route 44 Motel | Route | 44 | Motel | |

## Rule 10: Organizations and Institutions

Banks and other financial institutions, clubs, colleges, hospitals, hotels, lodges, motels, museums, religious institutions, schools, unions, universities, and other organizations and institutions are indexed and filed according to the names written on their letterheads. *The* used as the first word in these names is considered the last filing unit.

### Index Order of Units

| Name | Key Unit | Unit 2 | Unit 3 | Unit 4 |
|---|---|---|---|---|
| The Art Association | Art | Association | The | |
| Austin Bank & Trust | Austin | Bank | and | Trust |
| Bank of Berkley | Bank | of | Berkley | |
| Center of Technology | Center | of | Technology | |
| Christopher Columbus High School | Christopher | Columbus | High | School |
| Foundation for the Blind | Foundation | for | the | Blind |
| National Land Studies Department | National | Land | Studies | Department |

### Index Order of Units

| Name | Key Unit | Unit 2 | Unit 3 | Unit 4 |
|------|----------|--------|--------|--------|
| Political Science Club | Political | Science | Club | |
| South Plains Christian Church | South | Plains | Christian | Church |
| University of South Carolina | University | of | South | Carolina |

## Rule 11: Separated Single Words

**When a single word is separated into two or more parts in a business name, the parts are considered separate indexing units. If a name contains two compass directions separated by a space (South East Car Rental), each compass direction is a separate indexing unit.** *Southeast* **and** *south-east* **are considered single indexing units. Cross-reference if necessary. For example: South East SEE ALSO Southeast, South-East.**

### Index Order of Units

| Name | Key Unit | Unit 2 | Unit 3 | Unit 4 |
|------|----------|--------|--------|--------|
| South West Telestar | South | West | Telestar | |
| Southwest Telestar | Southwest | Telestar | | |
| South-West Vending Company | SouthWest | Vending | Company | |
| Sun Shine Car Wash | Sun | Shine | Car | Wash |
| Sunshine Tanning Salon | Sunshine | Tanning | Salon | |

## Rule 12: Hyphenated Names

A. **PERSONAL NAMES. Hyphenated personal names are considered one indexing unit and the hyphen is ignored.** *Jones-Bennett* **is a single indexing unit —** *JonesBennett.*

B. **BUSINESS NAMES. Hyphenated business and place names and coined business names are considered one indexing unit and the hyphen is ignored.** *La-Z-Boy* **is a single indexing unit —** *LaZBoy.*

### Index Order of Units

| Name | Key Unit | Unit 2 | Unit 3 |
|------|----------|--------|--------|
| Laura Armstrong-Jones | ArmstrongJones | Laura | |
| Browning-Ferris Ind. | BrowningFerris | Ind | |
| Dial-a-Gardener | DialaGardener | | |
| D-Signer's Shop | DSigners | Shop | |
| Northeast Realtors | Northeast | Realtors | |
| North-East Service Station | Northeast | Service | Station |

## Rule 13: Compound Names

A. **PERSONAL NAMES. When separated by a space, compound personal names are considered separate indexing units.** *Mary Lea Gerson* **is three units.**
   **Note: Although** *St. John* **is a compound name,** *St.* **(Saint) is a prefix and follows Rule 7 which considers it a single indexing unit.**

B. **BUSINESS NAMES. Compound business or place names with spaces between the parts of the name follow Rule 11, and the parts are considered separate units. New Jersey and Mid America are considered two indexing units each.**

### Index Order of Units

| Name | Key Unit | Unit 2 | Unit 3 | Unit 4 |
|------|----------|--------|--------|--------|
| Miss Anna Mae Abbott | Abbott | Anna | Mae | Miss |
| Miss Annamae Abbott | Abbott | Annamae | Miss | |
| East West Travel Agency | East | West | Travel | Agency |
| East-West Trucking Co. | EastWest | Trucking | Co | |
| Pre Fab Housing Sales | Pre | Fab | Housing | Sales |
| Pre-Fabricated Designers | PreFabricated | Designers | | |
| Prefabricated Products | Prefabricated | Products | | |
| St. Martins Home | StMartins | Home | | |

## Rule 14: Government Names

A. **FEDERAL. The name of a federal government agency is indexed by the name of the government unit (United States Government) followed by the most distinctive name of the office, bureau, department, etc., as written (Internal Revenue Service). The words "Office of," "Department of," "Bureau of," etc.,** *if needed* **for clarity and in the official name, are added and considered separate indexing units.**
   **Note: If "of" is not a part of the official name as written, it is not added.**

B. **STATE AND LOCAL. The names of state, province, county, parish, city, town, township, and village governments/political divisions are indexed by their distinctive names. The words "State of," "County of," "City of," "Department of," etc., are added only** *if needed* **for clarity and in the official name, and are considered separate indexing units (** *Wisconsin*/Transportation/Department/of**).**

C. **FOREIGN. The distinctive English name is the first indexing unit for foreign government names. This is followed,** *if needed* **and in the official name, by the balance of the formal name of the government. Branches, departments, and divisions follow in order by their distinctive names. States, colonies, provinces, cities, and other divisions of foreign governments are followed by their distinctive or official names as spelled in English (Canada; Poland; France, Paris). Cross-reference the written foreign name to the English name, if necessary.**

| Name | Index Form of Name |
|------|--------------------|
| Department of Public Safety<br>State of Arizona<br>Phoenix, Arizona | Arizona State of<br>    Public Safety Department of<br>    Phoenix Arizona |
| Administrative Division<br>Department of the Secretary of State<br>Dominion of Canada<br>Montreal, Quebec | Canada Dominion of<br>    State Secretary of Department of the<br>    Administrative Division<br>    Montreal Quebec |

Department of Health
Laramie, Wyoming

Lubbock County
Tax Assessor Collector
Lubbock, Texas

Food Safety and Inspection Service
Compliance Division
U.S. Department of Agriculture

Laramie
  Health Department of
  Laramie Wyoming

Lubbock County
  Tax Assessor Collector
  Lubbock Texas

United States Government
  Agriculture Department of
  Food Safety and Inspection Service
  Compliance Division

# Section G: LEGAL RIGHTS OF THE EMPLOYEE

As a result of federal and state legislation, American employees have many employment rights and benefits. Employees can act to correct violations of these rights and benefits without being disciplined by employers. Some of the more important employee rights and benefits are mentioned here.

## FAIR WAGES, OVERTIME PAY, AND EQUAL PAY

The Fair Labor Standards Act (FLSA) states that workers identified in the FLSA must be paid at least the legal minimum wage. The FLSA also includes provisions for overtime pay and equal pay for equal work. The Equal Pay Act amended the FLSA and states that it is illegal to have different pay scales or benefits for men and women who perform comparable work.

## FREEDOM FROM DISCRIMINATION

Title VII of the Civil Rights Act of 1964 prohibits employers from discriminating against individuals because of their race, color, religion, sex, or national origin. The Rehabilitation Act of 1973 prevents discrimination by government contractors against handicapped individuals. Discrimination against women because of pregnancy, childbirth, or other related medical conditions is forbidden by the Pregnancy Discrimination Act of 1978. The Age Discrimination in Employment Act of 1967 prohibits discrimination against anyone 40 years of age or older.

## FREEDOM FROM SEXUAL HARASSMENT

An amendment of Title VII of the Civil Rights Act of 1964 states that harassment is an unlawful employment practice. In addition, the Equal Employment Opportunity Commission (EEOC) has issued "Guidelines on Discrimination Because of Sex," which identifies sexual harassment as unwelcome sexual advances, requests for sexual favors, and other verbal or physical conduct when:
- submission to such conduct is made a term or condition of an individual's employment
- submission to or rejection of such conduct is used as the basis for employment decisions
- such conduct has the purpose or effect of unreasonably interfering with an individual's work performance or creating an undesirable working environment

## SAFE AND HEALTHY WORKPLACE

The Occupational Safety and Health Act (OSHA) of 1970 requires the employer to maintain a safe working environment for employees. Employees injured on the job may claim medical benefits and compensation for lost wages.

## UNEMPLOYMENT INSURANCE

Persons who have worked for a required period of time and who then become unemployed through no fault of their own are entitled to a percentage of their lost income for a stated period of time.

## SOCIAL SECURITY ACT BENEFITS

The federal Social Security Act, also known as the Federal Insurance Contribution Act (FICA), includes the following benefits:

*Retirement Income.* The Employee Retirement Income Security Act (ERISA) protects employees from unrestrained firing and the failure of employers to guarantee a pension plan for their employees.

*Benefits for Spouses of Retired or Disabled Workers.* At age 65, the spouse of a retired or disabled worker is entitled to a benefit equal to 50% of the worker's full benefit amount. Other family members, such as children, may also be eligible to receive benefits.

*Survivor Benefits.* A surviving spouse of a worker who was fully insured may be entitled to benefits on the deceased worker's employment record.

*Disability Benefits.* A worker under the age of 65 who is mentally or physically disabled, and whose disability is expected to prevent her or him from working for at least 12 months, or to result in death, may be eligible for monthly Social Security benefits.

*Health Insurance.* Medicare is health insurance for people aged 65 and over who are eligible for Social Security, and for people at any age who have been eligible to receive disability benefits for 24 months or more.

# PHOTO ACKNOWLEDGMENTS

# INDEX

## A

Access code, 572
Accession book, 534
Access log, 572
Accident prevention, 430
Accounts payable, 369
Accounts receivable, 345, 346, 362
Activities management, 390
Addressee, 209
Address format, 613; mailing labels *illus.*, 614
Adjustments, recording, 366
Administrative support services, 25
Advertisement, blind, 699
Agenda, 456; *illus.*, 458
Air mail, 209
Alarms, 440
Alphabetic filing systems, 526
Alphabetic general file, 534
Alphabetic indexing rules, 738
AMS simplified letter, 220, 221
Analog signals, 656
Aperture card, 508; *illus.*, 508, 578; organizing, 578
Appendix, 481
Application software, 190, 191
Appointments, making, 451, 454
Appostrophe, 722
Appraisal, 60
Appraisal form, 60; *illus.*, 61
Appreciation, expressing, 141
Archive, 510, 515
Assessing yourself, 684, 688
Assets, 483
Attachment notation, 232
Attitude, 122; how to exhibit yours, 124
Audio conference, 668
Automatic constant, 180; *illus.*, 181
Automatic document feed, 416
Automatic duplexing, 415
Automatic image shift, 415
Automatic redial, 660
Automatic teller transactions, 352
Auxiliary storage, 564

## B

Backup copies, 569
Balance sheet, 483; *illus.*, 484

Bank draft, 374
Bank statement, 352; *illus.*, 353
Bar graph, 487, 488; *illus.*, 488
BASIC, 190
Batch system, 187, 316
Bill of lading, 312; *illus.*, 313
Blank endorsement, *illus.*, 349
Blind advertisement, 699
Block format, *illus.*, 207
Block letter, 219; *illus.*, 221
Blue pages, 644
Board of directors, 24
Body, memorandum, 232; report, 477
Bonding, 347
Book copy mode, 416
Buffer storage, 295
Building evacuation, 436
Building security, 437
Business, 19
Business communication, oral, 105
Business letter formats, *see* letter formats
Business letter parts, *see* letter parts
Businesslike image, 127
Business meetings, 449, 456
Business reports, 475; formal, 476
Business travel, 463
Business writing, English skills for, 97; purpose, 90

## C

Calculators, 180
Calendars, 449, 450; coordinating, 454; entering recurring items, 454; group, *illus.*, 452
Call director 659
Call forwarding, 660
Call queing, 660
Call waiting/camp on, 660
Capital, 483
Capitalization, 729; basic rules, 729; business titles and positions, 729; geographic names, 730; hyphenated words, 730; individual names, 730
Caption, 521
CAR, *see* computer-assisted

retrieval
Card file, 556; *illus.*, 558
Career, focus on, 693; advancing, 678, 709; goal, 694; plan, 694; strategy, 694; review, 695
Cash, 345, 346; safeguards for, 346
Cashier's check, 374
CBX, *see* computerized branch exchange
Cellular phones, 659
Centralized copying, 418
Centralized dictation system, 241
Centralized structure, computer-assisted systems, 183
Centralized word/text processing unit, 257; *illus.*, 258
Central processing unit (CPU), 188
Centrex, 661, 662
Certificate of mailing, 619
Certified check, 374
Certified mail, 209, 620
Certified mail receipt, *illus.*, 620
Change, dealing with, 713; introducing, 58
Character, 686
Character keys, 274
Charging out, 503
Check, 372; cashier's, 374; certified, 374; *illus.*, 373; processing incoming, 347; voucher, 374
Check register, *illus.*, 356, 373
Chronologic filing system, 537
Chronologic order, 452
Circle graph, 487, 488; *illus.*, 488
Civil service examination, 701
Classification of workers, 47
Clearness, in writing, 94
Coated-paper copiers, 412
COBOL, 190
COD mail, 620
Code key, 286
Code record, 548; *illus.*, 549, 550
Coding, 521
Collating, 416
Collect calls, 648
Collection of goods, 311
Colloquialisms, 107
Colon, 723
Color-coded labels, 523; *illus.*, 523

COM, *see* computer output microfilm
Comma, 723
Command, 565
Commercial air travel, 463
Commission, 377
Communicating word processors, 667
Communication satellites, 657
Communication skills, 70
Communications network, 273
Company, learn about for interview, 705; loyalty to, 129; your role in representing to others, 126
Compilers, software, 190
Completeness, in writing, 96
Compliments, accept graciously, 713
Composing messages, 89
Comprehension, 79
Computer-assisted information processing system, 183
Computer-assisted retrieval (CAR), 579; advanced, 580; simple, 579
Computer-assisted systems, 183; centralized structure, 183; decentralized structure, 185; distributed structure, 185; equipment, 185; *illus.*, 184
Computer-assisted transcription, 281
Computer-based messaging, 667
Computer equipment, cleaning, 194
Computerized branch exchange (CBX), 662
Computerized business exchange, *see* computerized branch exchange
Computerized system inventory, 335; security, 193
Computer maintenance, 194
Computer output microfilm (COM), 508, 575, 576; *illus.*, 576
Computer technology, advanced, 574
Conciseness, in writing, 95
Conference call, 648; *illus.*, 649
Confidence, 685
Confirmation, 329; *illus.*, 330
Conflicting priorities, 136
Context, 80
Continuous paper feed, 416

Coping with unpleasant co-workers, 143
Copy notation, memo, 232; letter, 217
Control sheet, 316; *illus.*, 317
Convenience copiers, 410
Copier classification, 413; *illus.*, 414; speed, 413; volume capacity, 413
Copier costs, controlling, 417
Copier features, 415; symbols, *illus.*, 415
Copier paper, 417
Copier supplies, 417
Copying machines, 411
Copy log, 419; *illus.*, 420
Copy notation, 232
Copy preparation, 421
Corporation, 22
Correctness, in writing, 97
Courier delivery service, 621
Courses, 710
Courteous, being, 124
Courteousness, in writing, 96
Co-workers, interacting with, 140; unpleasant, coping with, 143, 145
CPU, *see* central processing unit
Credit, 363; establishment of, 309
Credit memoranda, 366
Credit memorandum, 314, 370; *illus.*, 314
Cross-reference, when to, 552
Cross-reference guides, 551
Cross-reference records, 549
Cross-reference sheet, 550; *illus.*, 551
Current liabilities, 369
Cursor, 274
Cursor positioning keys, 274
Customer service, 44, 305; basic skills required, 44; *illus.*, 45; where workers are employed, 45

**D**

Dash, 725
Data, 159
Database, 8
Database indexes, 579
Databases, 573
Data entry, nonkeyboarding, 279
Data processing, 40, 168, 169; basic skills required, 40; common applications, 304;

financial applications, 344; *illus.*, 170; opportunities for promotion, 41; where workers are employed, 41
Deadline, 134
Debit, 363
Decentralized structure, computer-assisted systems, 185
Decentralized word/text processing unit, 256; *illus.*, 257, 258
Dedicated word processor, 274; *illus.*, 275; internal storage (memory), 278; keyboard, 274; logic/intelligence unit, 278; monitor 277
Deductions, 377; paycheck, voluntary, 378
Defaults, 288
Department, 25
Deposits, preparing, 348; in transit, 356
Deposit slip, 350; *illus.*, 351
Desktop publishing system, 423
Detection system, 440
Dictation systems, centralized, 241
DID, *see* direct inward dialing
Digital signals, 656
Direct-dial calls, 647
Direct inward dialing (DID), 662
Directory assistance, 645
Diskettes, caring for, 195
Disposition, 684
Distributed structure, computer-assisted systems, 185
Distributed documents, 296
Distribution/transmission, 168, 171, 178; *illus.*, 171
Documentation, 477
Document formatting, 286
Document origination, 239; machine dictation methods, 241; manual methods, 240
Document storage, 296
Dot matrix printer, 293
Drafts, preparing, 87
Drawer labels, 522; *illus.*, 522
Duplicators, 423

**E**

Editing, 289; basic, 289; other, 289
Edit keys, 275; *illus.*, 276
Editor, 87
Edit program, 317

Effective writing, 94
EFT, *see* electronic funds transfer, 374
800 Service, 650
Electric typewriters, 270
Electrofax process, 412
Electronic blackboard, 668
Electronic calendar, 451; *illus.*, 453
Electronic copier/printer, 294
Electronic delivery systems, 296
Electronic dictionaries, 292
Electronic funds transfer, 374
Electronic mail, 663
Electronic messaging, 667
Electronic office, 8
Electronic shorthand, 281
Electronic storage, display, 272
Electronic system, integrated, 192
Electronic typewriter, 270; auxiliary storage, 273; common features, 270; communicating capabilities, 273; *illus.*, 271
Electrostatic copier process, 411
Electrostatic process, 411
Emergency office procedures, 435
Emergency telephone numbers, 435
Empathy, 124
Employee access, controlling, to the building, 438
Employees, bonded, 347
Employee's earnings record, *illus.*, 379
Employment agencies, 700; private, 700; temporary, 700
Employment application form, 703; *illus.*, 703
Employment changes, projected, *illus.*, 49
Employment commissions, state, 700
Employment requirements, 47
Enclosure notation, 232
Endnote method, 480
Endnotes, 480, 481
Endorsement, 349; blank, 349; in full, 349; restrictive, 349; special, 349
Enlargement, copier, 416
Enunciation, proper, 107
Envelopes, format, 222; *illus.*,

223; interoffice, 233; folding and inserting mail into, 606, 607; sealing, 607; special address notations, 222; special mailing notations, 223; stamped, 609; standard, 606; weighing, 607; window, 607
Equal Employment Opportunity Commission (EEOC), 146
Equipment checks, copier, 422
Equipment instruction, 57
Ergonomics, 12; *illus.*, 13
Ethical questions, 497
Evacuation, 436
Evaluation, based on work measurement, 62; by the supervisor 60; of performance, 60
Executive committee, 25
Express mail, 617
Express mail custom-designed service, 618
Express mail international service, 618
Express mail next-day service, 617

**F**

Facsimile (FAX), 666
FAX, *see* facsimile
Fiber optics, 412, 656
FICA, *see* social security tax
Fiche, *see* microfiche
Files, avoid overcrowded, 554; retrieving on magnetic media, 572; storing on magnetic media, 564
Filing, 503
Filing records, 553
Filing segment, 548
Filing systems, alphabetic, 526; chronologic, 537; numeric, 532
Film autoloader, 580
Financial reports, 482
Financial statements, 482; preparing, 485
Fires, 436
First aid procedures, 435
First-class mail, 615
First-class zone rated (priority) mail, 616
Flight reservations, 464
Flight schedules, 464
Flight tickets, 464
Floppy disk containers, 570

Floppy disk storage, 570; *illus.*, 570
Fluid duplicating, 423
Folder cuts, 523; *illus.*, 524
Folder labels, 522; *illus.*, 522
Folders, 523, 527, 529, 530; general, 526; *illus.*, 525; individual, 526; position, 524; special, 554
Footnote method, 479
Footnotes, 479, 481
Formal business meetings, 456
Formal business reports, 476
Formal memorandum, 229; *illus.*, 231; parts of, 230
Formal orientation program, 55
Format, 286; standard, 209
Format keys, 275; *illus.*, 276
Format line, 288
Formatting, 285; electric typewriters, 286; electronic typewriters, 286; text-editing systems, 287
Formatting rules, 249
Form letters, 242
Form paragraphs, 242
Fourth-class mail, 616
Full-rate cables, 664
Full-rate telegram, 664
Functional work area, 395
Future, prospects for, 48

**G**

General assistance, 44; basic skills required, 44; opportunities for promotion, 45; where workers are employed, 45
General folders, 526; *illus.*, 525, 528, 531
General offices, 6
Geographic file, 530; guides and folders, 530; *illus.*, 531
Gigabytes, 574
Goodwill, customer, 505
Government units, 19, 23
Government announcements, 701
Grammar, 98
Graphics, 43, 487; preparing, 488
Gross salary, 375
Growth, on-the-job, 709
Guides, 521, 527, 529, 530, 532; position, 524; primary, 521, *illus.*, 525; special, 521, 526

# H

Harassment, sexual, 146
Hard copy, 11, 505
Heading, memorandum, 230
Horizontal (flat) files, 555; *illus.*, 556
Hotel accommodations, 466
*Hotel/Motel Red Book*, 466
Hourly, 376
Human relations, 121; *illus.*, 142
Hyphen, 725

# I

Identification (ID) cards, 438
Impact printers, 293
Impression, good first, 705
Income statement, 483, *illus.*, 485
Incoming mail procedures, 591
Index card control file, 532, 534; *illus.*, 535
Indexing, 520, 739; articles and particles, 742; compound names, 746; government names, 746; hyphenated names, 745; identical names, 742; married women, 741; minor words in business names, 740; numbers in business names, 744; order of indexing units, 739; organizations and institutions, 744; punctuation and possessives, 740; separated single words, 745; single letters and abbreviations, 740; titles, 741
Indexing order, 548
Indexing units, 548
Index record, 548; *illus.*, 549, 550
Individual folders, 526; *illus.*, 525, 528, 529, 531
Informal meetings, 456
Informal orientation programs, 56
Informal report, 234; body, 236; *illus.*, 236; main heading, 235; page numbers, 237; secondary heading, 235; side headings, 237
Information, 159; accurate, 164; *illus.*, 159; timely, 163; transmitting, 656
Information distribution/ transmission, 42; basic skills required, 42; *illus.*, 43; opportunities for promotion, 43; where workers are employed, 42
Information management, 42; basic skills required, 42; *illus.*, 43; opportunities for promotion, 43; where workers are employed, 42
Information processing, 28, 156; computer-assisted system, 183; manual system for, 177; organization and technology for, 176
Information processing cycle, *illus.*, 178
Information processing system, 168
Information systems, 157; need for, 160
Information utilities, 574
Ink-jet printer, 294
Input, 178
Input media, 187; *illus.*, 188
Inputting, 42
Insured mail, 209, 619
Integrated communication systems, 669
Integrated electronic system, 192; equipment, 193; organization, 192
Integrated information network, 11
Integrated packages, 279
Integrated voice and data terminals (IVDT), 669
Intelligent copier, 414
Interacting, with co-workers, 140; with others, 120; with others in stressful situation, 142
Internal audit, 346
Internal control, 346
Internal networks, 662
International calls, 650
International mail, 621
Interoffice mail, 591, 621
Interoffice mail system, 605
Interoffice memos, *see* memorandum
Interpersonal skills, improving, 132
Interruptions, controlling, 146
Interview, anticipate questions, 706; before, 704; be on time, 707; dos and don'ts, 708; during, 707; following up, 709; prepare questions, 706; requesting, 701
Interviewing successfully, 704
Inventory, 325, 331
Inventory maintenance, 331
Invoice, from vendor, 370; *illus.*, 312, 364; preparation, 311
Itinerary, 468; *illus.*, 469
IVDT, *see* integrated voice and data terminals

# J

Job, new, introduction to, 54; starting right, 709
Job description, partial, *illus.*, 58
Job interview, dos and don'ts, 708
Job opportunities, exploring, 699
Job outlook through 1995 for office occupations, *illus.*, 48
Job performance appraisal, 60
Job search, planning, 695
Job specialization, 258

# K

Key, office functions, 4; telephone, 658

# L

Labels, 521, 522; color-coded, 523; drawer, 522; folder 522; preparing, 611
LANS, *see* local area networks
Laser beams, 412
Laser printer, 294
Lateral file cabinets, 555
Leftbound report, 476
Legal rights of the employee, 748
Letter, initial impact, 206
Letter address, 209; attention line, 212; city, state, ZIP Code, 212; company name, 211; delivery address, 211; name and title, 210
Letter formats, AMS simplified, 220; block, 219; *illus.*, 207; modified block, 219
Letter parts, attention line, 212; body, 214; complimentary close, 214; copy notation, 216; date, 208; enclosure notation, 216; *illus.*, 207; letter address, 209; mailing notation, 209; name, 210; postscript, 218;

printed letterhead, 208; reference initials, 216; salutation, 213; second-page heading, 218, *illus.*, 219; separate cover notation, 217; signature, 214; subject line, 213; title, 210
Letter punctuation styles, *illus.*, 221; mixed, 220; open, 220
Letterhead, printed, 208
Letter of application, 701; *illus.*, 702
Letter-quality printer, 292
Letter telegrams, 664
Letters, folding into envelope, 606, 607, 608
Liabilities, 369, 483
Library rate, 616
Line graph, 487; *illus.*, 488
Line printer, 293
Listening, 104, 111; attention, 112; attitude, 112; *illus.*, 113; notes, 114; questions, 114; summarize, 113
Local area networks (LANS), 192, 580, 657
Local telephone directory, 644
Locate keys, 274
Logo, 208
Long-distance calls, 646
Loyalty, to the company, 129

**M**

Machine dictation centralized dictation system, 241; desk-top units, 241; guidelines, 242; portable units, 241
Magnetic media, 506; advantages, 506; disadvantages, 506; managing, 563; retrieving files on, 572; storage, 570; storing files on, 564
Magnetic printer, 294
Mail, incoming, handling mail for supervisors, 594; procedures, 591; sorting and distributing, 592
Mail, outgoing, address requirements for automated handling, 612; classes of domestic, 615; courier/delivery service, 621; international, 621; interoffice, 621; procedures in a large company, 610; procedures in a small organi-

zation, 605; special postal services, 617; volume mailings, 611
Mailgram, 664
Mailing lists, 611
Mailing notations, 209
Mail orders, 308
Mailroom, 593
Mainframe computer, 185; *illus.*, 186
Maintenance, computer, 194
Management, 158; division, 25; middle, 25; top, 24
Management information systems (MIS), 165; administration of, 167; organization of, 166
Management support activities, 448
Manual information processing system, 177, 178; equipment for, 180; organization of, 179
Marketing your strengths, 694
Math, 732; addition, 732; averages, 736; calculating percentages, 735; converting decimals to percentages, 734; converting fractions and percentages to decimals, 734; division, 733; multiplication, 733; multiplying and dividing by 10 and multiples of 10, 735; percentage of increase or decrease, 735; rounding decimals, 734; subtraction, 732
Mature behavior, 689
Media, input, 187; storage, 502, 505
Meetings, after, 462; before, 457; during, 459; formal business, 456; informal, 456; small group, 456
Megabyte, 574
Memorandums, 229; computer generated, 230
Memorandum format, formal, 229; *illus.*, 231; simplified, 229, 233; *illus.*, 234
Memorandum parts, formal, 230; *illus.*, 221; simplified, 233; *illus.*, 234
Menu, 290, 565; *illus.*, 291, 567
Messages, 290, 291
Microcomputer, 185, 186; as word processor, 278; *illus.*, 186

Microdisks, 571
Microfiche, 509; *illus.*, 509, 577; organizing, 577
Microfilm, 507; advantages, 509; disadvantages, 510; retrieving records on, 578; roll, 508
Microfilm jacket, 509; *illus.*, 509
Microforms, 508; organizing, 577
Micrographics, 507
Microimage, 507
Microprocessors, 270, 413
Middle management, 25
Minicomputer, 185; *illus.*, 186
Minidisks, 571
Minutes, 459; correcting, 460; *illus.*, 461
MIS, *see* management information systems
Mixed punctuation, 220, 221
Mixed system of processing, 182
Mobile file, 556; *illus.*, 557
Mobile mail carts, *illus.*, 595
Modem, 656
Modified block letter, 219; *illus.*, 221
Modular components, 15
Modular furniture, 397
Monitor, 277
Monitoring devices, 418
Motel accommodations, 466
Multiline telephone, 658
Multi-station text-editing, 278

**N**

Name and subject file, 530
Name file, 527; guides and folders, 527; *illus.*, 525, 528
Net income, 483
Net loss, 483
Newspapers, 699
Non-add key, 180; *illus.*, 181
Nonimpact printer, 294
Nonverbal communication, 109
Not-for-profit entities, 19, 22
Not-for-profit organizations, *see* not-for-profit entities
Numeric file, *illus.*, 533, 535; general folders, 534; individual folders, 534
Numeric filing, guides, 532
Numeric filing system, 532

**O**

OCR, *see* optical character reader
Office, changes in, 7; general,

*illus.*, 6; place in the organization, 2; procedures when executive returns, 470; procedures when executive is away, 468; specialized, *illus.*, 6; state-of-the-art, 9, 11; technologically advanced, 11; traditional, 9; transitional, 10
Office accessories, 394
Office accident prevention, 430
Office assistant's procedures, 470
Office design, 11
Office environment, your role in, 122
Office equipment, using, 393
Office functioning, effective, 3; efficient, 3; smooth, 3
Office functions, key, 4
Office in transition, 9, 10
Office occupations, outlook for through 1995, *illus.*, 48
Office photocopiers, 411
Office procedures, emergency, 435
Office records, maintaining, 501
Office safety, 429; awareness/knowledge, 430
Office security, 429, 437
Office specialization, 37
Office supplies, 394
Office work, overall qualifications for, 46
Office workers, role of, 27, 172, 181
Office workforce, national overview of, 47
*Official Airline Guide*, 464; *illus.*, 465
*Official Guide of the Railways*, 466
Off line, 278, 572
Offset duplicating, 423
On line, 572
On-line agenda, 462
On-line system, 188, 318
Open punctuation, 220; *illus.*, 207, 221
Operating procedures, copier, 418
Operating software, 190
Operator-assisted calls, 647
Optical character reader (OCR), 280, 612; *illus.*, 280
Optical disk, 574; *illus.*, 575
Order form, *illus.*, 309

Order processing, 305; electronic, 314; manual, 306
Order receipt, 307
Orders, follow-up, 313
Organization chart, 26; *illus.*, 27, 28
Organization goals, 19
Organization structures, 26
Organizing your first job, 67
Orientation, 55
Orientation program, formal, 55; informal, 56
Originals, copier, 421
Out folder, 559
Out guide, 558; *illus.*, 559
Output, 40, 178; *illus.*, 189
Outputting devices, 189
Outsider access, controlling, 437
Outstanding checks, 356
Overnight telegram, 664
Owner's equity, 483

**P**

Packing list, 311
Paper feeders, 294
Paper files, managing, 545
Paper filing system, 519; components, 520; equipment, 520; procedures, 520; supplies, 521
Paperless office, 581
Paper trays, large capacity, 417
Parcel post, 616
Parentheses, 725
Partnership, 21
Password, 572
Paste-up materials, copier, 421
Payments received, 365
Payroll, 374
Payroll check distribution, 380
Payroll records, 379
Payroll register, 379
PBX, *see* private branch exchange
People interruptions, controlling, 146
Performance evaluation, 60
Period, 726
Periodic inventory control system, 333
Peripheral storage, 188
Perpetual inventory control system, 333
Personal directory, 646
Personality, 679

Personal profile folder, 712
Personal property, protecting, 436
Personal security 436
Personal telephone calls, 638
Person-to-person calls, 648
Petty cash book, 359; *illus.*, 360
Petty cash fund, 357; establishing, 358; keeping a record, 359; payments, 358; replenishing, 360
Petty cash receipt, *illus.*, 359
Petty cash summary report, 360, 361; *illus.*, 362
Photocomposition, 423
Photocompositors, 424
Photocopiers, 180; office, 411
Phototypesetting, 423
Physical count, of inventory, 334
Piece rate, 376
Pie chart, 488
Pitch, 126, 288
Plain-paper copiers, 412
Postage meter, 609; *illus.*, 610
Postal equipment, 181
Postal publications, 627
Postal services, special, 617
Power-down procedure, 434
Pre-employment tests, 708
Pressure, working under, 143
Pressure-sensitive labels, 611
Preventive maintenance, 393
Primary guides, 524; *illus.*, 525
Primary importance, 549
Primary storage, 188
Print, letter-quality, 292
Printer, 292; dot matrix, 293; electronic copier, 294; impact, 293; ink-jet, 294; laser, 294; magnetic, 294; nonimpact, 294
Printing documents, 292
Printout storage, 557; *illus.*, 558
Priorities, setting, 134, 135, 136
Priority mail, 616
Private branch exchange (PBX), 661
Private business exchange, *see* private branch exchange
Problems with co-workers, 145
Procedures, 158
Processing information, 178
Productivity, 12, 504
Professional, look, 713
Professional certificates of proficiency, 711

Professional image, projecting, 711
Professionalism, 143
Professional organizations, 710
Professional periodicals, 710
Professional Secretaries International (PSI), 710
Program, 190
Projected employment changes, *illus.*, 49
Prompts, 290, 565
Proofread, financial reports, 486
Proofreader's marks, standard, 720
Proprietorship, single, 20
Proximity readers, 438
PSI, *see* Professional Secretaries International
Punctuation styles, 220
Purchase order, 328, 370; computer-assisted preparation, 329; follow-up, 329; *illus.*, 328; manual preparation, 329
Purchase requisition, 326, 327, 370; *illus.*, 327
Purchasing, 325, 326; centralized, 326; decentralized, 326; mixed, 326

Q

Qualities, favorable, in others, 124
Question mark, 726
Quotation marks, 726
Quotations, 477

R

Reader, 507
Reader/printer, 507
Reading, 71, 72
Reading skills, improving, 78
Ream, 417
Receipt of goods, 331
Receiving goods, 330
Receiving report, 370
Reconciling a bank account balance, 352
Reconciling a bank statement, purpose, 354; steps, 355; worksheet, *illus.*, 355
Record, 502
Record categories, *illus.*, 514
Record destruction, 504
Record life cycle, 512; *illus.*, 513

Record maintenance, stockroom, 332
Record retention, 504
Record retrieval, 503
Records, collecting, 546, 547; copies of instead of cross-reference sheets, 551; cross-reference, 549; filing, 553; index/code, 547, 548; inspecting, 547; managing, 544; office, 501; photographing, 575; preparing for filing, *illus.*, 547; preparing for storage, 546; removing from active storage, 514, 559; retrieving, 558; retrieving on microfilm, 578; sort, 552
Records management, 168, 169, 500; a future in, 543; costs, 510; *illus.*, 170; personnel, 511; storage space, 511
Records management filing system, 502
Records management system, benefits, 504; overview, 502
Reduction, copier, 416
Reduction ratio, 575
Reel tape storage, 571; *illus.*, 571
Reference initials, 232
References, 481
References sources, 57
Registered mail, 209, 619
Release mark, 547
Reminder systems, 449
Remote meter resetting system, 609
Rental car, 464
Report, formal, 476; guidelines for setting up, *illus.*, 479; informal, 234; microcomputer assistance, 486
Report formats, *illus.*, 478; leftbound, 476; topbound, 476; unbound, 476
Report parts, appendices, 481; body, 236, 477; endnotes, 480; footnotes, 479; *illus.*, 236; main heading, 235; page numbers, 237; quotations, 477; secondary heading, 235; side headings, 237; table of contents, 477; textual citations, 480; title page, 477
Reprographic equipment, 423
Reprographics, 168, 169, 410;

*illus.*, 171
Reprographic services, 410
Requisition card, 558; *illus.*, 559
Requisition of goods, 334
Restriction endorsement, *illus.*, 349
Resume, 696; career goal, 696; categories of, 696; education, 697; extracurricular activities, 697; *illus.*, 698; keep current, 699; personal information, 697; preparing, 696; references, 697; work experience, 697
Retention schedule, 504, 514
Retrieving files, magnetic media, 572
Retrieving records, 558; on microfilm, 578
Return receipt, 619
Revenues, 19
Role play, 706
Roll microfilm, 508; *illus.*, 508; organizing, 578
Rough drafts, 289

S

Safety, work area, 432; workstation, 431
Salaries, 374
Salary, 375; gross, 375
Sales order, *illus.*, 310
Satellite clusters, 257
Satellite communications, 657
Satellite dishes, 657
School placement and counseling services, 699
Screening, 634
Scrolling, 290
Secondary storage, 188, 564; *illus.*, 189; importance of, 564
Secondary storage media, policies and procedures, 568
Second-class mail, 616
Sector, 614
Secured file, 573
Security, building, 437; computer systems, 193; files, 572; office, 437; personal, 436
Segment, 614
Self-acceptance, 680; being aware of your own worthiness, 682; others, being aware of, 681; yourself, be honest with, 680; yourself, perceiving, 680